THE MARKET, THE STATE, AND THE EXPORT-IMPORT BANK OF THE UNITED STATES, 1934–2000

This is the first history of the Export-Import Bank of the United States (Ex-Im) based on archival sources. As the government's export credit agency, Ex-Im promotes exports through loans, guarantees, and insurance and has had an unusual history as a public institution shaped by market principles. Congress mandated that the Bank only provide credit with a reasonable assurance of repayment. But the rules of the market and the needs of the state conflicted at times. Ex-Im has played a part in all the major events that marked the growing involvement of the United States in the international economy. In the last two decades, the Bank has carried on its congressionally mandated mission in an increasingly complicated environment brought on by changes in private capital markets; congressional constraints on its budgets; major financial crises in Latin America and Southeast Asia; fast-moving developments in communications and information technology; and the demands of nongovernmental organizations devoted to environmental protection.

William H. Becker is Professor of History at The George Washington University, where he also teaches in the Strategic Management and Public Policy Department in the School of Business and Public Management. His published works include *From the Atlantic to the Great Lakes* (1984) and *The Dynamics of Business-Government Relations: Industry and Exports, 1890–1921* (1982), which won the 1982 Newcomen Award for Outstanding Book in Business History 1979–1982. He was the general editor of the *Encyclopedia of American Business History and Biography* and is the editor of "Business, Society, and the State," a series for the University of North Carolina Press.

William M. McClenahan, Jr., is Lecturer in business law and public policy at the Robert H. Smith School of Business at the University of Maryland, College Park. His published works include co-authorship of *Voice of the Marketplace: A History of the National Petroleum Council* (2002). He is also an attorney and practiced for 12 years with the Interstate Commerce Commission between 1974 and 1986.

THE MARKET, THE STATE, AND THE EXPORT-IMPORT BANK OF THE UNITED STATES, 1934–2000

WILLIAM H. BECKER
The George Washington University

WILLIAM M. McCLENAHAN, JR.
University of Maryland, College Park

CAMBRIDGE
UNIVERSITY PRESS

PUBLISHED BY THE PRESS SYNDICATE OF THE UNIVERSITY OF CAMBRIDGE
The Pitt Building, Trumpington Street, Cambridge, United Kingdom

CAMBRIDGE UNIVERSITY PRESS
The Edinburgh Building, Cambridge CB2 2RU, UK
40 West 20th Street, New York, NY 10011-4211, USA
477 Williamstown Road, Port Melbourne, VIC 3207, Australia
Ruiz de Alarcón 13, 28014 Madrid, Spain
Dock House, The Waterfront, Cape Town 8001, South Africa

http://www.cambridge.org

First published 2003

Printed in the United States of America

Typeface Sabon 10.25/14 pt. *System* LaTeX 2ε [TB]

A catalog record for this book is available from the British Library.

Library of Congress Cataloging in Publication Data

Becker, William H.
The market, the state, and the Export-Import Bank of the United States, 1934–2000 /
William H. Becker, William M. McClenahan, Jr.
p. cm.
Includes bibliographical references and index.
ISBN 0-521-81143-0
1. Export-Import Bank of the United States. 2. Export credit – United States.
3. United States – Commercial policy. I. McClenahan, William M. II. Title.
HG3754.U5 B43 2002
332.1′54′0973–dc21 2002066521

ISBN 0 521 81143 0 hardback

TO OUR WIVES

Ruth Anne Becker
Cheryl Bailey

CONTENTS

PREFACE AND ACKNOWLEDGMENTS

In 2000, the Export-Import Bank of the United States (Ex-Im) marked its sixty-fifth anniversary. Ex-Im is the United States' export credit agency (ECA). It is a federal entity dedicated to promoting American exports by providing loans, guarantees, and insurance, without competing with the private sector. Many other countries have ECAs, including all the world's major industrial exporting countries. Throughout its history, Ex-Im has served the interests of the American exporter community, while also attending to the public policy goals of the executive branch and Congress. For almost half of its recent history, Ex-Im has played a part on the world scene by contributing to the United States' efforts to promote freer trade – leveling the playing field by standardizing practices among ECAs – through negotiations at the Organization for Economic Cooperation and Development (OECD).

At the turn of the century, the Bank was confronting a series of changes in private international capital markets and in the practices of other ECAs. In the last two decades, Ex-Im conducted its business in the midst of major international financial crises in Latin America in the 1980s and Southeast Asia in the late 1990s. Like other private and public institutions, Ex-Im also had to face up to the opportunities and challenges of the revolution in information technology and the arrival of the Internet. In addition, as an institution operating on the world scene, Ex-Im had to pay heed to the demands of nongovernmental institutions devoted to environmental causes.

Anniversaries are often a time to take stock, to look backward to understand better the present and thus to plan for the future. The turn of a century, and a new millennium, added force to the desire within the

Bank to make use of its anniversary for a reflective view of the institution as it planned on how to adjust to a fast-changing environment. As the anniversary approached, Dr. Rita M. Rodriguez, a bank director, suggested that an appropriate way to mark the institution's sixty-fifth year in 2000 would be to commission a scholarly history. The board of directors agreed and, to manage the project, established a history committee chaired by the Bank's then president and chairman, James A. Harmon. Other members of the committee were James C. Cruse, group vice president – policy; Eugene Ferguson, librarian; James K. Hess, chief financial officer; James A. Mahoney, vice president – engineering and environment; Carol Miller, personnel management specialist; John Niehuss, general counsel; and Dr. Rita M. Rodriguez, director.

The Bank, as a federal agency, publicly requested proposals and bids through a standard mandated process. The authors were the successful bidders and received a contract to write the history. Both of the authors are professional academic historians, associated with the Business History Group, Inc. (BHG). William H. Becker is Professor of History at the George Washington University, where he also teaches in the School of Business and Public Management. Professor McClenahan also holds a law degree and was professionally engaged as a government attorney for twelve years before successfully completing a Ph.D. program in history. Our scholarly interests have focused on the history of business, of business–government relations, and of the United States' role in the international economy.

In writing this book, we had full access to the Bank's records and to its personnel. Ex-Im's library and archives included numerous files of use to historians, as well as copies of relevant secondary material and government documents. The Bank's Policy Office files also contained valuable historical material. We relied on Ex-Im's records in the National Archives at College Park, Maryland, and information about the Bank contained in the archival collections of the Departments of State, Treasury, and Commerce, along with several other relevant collections. As the footnotes indicate, we made extensive use of oral history interviews with numerous current and previous officials of the Bank, as well as many individuals who had dealings with Ex-Im or were observers of its operations. Transcripts of all of our interviews are now deposited in the Bank's archives for the use of other scholars.

From the outset of this project, both the authors and the Bank were determined to produce a scholarly work published by a university press. The authors and Ex-Im understood from the beginning that the manuscript would undergo the scrutiny of other professional scholars before publication. Toward that end, we proposed that the Bank have drafts of chapters reviewed by a respected scholar who could make comments and suggestions as the work was being written. The Bank agreed, and draft chapters were reviewed by Richard Sylla, Henry Kaufman Professor of the History of Financial Institutions and Markets, and Professor of Economics, New York University. Throughout the process of writing the book, Professor Sylla proved enormously helpful to us and to the committee in his suggestions about the manuscript. We are grateful for his careful reading of chapters over the many months that we have worked on the book. Of course, he bears no responsibility for any errors of fact or interpretation that might remain in the work, despite his good efforts.

Members of the Bank's history committee also read and provided suggestions about draft chapters and the final version of the manuscript. We also appreciate the many opportunities that we had to discuss our work with members of the committee. In particular, we are grateful for the time given to the careful reading of our work, and to us personally for discussion, by James A. Harmon, chairman and president of the Bank (1997–2001); Dr. Rita M. Rodriguez, director (1982–1999); James C. Cruse, group vice president – policy; and James K. Hess, chief financial officer. In addition, Mr. Hess was the history committee's secretary and our liaison with the Bank, providing us with office space and helping in arranging oral history interviews. His staff made an invaluable contribution to our work by compiling the Bank's historical financial data found in the appendix. We would also like to acknowledge the assistance provided throughout the project by the Bank's librarian and archivist, Eugene Ferguson, and his staff. Despite all the assistance that we have had in writing this book, we take full responsibility for any errors.

One final word about usage is appropriate. Over the course of its history, the Export-Import Bank of the United States has been known by slightly different names. The major changes in its name are included as part of the history that follows. In addition, the Bank was known by various abbreviations, including Eximbank, EXIM, EIB, and Ex-Im

Bank. Throughout the text that follows, for reasons of consistency, we use Ex-Im or Ex-Im Bank, except in direct quotations in which another abbreviation was commonly in use at the time.

William H. Becker, *The George Washington University*
William M. McClenahan, Jr., *University of Maryland, College Park*

INTRODUCTION

The Export-Import Bank of the United States is the government's official export credit agency (ECA). Throughout its history the Bank has promoted the financial needs of American exporters, but it has also served the goals of policy makers in the White House, as well as the Departments of the Treasury, State, and War (later Defense). In that sense, Ex-Im was not atypical when compared to the ECAs of other governments. What has been unusual in Ex-Im's history was the need to compete with foreign ECAs, which were the products of different political economies, serving governments that often had domestic and foreign agendas unlike those of the United States. Ex-Im has avoided competing with private sector institutions. That stricture, a part of its early congressional mandate, has shaped a government institution keenly attuned to the practices of financial market institutions. Additionally, the Bank focused on market principles because of the requirement that its lending be based on the assumption of a reasonable assurance of repayment.

Franklin D. Roosevelt created the Export-Import Bank in 1934 during the New Deal's earliest zeal for planning and building the power of the state. It now exists in an environment where leaders extol market solutions to economic growth and development in most places in the world. As this transformation suggests, Ex-Im has long conducted its business in an ever-changing realm defined by the shifting demands of both the state and the market. The Bank's experience over the last sixty-five years provides a telling perspective on the achievements, failures, and future possibilities of a public institution committed to operate by the rules of the market. Ex-Im's history tells us much about the use of market principles over many decades to attain the objectives of the American state.

Belying the common image of sclerotic public institutions, Ex-Im proved itself flexible, indeed entrepreneurial, in addressing the shifting relationships between the power of the state and of the market. Some of the shifts – such as the end of the Bretton Woods fixed exchange system in 1971 – were of tectonic proportions. So the required adjustments were not accomplished without tension and difficulty; nor did they all work out as Ex-Im would have liked. But overall, the Bank and its leaders were adroit in continuing to serve the financial needs of American exporters *and* the public policy interests of the United States. This was as true throughout the depression of the 1930s, as during post–World War II European reconstruction, the initial sponsorship of Third World economic development in the 1950s, the Alliance for Progress in the 1960s, the oil shocks of the 1970s, the international debt crisis of the 1980s, the aftermath of the disintegration of the Soviet Union in the 1990s, and the Asian financial collapse of 1997–8.

As the United States' export credit agency, the Bank's supporters and critics measured it against similar bodies in other industrial countries. Ex-Im's history, as such, provides a comparative perspective on ECAs, a key twentieth century international economic institution. Roosevelt had created the Export-Import Bank in part to provide American exporters with services comparable to those available from the government ECAs of competing industrial powers. After the early 1950s, how Ex-Im's services stacked up against those of the United States' European and Japanese competitors became a vigorously contested policy issue. This was especially true in the heated debates over the causes of America's declining competitiveness in the 1970s and 1980s.

At the same time, Ex-Im joined in the United States' campaign to liberalize international trade and finance. Since the 1970s, Bank officials have helped represent the United States in Organization for Economic Cooperation and Development (OECD) negotiations to level the global playing fields. Practically, the resulting OECD agreements helped American businesses breach international trade barriers in the financing of exports.

Sustaining the Bank throughout its history has been an unusual organizational culture for a public institution. Key Ex-Im leaders – including, among others, Jesse H. Jones, Warren Pierson, William McChesney Martin, Walter Sauer, William J. Casey, Jr., and Henry Kearns – fostered businesslike values among the Bank's staff. Together they embraced the standards of the financial marketplace in analyzing risk, structuring loans, and scheduling payments. Ex-Im earned profits and paid dividends to the U.S. treasury through the 1970s.

Initially, the Roosevelt administration designed the Bank for two purposes. It was to serve as the government's agent in trading with the Soviet Union, which the United States recognized in 1933. Second, Ex-Im was to cope with the "market failure" of a commercial banking sector, which was unable during the Great Depression to offer sufficient export financing. For the most part, Ex-Im during its history extended credit, or guaranteed the extension of credit, to foreign purchasers of American exports. In making its loans, the Bank by statute had to avoid competing with commercial banks while still expecting a reasonable assurance of repayment. It was not to be a concessional lender nor an aid-giving institution.

This core market orientation has been tested many times during the Bank's history. For much of this time, but certainly in its first decades, government officials treated Ex-Im's export support activities as fundamentally an instrument of American foreign policy. Its responsibility as the U.S. agent for a hoped-for large trade with the USSR was only the first in a number of instances in which the Bank served the needs of diplomacy. The demands of high-level foreign policy on occasion conflicted with the Bank's basic principles. Ex-Im did not always prevail in these struggles. Acting against its market principles at times caused the Bank both political and financial problems. But out of the conflicts grew an extraordinarily resilient and flexible – indeed at times entrepreneurial – institution. These qualities equipped Ex-Im to adjust itself not only to the demands of the American foreign policy establishment but also to the agendas of the Department of the Treasury, presidents of the United States, and powerful members of Congress. These organizational traits also prepared Ex-Im to confront other transformations in its environment – shifts in the domestic and international economy, changing relationships between market and state power, and the United States' varying role in the postwar economic order.

Ex-Im's record was entwined with the United States' growing private and public role in the international economy since the 1930s. Its history demonstrates how American exports influenced the country's foreign policy toward countries on almost every continent. Beginning in the 1930s, Latin America became an important focus of the Bank's activities, which both complemented and at times conflicted with Roosevelt's "Good Neighbor Policy." During World War II, the Bank financed Latin America's acquisition of American capital goods, purchases used to produce strategic materials sold back to the United States. Because of its experience in making and administering these large-scale loans, Harry Truman drafted Ex-Im to begin European reconstruction immediately after the war. Between 1945 and 1948, the Bank served as a crucial bridge between the end of lend–lease and the beginning of the Marshall Plan. This role created great tensions within the Bank. The Truman administration expected the Bank to satisfy the huge capital needs of countries in situations that frequently did not meet the Bank's prudential standards for lending.

In the 1950s and the 1960s, Ex-Im focused more intently on Latin America. Its lending complemented a growing foreign policy interest in economic development there and in other underdeveloped regions. Ex-Im's interest in development was not new. Indeed, the Bank's leadership in the 1930s had articulated one of the earliest policy rationales for promoting economic development. Ex-Im preferred to finance the overseas sale of capital goods used in development projects. The latter, the Bank's leaders believed, contributed to the development of an industrial base that in turn later would promote markets for U.S. goods.

The Department of State embraced the Bank's development arguments, as Cold War tensions between the United States and the Soviet Union spilled over into the Third World. Thus, initial skepticism about Ex-Im in the early Eisenhower administration's Department of the Treasury was balanced and then was subsumed by support in John Foster Dulles' State Department. Organized exporter and banker groups pressed Congress to protect Ex-Im from treasury's budget cutters. In Dulles' view, the Bank's promotion of exports, and the private foreign firms that at times received credits to purchase them, helped counter growing leftist movements in Latin America.

Radical changes in the 1960s and especially the 1970s changed the United States' standing in world trade and finance. Ex-Im had to adjust itself accordingly. Western Europe and Japan had recovered from the destruction of WW II. Increasingly, their exports entered the American market, eventually ending the United States' trade surpluses. Trade deficits – and the balance of payment deficits that followed – unnerved American officials. Many of them now extolled the Bank's promotion of exports as helping address the country's balance of payments problems. In addition, because the Bretton Woods system of fixed exchange rates artificially kept the relative value of the dollar high – increasing the foreign cost of American goods – policy makers saw Ex-Im lending to foreign purchasers as offsetting the negative consequences of the expensive dollar.

President Richard M. Nixon revolutionized international finance when he abandoned the Bretton Woods' fixed-exchange-rate regime in 1971. This policy decision fundamentally altered the international economic environment in which the United States had operated since the end of World War II. By 1973, the rates of exchange among the major currencies floated. Floating currencies – at least in the minds of economic theorists and some treasury officials – challenged the traditional rationale for the Bank's promotion of exports. Because ending Bretton Woods led to a devaluation of the dollar, in theory a cheaper American currency would lower the price of exports, making them more attractive to foreign buyers. In fact, currencies did not float freely, as governments intervened in currency markets to influence rates of exchange.

In the 1970s, the importance of exports increased dramatically in many countries following OPEC's tripling of oil prices in 1973–4. Overnight, oil importing countries – including the United States – saw the costs of imports explode. In response, foreign export credit agencies upped assistance to their exporters through highly subsidized financing. Such practices heightened competition for export markets. They added some urgency to Congress' 1971 mandate that Ex-Im play a direct role in helping American exporters cope with heavily subsidized foreign competition. One aspect of the Bank's new responsibility involved participating in Organization for Economic Cooperation and Development (OECD) negotiations. These discussions focused on the devices governments used to assist their countries' exporters. The United States' goal has been to establish a common ground of standards on interest rates, length of credits, levels of concessionary lending, and so on. By helping level the playing field, the Bank became a key instrument in the United States' effort to promote fairer and larger international trade in the last thirty years.

Also sharply influencing the Bank were changes in the domestic economic situation in the 1950s, 1960s, and 1970s. Beginning with the economy-minded Eisenhower administration and carrying through the era of persistent and increasing federal deficits that began in the late 1960s, budget officials attempted to reduce the government's borrowing. As a result, the treasury and the Office of Management and Budget (OMB) pressed Ex-Im to cut its reliance on the treasury for funds. Ex-Im responded innovatively to these demands after 1960 by encouraging partnerships with commercial banks offering export financing. These efforts increasingly employed Bank guarantees to back up private lenders by reducing their risks and initiated a partnership with foreign credit insurers where the Bank assumed significant liability exposure.

The impact of other economic shifts, however, was not so easily managed. Boom conditions in the 1960s gave way in the 1970s to "stagflation" – declining growth rates accompanied by increasing inflation and unemployment. These circumstances confounded both the Republican and Democratic administrations in the 1970s, neither of which devised economic policies able to cope with this unprecedented economic problem. At times, the Federal Reserve met increasing inflation by raising interest rates. This boosted the cost of the Bank's funds, along with those of other financial institutions. As a result, the Bank during the 1970s lent funds – increasingly to meet the practices of other ECAs – at rates below its own cost of capital. The Bank thus jeopardized its profitability – it abandoned paying a dividend in 1980. Moreover, this policy opened the Bank to persistent criticism about offering subsidies, defined by its critics as the difference between the rates it paid on borrowed funds and the rates it charged to lend money.

Subsidization became a contentious political issue in the 1970s. Part of the criticism's sting was a result of the small number of firms that seemed to benefit most from the Bank's lending. Late in the 1960s, Ex-Im focused on American capital goods with comparative advantage. These included the "high-tech" products of the time – jet aircraft, nuclear power stations, and the ground facilities for satellite communications – that required substantial financial support to foreign purchasers. Consequently, by the 1970s, almost half of the Bank's lending bolstered exports from these industries. Because these goods were manufactured by large, profitable companies – Boeing, McDonnel Douglas, Lockheed, General Electric, Westinghouse – antagonists in Congress questioned the Bank's large expenditures for such money-making enterprises in a period of budget deficits and fiscal restraint. The Bank defended itself by arguing that financing high-tech exports boosted employment in key industries and helped the U.S. balance of payments. These arguments, of course, resonated among exporters and members of Congress whose districts included the favored companies and their employees. But criticism of Ex-Im's subsidies did not subside in the 1970s, as academics and journalists joined several prominent members of Congress in probing how and why the Bank did business.

Critics had much to complain about in the 1980s. By then, Ex-Im was losing substantial sums of money because of a high level of business in the late 1970s and early 1980s financed at "subsidized" rates. With the arrival of the Reagan administration in 1981, the Bank faced an additional challenge. The administration espoused an ideology opposed to large government programs. That mind set, along with the fact that the Bank was losing money, weakened Ex-Im's position. So too did the domestic and international economic situation in the 1980s. Reagan and the Fed purged inflation out of the domestic economy. The result was a strong dollar, which in turn depressed exports. In addition, the Latin American debt crisis of the 1980s dampened demand and reduced economic activity in that region and elsewhere.

Consequently, Bank losses and nonperforming loans increased. The period from the mid-1980s through 1990–1 was characterized by dramatically reduced demand for Ex-Im products (credits, guarantees, and insurance). The Bank, however, was able to use this period to begin to realign its institutional relationships with the finance and insurance industries and to adjust its own internal policies and procedures to this new environment.

In 1990, Congress overhauled the way the federal government budgeted its credit operations in the wake of the domestic savings and loan crisis. Credit reform and continuing budget pressures presented challenges to traditional assumptions about how the Bank could best perform its function of complementing, not displacing, private markets. Vexing problems about the Ex-Im's relationship with the private sector were also a factor in the decision in 1992 to end its thirty-year relationship with a consortium of private insurers. In addition, the maturation of the OECD arrangements and the increasing sophistication of international capital markets ensured that the mix of Ex-Im activity would be primarily loan guarantees and not credits.

During the 1990s, the environment for the financial services of the Ex-Im again underwent a dramatic transformation. Early in the decade, the levels of Bank activity had increased dramatically over the doldrums of the mid to late 1980s and exceeded those of the mid 1970s. OECD negotiations led in 1991 to an arrangement to limit concessional finance in export credits, a practice that had begun to challenge the Bank in the 1980s. By 1997, participants in OECD bargaining also had reached an accord on setting minimum risk premium fees for dealing with country and sovereign risk. The collapse of the Soviet Union increased demands on Ex-Im resources, as did the increasing role of market-based solutions (as opposed to sovereign guarantees) for development outside of the former Soviet bloc. Commercial and investment banks remained cautious participants in trade finance, even though new sources of investment capital became available in international markets. Despite the widening of capital resources, traditional providers fled Asia following the 1997 crisis in the region. Ex-Im then provided a substantial amount of the short-term credit needed to cope with the harrowing consequences of private capital flight.

At the beginning of a new century, the Bank again faced how to position itself between the state and the market. While private investment capital returned to Southeast Asia following the crisis of 1997–8, traditional export financing did not for the most part. Consequently, the Bank had to determine how it would cope with the risks in that region and in those other parts of the world – such as Sub-Saharan Africa and Russia – where traditional commercial export finance was likely to be scarce. It also had to decide whether to follow or counter Canadian and German government agencies that were directly competing with the private sector for business. That trend, which accelerated during the 1990s, challenged the United States' commitment to creating an orderly foreign export credit regime through OECD understandings. However that issue is resolved, Ex-Im will also probably need to reaffirm its role as a provider of credit – a lender of last resort – a task it will need to take up again when the next international financial crisis further drives private commercial finance from export markets.

In the book that follows, we turn in Chapter 1 to the founding of the Bank, its early lending, and the beginnings of a distinct business-oriented culture. The chapter that follows (Chapter 2) traces Ex-Im through World War II and its role in postwar reconstruction. Chapter 3 discusses how the Cold War influenced the work of the Bank and the next chapter (Chapter 4) explores how Ex-Im increasingly used guarantees and insurance to meet the needs of its customers and the United States government. In Chapter 5, we examine how the end of the Bretton Woods system and the oil crisis of the 1970s changed the international economy, which in turn had profound effects on Ex-Im's business and the role Congress mandated for the Bank. Chapter 6 investigates how the Bank managed its business in the face of troubled domestic and international economic conditions, especially after the onset of the international debt crisis in the 1980s. The last chapter (Chapter 7) focuses on how the economic boom of the mid and late 1990s, the opening of new overseas markets for the United States, and the Asian financial crisis yet again required Ex-Im to adjust its practices to meet rapidly changing circumstances. Lastly, the epilogue takes stock of how the Bank has responded to rapid economic change, both in the United States and overseas, and the issues and conditions it faced at the beginning of a new century.

1

SETTING A FLEXIBLE COURSE

The Export-Import Bank, 1934–1939

INTRODUCTION

Franklin D. Roosevelt established the first Export-Import Bank of Washington in February 1934 to serve his foreign policy and promote economic recovery in the United States. He wanted the Bank to help normalize relations with the Soviet Union. The effort bogged down and failed following protracted discussions over previously unpaid Soviet debts. Another diplomatic objective – improving relations with a turbulent Cuba – prompted the Roosevelt administration to establish the second Export-Import Bank of Washington a few weeks later in March 1934. In June 1935, after officials determined that no business would be done with the Soviet Union, the two banks merged to form one Export-Import Bank of Washington (Ex-Im).

From the first, organized groups of American exporters and bankers supported the new government banking institutions. Exporters needed the Bank's services during the 1930s because of depressed conditions and the rapid deterioration of international trade and finance. Officials of the Roosevelt administration were sensitive to their needs and saw the Banks as contributing to economic recovery.[1]

In its first decade, the Bank struggled to define its own mission. Ex-Im officials created an official dialogue with organized export and banker groups as the Bank developed its operating policies and procedures. Increasingly in the 1930s, Bank officials and staff defined the Ex-Im's role as promoting American export of agricultural and manufactured goods. But there were constraints on what the Bank could do. Senior Ex-Im

1 Earl Mazo, "The Export-Import Bank of the United States," 1976, pp. 3–4, ms in Library, Ex-Im.

officials had to accommodate the Department of State, as well as other government agencies that perceived the Bank as having an impact on their responsibilities. State Department officials closely monitored the Bank's activities because the decisions and actions of Ex-Im could affect the economies – and possibly the diplomacy – of foreign countries. At the end of the 1930s, as Europe prepared for war, isolationist members of Congress also paid close attention to the work of the Bank lest it compromise America's nominal neutrality.

Throughout the 1930s, the Bank's leaders endeavored to balance the needs of its government and private sector constituencies. At the same time, they sought to define a distinct organization identified with, but not subservient to, their constituencies' views of what the Bank needed to do and how it was to conduct its business. All of this was accomplished by a small cadre of top leaders, working with a modest staff. In a period of tight government budgets, the latter never seemed to grow fast enough to meet the increasing demands put on the new institution. At the senior levels, Bank officials determined policies that guided the Bank in assisting exporters and working with the private banking sector. Its staff defined the day-to-day procedures necessary to process and evaluate applications and to disburse funds and receive payments.

The Ex-Im's experiences in the 1930s provided the Bank with organizational qualities that would characterize the institution for decades to come. In its dealings with exporters, private sector lenders, and foreign purchasers of American goods, the Bank aspired to be businesslike in assessing risk and serving its loans. Its policies and procedures conformed to prevailing private sector commercial and financial practice. At the same time, the Bank's leaders learned to be flexible in accommodating the State Department in what it saw as the demands of American foreign policy. These qualities – orderliness and flexibility – endowed Ex-Im with a resilient organizational culture.

ESTABLISHING THE BANK

Franklin D. Roosevelt took office in March 1933 in the midst of an unprecedented economic depression. Bringing about economic recovery was the new president's first priority. But there were also major related international issues that needed attention. None was perhaps more contentious than that of extending diplomatic recognition to the

Soviet Union. Weeks after becoming president, Roosevelt authorized negotiations with the USSR over the terms of recognition, and he extended it in December 1933. In doing so, he satisfied his foreign policy advisers and American businesses interested in increased trade with the Soviet Union.

Roosevelt also ended a long-running public policy quarrel. Since the Bolsheviks had seized power in Russia in 1917, the United States had refused to accept the legitimacy of the new Soviet regime. Throughout the 1920s, Presidents Harding, Coolidge, and Hoover conditioned recognition on the USSR agreeing to accepted standards of international conduct. That is, they wanted the Soviet government to end its support of revolutionary activities in other countries, return confiscated property, and accept the international financial obligations of its predecessor government.[2]

During the 1920s, discussions of U.S. recognition of the Soviet Union increasingly turned on its willingness to honor pre-revolutionary financial obligations. For Secretary of Commerce, and then President, Herbert Hoover these debts were a matter of basic principle, as well as of American self-interest. The debts owed were not large, but as an expanding creditor nation the United States, he thought, could not ignore repudiation of financial responsibilities. Hoover believed firmly that the recognition of basic property rights held together the "whole fabric of international life."[3] The president was not alone in his views. Officials in the Department of State embraced a similar ideological stance. Indeed, a small group of department specialists on the Soviet Union became articulate spokesmen for a policy of nonrecognition.

Nevertheless, the government's tough position did not prevent some American firms from developing a strong interest in the USSR. American officials usually did not interfere with Americans selling goods and furnishing credits to the Soviet Union, so long as these were private transactions. In fact, by 1926, the United States exported more to the Soviet Union than to any other country, and Americans were the second largest providers of foreign capital. American firms also became heavily involved in providing the USSR with technical assistance. Indeed, these

[2] Frederick C. Adams, *Economic Diplomacy: The Export-Import Bank and American Foreign Policy, 1934–1939* (Columbia, MO: University of Missouri Press, 1976), pp. 98–9.
[3] Quoted in Adams, p. 99.

efforts received a lot of publicity when Henry Ford agreed to assist the Soviet Union's automobile industry and W. Averell Harriman, the mining of magnesium.[4]

Ford and Harriman, of course, were not alone. In the 1920s, less-prominent American businessmen created associations to promote business with the USSR. They established the American Commercial Association to Promote Trade with Russia, the American-Russian Chamber of Commerce, and the Allied American Corporation. Chase National Bank of New York led other banks in exploring ways to increase credit for trade with Russia. For its part, the USSR set up an agent in New York, the Amtorg Trading Corporation, to represent the Soviet bureaucracies responsible for exports, imports, and foreign credits.[5]

Increased economic ties with the Soviet Union in the 1920s prompted some prominent business leaders to question the United States' nonrecognition policy. Because of the Soviets' first five-year plan in 1928, purchases of American producers' goods increased sharply. As the Soviet Union promoted rapid industrialization, it appeared that the Russian market would be limited only by the ability of American manufacturers to finance the new business. In the face of the deepening depression in the early 1930s, support increased among businessmen for U.S. recognition of the USSR.[6]

Foreign policy concerns also prompted doubts about the wisdom of nonrecognition. In the late 1920s and early 1930s, the world situation became more ominous. There were growing threats to the USSR from militarists in Japan and the increasing influence of the virulently antibolshevik Nazis in Germany. Recognizing the Soviet Union, some State Department officials believed, would throw American power into the balance, perhaps moderating the dangerous tendencies of the time.[7]

So in extending diplomatic recognition to the USSR in December 1933, Roosevelt heeded his foreign policy advisers and pleased businesses interested in markets in the USSR. It was also from these two

[4] Ibid., pp. 101–2.

[5] Ibid., pp. 100–1; "The Amtorg Trading Corporation," Office of Secretary, Reconstruction Finance Corporation, Administrative Subject Files, 1932–1957, Box 3, "Amtorg Trading Corp." folder, Record Group 234, Records of the Reconstruction Finance Corporation, National Archives.

[6] Russian Business" (nd), Office of Secretary, RFC, Administrative Subject Files, 1932–1957, Box 34, "Loans – Russia" folder, RG 234; Adams, p. 105.

[7] Adams, pp. 105–6.

groups that the idea of a government export-import bank originated. Leading the way within the circle of the president's advisers were officials with a keen interest in the Soviet Union. They included William Bullitt, the United States' first ambassador to the Soviet Union; the general counsel of the Reconstruction Finance Corporation (RFC), Stanley F. Reed (later a Supreme Court Justice); and Assistant Secretary of State R. Walton Moore. Perhaps the most influential figure in the discussions was Robert F. Kelley, the State Department's most senior specialist on the Soviet Union. Kelley for many years had vigorously opposed diplomatic recognition of the USSR because of the outstanding loans. Following FDR's decision to recognize the USSR, Kelley and others who shared his views came up with the idea of an official bank. A governmental institution controlling access to credits, Kelley thought, would gain leverage for the United States with the Soviet Union. Such influence, he believed, was necessary to ensure that the Russians would eventually come to an agreement on the debt issue. Centralizing authority over credits would also reduce the opportunity for the USSR's trading company to play off American exporters against each other for better terms.[8]

Bullitt oversaw the preparation of the president's executive order creating the first export-import bank. Two RFC[9] attorneys drafted the official document for Roosevelt's signature. One of the lawyers was special RFC counsel Warren Lee Pierson – later president of the Bank. Following a review of the document by the attorney general and officials in the treasury, the executive order went to the president for his signature. Roosevelt selected the name for the new institution, writing in the blank space for a name left on the executive order.[10]

Roosevelt's executive order of February 2, 1934, authorized the new bank to finance American trade with the USSR. It operated under the laws of the District of Columbia, with authority to conduct general banking activities including the purchase and sale of government securities and gold. The Bank raised its capital by selling $10 million in preferred stock to the Reconstruction Finance Corporation and $1 million in common stock to the Departments of State and Commerce

[8] Ibid., pp. 110–12; Warren Lee Pierson, "The Export-Import Bank of Washington," chapter 1, ms in Library, Ex-Im.

[9] Congress set up the Reconstruction Finance Corporation in 1932 to lend funds to struggling banks, railroads, insurance companies, and state governments.

[10] Mazo, p. 1.

under the provisions of the National Industrial Recovery Act (NIRA) of 1933. The National Recovery Administration (NRA) of 1933 was an umbrella agency that gave the president considerable latitude in promoting an economic turnaround.[11]

In any event, the Soviet Union was not the only country that required American diplomatic attention in the first years of the Roosevelt administration. Closer to home there was a volatile situation in Cuba. Since the Spanish-American War, the United States had taken a special interest in Cuba. By the 1920s, private U.S. investment in the island had given Americans a major role in Cuba's economy. Even so, high American tariffs cut sugar exports to the United States, and exports of American goods to Cuba fell dramatically in the late 1920s and early 1930s. The intensifying world depression only served to make worse an already bad Cuban economic situation. These conditions heightened nationalistic, and anti-American, sentiment in Cuba and contributed to growing unrest, which led to coups and countercoups in 1933.[12]

In January 1934, a coup empowered a government with which the United States felt it could work. Consequently, as part of an effort to improve relations with Cuba, President Roosevelt created a second Export-Import Bank of the United States on March 9, 1934. Its capitalization was based on a RFC subscription of $2.5 million in preferred stock and $250,000 in common stock officially held by the State and Commerce Departments under the NRA. By September, the Bank had worked out an agreement with the new Cuban government to finance the purchase of silver to be coined into pesos at the U.S. mint in Philadelphia. In December 1934, Cuba signed a second agreement to obtain additional silver for coinage. This program increased Cuba's supply of currency and was less onerous financially than floating government bonds.[13]

Meanwhile, negotiations over the unpaid Russian loans were proving tedious, tense, and at times acrimonious. Until an agreement was reached, however, the Bank would conduct no business with the Soviet Union. In July 1934, the Bank's trustees enlarged the scope of the second bank to allow it to do business anywhere else in the world, with the exception of the USSR. Loan discussions bogged down later

[11] Ibid., pp. 6–7; Rosemary Mazon, "Highlights in Evolution," June 6, 1991, pp. 1–5, ms in Library, Ex-Im.

[12] Adams, pp. 136–7.

[13] Ibid., pp. 138–9.

in 1934 over the amounts to be repaid and the number of years for repayment. Ultimately, the debt negotiations failed. At the end of January 1935, both sides concluded that they could not come to a satisfactory understanding.[14]

In June 1935, the two banks merged because the first bank would never do any business with the Soviet Union. Outstanding loans and commitments of the second Ex-Im were eventually transferred to the first bank to effect the merger.[15] Putting the two banks together was not difficult administratively. A single board of trustees had governed the two banks. Its members included representatives from the two banks (which had exactly the same officers), the Reconstruction Finance Corporation, and the State, Treasury, Commerce, and Agriculture Departments. Assistant Secretary of State, and later State Department Legal Counsel, R. Walton Moore chaired the board resulting from the merger until his death in 1941. As president of the first and second Ex-Im banks, Roosevelt appointed George N. Peek, who also served as his Special Adviser on Foreign Trade (SAFT). Peek added the presidency of the Ex-Im banks to his SAFT responsibilities and used the same staff to carry out the duties of both posts.[16]

The newly merged Bank began its work with increased powers. In January 1935, the administration received congressional authority to continue an export-import bank as part of legislation to reauthorize the RFC. The administration required new legislative authority, since the Bank's original mandate under the National Industrial Recovery Act would expire in June 1935. Roosevelt did not seek to recharter the NRA. It was controversial and eventually in 1935 the Supreme Court declared significant portions of its activities unconstitutional. In any event, under

[14] The course of the negotiations can be followed in the documents published by the Department of State in *Foreign Relations of the United States: The Soviet Union, 1933–1939* (Washington, DC: Government Printing Office, 1952), pp. 66–81, 86–101, 108–61 (hereafter *FRUS*). See also Adams, pp. 112–28.

[15] Adams, pp. 70–3; Executive Order No. 6581, "Authorizing the Formation of a Banking Corporation to be Known as Export-Import Bank of Washington," February 2, 1934, Office of Secretary, RFC, General Correspondence . . . , Box 21,"Exim Bank" folders, RG 234.

[16] Memorandum, Peek to McHugh, U.S. Department of Agriculture, Agricultural Adjustment Administration, February 13, 1934, Special Adviser on Foreign Trade (SAFT), Records of the Secretary, General Records, 1933–1935, Box 6, "George N. Peek" folder and "Statement by Mr. George Peek," February 26, 1934, SAFT, Records of the Public Relations Office, Box 1, "Publicity Materials, 1933–1935" folder, RG 19, Records of the Special Adviser on Foreign Trade, National Archives.

the auspices of rechartering the RFC, Congress reauthorized the Bank for two years and enlarged its powers. The new legislation permitted the Bank to discount notes and borrow funds for its business up to limits set by the secretary of the treasury. These provisions freed the Bank from the restrictions of District of Columbia law that had limited the size of loans the Banks could make and prohibited the discounting of notes. The new legislation also led to a larger capital base for the Bank. In September 1935, the RFC approved the purchase of $25 million in preferred capital stock, contingent on the approval of the secretary of the treasury.[17]

Thus, within two years of Ex-Im's founding, Roosevelt had enlarged the scope of its activities beyond the USSR and Cuba, and Congress had broadened its powers and increased its funding. Foreign policy personnel were instrumental in establishing the banks. Indeed, Secretary of State Hull hosted the organization meeting of the Ex-Im in his office on February 13, 1934. Similarly, Assistant Secretary of State Sumner Wells, a former ambassador to Cuba, presided over the second Ex-Im's first meeting on March 12, 1934. But the private sector came to play a larger role in the life of the Bank as the years passed. The strong support that organized business groups offered the Ex-Im strengthened the hands of those in the Bank who increasingly saw the institution as an instrument to assist the private sector.

FORGING TIES TO BUSINESS

Organized American exporter and banker groups applauded the founding of the Export-Import Banks. Their representatives promptly established ties to Bank officials – contacts that matured during the decade. The economic debacle of the early 1930s severely disrupted the export sector in the United States, as well as the banks whose lending had facilitated the business.

For exporters, the situation in the early 1930s was dire indeed, as private sources of export financing almost evaporated. These circumstances represented a sharp reversal from the 1920s. During that decade, private American capital easily met the needs of American foreign trade. Over this same period, U.S. investment abroad climbed to $700 million

[17] Pierson, pp. 6–8; Memo, "Financing Export Trade to Russia," January 9, 1934, Office of Secretary, RFC, General Correspondence . . . , Box 21, "Exim Bank" folders, RG 234.

and short-term lending, which supported much foreign trade, reached $100 million a year on average in the 1920s. Generally, exporters obtained ninety-day loans, which commercial banks frequently extended, as needed. Federal Reserve policy prohibited commercial banks from discounting longer-term credits.[18] By the early 1930s, the depression crippled financial support for American foreign trade. Short-term lending dropped to $4 million a year in 1934; long-term lending was only about $9 million. American foreign trade had grown rapidly between 1920 and 1929. In 1929, exports of merchandise reached $5.2 billion. By 1933, it had dropped to $1.7 billion; it rose slowly but only reached $3.2 billion by 1939. This latter increase was generally not the result of improved basic economic conditions in the world economy. It was unhappily the consequence of war preparations and war itself.[19]

There was more to the problems of the depression for export interests than the loss of markets. Many countries had balance-of-payments difficulties, which led to restrictions on foreign exchange payments. As governments moved away from traditional channels and methods of trade, the world's commerce was further restricted. Under the circumstances, American banks were reluctant to lend to exporters whose payments for goods might be delayed because of exchange controls.[20]

As international trade contracted, American exporters turned to the government for assistance. In 1931, the National Foreign Trade Council (NFTC) supported the establishment of a government program to promote exports and imports. The group advocated an agency similar to those developed in other industrial countries in the 1920s. Indeed, Germany and Great Britain had generally been encouraging foreign

[18] Many observers at the time attributed Federal Reserve rules to the fact that Congress created the United States' central bank before the country had become a creditor nation. Generally, the argument was that the United States' commercial, banking, and credit system had developed when the United States was a debtor nation. The system proved inadequate as the United States became a creditor nation after World War I. See "The Export-Import Banks," Address by Charles E. Stuart, Executive Vice President of the Second Export-Import Bank Washington, delivered to Export Managers' Club, New York, August 21, 1934, Subject Files, 1933–1975, "Policy & Scope Documents," Box 41, Record Group 275, Records of The Export-Import Bank of the United States, National Archives (hereafter Stuart, "The Export-Import Banks").

[19] R. Tirana, "Fifteen Years of Export-Import Bank of Washington," October 1948, pp. 1–2, ms in Library, "(William McChesney) Martin Term" files, Library, Ex-Im. U.S. Department of Commerce, *Historical Statistics of the United States* (Washington, DC: Government Printing Office, 1977), p. 537.

[20] Tirana, pp. 1–2; Adams, p. 68.

trade since the early twentieth century through the commercial activities of their diplomatic services. In the early 1920s, both countries established agencies explicitly designed to provide credit to exporters. France, Italy, and Japan followed their lead later in the 1920s.[21]

Interest in governmental assistance increased as economic conditions worsened. In the fall of 1933, export-oriented business organizations formed a joint study committee on creating a public agency to finance foreign commerce. Leaders with important export interests joined well-established advocacy groups – the NFTC, the American Manufacturers' Export Association (AMEA), and the Council on Inter-American Relations – in forming the committee. Once constituted, the committee reached out to other potential allies, including bankers and importers, and sought out government officials. At about the same time, the National Association of Manufacturers and the Russian-American Chamber of Commerce also weighed in with plans for financing trade with the USSR.[22]

Committee members quickly came up with a proposal. In January 1934, they advanced the idea of a cooperative arrangement with government to provide the credit needed for foreign trade. Funds and credit for the initiative would come primarily from the Reconstruction Finance Corporation, which would provide $25 million of an initial $30 million in capital – the balance to be raised privately. Even though the government would have a role in managing the institution, the committee wanted private sector managers substantially to be involved, if not totally running things. The committee thought that practical businessmen like themselves were best equipped to manage the day-to-day business of helping American agriculture and industry. Government representation, however, figured into their proposal because coping with blocked exchange accounts would require government-to-government negotiations. The committee also contemplated an agency capable of issuing insurance and of resolving disputes about foreign investments, credits, and business agreements.[23]

[21] Stuart, "The Export-Import Banks"; Adams, p. 69.

[22] "Russian Business," n.d., and "Memorandum Relating to the Formation of a Discount Corporation for Financing Trade with Soviet Russia," February 1934, Office of Secretary, RFC, Administrative Subject Files, 1932–1957, Box 34, "Loans – Russia" folder, RG 234; Adams, p. 69.

[23] Adams, p. 70.

In the end, the committee did not get what it wanted. The two new Ex-Im institutions were wholly governmental agencies, fully funded by the RFC. Roosevelt and the State Department appointed their leaders more for reasons of foreign policy expertise and political connections than for their experience in commercial matters. But Roosevelt administration officials were sympathetic to the difficulties exporters faced, which provided an opening for organized business groups to develop ties to the Bank. Increasing exports clearly would contribute to recovery.

Soon after the trustees authorized the Bank to do business everywhere but the USSR, Peek published the Bank's first general policy statement. The statement was, he said, prepared following "a comprehensive canvass of the situation during the past 6 months with American producers and business men, whose actual needs in relation to export and import business have been carefully studied case by case." In this document of July 30, 1934, the Bank declared that its goal was to supplement the work of existing commercial banks and financial institutions. It was not the Bank's mission to compete with or take business away from them. Indeed, the statement went on to say that the Bank would "deal with proposals directly and through regular banking channels," and it invited commercial banks to participate in special loans. Ex-Im loans were defined as short term (less than 180 days), intermediate (180 days to one year), and long term (one to five years). The Bank's interest rates were to be 0.75 percent over funds borrowed from RFC on loans of one year or less, and one percent over RFC funds for those between one and five years. For unusual, generally riskier transactions, the Banks would charge higher rates of interest and participate only up to 75 percent of the credit needed. The statement explicitly ruled out as a primary responsibility of the Bank, "the guaranteeing of a credit risk or the acceptance of paper without recourse." A few days earlier Peek had also said at a news conference that the Bank did not expect to extend credit to sovereign governments.[24]

Despite an extensive publicity campaign that accompanied the issuance of the policy statement, potential customers among exporters

[24] Second Export-Import Bank of Washington, DC, General Policy Statement, July 30, 1934, Subject Files, 1933–75, Box 41, "Policies and Scope" folders, RG 275; Press Conference, July 27, 1934 (p. 2) , SAFT, Records of the Secretary, General Records, Box 7, "Press Conference" folder, RG 19; Adams, pp. 76–7.

and importers remained unsure of what the Bank had to offer. Indeed, Peek pointed out that the Bank in its first months had received numerous inquiries, almost all of which did not lead to bank assistance. Then, too, internally there were administrative difficulties that complicated the review of applications. Lines of authority crossed between those working on tasks for SAFT and Ex-Im matters. Compounding these difficulties were the Bank's close quarters. In July 1934, the Bank's 13 designated senior executive employees and their support staff had only about 1600 square feet of space in the offices occupied by RFC at 1825 H Street.[25]

In the fall of 1934, Peek formalized ties to organized exporter and banking groups to increase the visibility of the Banks. As a former business executive – he had been a vice president of John Deere and Company and president of the Moline Plow Company – he understood how the banker and exporter communities could get out the word about the Bank. He also wanted to gain their confidence. In an October 1934 speech, Peek invited the American Banker's Association (ABA) to set up an advisory committee to cooperate with the Bank. Within weeks, in November 1934, he made the same offer at a meeting of the influential NFTC. For twenty years, that group had advocated government policies to promote American foreign trade. Its president since 1932, Eugene P. Thomas, a former vice president of US Steel, had been a vocal advocate of government assistance to exporters. NFTC's membership included leaders from some of the country's most powerful manufacturing companies: Standard Oil of New Jersey, Caterpillar Tractor, General Electric, Westinghouse, General Motors, and Chrysler. Leaders of key banks were also members: National City Bank of New York, Bankers Trust, Guaranty Trust, and Chase National Bank.[26]

Thomas and the NFTC got right to work. Its advisory committee joined with the one set up by the ABA. The latter had already formulated ideas about how the Ex-Im should operate. They proposed an executive

25 Memorandum, RFC to George N. Peek, August 31, 1934, Office of Secretary, RFC, General Correspondence..., Box 2, "Ex-Im Bank" folder, RG 234. R. W. Burgess to Charles E. Stuart, Memoranda: "Export-Import Bank Credit Investigation" and "Analysis Source Material and Bank Policy Comments," September 27, 1934; Summary of Bank Policy Proposal by Mr. Burgess, October 1, 1934; Peek to Director of the Budget, June 26, 1935, Subject Files, 1933–1975, Box 41, "Policies & Scope" folders, RG 275.

26 Adams, p. 75.

committee of bankers to take on a consulting role to assist the Ex-Im on foreign business and special overseas problems, in particular unblocking foreign exchange. Overall, in regard to lending, the committee thought that the Ex-Im should concentrate on what commercial banks were not able to do: provide longer-term – and at times riskier – loans. To prevent unwanted competition and to expedite the lending process, the committee suggested that requests for Ex-Im loans be channeled through commercial banks.[27]

In March 1935, the advisory committees arranged a two-day session in Washington with Ex-Im officials and representatives from the Agricultural Advisory Committee and the Cotton Advisory Committee. The latter two groups were interested in the Bank's financing the sale of agricultural products abroad. In fact, in future years supporting overseas sales of cotton and tobacco were among the Ex-Im's first and most important transactions.[28] The upshot of these meetings was a series of recommendations that laid out how the private sector groups wanted to shape the Ex-Im to serve their interests. Keenly aware of what foreign governments did to support their exporters, the advisory committees desired the Bank to be as helpful as comparable agencies in Europe and Japan. To be competitive with these foreign agencies would have required Ex-Im to take on greater risk than commercial banks usually would at the time and, on occasion, provide a general line of credit above the value of exports in a particular deal. Finally, they favored that the Ex-Im take the initiative with the State Department in freeing up blocked foreign exchange balances.[29]

In the meantime, though, the Bank's officers had been working independently on an organizational structure and internal procedures. In April 1935, its practices were codified through several memoranda.

[27] Press Releases: "Commercial Bankers Present Nation-Wide Plan of Cooperation with Export-Import Banks" and "Joint Statement By Advisory Committee of the American Bankers Association and the Export-Import Banks," in SAFT, Records of Public Relations Office, Box 1, "Publicity Materials, 1933–1935" folder, RG 19; Memorandum, "A Plan of Cooperation with The Export-Import Banks," American Bankers Association, December 3, 1934, RFC, Office of Secretary, General Correspondence . . . , Box 21, Ex-Im Bank folders, RG 234; Pierson, pp. 13–16.

[28] Annual Report for the Export-Import Bank of Washington for 1936, typescript in Library, Ex-Im (hereafter Annual Report).

[29] Letter, E. P. Thomas, NFTC, to Earl B. Schwulst, RFC, April 8, 1935, Office of Secretary, General Correspondence . . . , Box 21, "Export-Import Bank of Washington" folders, RG 234.

These indicated that daily operations of the Bank were the responsibility of an executive committee of the board of trustees. The latter legally had the final authority over the authorization of credits. The Bank's president presided over the executive committee, which also included the Bank's treasurer, Lynn P. Taley, and Robert F. Kelley, an assistant secretary of state. Also attending the executive committee meetings on a regular basis were Charles E. Stuart, the Bank's vice president; Peek's assistant, Wayne C. Taylor; the chairman of the credit committee, J. W. Pole; and Warren Lee Pierson, secretary and general counsel. Other aspects of daily operations were carried out by two committees: operations and credit. There were also legal, commercial, accounting, and administrative departments. The operations committee had responsibility for regularly reviewing the Bank's policies, procedures, and practices. Applications for credit were routinely to be referred to a member each of the credit and commercial committees. These two individuals were to prepare independent reports on the application, which were then to be forwarded to the legal department and the credit committee for review, and finally to the executive committee for decision. If there was a commitment on the basis of the applications, the two officers who originally examined the application were to be in charge of monitoring the loan.[30]

Soon after determining these procedures, the Bank was faced with a crisis. In June 1935, President Roosevelt decided to do away with the office of special adviser on foreign trade (SAFT). While FDR wanted the work of the Bank to continue, it would have to do so with a reduced budget and fewer personnel as Peek's office of SAFT suspended operations. The resulting reorganization, approved in July 1935, more or less retained the basic organizational structure and operating procedures of the Bank's executive personnel. In 1935, the Ex-Im's operating expenses were $125,000. They went down to $50,000 in early 1936 and stayed there into 1939. By then, the Bank's leadership thought that it was seriously understaffed. In 1937, the Bank authorized credits of $22.9 million, disbursed $7.7 million, and received payments of $7.9 million. A year later, commitments were $31.3 million; disbursements $18.6 million; and payments $9.7 million. Officials argued that their work was more complicated; proposed loans took more time to

[30] Minutes, Meeting of the Executive Committee, Export-Import Bank, April 15, 1934, Minutes, Box 2, RG 275; Mazon, p. 8.

examine and service than the relatively simple large agricultural credits of the Bank's initial lending. At the end of 1936, for example, the Bank had authorized $26.7 million for agricultural exports and disbursed $17.4 million since its inception.[31]

Talk of reduced budgets and fewer staff did not reassure the export and banking groups looking to the Ex-Im for assistance. Indeed, they only added to already existing concerns about the Bank. To the National Association of Credit Men, the Bank needed to focus more clearly on exchange problems. It reported in 1934 that a survey of 200 of its members found that almost all of those replying thought that the major impediment to foreign trade was the "exchange transfer problem." The NFTC, in surveys conducted among its members in 1935, recounted that an overwhelming number did not believe that "with recourse" financing was useful to them. Under "with recourse" financing, the Bank expected payment from the exporter in the event that a customer failed to pay for his goods. Early statements of Bank policy did not rule out the possibility of "without recourse" financing. But the Bank officially would undertake it only in special circumstances, and rates would be higher to reflect what might be riskier business. In fact, unofficially, internal Bank procedure instructed employees to turn back requests for without recourse financing as a matter of routine.[32]

Peek strongly opposed without recourse financing, as did the State Department's representative on the Bank's executive committee, Robert F. Kelley. The Bank's president believed that without recourse loans were not a sound way to do business. He feared that such lending (even for only a percentage of a financed transaction) would reduce the recipient's diligence in overseeing business financed in such a way. Kelley's concern was that if without recourse lending supported sales to a foreign

[31] Memorandum, George N. Peek to Executive Committee, July 12, 1935 and Minutes, Board of Trustees, July 15, 1935, Minutes, Box 2, RG 275; Memorandum, Pierson, "Explanation of Estimates of Administrative Expenses of the Export-Import Bank of Washington for 1940," May 3, 1939, Subject Files, 1933–1975, Box 3, "Budget 1940" folder, RG 275; Annual Report for 1936, p. 6; Annual Report for 1937, p. 6; Annual Report for 1938, p. 4.

[32] "Result of Survey on Current Export Credit and Exchange Problem," *Weekly Confidential Bulletin* of the Foreign Department and Foreign Credit Interchange Bureau, National Association of Credit Men, June 9, 1934, in Office of Secretary, RFC, Administrative Subject File, 1932–57, Box 34, "Loans – Russia" folder, RG 234; Summary of Bank Policy Proposal by Mr. Burgess, October 1, 1934, Subject Files, 1933–1975, Box 41, "Policies & Scope" folders, RG 275; Adams, pp. 76–9.

government entity, the United States could become a creditor of a foreign government, an entanglement the administration wished to avoid.[33]

In place of without recourse financing, Peek said he favored the Ex-Im providing insurance for exporters. This proved to be a popular position. NFTC polls indicated that over half the members surveyed believed that the government should emulate Great Britain and provide insurance for exporters against the insolvency of their customers. But Peek's support for insurance never went beyond the rhetorical, and in any event there was little interest in Congress in such a program. Peek was also too busy with other responsibilities to mount a campaign to build the congressional support necessary to create an insurance program.[34]

Not much progress occurred in building cooperation with the private sector, despite hearty assurances of collaboration between the Bank and the exporter and banking committees in March 1935, following the joint meeting in Washington. By early 1936, Fred I. Kent, a leading member of the ABA's advisory committee to the Ex-Im, bluntly summed up almost two years of the Bank's work. The Ex-Im, he said, "has not as yet made sufficient headway in meeting the need [of exporters, importers, and bankers] to be effective."[35]

Nevertheless, key Bank officials and staff in 1935 were coming around to the view of the export community on a number of issues: without recourse lending, longer credit terms, the provision of finance to foreign purchasers of American goods, and the problems of blocked exchange. In particular, Charles E. Stuart, executive vice-president of the Bank, became a spokesman for a more expansive view of the Bank's products and facilities. In 1935, Stuart toured Europe where he observed first hand the operations of different government agencies designed to finance trade. He learned that difficulty in getting without recourse financing put American traders at a competitive disadvantage against more liberally financed foreign exporters.[36]

33 Adams, pp. 76–7.

34 Minutes, Executive Committee (pp. 522–3), Export-Import Bank, May 26, 1936, Minutes, Box 2, RG 275; Adams, pp. 78–9.

35 Letter, Fred I. Kent to Jesse Jones, RFC, January 10, 1936 and Address by Charles E. Stuart, "European Conditions in their Relationship to International Trade and Export Credits, November 19, 1935, p. 26, both in Office of Secretary, RFC, General Correspondence... Box 21, "Ex-Im Bank" folders, RG 234.

36 Address by Charles E. Stuart, "European Conditions in their Relationship to International Trade and Export Credits," November 19, 1935, p. 26, Office of Secretary, RFC, General Correspondence... Box 21, "Ex-Im Bank" folders, RG 234; Adams, p. 79.

Stuart, Peek, and others were also influenced by the well-organized export and banker groups – highly focused and vocal proponents of what business thought it needed to expand export trade. Their interest in the Bank, if anything, increased when, after a few years of moderate recovery from the worst of the depression, economic conditions degenerated in the fall of 1937. The dramatic economic reversal – the so-called Roosevelt recession – led to a short-lived, but sharp drop in output, employment, and profits of American industry.

Changing attitudes toward without recourse financing, however, raised tensions with State Department officials involved with the Bank. This issue, though, was not the only source of strain for the fledgling Ex-Im. There were also disputes over how to cope with exchange restrictions that harmed American export trade. In 1935, the Bank's president, George N. Peek, became embroiled in what became a major public dispute with Secretary of State Cordell Hull. The issue revolved around Peek's statist approach to trade policy, a stance sharply antithetical to Hull's commitment to the principles of unconditional most-favored-nation (MFN) trade and reciprocal trade agreements. The upshot of the dispute was Peek's resignation in November 1935.[37]

THE BANK AND AMERICAN FOREIGN POLICY

The dispute between Hull and Peek proved to be a major distraction for the Bank and its private sector supporters. If FDR established the Ex-Im Banks to aid the country's foreign policy and economic recovery, he had appointed George N. Peek to satisfy agricultural interests in the Democratic Party. Peek was a well-known spokesman for agricultural interests; they applauded his appointment as FDR's special advisor on foreign trade. Peek's career as an executive in the agricultural implement manufacturing business schooled him in the problems of American agriculture. In the 1920s, Peek became one of the leaders of a movement for farm price supports, which included schemes devised to maintain farm prices by dumping surplus agricultural products overseas.[38]

Peek and Secretary of State Hull quickly became rivals. Hull's diplomacy revolved around the issue of foreign trade. He believed that

[37] Adams, pp. 80 ff.

[38] Michael A. Butler, *Cautious Visionary: Corell Hull and Trade Reform, 1933–1937* (Kent, OH: The Kent State University Press, 1998), p. 98.

multiplying trade relations among countries was both economically and politically beneficial. Hull spearheaded the successful effort to change the country's basic approach to trade policy. The Reciprocal Trade Act of June 1934 gave authority to the executive branch to negotiate bilateral trade agreements, within limits set by Congress. But the legislation was revolutionary in that it gave the president authority to negotiate trade agreements without Senate ratification of a treaty. As such, these agreements would avoid the "horse trading" of previous tariff legislation that protected rates on specific categories of goods favored by influential members of the Senate. Essential to Hull's approach to these treaties was the unconditional MFN principle. U.S. tariff concessions with one country would pass to others, so long as that country did not discriminate against American exports. In this way, Hull believed, trade barriers would come down and an intricate, interdependent web of trading relations would promote the kind of mutual interest among countries that would lessen the likelihood of international conflict.[39]

Peek had a different view of the ideal trading relationship. He saw the terms of trade as something to be arranged bilaterally between two countries. Because foreign governments had responded to the depression by trying to manage trade relations, Peek believed that the United States would have to adopt similar policies. Peek after taking his SAFT post in January 1934 tried to use his position to take command of American trade policy.[40]

It was in the midst of this unfolding dispute between Hull and Peek that the White House announced the formation of the Export-Import Bank, and Peek's appointment as its first president. At the same time, FDR continued Peek on as his special trade adviser with an increased budget. Peek used his new positions to further his programs on trade, embroiling the Ex-Im at times in the disputes that erupted as he tried to forward his agenda on managed trade in opposition to that of Hull's in favor of reciprocal trade agreements.[41]

Ultimately, after many months of bureaucratic infighting, Roosevelt favored Hull's approach over that of Peek. In June 1935, the president gave the Department of State authority to investigate and negotiate

[39] Ibid., pp. 1–14, 82–96.
[40] Ibid., pp. 98–120.
[41] Ibid., pp. 99–102.

trade agreements under the Reciprocal Trade Act of 1934. Having lost out to Hull, Peek left office in November 1935. Warren Lee Pierson got the nod as the new president of the Bank in February 1936, after Jesse Jones – who served as president for two months and was the unanimous choice of the Bank's board of trustees – turned the job down.[42] Pierson, a young Los Angeles attorney – he was 37 in 1936 – had come to Washington to work in the Reconstruction Finance Corporation as a special counsel. He impressed its head, Jesse Jones, who recommended Pierson as the first counsel to the Bank.[43]

THE BANK, BUSINESS, AND FOREIGN POLICY

With the appointment of Warren Lee Pierson to succeed George N. Peek, the Export-Import Bank had a president who focused full-time on the work of the new institution. During Pierson's tenure, those responsible for the day-to-day work of the Bank developed a business-oriented "deal-making" and "contract-administering" culture. The Bank's credit and commercial committees – where exporter requests for assistance were considered and when approved monitored – were committed to assisting exporters with sound businesslike proposals. Pierson, as president and convener of the executive committee, was clearly in their camp and became known as being "distinctly ambitious for the Bank" and willing "to push out vigorously for business."[44]

But throughout the 1930s, the Bank regularly also had to attend to concerns of American foreign policy. The Department of State loomed large in the life and work of the Bank. E. Walton Moore, assistant secretary of state and department legal counsel, remained as chairman of the Bank's board of trustees until 1941. Assistant Secretary of State Robert F. Kelley, a full member of the Bank's three-person executive committee, routinely consulted with his State Department colleagues about issues considered by the Bank's executive committee. Indeed, the executive committee itself often took the initiative and postponed

[42] Press Release, RFC, February 19, 1936, Office of Secretary, General Correspondence... Box 21, "Ex-Im Bank" folders, RG 234. Jones served as president between December 2, 1935, and February 17, 1936.

[43] Pierson, chapter 1.

[44] Comment of Herbert Feis, Economic Adviser to the Department of State, quoted in Adams, p. 195.

matters before it until the State Department rendered an opinion on the foreign policy implications of pending matters.

Pierson and his Bank colleagues never confronted the Department of State in the aggressive manner that Peek did. But Peek's departure did not guarantee altogether smooth relations. Hull and his departmental associates continued to view the Bank as an institution that required close attention. At first, they worried that the Bank might hinder American foreign policy goals, especially in Latin America. State Department officers thwarted Ex-Im efforts whenever they believed they came in conflict with the larger objectives of the Roosevelt administration's foreign policy. Some in the foreign affairs bureaucracy, like Assistant Secretary of State Frances Sayre, frankly looked upon the Bank and its private sector constituencies as having narrow self-interests that needed to be subordinated to the long-term concerns of the United States.

During the 1930s, the State Department's relationship with the Bank shifted as American foreign policy concerns changed. Generally, the early Roosevelt administration expended the most energy on improving relations in the western hemisphere. By the later 1930s, the government had to concentrate more on Europe and Asia, in particular the increasingly aggressive behavior of Germany and Japan. But Latin America remained an important focus of attention. For one thing, toward the end of the decade, foreign policy officials feared Germany's growing influence in the region. For another, confiscation of American oil properties in Bolivia in 1937 and Mexico in 1938 created a new set of problems in protecting Americans' rights and property. Additionally, foreign exchange problems remained a constant issue through all the years of the decade.

But in the Bank's early history, Roosevelt's hemispheric diplomacy figured most significantly in its operations. FDR had made improving relations with Latin America a central aspect of his foreign policy. It had two primary goals. First was the increasing commitment to the notion of a liberalizing international trade order. A centerpiece of this effort was Hull's reciprocal trade agreements.

The other major aspect of New Deal foreign policy was the commitment to what became known as the Good Neighbor Policy. Roosevelt in the 1932 presidential campaign had sharply criticized previous Republican policies toward Latin America, castigating what he saw as a history of heavy handedness and frequent armed interventions. Instead, he promised Latin American nations that the United States would intervene only in an emergency when Americans and their property were in direct danger. Never, according to FDR, should the United States intervene to force payment of debts. In effect, Roosevelt and his close advisers on Latin America proposed a rethinking of the Monroe Doctrine. They argued that every nation in the Americas had a stake in working together. Toward that end, the United States advocated consultation and joint action if necessary to protect the hemisphere. Administration officials also advocated lower tariffs to stimulate trade with the United States and thereby, from their point of view, benefit Latin America economically. A commitment to nonintervention was an important part of the government's thinking about improving economic conditions there. A growing American economic presence through trade or investment should not be, from the Roosevelt administration's perspective, cast in a threatening way.[45]

But the Roosevelt administration was also keenly attuned to the dangerous consequences for the hemisphere of the international depression. Declining economic circumstances, the United States feared, opened the continent to nationalistic, anti-American sentiments, as well as social and political instability. There was also the possibility of unwanted foreign influence, especially from Nazi Germany.

Once the trustees expanded the Bank's geographical scope in July 1934, exporters of heavy manufactured goods turned to the Ex-Im for assistance in developing what they saw as a promising market in Latin America. Increased interest in export business there raised a set of perplexing issues for the Bank about foreign exchange. Most Latin American countries had serious balance of payments problems, which led to restrictions on exchange and trade. Germany in particular solved this problem with arrangements that directed commerce and payments back and forth bilaterally. State Department officials saw these developments as threatening U.S. goals for increasing multilateral trade and, as such, ultimately hindering economic recovery. But from a practical point of view of promoting exports, something had to be done about blocked payments.[46]

[45] Adams, pp. 134–6.
[46] Ibid., pp. 139–40.

In 1935, the Bank advocated that it purchase without recourse the obligations of Latin American governments to free up blocked exchange. As a result, the Bank recommended, for example, that it acquire the obligations of the Bank of Nicaragua. This proved to be a controversial recommendation because Nicaragua had a poor credit history and had defaulted on past debts to the U.S. government. In addition, the State Department took the position that the arrangement would make the United States a creditor of a Nicaraguan governmental agency. The latter concern of the department became something of a regular refrain in considering other Ex-Im proposals in regard to Latin American countries. From the department's point of view, without recourse financing would undermine the goals of the Good Neighbor Policy if a default led the Bank to become a creditor of a governmental entity in a Latin American country.[47]

Providing assistance to exporters interested in doing business with Brazil presented the Bank and the State Department with similar but knottier issues. Because of Brazil's size, potential wealth, and strategic location, the department saw it as one of the most important countries in Latin America. Frozen exchange balances were a persistent problem for American exporters to Brazil; at the beginning of 1935, about $35 million of payments to Americans were blocked because of exchange problems. In that same year, to provide liquidity, Peek suggested that the Brazilian government issue long-term bonds to those with deferred balances; the bonds would be secured by a lien against revenue generated by the sale of Brazilian coffee in the United States. The State Department challenged the proposal. Officials argued that it would not necessarily lead to increased exports and that it undermined multilateralism. Similarly, the department refused to support a series of proposals from the National Foreign Trade Council in which the Bank would purchase on a without recourse basis Brazilian government obligations as a way to free foreign exchange. Ex-Im officials, including Jesse Jones, were skeptical of some of these arrangements. They believed that the proposals would aid large industrial corporations, which should have been able to deal with blocked exchange on their own. Ultimately, in February 1936, the Bank signed an agreement in which it would purchase on a

47 Minutes, Executive Committee, Ex-Im, June 10, 1935, Minutes, Box 2, RG 275; Adams, pp. 142–3.

recourse basis $27.75 million of notes issued by the Bank of Brazil to pay for blocked accounts.[48]

Overall, the State Department was not willing to take what it saw as steps that undermined larger foreign policy goals to deal with blocked exchange. So, in 1935 and 1936, officials continued to reject Bank proposals to use without recourse financing to free up blocked exchange balances in Peru, Costa Rica, and Nicaragua. Not surprisingly, State Department officials preferred to deal with blocked exchange through diplomatic means. In negotiating a reciprocal trade agreement with Brazil (ratified in January 1936), American diplomats successfully included in the treaty promises from the Brazilians that future deals with American businesses would not be hindered by the lack of exchange and that arrears would be addressed.[49]

If the State Department showed any flexibility in the early 1930s, it was in regard to Mexico. When the Bank pushed the department, there was some movement. Before Mexico confiscated American oil facilities in 1938, the Bank made a number of without recourse loans involving state and federal government agencies. There was disagreement within the department over how to deal with Mexico, as some Latin American specialists applied the same unyielding criteria to Mexico as to other countries in the hemisphere. But others apparently believed that Mexico's tax collection system was strong enough to prevent default on its liabilities. In 1935, for example, the Bank acquired the notes of Chihuahua state. Later that year, to assist in the sale of equipment for a waterworks in Vera Cruz, the Bank provided without recourse financing and became a creditor of both the Mexican government and Vera Cruz.[50]

Over time, changing circumstances in Latin America ultimately forced the State Department to further relax its policies toward the terms upon which the Bank could do business there. Growing evidence

[48] See the correspondence between the American charge in Rio de Janeiro and the Secretary of State, February 20, 1935 to December 21, 1935 in U.S. Department of State, *FRUS, 1935*, Vol. IV, pp. 349–86 and the correspondence between Secretary of State and U.S. Ambassador to Brazil, January 4 to June 11, 1936, in *FRUS, 1936*, Vol. V, pp. 282–96; Minutes, Board of Trustees, Ex-Im, February 17, 1936, Minutes, Box 2, RG 275; Credit No. 80, "National Foreign Trade Council," Credit Files, 1934–1951, Box 1, RG 275; Mazo, p. 11; Adams, pp. 146–52.

[49] Adams, pp. 147–8.

[50] Ibid., pp. 154–6.

of German influence in Latin America alarmed U.S. officials as the Nazi regime's policies at home and toward its neighbors became more extreme. The severe economic setback the United States suffered in 1937 added urgency to the requests of exporter and banker groups for assistance in expanding trade to Latin America. In 1938, industrial production contracted by a third, which eventually impacted Latin America, as its trade with the important American market declined. Multiplying economic difficulties in Latin America fueled nationalistic sentiments, embodied in the confiscation of property of American oil companies in Bolivia and Mexico.[51]

During the 1930s, German influence grew fastest in Argentina, Brazil, Chile, and Mexico. Developments in Brazil proved particularly worrisome. The country had been moving erratically toward a nationalistic economic policy ever since an avowedly nationalist president came to power in 1930. More troubling than the possible discrimination against U.S. business and financial interests was evidence of growing commercial ties between Brazil and Germany. In the mid 1930s, Germany endeavored to pull Brazil into its trading orbit. Indeed, in 1934, Germany became Brazil's single largest trading partner, following a series of bilateral arrangements. Between 1934 and 1937, German imports went from 14 to 24 percent of the country's total imports in dollar terms. German imports also grew in percentage terms in Argentina, Chile, and Mexico. Equally troubling to the United States was that these economic inroads were often accompanied by stronger political ties. In Brazil, for instance, the military enthusiastically supported the bilateral swapping arrangements because it gave them access to Germany's weapons industry.[52]

In this atmosphere of growing concerns about Germany, Ex-Im officials argued that the Bank should be allowed to liberalize its policies. Bank officials portrayed increased American export trade to Latin America as helping lessen German influence in the region. The Ex-Im also depicted assistance to American exporters as a way to counter shrinking markets at home following the sharp downturn in the economy between 1937 and 1938. These arguments resonated with high-ranking

[51] Ibid., pp. 188, 203–15, 222; Michael A. Bernstein, *The Great Depression: Delayed Recovery and Economic Change in America, 1929–1939* (New York: Cambridge University Press, 1989).

[52] Adams, pp. 143–5, 197–8.

officials in the State Department – especially Roosevelt's friend Undersecretary of State Sumner Welles – who came around more or less to the Bank's view.[53]

Similarly, Assistant Secretary of State Francis B. Sayre, who had been in charge of trade negotiations under the reciprocal trade agreements program also changed his thinking in 1937–8. Officials of the NFTC made a persuasive case that exporters would abandon reciprocal trade if something were not done about the exchange problem. Exporters believed that, under the German bilateral arrangements, their exports would be paid for in hard currency.[54]

In 1938 and 1939, the State Department acquiesced to Pierson's strong stand on the need for the United States to do more about the exchange problems Latin American countries continued to face, especially in the aftermath of the 1937 collapse in the American economy. In the fall of 1938, Pierson toured several Latin American countries. On his return, he made a strong case that the Bank deal with the dollar exchange shortage by providing credits to central banks in Uraguay, Brazil, and Argentina. These credits would provide the dollar exchange needed to allow for the purchase of American goods.[55]

Three different railway loans in 1937 and 1938 further illustrate the evolution in State Department thinking. In October 1937, Pierson championed a 50 percent without recourse financing of locomotives to the government-owned railroads in Chile. At first, the State Department opposed the deal for the usual reasons: the United States would become a creditor of Chile, which had not been diligent in paying back American bondholders. But the Bank persisted, and high-level State Department officials relented. After all, the latter concluded, the Germans were capable of supplying Chile's needs if American business did not. A similar situation developed in regard to financing for the Central Railway of Brazil. Originally, in December 1937, the State Department objected because Brazil had not made arrangements to compensate Americans for the default on Brazilian bonds. Also, Brazil had not lived up to its 1936 agreement to free up blocked exchange. Discussions of the loan for railroad equipment dragged on through

53 Adams, p. 196.

54 Memorandum of Conversation, October 24, 1938, Eugene P. Thomas et al., NFTC, Frances B. Sayre et al., U.S. Department of State, *FRUS, 1938*, Vol. V, pp. 57–9.

55 Adams., pp. 203–15.

early 1938, when the department again rejected the Bank's proposal. By May 1938, however, Welles overrode those in the department objecting to the loans, and the deal went through. Similarly, in 1938, Welles rejected complaints about Bank assistance for exporters of railroad equipment to the Sorocabana Railway of Brazil in the state of Sao Paulo.[56]

But there was more change to come in the role the Bank played in Latin America. Deteriorating economic conditions in Haiti in the late 1930s – and the threat of increased German economic influence there – provided the occasion for something of a turnabout in State Department thinking about the Bank. As a result, for probably the first time, the State Department turned to the Bank for assistance in 1938. The role Ex-Im came to play in Haiti also marked an important turning point for the Bank. Not only did it represent a maturer relationship with the State Department, but it also led to an entirely new kind of lending for the Bank – so-called development lending – and new responsibilities in monitoring the projects financed.

By early 1938, Haiti was in desperate economic shape. It had an economy marked by a high rate of unemployment and business failures. The long-term ill effects of the depression were exacerbated by fast-falling international coffee prices, the destruction of the country's cotton crop by insects, and disappointing overseas markets for bananas. Strained border relations with Santo Domingo only worsened the situation, as did the repatriation of Haitian workers from that country and Cuba.[57]

Because of the demands for social services and declining tax revenues, the Haitian government in 1937 defaulted on U.S. loans originally made in 1922. To cope with the situation, Haiti needed another foreign loan. State Department officials were solicitous when Haitian officials approached the United States for advice. But true to the tenets of the good neighbor policy, the department was also concerned lest the United States be perceived as interfering. Certainly, the U.S. government was not at first inclined to assist Haiti in floating a loan among private

[56] Credit No. 174, "The Westinghouse Electric International Company (Chile)," Credit Files, 1934–1951, Box 2, RG 275; Credit No. 200, "Central Railway of Brazil," Credit Files, 1934–1951, Box 4, RG 275; Adams, pp. 193–8.

[57] For background discussion of the Bank's role in Haiti see Memorandum, Whittemore to Pierson, June 16, 1938, in Credit No. 201, "J. G. White Engineering Corporation," Credit Files, 1934–1951, Box 50, RG 275 (note file misfiled in Subject Files, 1933–1975).

investors, although it supported the idea of a continued payments moratorium on the 1922 bonds.[58]

The department's reserved approach to Haiti's problems changed quickly when German influence became a possibility. In turning to private capital markets for assistance, Haiti found a sponsor for refunding its loans in a group of European investors willing to support a major public works program for the country. What alarmed the United States was the investors' intention of using a German engineering firm to carry out the project. In the spring 1937, State Department officials encouraged Wall Street investment houses to take on the funding. While none of the investment bankers wanted to see foreign influence increase in Haiti, they refused to support what they considered an unusually risky endeavor.[59]

As a result, the department turned to the Export-Import Bank to provide the funding for the Haitian public works project. In its own analysis of the deal, the Bank concluded that there were great risks and that it was probably not a prudent loan in terms of standard U.S. banking practice. Hence, there was reluctance in the Bank to take it on. Even so, on June 18, 1937, Ex-Im's executive committee approved the loan. It came down on the side of promoting the national interest in keeping foreign, especially German, influence out of a country so close to the United States. Such influence, the Bank concluded, would not be in the interest of Haiti, nor of Americans with economic and financial stakes there. Because of the riskiness of the loan, Pierson insisted that the Bank have greater than usual oversight of the financial and engineering aspects of the deal. In the agreement with Haiti and the American engineering firm retained to do the work, the Bank stipulated that it could reject particularly risky aspects of the 100 or so parts of the project.[60]

The arrangement was significant for the Bank in several respects. Under the terms of the understanding approved by the executive committee, Haiti would issue no more than $5 million in notes to finance a public works program. The American engineering firm, J. G. White Engineering Corporation, would plan and carry out the project and, acting as the agent of the Haitian government, be responsible for

[58] Adams, pp. 198–9.

[59] Minutes, Executive Committee, Ex-Im, June 18, 1938, Minutes, Box 3, RG 275; Adams, pp. 199–201.

[60] Mazo, p. 16; Adams, pp. 202–3.

purchasing supplies and equipment in the United States, and when necessary hiring local workers and acquiring supplies in Haiti. The Bank agreed to purchase the Haitian notes issued to the engineering firm on a without recourse basis.[61]

In assisting Haiti, the Bank at the State Department's behest markedly increased the scope of its activities. It overtly became a creditor of a foreign government, and it also allowed some of its funds to be spent on local labor and materials. In addition, the terms of the arrangement called for the Bank to take on a role in monitoring the engineering aspects of the project.[62]

The deal with Haiti encouraged other governments in Latin America to seek such loans with the United States through the Ex-Im. This new form of lending program won the enthusiastic support of organized American export groups. In 1939, the Bank reached agreements with Brazil, Paraguay, and Nicaragua to provide loans for development projects. In the latter two agreements, both countries promised to retain American financial experts to oversee central bank operations. Both countries also appointed a chief engineer to supervise planning and implementation of the development projects; the engineer in each case was subject to the Bank's approval.[63]

Changing foreign policy concerns about Latin America led to another departure for the Bank in 1938. In December of that year, the Bank provided International Telephone and Telegraph Corporation (ITT) with a loan of $10 million. These funds were needed to expand facilities in Latin America and to pay off some bonds and loans that came due January 1, 1939. Normally, the company would have raised the money in private markets. But the sharp economic reversal of 1937, and a war scare in Europe in 1938, made it impossible for ITT to acquire the funds it needed through traditional financial channels.[64]

State Department officials approved the deal with the Bank in large part because of the strategic importance of ITT. The company

[61] Ibid., pp. 198–203.

[62] Credit No. 201, "J. G. White Engineering Corporation," Credit Files, 1934–1951, Box 50, RG 275.

[63] Adams, pp. 203–17.

[64] Credit No. 215, "International Telephone and Telegraph Company," Credit Files, 1934–1951, Box 4, RG 275; Minutes, Executive Committee, Ex-Im, December 1, 1938, Minutes, Box 3, RG 275; Adams, p. 208.

provided telephone and cable service in a number of countries, including Argentina, Chile, Peru, Cuba, Puerto Rico, and the southern parts of Brazil. It also owned one of the two telephone companies in Mexico, along with operations in Spain, Rumania, and China (Shanghai). Pierson made the case for the importance of having an American firm provide these services. Both Ex-Im and the State Department believed that failure to pay its debts would have forced ITT to sell some of its subsidiaries to foreign companies. The prospect that German interests might have been able to purchase these properties was unacceptable to American officials. [65]

Latin America was not the only foreign policy arena in which the Bank came to play a larger role in the late 1930s. Because of Japanese expansion into China in 1937, the fate of the latter country became a major concern to the United States. Pierson had been interested in promoting American exports to China for some years. He had traveled to Asia in 1937 to assess American prospects. Earlier, in 1935, the Bank had assumed close to $16 million in loans that the RFC had provided to China for the purchase of American cotton and wheat.[66] But the Japanese invasion of China in 1937 rendered normal trade impossible. The war in China eclipsed the commercial role for the Bank Pierson had envisioned, but it did not foreclose a place in the U.S. government's diplomatic response to the Asian crisis.

In the year following the Japanese attack, the U.S. government went through a slow process of evaluating what should be done. It took time for a consensus to emerge. Generally, officials were reluctant to confront Japan directly, although the United States wanted to make clear its displeasure with the invasion of China. During 1938, American officials decided to assist China to help the country hold out against the Japanese. Pierson supported this course of action and worked closely with American officials in the Treasury, Commerce, and Agriculture Departments, as well as with the Commodity Credit Corporation and the Reconstruction Finance Corporation. At first, they thought that China would need agricultural products, but as the Japanese onslaught intensified in 1938 (by October only one Chinese port remained in the government's hands), the Chinese requested trucks, spare parts, lubricants,

[65] Memorandum, Pierson to Files, June 10, 1938, in Credit No. 215, "International Telephone and Telegraph Company," Credit Files, 1934–1951, Box 4, RG 275; Adams, p. 208.
[66] Mazo, p. 13.

and gasoline. These would be used on the Burma–Yuannan highway – the "Burma Road" – the last major transportation link in the country still under the government's control.[67]

In December 1938, the Export-Import Bank reached an agreement to assist the Chinese. The Bank extended a $25 million loan to the Universal Trading Corporation, set up by the Chinese in the United States, to buy American and sell Chinese goods. The five-year term loan would be repaid essentially from the proceeds of tung oil (used in making paints) sold in the United States over the years of the loan. Government officials went out of their way to portray the loan as a commercial endeavor. The Japanese, of course, had few illusions about what the United States was trying to do.

But there were also those in the United States who questioned the obviously political aspects of the loan to China. In becoming involved in the war in Asia, the Bank found itself clearly identified as an overt instrument of American foreign policy. Since FDR's approach to the world came in for sharp criticism in the late 1930s, the Bank found itself involved in often highly partisan congressional maneuvering. As such, the environment that Bank officials had to cope with became more complicated as the Bank proved its utility to the State Department and the Roosevelt administration.[68]

THE BANK, CONGRESS, AND THE FUTURE

The Bank's role in Haiti and China sparked a congressional debate about its future. Leading Republican opponents of the Roosevelt administration proposed that the Bank be forbidden from doing business with foreign governments. Isolationists in general worried that the Ex-Im could ensnare the United States in the affairs of foreign countries without congressional authorization.

These concerns arose early in 1939 at the same time that the Bank's charter was up for renewal. Leading the defense of the Bank was Cordell Hull and Jesse Jones, both of whom made the case for the Bank's contributions to the broader interests of U.S. foreign policy, especially in Latin America. Administration supporters in Congress were able to beat

67 Minutes, Executive Committee, Ex-Im, December 13, 1938, Minutes, Box 3, RG 275; Mazo, p. 17; Adams, 226–37.

68 Adams, pp. 238, 245.

back an attempt to close the Bank down – a position supported by most Republicans – but the resulting compromise gave proponents less than they had hoped for. Congress in February 1939 extended the Bank's charter for two years, not four as requested, and put a ceiling of $100 million on obligations. The ceiling itself was suggested by Jones in an effort to placate opponents of the Bank.[69]

Even though the focus of congressional debate was the Bank's role in American foreign policy, there was also a recognition in the government and among exporters that the Ex-Im had become a capable financial institution. In fact, the organizational capabilities developed during the 1930s proved essential to the mission the Bank followed in the 1940s. During World War II and its aftermath, the Bank came to play a role much enlarged from what any of its government or private sector supporters had envisioned early in the 1930s. In the future, though, it became clear that the basic principles upon which the Bank had originally established its policies in promoting exports had taken firm root. There was a businesslike tradition to which the Bank could return once the United States fulfilled its role in World War II and the reconstruction of Europe that followed.[70] But the Bank had also shown itself to be flexible, an institution capable of adjusting to changing circumstances.

[69] Mazo, pp. 17–18; Adams, pp. 250–1; Congress, Senate, Committee on Banking and Currency, "To Continue the Functions of . . . the Export-Import Bank of Washington . . . ," 67th Congress, 1st Session, 1939, p. 34.

[70] Adams, p. 252–3.

2

WORLD WAR AND ITS AFTERMATH

INTRODUCTION

During World War II and in its aftermath, the Export-Import Bank showed itself to be a remarkably flexible and resilient institution. The volume, scope, and complexity of its activity increased rapidly in these years. When war broke out in Europe in 1939,[1] the Bank to that point principally financed the export of surplus agricultural products and aided manufacturers to meet overseas competition. During World War II, the Bank's focus narrowed essentially to dealing with Latin America. But its activities there broadened. It helped Latin American countries to cope with the dislocations in world markets and finance brought about by the conflict. Ex-Im financed – in cooperation at times with other U.S. government agencies – equipment, facilities, and strategic materials for the war effort. The Bank embarked on a program of developmental lending to improve the export capabilities of Latin American countries. In doing so, it reoriented its financing from relatively simple transactions to complex project-type lending that involved literally hundreds or thousands of separate transactions.

Following the war, the U.S. government refocused the Bank on Europe instead of Latin America. In coping with the destruction in Europe, the Ex-Im became the first government agency to provide loans in the emergency reconstruction effort of the immediate postwar years. It was the only agency of the U.S. government still in business in 1945

[1] In discussing the prewar period, we refer to the time between the beginning of hostilities in Europe (September 1, 1939) and the United States' entry into the war (December 7, 1941); the war period is from December 8, 1941, to the end of hostilities in the Pacific, August 14, 1945 (Japan formally surrendered on September 2, 1945); the European phase of the war ended on May 8, 1945 when Germany surrendered unconditionally.

with the experience to take up the task of extending and managing large credits overseas.

In responding to all of the new demands of the 1940s, the Bank's leadership and staff adhered to, as best they could, the basic businesslike principles of making and administering loans devised during the 1930s. Consequently, these were years of testing for the Bank as an organization. Providing credits – very large credits after the war – was frequently connected to the achievement of the government's goals in foreign policy and national security. Under such circumstances, high-ranking government officials pressed the Bank to speed up its approval of credits and ease somewhat its terms. Nevertheless, at the end of the emergency reconstruction period in 1947, it was clear that the Bank had survived the tests of the 1940s. Ex-Im emerged as a prudent loan-making organization, with a commitment to careful and detailed processes for extending and managing loans, which in fact had become the essence of the Export-Import Bank's culture.

BEFORE AMERICAN ENTRY INTO WORLD WAR II

As war approached in Europe in the late 1930s, the United States could not help but be affected. When in 1939 European governments intensified their war preparations, American industry received numerous orders, and the economy picked up. At the same time, the debate over American involvement in Europe sharpened as Germany became more aggressive and threatening to her neighbors. For his part, FDR determined that the United States should aid those imperilled by Germany, despite frequent public statements that America itself would not become belligerent.

Ex-Im became a part of Roosevelt's controversial effort. In the winter 1939–40, the Bank responded positively to a request for a loan from Finland, after the USSR had attacked that country in December 1939. This aggression flowed from the understanding reached in a secret pact that Germany's Adolph Hitler and the USSR's Joseph Stalin signed in August 1939. Finnish government authorities requested that the Bank provide a five-year $10 million credit for the benefit of the Finnish American Trading Corporation in New York. In deference to American neutrality laws, the Finns promised not to purchase military supplies and equipment with the proceeds. Ex-Im did not have the funds to meet the request fully. Congress in January 1939 had limited the Bank's outstanding loans to $100 million, and by the end of the year most of that was committed. The Bank was able to put up $3 million for Finland, and the Reconstruction Finance Corporation the remaining $7 million.[2]

Public sympathy grew for the Finns early in 1940 as they resolutely resisted the superior numbers of invading Soviet troops. Congress debated bills that would have permitted the RFC to provide substantially greater, unrestricted assistance to Finland. Meanwhile, the Roosevelt administration requested that Congress increase the Ex-Im's lending limits. Eventually, Congress doubled the Bank's commitment authority from $100 million to $200 million in March 1940, with the assumption that some would be used to aid Finland. Despite the substantial public support for Finland, congressional debate on the funding legislation indicated that many members continued to resist the United States being drawn into the European conflict. Consequently, they succeeded in putting some restrictions on the Bank in the legislation that Roosevelt signed into law in March 1940. Loans could not exceed $20 million for any one country, and such advances were subject to the restrictions of the 1939 Neutrality Act, which prohibited funding purchases of war materials. In addition, Congress subjected the Bank's lending to the provisions of the Johnson Act of 1934. That legislation prohibited government agencies and private American citizens from making loans to governments that had defaulted on debts to the U.S. government as of April 1934.[3]

The Bank promptly increased its loan to the Finnish American Trading Company to $20 million. At the same time, in March 1940, the Bank approved credits totaling $36 million to the other Scandinavian countries (Norway, Sweden, and Denmark), which had been pending since December. As it turned out, most of these credits were not used. The Bank suspended them when Germany overran Norway and Denmark in April 1940. Ex-Im officials did not want, in effect, to provide credits that might be used for the German war effort.[4]

[2] Rifat Tirana, ms, "Fifteen Years of Export-Import Bank of Washington," October 1948, pp. 7–10, "(William McChesney) Martin Term" file, Library, Ex-Im (hereafter "Martin Term" file).

[3] Act Extending the Export-Import Bank of Washington (Including Amendments), PL 420, 76th Congress, approved March 2, 1940.

[4] Tirana, pp. 7–10.

Subsequent events in 1940 ultimately had an even greater affect on the Bank. Germany followed the invasions of Norway and Denmark with attacks in May on France, the Netherlands, Luxembourg, and Belgium. On June 22, 1940, the American public was stunned as Hitler's troops occupied Paris after France capitulated to Germany. These developments prompted the United States to accelerate its preparedness program, fashion closer ties to Great Britain, and reassess the country's strategic position in a world where Nazi Germany virtually dominated Western Europe. One consequence of the reassessment was the Roosevelt administration's heightened attention to the western hemisphere, a region that produced strategic materials and where German influence had increased during the 1930s.

The Bank came to play an important role in the government's evolving war-time policy toward Latin America. After war broke out in Europe, the United States joined the other American republics in planning a common response to the loss of Latin American markets in Europe. Following the fall of France, the foreign ministers of the American republics met in Havana in July 1940. While neutrality and the common defense of the hemisphere dominated the agenda, economic cooperation remained an important issue. Trade with Europe had virtually shut down, causing serious economic dislocations all over the region. Not only had Latin American nations previously sold large quantities of their agricultural products in Europe, but they had also made significant purchases of equipment (both industrial and agricultural) from Europe. While the United States could supply the producers goods that the hemisphere needed, it was not in a position to increase its purchase of the region's agricultural products. American farmers continued to supply more than could be sold in the American market. Nevertheless, the signatories pledged to increase their cooperation with each other and "to devise and apply appropriate means of effective action to cope with the problems arising from the present disturbed world conditions."[5]

Coincident with the meeting in Havana, the president formally asked Congress to increase the Bank's capital by $500 million and to remove the recently imposed restrictions on its operations. These changes

[5] Memorandum, Emilio G. Collado, Division of the American Republics, June 10, 1940, *Foreign Relations of the United States, 1940*, Volume V (Washington, DC: Government Printing Office, 1941), pp. 354–67 (hereafter *FRUS*).

were needed, the president said in a message of July 22, 1940, "to the end that the bank may be of greater assistance to our neighbors south of the Rio Grande, including financing the handling and orderly marketing of some part of their surpluses."[6] Jesse Jones, head of RFC and chairman of the Bank's board of trustees, emphasized – in a theme that became a common refrain – that the legislation would allow the Bank "to assist these [Latin American] countries to develop their natural resources, to produce more of the things we import from them and which are not competitive with our own products."[7]

The president got almost all that he wanted for the Bank. There was little real opposition on Capital Hill following France's capitulation. Congress, in September 1940, increased Ex-Im's lending authority from $200 million to $700 million and continued the Bank to January 1947. The legislation, however, still required adherence to the 1934 Johnson Act and the 1939 neutrality legislation. But the Congress followed the president in his other requests and, in effect, legislated a change in focus for the institution. In its preamble, the act stated that the purpose of the new legislation was "to assist in the development of the resources, the stabilization of the economies, and the orderly marketing of the products of the countries of the Western Hemisphere." The act went on to authorize the Bank "to make loans to any governments, their central banks, or any other acceptable banking institution and, when guaranteed by any such government, a central bank, or any other acceptable banking institution, to a political subdivision, agency, or national of any such government."[8]

For most of the war, then, the Bank focused its activities on Latin America. A major exception were two large credits (totaling $75 million) extended to China in late 1940.[9] But for the most part, Ex-Im became deeply engrossed in various kinds of lending in the

6 Quoted in Earl Mazo, "The Export-Import Bank of the United States," 1976, p. 31, ms in Library, Ex-Im.

7 Mimeographed Statement of Jesse Jones, Federal Loan Administrator, Before House Banking and Currency Committee, August 6, 1940; Statutes Pertaining to the Export-Import Bank of Washington (as of October 1, 1940); Memorandum, Hampson Gary to Warren Lee Pierson, November 18, 1940, in Office of Secretary, General Correspondence with Other Government Departments, 1932–1957, Box 21, "EximBank" folder, Record Group 234, Records of the Reconstruction Finance Corporation, National Archives.

8 Public Law 792, 76th Congress, approved September 26, 1940.

9 Mazo, p. 40.

western hemisphere. The Bank's officials and staff developed expertise about the countries in which they made loans, and the institution developed a strong commitment to Latin America. Ex-Im's commitment to the region, however, was not entirely on its own terms. The War and State Departments, and other governmental agencies, came to the Bank to further their own objectives in Latin America.

After Congress substantially increased its lending authority in September 1940, Ex-Im turned to exchange problems. Because of shortages in reserves, Latin American exchange rates came under increased pressure, and there were delays in settling balances. To make dollars available, Ex-Im authorized lines of credit to central banking authorities in Argentina ($60 million), Brazil ($25 million), Uruguay ($5 million), and Peru ($10 million). There were smaller credits to Cuba and Costa Rica. A Venezuelan agricultural bank received $4 million to cover the amount of funds previously obtained from European sources and lent to the country's farmers. As with previous Bank credits, not all the recipients utilized these new lines of credit. In Uruguay and Peru, the knowledge of the availability of the dollar funds increased confidence that there were adequate reserves. In Argentina, the parliament refused to approve the loan. Brazil also did not make use of its full credit. Increasing earnings from the sale of the country's strategic materials markedly improved its exchange situation in the early 1940s.[10]

Another aspect of Ex-Im's assistance to Latin America was exhibited in the significant credits it extended for public works programs. Loans went to Cuba, Mexico, and Panama for road-building projects. The projects in Mexico included work on the strategically important Inter-American highway, for which Congress had agreed to defray two

[10] Annual Reports of the Export-Import Bank of Washington for 1940–1945, typescripts in Library, Ex-Im; Bulletin No. 10, "Activities of the Export-Import Bank of Washington and its Participation in Financial Transactions in Latin America," July 1942, Inter-American Development Commission, Washington, DC, Subject Files, 1933–1975, Box 36, "Inter-American Development Commission, 1940–1948" folder, RG 275, Records of the Export-Import Bank of the United States, National Archives; An Address, Warren Lee Pierson, "The Export-Import Bank and American Industry," April 26, 1943, Office of Secretary, General Correspondence with other Government Departments, Box 21, "EximBank" folders, RG 234 (hereafter Pierson Address, 1943); Memorandum, "Future Operations of the Export-Import Bank," April 22, 1942, Subject Files, 1933–1975, Box 39, "Legislation 1935–1945" folder, RG 275.

thirds of the cost. Similarly, the loans to Panama aided the building of an important highway across the isthmus. Argentina received loans to purchase equipment for its railways and for the building of two dams.[11]

Because of the distressed economic circumstances in the region, the Bank became even more flexible in regard to its previous policies that limited local expenditures. As in the 1938 Haitian loan for internal improvements, the Ex-Im allowed some of its funds to be used for the local purchase of materials and for hiring workers in highway and other public works projects. Both practices helped local economic conditions in the Dominican Republic, Colombia, Costa Rica, and Ecuador. In doing so, recipients could use their own currency, which ultimately freed up foreign exchange to pay arrears and make new purchases in the United States.[12]

As part of its mandate to assist in stabilizing Latin American economies, the Bank involved itself in helping the hemisphere's agricultural sector adjust to the disruptions brought about by the European war. Cuba received $11.3 million to stabilize the sugar-growing sector. The Bank's finance supported the growth of new varieties of crops or the storage of sugar that could not be sold in former markets. Similarly, Haiti received about $5 million to support experiments in growing rubber trees and commercializing other agricultural and forestry resources. Ultimately, the Bank approved Haiti using the bulk of these funds to expand production of sisal, a fiber much in demand after the Japanese occupied the Phillippines and cut off traditional supplies of hemp and related products.[13]

The Bank independently departed most from previous thinking about its mission in Brazil. In November 1940, the Bank authorized $25 million toward the construction of a large, fully integrated steel mill in Brazil at Volta Redonda. In doing so, Ex-Im committed

[11] Annual Reports for 1940–1945; Minutes, Executive Committee, Ex-Im, March 6, 1942, Minutes, Box 2, RG 275; Credit No. 294, "Republic of Cuba – Comision de Fomento Nacional," Authorized 5/1/41, Credit Files, 1934–1951, Box 7, RG 275.

[12] Annual Reports for 1940, 1941, 1942; Minutes, Meeting of the Executive Committee, Export-Import Bank of Washington (hereafter Minutes, Executive Committee, Ex-Im) June 6, 1941, October 27, 1941, Minutes, Box 2, RG 275; Minister in Ecuador to Secretary of State, May 31, 1940; Secretary of State to Minister in Ecuador, June 4, 1940, *FRUS, 1940*, Vol. V, pp. 874–6.

[13] Minutes, Executive Committee, Ex-Im, January 9, 1941, May 1, 1941, December 18, 1942, Minutes, Boxes 2, 5, RG 275.

itself to promoting industrial development. Pierson made the case that supporting the development of industry would contribute to nation building, ending the colonial psychology that had so bedeviled Latin American history. The Bank's president also argued that the United States would ultimately benefit from Brazilian economic development. He observed that the United States' best markets were found in industrialized countries. Generally, he argued that it was in America's interest to have Latin American countries build stable and independent economies. As standards of living rose, they would become better markets for American goods.[14]

There were immediate and longer-term gains to support funding the Brazilian project. The country's increased steel capacity – Brazil already had several small steel operations – would contribute to the hemisphere's defense needs. Then, too, there were the benefits to American businesses, which furnished equipment and technical assistance for the project.

Despite Pierson's new thinking about the role of the Bank in fostering industrial development, the Brazilian steel plant project had come to the Bank in a conventional way. Officials in Brazil only approached Ex-Im after they had failed to attract private sources of American capital. In 1939, the United States Steel Corporation (USS) produced a positive feasibility study on building a large-scale steel mill in Brazil. The Brazilian government organized an initiative that included both private and public subscription to $25 million in stock in the new company, Companhia Siderugica Nacional. When USS decided against a small $5 million equity stake in the business, and U.S. capital markets showed little interest in the undertaking, the Brazilian government turned to the Export-Import Bank for substantially all the needed dollar expenditures – $20 million. The organizers planned to use these funds for American equipment and technical assistance – that is, the engineers to design, construct, and get operations underway. In considering the technical features of the proposed project, the Bank turned for advice to consulting engineers suggested by American steel company executives. Ex-Im

14 Pierson Address, 1943; other sources on Pierson's thinking include "Warren Lee Pierson, February 17, 1936–March 31, 1945" and Memorandum, Walter Sauer to Judy Mazo, "Impetus for Establishment of Eximbank," August 1, 1973, in Mazo-Mazon Files, Library, Ex-Im. Also, Memorandum (Ex-Im), "Government Foreign Lending," June 1, 1943, Central Decimal File (CDF), Box 3919 (811.516 Export-Import Bank/1-143), RG 59, U.S. Department of State, National Archives.

signed a contract in May 1941, which included a repayment guarantee from the Brazilian central bank.[15]

The initial credit to the Brazilian National Steel Company marked the Bank's first major financing of industrial development overseas. Afterward, the Bank provided other credits. In December 1941, Ex-Im supplied an additional $5 million, and in 1943 a further $25 million. The Brazilians also upped their contributions to the project, which was finally completed in 1946. Ex-Im would finance additional expansions of Volta Redonda into the 1970s, and the plant became the impetus for related industrial development. As the Brazilian project progressed, other Latin American countries also proposed steel mill construction. Subsequently, the Bank financed the purchase of equipment from the United States to support such projects. In 1945, Ex-Im provided $33 million for construction of a steel mill (and related hydroelectric projects) in Conception, Chile. The Chilean government requested support for the project to diversify the country's economy beyond dependence on copper and nitrates. After careful scrutiny, the board approved the loan in the interest of diversification, even though the steel mill was economically marginal, in view of the small size of the Chilean market.[16]

Thus, Volta Redonda set the Bank on an important new course. By promoting industrial development, Ex-Im became involved in project lending. The latter required its staff to administer the credit for the construction of a complex industrial facility, which led to a sharpening of their skills and an elaboration of the Bank's procedures. Credits for Volta Redonda were disbursed slowly as the project proceeded. Because of the complexity of the project, it involved literally thousands of individual disbursements.[17] Volta Redonda was thus something very different from supporting the simple export of transportation equipment

[15] Memorandum, "United States Interest in Brazilian Steel Plant," April 25, 1941, CDF, 1940–1944, Box 4523 (832.6511/195), RG 59; Memorandum of Conversation, "Proposed Iron and Steel development in Brazil," December 14, 1939, CDF, 1940–1944, Box 4523 (832.6511/45), RG 59; Minutes, Executive Committee, Ex-Im, October 17, 1940, Minutes, Box 5, RG 275.

[16] Minutes, Executive Committee, Ex-Im, October 25, 1944, and July 13, 1945, Minutes, Box 5, RG 275; see also Memorandum, untitled, Knox to Haley, October 13, 1944, CDF, 1940–1944, Box 4295 (825.51/10-1344), RG 59; Memorandum, Chief of the Division of Foreign Economic Development, Department of State, September 20, 1945, and Secretary of State to the Ambassador in Chile, November 27, 1945, *FRUS, 1945*, Vol. IX, pp. 818–19, 822–3.

[17] Letter, Pierson to Smith, January 20, 1943, Subject Files, 1933–1975, Box 4, "Budget, 1943" folder, RG 275.

or agricultural goods that had been the bread and butter of the Bank's work until this time. The further development of project lending in the 1940s created a parallel need for more careful Ex-Im staff analysis in the planning, design, and construction phases, as well as at times in postproject evaluations.

Meanwhile, as German and Japanese territorial aggression accelerated in 1940 and 1941, the Bank cooperated with U.S. government agencies set up to ensure adequate supplies of strategic materials. As part of this preparedness effort, the Reconstruction Finance Corporation in June 28, 1940, incorporated both the Metals Reserve Company (MRC) and the Rubber Reserve Company (RRC) to stockpile critical materials. The Bank had its earliest dealings with these corporations in the fall of 1940 in a $75 million credit extended to the Central Bank of China to pay for purchases in the United States. These loans were secured by the proceeds generated by contracts with the Metals Reserve Company for the sale of Chinese tungsten, tin, and other strategic materials. Similarly, a $25 million credit in 1940 to the Aluminum Company of Canada (ALCAN) – and another loan made to the company during the war – was secured by the proceeds of the sale of aluminum ingots to the MRC. The Bank lent the money to ALCAN to finance American-made equipment purchased for the expansion of plant capacity, the output of which was slated for sale to the MRC.[18]

In December 1940, the War Department first approached the Bank for assistance. At the department's request, Ex-Im provided funds for equipment and technical assistance to Latin American countries improving airport landing facilities. These improvements initially helped private commercial aviation, but as the war progressed they also proved important in the delivery of war-related materials through lend–lease and other programs.[19]

THE BANK AND WORLD WAR II

The Japanese attack on Pearl Harbor on December 7, 1941, brought the United States fully into the conflict. On December 8, 1941, the United States declared war on Japan; in the next days, Germany and Italy

[18] Memorandum, Pierson to Jesse Jones, March 12, 1942, Subject Files, 1933–1975, Box 39, "Legislation 1935/45" folder, RG 275.
[19] Credit No. 278, "Pan American Airports Corp.," Credit Files, 1934–1951, Box 6, RG 275.

Table 2.1 *Authorizations 1941–1945*

Year	Authorizations ($ million)
1941	308.6
1942	357.9
1943	22.2
1944	36.8
1945	70.4

Source: Appendix B, Summary of Authorizations.

each declared war on the United States. Despite the demands put on the government in prosecuting the war, the United States' interest in Latin America did not diminish. On December 9, 1941, the United States called an urgent meeting of the Foreign Ministers of the American Republics, which convened in Rio de Janeiro on January 15, 1942. By then, many of the Latin American countries were already at war with Germany or at least had broken diplomatic relations. In any event, the conferees pledged to cooperate in protecting the hemisphere militarily and economically. In regard to the latter, they vowed to increase the production of needed strategic materials for the Allied powers.

There was no question that the United States' war effort required a host of the strategic materials produced in the region. American officials also wanted to ensure that war-time economic disruption did not provide an opening for German influence. In 1942 and 1943, the Bank found itself an important player in promoting both of these U.S. objectives. But by the last two years of the war (1943–1945) the United States' intense military campaigns in Europe and Asia reduced new credit authorizations to Latin American countries by the Bank, only to rise again after mid 1945. During this period Ex-Im activity declined in terms of new authorizations. (See Table 2.1.) In part, this was also the result of the improved economic condition of key Latin American countries, which were earning ample reserves from the sale of strategic materials to the United States. Indeed, by the end of the war Brazil, Venezuela, and Mexico found it difficult to spend their dollar reserves as the U.S. economy maximized war-related production for the war effort.[20]

[20] *First Semiannual Report to Congress for the Period July–December 1945*, pp. 3–4 (hereafter Semiannual Report).

Initially, however, American entry into World War II intensified the already considerable negative economic effects the conflict had on Latin America. U.S. officials continued to view the Bank as an instrument to help cope with these changes. U.S. officials watched closely German activity in the region. To reduce the possibility of Nazi influence, the Bank provided modest credits for the purchase of German holdings in several Latin American industries.[21]

Early in the war, the Bank attempted something more ambitious to assist hemispheric commerce, especially in strategic materials. In a departure from the practices of the 1930s, Ex-Im set up lines of credit at major Latin American banks to facilitate the shipment of both imports and exports. Because of the uncertain shipping situation – merchant ships were pressed into military service and Germany waged a full-scale submarine campaign against shipping – buyers and sellers could not know when shipments might arrive. In response to these circumstances, the Bank enlarged its services to assist both sellers and buyers. The foreign commercial banks receiving Ex-Im credits could open letters of credit for buyers of American goods with commercial banks in the United States. Ex-Im promised to reimburse the American banks against advances on the letters of credit used by purchasers of goods. Under the terms of the program, manufacturers could also receive payment upon completion of the manufacture of their goods from cooperating American banks whose advances were underwritten by the Ex-Im. In total, the Bank authorized $50 million for this program, although only $22 million of the credits was ever used. Increasing war-production demands in the United States reduced goods available for export. Then, too, the government's need for strategic goods took priority for the scarce shipping tonnage available.[22]

In 1942, the Bank enlarged its efforts to help Latin American countries cope with war-related dislocations, in large part to ensure that

[21] See, for example, in regard to Uruguay, The Charge in Uruguay to Secretary of State, May 7, 1941, in *FRUS, 1941*, Vol. VII, pp. 595–6; Bolivia, Telegram, Hull to Bolivian Ambassador (Boal), April 10, 1943, *FRUS, 1943*, Vol. V, p. 584; and Brazil, *FRUS, 1943*, Vol. V, pp. 756–61.

[22] "Questions and Answers Regarding The Export-Import Bank Letter of Credit Plan for Financing United States Exports Under War Conditions," National Foreign Trade Council, Inc., October 7, 1942, Subject File, 1933–1975, Box 4, "Budget, 1942–1943" folder; RG 275; Credit No. 306, "Misc. Latin America: Special Bank-Export Credit Line," Credit Files, 1934–1951, Box 11, RG 275.

they continued to provide needed strategic materials. Bank assistance to programs to diversify agriculture programs in Venezuela, Colombia, Bolivia, and Ecuador provided funds to improve food supplies, lessening the need for imports. These credits likewise promoted projects designed to expand the productive capacity of strategic materials, such as rubber, metals, fibers, and plants needed for medicines. Similarly, while public works projects helped relieve the immediate impact of unemployment, they usually had a strategic aspect too. A large part of the Bank's credits for road construction in Mexico, El Salvador, Honduras, Nicaragua, and Equador went to the building of the strategic Inter-American Highway. Other road construction opened supply channels to areas producing needed crops and strategic materials.[23]

The Bank's credits also mobilized other Latin American resources for the war effort. Companies in Argentina and Bolivia received loans to purchase mining equipment to enlarge the output of tungsten ores procured by the Metals Reserve Company. Brazil, at the behest of the War Department, received Bank funds to purchase machinery for an airplane engine factory that made its product under license to American manufacturers. Similarly, Ex-Im funded Mexico's construction of a refinery that produced high-octane aviation fuel, which was urgently needed to fly the fastest fighter planes.[24]

One of the largest and most complicated of the Bank's efforts to promote strategic materials production occurred in Brazil's Itabira region, an area rich in low-phosphorous iron ore. Scandinavia, Spain, and North Africa had been a traditional source of high-grade iron ores for the European steel industry. German conquests in Scandinavia gave it access to the region's iron mines. Particularly hard hit by this turn of events was the British steel industry. It turned, as a result, to Spanish and North African sources of high grade iron ore. Neither was particularly reliable. Spain's leader General Francisco Franco was sympathetic to Hitler, and so it was conceivable that Spanish supplies would be cut off. The German military campaign in North Africa between

[23] Annual Reports for 1940–1945; Minutes, Executive Committee, Ex-Im, March 6, 1942, Minutes, Box 2, RG 275.

[24] Credit No. 350, "Gasoline Refinery Equipment – Petroleos Mexicanos," Credit Files, 1934–1951, Box 9, RG 275; Mazo, p. 43.

1941 and 1942 disrupted access to supplies of the prized ore found there.[25]

The precariousness of British iron-ore supplies heightened interest in the Itabira mines in the interior Brazilian province of Minas Gerais. Production, however, was insignificant, and increasing it would be difficult. The mines, partly owned by British interests, were almost two hundred miles from the ocean port of Vitoria. The railroad that served the mines – the Vitoria a Minas Railway – was not in a condition to handle increased ore shipments. Further complicating the situation, the railroad was in bankruptcy, and many of its bondholders were in German-occupied Europe.

As Britain faced potential shortages of iron ore in 1941, the War Department pressed both the Bank and the Metals Reserve Company to come up with a plan for the mines in Brazil. Pierson in October 1941 visited the region. Afterward, he proposed a dramatic project in which the Ex-Im would oversee both the rebuilding of the railroad and the development and operation of the mine while giving "Brazilians nominal control" and permitting "the employment of a substantial number of Brazilian engineers."[26]

As it turned out, the deal struck in March 1942 did not authorize the Bank to take the role Pierson had envisaged. The United States' entry into the war and the increasing precariousness of British iron ore supplies prompted the participants to come to an arrangement for the credit and project that failed to give the Bank the control that it thought it needed. The understanding centered around a complex transaction among British shareholders and the governments of Brazil and the United States, the latter represented by the Export-Import Bank and the Metals Reserve Company. British companies sold their interest in the existing mines to the Brazilian government, which would create a corporation (Companhia Vale do Rico Doce; Rio Doce Company) with stock owned by the government and private investors. Rio Doce would rehabilitate the Itabira iron ore mines, improve the existing railroad line between the mines and the port of Vitoria, and refurbish and expand the

[25] *FRUS, 1940*, Vol. V, pp. 600–15; *FRUS, 1942*, Vol. V, pp. 674–83; *FRUS, 1943*, Vol. V, pp. 656–63, 754–65.

[26] Telegram, Hull to American Embassy (Rio), October 3, 1941, CDF, 1940–45, Box 4519 (832.6511/195), RG 59; Letter, Pierson to Tawresey, August 4, 1944, Subject Files 1933–1975, Box 13, "Commerce Department 1936–1956" folder, RG 275.

port and docks to handle the projected increase in iron ore. The arrangement called for shipments to the Metals Reserve Company through 1945 of 1.5 million tons a year, half of which the British agreed to purchase.[27]

By the terms of the credit agreement of March 18, 1943, the Bank extended a credit of $14 million to cover the dollar costs of rehabilitating the mines, railroad, docks, and harbor. The repayment of the $14 million credit – half of which was provided through lend–lease funds – was not unconditionally guaranteed by the government of Brazil or one of its agencies, an aspect of the project that troubled Bank officials. Equally problematic was the provision that notes given as evidence of advances against the credit were payable out of proceeds of iron ore sold in the next 25 years, and that the Ex-Im was only entitled to 15 percent of the value of the ore plus a fixed fee per ton. In May 1944, the Bank extended an additional credit of $5 million for the purchase of rolling stock for the railway. In this instance, the Brazilian government guaranteed the loan.[28]

From the first, the project proved troublesome. There were difficulties in organization. The American engineers and other contracting company personnel on the scene viewed the Brazilian company's management as inept. Indeed, at one point, this group of Americans were "disgusted and threaten[ed] to withdraw from the project."[29] Not surprisingly, such criticisms created great friction between Americans and Brazilians. But there were other difficulties. Shortages of construction materials in the United States and the inability to get the highest priority ratings from the War Production Board for the project delayed construction. As a result, ore shipments were much below projections – only about 250,000 tons for all of 1942 and 1943. The following year was better, with a total shipped close to that of the previous two years, but still well below original projections.

A change in Britain's need for the ore also affected the project. An improvement in the fortunes of Allied operations in Europe and in North

[27] Memorandum, to Ex-Im Board of Directors, February 7, 1947, CDF, 1945–49, Box 5054 (832.51/2-1347), RG 59; Arey, "History of the Export-Import Bank," pp. 52–3, ms in Library, Ex-Im.

[28] Memorandum, "Regarding Conversation with the Minister of Finance," May 22, 1944, CDF, 1940–44, Box 3918 (811.516/859), RG 59.

[29] Letter, Blocher to Caffery, December 14, 1943, CDF 1940–1944, Box 4519 (832.6351/140), RG 59; Telegram, Caffery to Hull and Pierson, December 21, 1943, CDF, 1940–1944, Box 3918 (811.516/859), RG 59.

Africa after 1942 raised serious questions about how much British steelmakers would really need from the Brazilian mines. By mid 1944, Bank officials unhappily anticipated that shipments on which repayment of the credit was based would soon have to find new markets. The British contract to purchase up to 750,000 tons a year expired in mid 1945. Pierson, to no avail, approached the Bethlehem Steel Company to take the ore, while continuing problems and delays also required attention from Bank officials. Ex-Im's first full-time engineer, R. K. West, hired in 1941, spent almost three years in Brazil primarily working on the project, which took until 1950 to complete.[30]

Overall, by the end of World War II, the complexity of the Bank's business had increased. The Bank's officers and staff had experienced more than a greater volume of business at the beginning of the conflict. War-time demands required them to adapt the procedures established in the 1930s to many more transactions, while also performing entirely new tasks. Development lending in particular involved numerous transactions. As Pierson observed to the head of the Bureau of the Budget in 1943, "no two loans are of the same nature." Thus, "a statement of the number of loans or the amounts disbursed by the Bank fails to reflect fully the amount of work required by the Bank in connection with the authorization, disbursement and the collection of loans. Each application requires careful and individual study by the staff of the Bank. Frequently the officers are called upon to spend many days in conferences with representatives of foreign governments... and to carry on voluminous correspondence."[31]

Indeed, the Ex-Im's paperwork was daunting. Reviewing applications alone could require more than one round of correspondence to ascertain whether the proposed loan was something for which the Bank might provide funding. Furthermore, approved loans to Latin American countries required the Bank to send out contracts, other legal

[30] Memorandum, Barber to Pratt, "Iron Ore Development in Brazil," June 15, 1944 (832.8351/ITI/195); Memorandum, Pratt to Stettinius, "Lend-Lease Itabira Mine, Brazil," May 17, 1944 (832.6351/ITI/116); Letter, Pierson to Stettinius, June 14, 1944 (832.6352/ITI/16-1444); Letter, Walmsley to Acheson, June 1, 1944 (832.6351/ITI/6-144), all CDF 1940–44, Box 4519, RG 59. The Rio Doce Company became the largest independent iron-ore company in the world by the 1970s and continued to finance expansion through Ex-Im into the 1980s.

[31] Letter, Pierson to Harold D. Smith, Director, Bureau of the Budget, January 23, 1943, p. 3, Subject Files, 1934–1975, Box 4, "Budget, 1943" folder, RG 275.

documents, and technical reports in Spanish or Portuguese, as well as English. Because disbursements and collections were made over a period of time, elaborate record keeping was necessary if they were to be properly monitored. Similarly, in that the Bank frequently partnered with private financial institutions to disburse and service loans, there was further legal documentation and regular reporting requirements from those dispensing funds, all of which required careful record keeping. In 1945, the Bank had agency agreements with thirty-nine private financial institutions.[32]

As in many organizations, staff work could make or break an institution. This was certainly the case at the Ex-Im. In making decisions about extending loans, the Executive Committee of the board, acting for the board, depended on the staff to generate the data needed to make informed decisions. The Bank's five full-time top-level officers presided over this process, as well as having responsibility for administering the loans that the board authorized. Pierson, the Bank's president, also served as its general counsel. In addition, there were two vice presidents, the board's secretary, and an assistant secretary. One of the two vice presidents was the assistant counsel, and the secretary was also a counsel.[33]

Generally, Pierson assigned one vice president to oversee all the Ex-Im's credit and banking activities, while the other – the assistant counsel – had responsibility for legal matters. These included drafting the contracts and other documents needed in extending credit. In addition, they handled the legal work for agreements with commercial banks that either participated in the credit or acted as an agent for the Bank in dispursing and collecting payments. Supporting this work was an accounting department under the direction of a chief accountant who had a staff of assistants, audit clerks, and clerical workers.[34]

Beginning in 1941, the Bank added an engineer to its staff of professional employees for the first time. Because of the technical complexities of many projects, the Bank added a total of five engineers by 1945. They became routine participants in the analysis of many proposed projects,

[32] Ibid.; Export-Import Bank of Washington, "Justification of Budget Programs," February 25, 1946, Subject Files, 1934–1975, Box 5, "Budget, 1943" folder, RG 275.

[33] Letter, Pierson to Smith, January 23, 1943, p. 3, Subject Files, 1933–1975, Box 4 "Budget, 1948" Folder, RG 275.

[34] Ibid.

and later they were called on to take part in the assessment of on-going loans. They also traveled abroad with the Bank's examiners and legal personnel, since the Bank did not maintain field offices. On these Bank trips, Ex-Im officers and staff negotiated about the terms and circumstances surrounding the authorization of credits, investigated the operations of on-going projects, or helped devise the financial arrangement for new projects.[35]

To support the work of the Bank's operations, the leadership could call on a clerical staff of secretaries, stenographers, typists, and file clerks. Between 1943 and 1945, twenty-nine additional employees joined the Bank's staff, increasing its total number to seventy-nine. Even so, Pierson still made the case at the time that the staff was often hard pressed to handle its workload. In fiscal 1945, for example, the Bank authorized twenty new credits valued at $70.4 million.[36] There were in that year 2,908 disbursement transactions totaling almost $44 million and 2,352 repayments transactions of $52 million.[37] To manage the workload of its professional employees, the Bank had to turn to other government agencies for specialized assistance and information. Data came from the Departments of State, Treasury, Agriculture, and Commerce (in particular its Bureau of Foreign and Domestic Commerce), as well as smaller operations such as the Inter-American Regional Office of the Public Roads Administration.[38]

In meeting its expanded responsibilities, the Bank continued to work with private sector financial institutions in managing its authorized credits. The Bank routinely sold preferred stock to the Reconstruction Finance Corporation for its capital requirements. This was itself a complex activity. But private banks also helped the Ex-Im by disbursing funds and providing loans guaranteed by the Ex-Im, which allowed them to remain active in the foreign field. Thus, financial institutions working with the Bank extended and then serviced loans approved and guaranteed by

[35] Ibid.

[36] Until 1977, the government's fiscal year was from July 1 through June 30. See Appendix B.

[37] Memorandum, D. B. Griffin, Treasurer, to Wayne C. Taylor, President, November 9, 1945, Subject Files, 1933–1975, Box 5, "Budget, 1946" folder, RG 275.

[38] Congress, House, "Second Deficiency Appropriations Bill, 1945," 79th Congress, 1st Session, H.R. No. 785, 1945, p. 8; Export-Import Bank of Washington, "Justification of Estimates," Subject Files, Box 3,"Budget, 1945" folder, RG 275; Letter, Pierson to Smith, January 23, 1943, Subject Files, Box 4,"Budget, 1943" folder, RG 275; Memorandum (and Explanatory Statement), Pierson to Leo T. Crowley, Re: Eximbank Budget, February 12, 1944, Subject Files, 1933–1975, Box 4, "Budget, 1944" folder, RG 275.

the Bank. By the end of the war in 1945, guaranteed funds represented about 40 percent of total outstanding Ex-Im authorizations.[39]

Garnering the budgetary resources for an expanded staff was a constant concern to the Bank's president. Even though the Bank paid expenses out of its own earnings, it had to obtain congressional approval for its administrative expenditures. At times in the 1940s, the president of the Bank had to cope with appropriations below what he had requested. Indeed, in 1942, the Bank was rocked when Congress dropped its entire authorization in the midst of a dispute over funding agencies for the war effort. Pierson had to scramble to salvage the situation; henceforth, the Bank was more attentive to Congress.[40]

Tested as the Bank was during World War II, it faced even greater demands in the immediate postwar period. U.S. officials concluded that the Bank was the only institution prepared to handle large-scale lending to meet urgent European demands for reconstruction assistance. Because of the Bank's organizational capabilities in 1945, it seemed the logical government agency able to take on new kinds of overseas credits.

THE BANK AND POSTWAR RECONSTRUCTION

When it looked like the Allies would win the war, U.S. officials had to confront the monumental problems of postwar reconstruction. In coping with these demands, the Bank came to play an important part. Allied troops landing at Normandy, France, in June 1944 marked the beginning of the end for Hitler's Germany, even though there were many tough months of fighting before the war in Europe ended in May 1945. President Roosevelt and his closest advisers were determined that the United States would take the lead in rebuilding the international political and economic system after the war. They believed that the lessons of World War I demanded an activist role for the United States. Roosevelt concluded that the political and economic chaos of the 1920s and 1930s

[39] Memorandum, Hawthorne Avery to Mr. Waugh (Subject: Guarantees), March 3, 1959, Subject Files, 1933–1975, Box 32, "Guarantees and Insurance, 1950–1959" folder, RG 275; Annual Report for 1945.

[40] Memorandum, Pierson to Jesse Jones, April 26, 1942, Subject Files, Box 39, "Legislation Folder, 1935–1945" folder, RG 275; Memorandum, D. B. Griffin, Assistant Treasurer, to Pierson, December 21, 1942, Subject File 1933–1975, Box 4, "Budget, 1942–43" folder, RG 275.

had resulted in large part from the refusal of the United States to remain fully engaged in international affairs. Indeed, in regard to managing the postwar world economy, the United States and Great Britain had set up joint study groups as early as 1940 to plan new international economic institutions for the postwar world. Ultimately, emerging from these discussions were the proposals for the multilateral International Bank for Reconstruction and Development (IBRD) – later commonly referred to as the World Bank – and the International Monetary Fund (IMF).

As the war in Europe ended, however, American leaders realized that the IBRD would not be ready to make loans. Ultimately, they turned to the Ex-Im to meet the immediate demands of postwar reconstruction.[41] That the Bank would be called on to help in the postwar reconstruction effort did not come as a surprise to its leadership. Pierson and his colleagues had committed their thoughts about the structure and dimension of postwar lending in a wide-ranging policy paper in early 1943.[42] Indeed, the Ex-Im was making loans for rehabilitation in liberated areas even before the war ended. Ethiopia was the first candidate for such lending. With the help of the British, the Ethiopians forced the Italian army out of the country in 1941, after six years of occupation. In August 1944, Ethiopia received a half million dollar credit from the Bank. Part of it was to pay for American experts to assist the government in operating a railroad running through its territory; the balance of the funds were for engraving and printing new currency. The Bank, early in 1945, provided a $750,000 credit for American equipment to a Norwegian coal mining company for restoring operations at mines in Spitsbergen. Soon after the German surrender, the Bank also authorized the expenditure of the $10 million for Norway that was committed before the German invasion in 1940. In July 1945, however, the Bank canceled the $10 million credit and approved an increase to $50 million for the acquisition of American agricultural and industrial

[41] Transcript, Interview with William McChesney Martin, November 20, 1973, in Earl Mazo-Rosemary Mazon Research Materials, Library, Ex-Im, pp. 1–3 (hereafter Martin Interview); for concerns about reconstruction and managing the international economy see Congress, House, Sixth Report of the Special Committee on Post-War Economic Policy and Planning (H.R. No. 541), "Post-War Economic Policy and Planning," 79th Congress, 1st Session, 1945, pp. 1–2.

[42] Memorandum (Ex-Im), "Government Foreign Lending," June 1, 1943, CDF, 1940–44, Box 3919 (811.56 Export-Import Bank/6-143), RG 59.

products approved by the Bank. Denmark received $20 million from the Bank under similar terms.[43]

At the same time, in the last half of 1945, Ex-Im accelerated new authorizations to Latin America – almost $106 million, including an integrated steel mill in Chile, cargo vessels for Brazil, and rural electrification in Mexico. This level was almost three times that of all of Fiscal 1945.[44]

After the war in Europe came to an end on May 8, 1945, Harry Truman – who had become president upon the death of Franklin D. Roosevelt on April 12, 1945 – needed to move quickly to cope with Europe's reconstruction needs. The lend–lease program would have been the logical place to turn. It had an enviable record of providing America's allies with military and industrial materials. Because Congress had only authorized lend–lease assistance until the end of hostilities (Japan surrendered on August 14, 1945) – months earlier than anticipated – the program could not be used to meet the urgent needs for rebuilding in a devastated Europe.[45]

Secretary of State James K. Byrnes convinced Truman to use the Export-Import Bank for immediate postwar reconstruction purposes. At the time, American officials contemplated at least one billion dollars in credits for the Soviet Union, which had suffered massive destruction during the war. Byrnes collaborated with Leo T. Crowley, chairman of the Ex-Im's board of trustees, on the outline of the proposed legislation to empower the Export-Import Bank to cope with this new task. Crowley, like Byrnes, was from South Carolina, a lawyer, and an experienced high-level New Deal official. Both men were among the group of government officials who believed that eventually European reconstruction would become the responsibility of the IBRD, which was undergoing close scrutiny in congressional hearings in the spring and summer of 1945.[46] Byrnes and Crowley appreciated the Ex-Im as the only already functioning governmental institution

[43] Minutes, Executive Committee, Ex-Im, August 7, 1944, Minutes, Box 2, RG 275; Annual Reports for 1944 and 1945; Mazo, pp. 51, 56.

[44] Semiannual Report for July–December 1945.

[45] Minutes, Meeting of Board of Directors, Ex-Im, September 11, 1945, Minutes, Box 6, RG 275.

[46] These efforts also led to the establishment of an international trade organization (ITO) to liberalize trade. The treaty needed to set up the ITO did not receive Senate approval.

with substantial experience in making and administering large loans overseas.[47]

But what the Bank needed to meet the demands of reconstruction, Byrnes and Crowley believed, was enhanced standing, a clarification of mission, and more money.[48] From 1939, the Roosevelt administration had frequently shifted Ex-Im around as part of its efforts to cope with preparedness and then full-scale conflict. Even though the Bank's leadership endeavored to keep its procedures for making and administering loans unchanged, Ex-Im's odyssey suggested a lack of permanence. The government's Reorganization Plan No. 1 of 1939 placed the Ex-Im in the Federal Loan Agency. In February 1942, FDR issued an executive order that transferred the Bank to the Department of Commerce. He moved it again in July 1943, when Ex-Im became a part of the Office of Economic Warfare (OEW), a catchall agency that included the Board of Economic Warfare. At that time, Leo T. Crowley, director of OEW, succeeded Jesse Jones, then secretary of commerce, as chairman of the Ex-Im's board of directors, although Jones remained a member of the Bank's board. But this was not the end of changing the Bank's location in the government's administrative hierarchy. In September 1943, President Roosevelt put Crowley in charge of the newly established Foreign Economic Administration, which gained authority for, among others, the Office of Economic Warfare (including the Export-Import Bank) and the Office of Lend–Lease Administration.[49]

In any event, Truman in a June 4 message to Congress announced plans to use the Bank for emergency reconstruction assistance in Europe. Truman's proposed legislation requested a substantial enlargement of the Bank's funding from $700 million to $3.5 billion. Included in his proposal was the removal of the 1934 Johnson Act prohibitions on making loans to countries that had defaulted on U.S. loans and an extension of the Bank for ten years.[50]

The legislation essentially faced no opposition, although it underwent some changes by the House Banking and Currency Committee.

[47] Martin Interview, p. 41.

[48] Ibid., pp. 1–6.

[49] Memorandum, Pierson to Crowley, Re: "Eximbank Budget," February 12, 1944, Subject Files, Box 4, "Budget, 1944" folder, RG 275.

[50] "Legislative History on Selected Points in The Export-Import Bank Act of 1945," Mazo-Mazon Research Materials, Library, EX-Im, pp. 1–15 (hereafter Legislative History).

These alterations reshaped several aspects of the original bill, which resulted in several far-reaching changes in the Bank. President Truman signed The Export-Import Bank Act of 1945 (P.L. 173, 79th Congress) on July 31, the same day he approved the Bretton Woods Agreement Act. The latter authorized the United States to participate and invest in the International Bank for Reconstruction and Development and the International Monetary Fund.[51]

Significantly, Congress' alterations in Truman's proposal included making the Bank an independent governmental agency. As the chairman of the House Banking Committee said, the Bank "will have an independent existence, not connected with or under the domination of any department of Government."[52] Congress' maneuver, however, further subjected the Bank to Congress. Its authority over the Bank became even stronger with the passage in March 1947 of the Government Corporation Control Act (Public Law No. 248, 79th Congress) and the Reincorporation of the Export-Import Bank of Washington Act in October 1947. The Government Corporation Control Act stipulated that government-owned corporations organized under state (including District of Columbia) law would be liquidated, if not reincorporated by Congress by June 30, 1948. Accordingly, Congress reincorporated the Bank and, in doing so, extended its life to June 30, 1953. Clearly, in the future, it would be up to Congress whether or not the Bank would be extended beyond that date. Thereafter, the Ex-Im would regularly have to seek Congressional reauthorization at intervals set by Congress.[53]

The 1945 act also changed Ex-Im's management and governance structures. Perhaps of greatest significance for the Bank's day-to-day exercise of its authority was Congress' vesting final decision-making responsibility in a bipartisan presidentially appointed board of directors of five full-time members, subject to Senate confirmation. Of the five members of the board, no more than three could come from the same political party. The president also received responsibility to appoint one of them chairman. Significantly, the act mandated that the board draw up its own rules of procedure. Indicative of Congress' view that the Bank should continue to serve the foreign policy interests of the United States

[51] Martin Interview, pp. 1–6; Legislative History, pp. 1–15.
[52] Quoted from *Congressional Record*, July 13, 1945, p. 7535, in Legislative History, p. 8.
[53] Congress, Senate, Report (to accompany S. 993): Reincorporation of Export-Import Bank of Washington, April 17, 1947, 80th Congress, 1st Session, 1947, pp. 1–2.

was the requirement that the secretary of state be one of the five on the board of directors ex officio.[54]

Truman selected William McChesney Martin, a former head of the New York Stock Exchange, to become the Bank's chairman. Martin, while serving in the military in Washington during the war, worked with officials, including Crowley, who spearheaded the effort to utilize the Bank to help with emergency reconstruction. To serve with Martin and Secretary of State Byrnes, the president appointed Herbert E. Gaston, a former assistant secretary of the treasury; Clarence E. Gauss, a career diplomat who had been U.S. ambassador to China; and Lynn U. Stambaugh, a Washington-based attorney. Following hearings held during November and December 1945, the Senate confirmed the president's appointments.

Congress in the 1945 act also mandated that the Bank be incorporated into the larger structure of the United States' emerging postwar foreign economic policy apparatus. Thus, the legislation established an advisory committee, presided over by the Bank's chairman, and consisting of the secretaries of state, treasury, and commerce, as well as the chairman of the Federal Reserve System. Congress envisioned this committee as ensuring that the Bank's policies were in step with overall government economic policy. Moreover, the advisory committee included the same members as the National Advisory Council (NAC) on International Monetary and Financial Problems, a committee set up under the Bretton Woods legislation. The latter designed the NAC to coordinate the activities of the American representatives to the World Bank and the International Monetary Fund with major government departments. These oversight and coordinating entities were in part a result of congressional concern that the Export-Import Bank and the new World Bank would duplicate efforts and come into conflict with each other.[55]

As it turned out, the Bank's advisory committee never met. But the National Advisory Council became an integral part of how the Bank conducted its business. The NAC, chaired by the secretary of the treasury, emerged as the coordinating agency that Congress had envisioned. It took some experimentation to determine the working relationship between the Bank and the NAC, but a policy was in place by

[54] The Export-Import Bank Act of 1945 (P.L. 173, 79th Congress).
[55] Legislative History, pp. 11–15.

January 1946. As a matter of routine, the Bank referred requests for credits it had under consideration to the NAC. After review, the NAC informed the Bank whether there was a reason of policy not to consider a particular request for a loan. In this way, the NAC ruled on the Bank's consideration of a potential loan and not whether ultimately to extend a credit. The procedure, at its best, allowed the Bank to exercise its financial judgement about potential credits, and freed the NAC staff from making the kinds of feasibility assessments that the Bank's experienced personnel were clearly better equipped to make.[56]

Despite the changes that Congress made in President Truman's original legislative proposal, it did accede to several of his requests. Ex-Im received an increase in lending authority from $700 million to $3.5 billion. The legislation authorized the Bank to issue one billion dollars in capital stock, which the treasury purchased in its entirety. In addition, Congress empowered the Ex-Im to borrow from the treasury an amount up to two and one half times its outstanding capital stock. The act also ended the restrictions that prohibited private and public entities from making loans to countries that had defaulted on obligations to the United States. In removing such restrictions, Congress hoped to encourage private banks to participate in Export-Import Bank lending.[57]

The act also gave statutory authority to provisions that first appeared in Roosevelt's 1934 executive orders setting up the Bank. Congress included language stating that the Bank "in the exercise of its functions should supplement and encourage and not compete with private capital." In addition, the act stipulated that the Bank's loans "should be for specific purposes, and, in the judgement of the Board of Directors, offer reasonable assurance of repayment." From the Bank's point of view, this language simply sanctioned what had been its policy and preferences from the beginning of its operations.[58]

Within weeks of the president's assenting to the 1945 act, Martin and his board colleagues got down to work on the fourth floor of the Lafayette Building. After a few months of operations, however, they

56 Minutes, Board of Directors, Ex-Im, January 3, 1946 and January 23, 1946, Minutes, Box 2, RG 275.

57 Congress, House of Representatives, Hearings: Export-Import Bank Act of 1945, Committee on Banking and Currency, 79th Congress, 1st Session, July 11–12, 1945, pp. 6–7, 10, 14, 62–3; Legislative History, pp. 1–15.

58 Legislative History, pp. 1–15.

realized that the 1945 act left the Bank's president in limbo. Wayne C. Taylor, a vice president, had succeeded Warren Lee Pierson who had resigned the Bank's presidency on March 31, 1945. Taylor had begun his career at the Bank as an assistant to George N. Peek. After the new board was constituted, Martin and his colleagues devised procedures that did not depart substantially from those of the Executive Committee that for twelve years had exercised top-level decision-making authority.[59] As before, they relied on the work of the staff for the information they needed to make decisions. They met weekly, and more frequently, if necessary. But the new operations of the Board, in effect, bypassed the president, diminishing his previous role in the Bank. By early 1946, Taylor and Martin agreed that "the present set-up of the Bank was not feasible." They discussed the situation with President Truman who assented to Taylor's decision to leave. At a special meeting of the board on February 6, 1946, the directors accepted Taylor's resignation and elected its chairman, William McChesney Martin, to also fill the office of president. This dual role of leadership became the Bank's regular practice in the following years. It was a way to avoid the potential for conflict with the Bank's president inherent in Congress investing the chairman with the authority granted in the 1945 act.[60]

By the time these changes took place, Martin and the directors had already been heavily involved in authorizing funds for reconstruction. In early September 1945, the board consented to fund three "lend-lease termination credits." France was the major recipient, with a credit of $550 million; the other two were Belgium ($55 million) and the Netherlands ($50 million). These funds were for the purchase of American industrial goods, as well as consumables like food and fuel, something that the Bank had never funded before. Originally, these countries' governments had received approval for assistance from the

[59] Martin and the directors did effect a reorganization in the next two years. They added departments devoted to developing private sector interest in Bank loans in 1946. Engineering also became a separate department. Letter, Martin to Senator Aiken, January 29, 1948, Subject Files, 1933–1975, Box 6, "Budget, 1948" folder, RG 275; A. Carl Cass, "The Role of the Engineering Division in the Operations of the Export-Import Bank of Washington," Subject Files, 1933–1975, Box 11, "Capehart Committee, 1953" folder, RG 275.

[60] Minutes, Special Meeting, Ex-Im, in Executive Session, February 6, 1946, Minutes, Box 2, RG 275; Letter, Taylor to Charles B. Henderson, RFC, September 6, 1945, Office of Secretary, General Correspondence With Other Government Agencies, 1932–1957, Box 22, RG 234.

lend–lease authorities. Consequently, the recipients contracted with suppliers in the United States, who then proceeded to work on fulfilling the often large orders. But by the time the funding was needed for payment, the lend–lease program had ended with Japan's surrender on August 14.

Government officials considered the promised lend–lease credits legitimate obligations of the United States. As a result, the foreign economic administrator requested that the Bank take up these credits, accepting the thirty-year maturity and $2^3/_8$ percent interest rate promised by lend–lease authorities. Neither of these were standard Bank terms, nor was the speed at which the Ex-Im disbursed the funds. They were fully expended by the end of June 1946.

As it turned out, ensuing requests for reconstruction lending also included longer maturities and lower interest rates than the Bank would routinely have made on its own. The Bank preferred a maximum maturity of fifteen years, with a five year grace period. At the time, it also expected at least 3 percent in interest, a minimum needed to attract private participation in lending. Despite considerable pressure to accept the lend–lease terms in subsequent lending, Martin and his board colleagues fought for their established – in their view – "prudent" practices.[61]

The lend–lease termination credits were only the beginning of the Bank's reconstruction assistance. European economic conditions in the winter of 1945–6 were desperate: shortages of all kinds of goods, large numbers of homeless refugees, and significant damage to the infrastructure in many devastated major European cities. In addition, relations between the United States and the Soviet Union were becoming tense over the USSR's behavior in Eastern Europe, especially Poland. In these strained circumstances, substantial credits to the USSR were becoming less and less likely, itself an issue in the deteriorating relationship between the two countries. President Truman's diplomatic and military advisers feared that the economic dislocations brought on by war-time destruction would enhance support for communist movements in Western Europe. Political conditions in France and Italy were particularly worrisome, with the growth of large communist parties in both countries.[62]

[61] Mazo, pp. 56–7; Tirana, pp. 10–11; "1949 FY Budget," Subject Files, 1933–1975, Box 6, "Budget, 1949" folder, RG 275.

[62] "Formulation of a Foreign Financial Program: Policy to Help War-Devastated and Liberated Countries Meet Their Dollar Requirements Pending the Beginning of Loan

In the first half of 1946, the Truman administration supported emergency reconstruction loans beyond those obtained through the lend–lease credits. They favored an additional $650 million to France, $45 million to Belgium, and $50 million to the Netherlands. There was also to be new funding to Greece ($25 million) and Poland ($40 million). Meanwhile, Italian officials hinted that they were preparing a large request for reconstruction aid, in the neighborhood of $950 million. In any event, coupled with credits already extended to Denmark ($25 million) and Norway ($50 million), the Bank authorized a total of $885 million for emergency reconstruction assistance by the middle of 1946, in addition to the $655 million committed on behalf of the lend–lease credits.[63]

The emergency credits extended to Norway, Denmark, Belgium, and the Netherlands had unusual features. For these countries, the Bank established lists of a variety of agricultural and industrial goods without specifying in the contracts for the credits what the countries would in fact select for purchase, and what the articles would be used for. In drawing up these "shopping" lists, as they were called at the time, the Bank collaborated with the Department of Commerce to ensure that selected items were not in short supply, which would have contributed to American inflation.[64]

Despite the scale of the emergency lending, Martin and the board did not ignore the Bank's other business. In October 1945, for example, Ex-Im extended credits of $100 million for the export of about 800,000 pounds of raw cotton to Europe. This was an American commodity very much in oversupply, and there was demand for the cotton to restart cotton textile manufacture in Europe. There was also a special cotton credit of $33 million to China, as well as traditional credits to American exporters of manufactured goods. In July 1946, for example, in cooperation with American manufacturers, the Bank arranged a $25 million credit for Turkey to purchase aircraft. In December 1947, the Ex-Im board authorized a $300 million, midterm loan to Canada. That country had encountered severe, but ultimately temporary, balance of payments problems that could have compromised existing levels of American exports. Politically, the loan was important because Canada

Operations by the International Bank for Reconstruction and Development," *FRUS, 1946*, Vol. I, pp. 1390–1438.

[63] Ibid.; Semiannual Reports for January–June 1946 and July–December 1946.

[64] Ibid.

also had made significant commitments to aid the postwar reconstruction of Europe that might be jeopardized. Private American banks were unwilling to extend help, and the Ottawa government turned to the Export-Import Bank. Canada only drew $140 million by mid-1948, when she was able to borrow from American insurance companies.[65]

Latin America also received attention from the Bank, despite the focus on Europe. It had to continue monitoring and supporting development projects begun earlier in the 1940s. At the beginning of 1946, the Bank had undisbursed commitments to Latin America of $339 million. In the next two years, Ex-Im authorized an additional $108 million for export financing. This lending included the first in a series of loans stretching into the 1950s to build hotels in Colombia, Panama, and Venezuela. There was also support for purchases of a range of capital goods, among them railroad equipment, aircraft, construction machinery, barges, and the like.[66]

Receiving the particular attention of the Bank's president in the postwar years was the complicated and troubled Rio Doce project in Brazil. Martin was determined to get a grip on the seeming ever-present concern to the Bank. In the mid 1940s, two of the Bank's five engineers devoted themselves full-time to the project. Following delays in coming to terms on new credits for the project in the summer 1946, Martin held up new Brazilian credit authorizations until sovereign guarantees were made for the new lending. Martin delivered this message in a blunt confrontation with the Brazilian ambassador, which caused something of a diplomatic furor. But Martin held firm, and the Brazilians acceded to the Bank's terms.[67]

The troubled project in Latin America was not the only concern of the board in 1946–7. Indeed, after dealing with the lend–lease credits, Martin and the other directors struggled to discipline other foreign policy-driven lending, to have it conform to the Bank's standard

[65] Semiannual Report for July–December 1945; "FY 49 Budget," in Subject Files, 1933–1975, Box 7, "Budget, 1949" folders, RG 275; "1947 FY Budget," pp. 36–37, Box 4, in Subject Files, 1933–1975, "Budget, 1947" folder, RG 275; Credit No. 433, "Dominion of Canada," Credit Files, 1933–51, Box 10, RG 275.

[66] Semiannual Reports for July–December 1945, January–June 1946, July–December 1946, January–June 1947.

[67] Semiannual Report for January–June 1946; U.S. Ambassador to Secretary of State, August 29, 1946; Memorandum, Richard F. O'Toole, Division, Brazilian Affairs, September 6, 1946, *FRUS, 1946*, Vol. XI, pp. 499–501.

practices. Essentially, right after the war, State and War Department officials often raised expectations about the leniency of terms and availability of financial assistance among beleaguered officials in potential borrower countries. The Bank then had to cope with these expectations in working out the terms of credits with their postwar governments.[68]

Two large and important loans in 1946 illustrate the Bank's growing insistence on its standard procedures for negotiating and administering credits. Each of the countries involved, China and France, was important to American foreign policy and strategic goals in Asia and in Europe. In December 1945, President Truman laid out a policy of support toward China, a country wracked by a civil war between its government and a communist insurgency. After much discussion with American foreign policy officials, the Chinese requested $500 million from the Export-Import Bank. The board had deep misgivings about the ability of China to make appropriate use of the credits and of its ability to repay. But the NAC approved the Bank's consideration of the loan, and Assistant Secretary of State Will Clayton, who usually represented the secretary of state on the Bank's board, emphasized the importance of the loan to U.S. policy toward China.[69]

Under the circumstances, the board approved the credit of $500 million. But the Ex-Im attached provisions and a deadline that offered it substantial control over its funds. In a statement on the China credit, the board observed that "it is understood that funds will be disbursed against specific projects to be approved by the Bank." The Bank also only extended the credits to June 30, 1947, pending China's submission of fully developed project proposals for assistance. As it turned out, the Chinese did not meet the deadline, and the Bank was able to withdraw the commitment.[70]

Similarly, the Bank succeeded in shaping the 1946 French emergency reconstruction loan more closely to its operational preferences. For reasons of American policy – the United States saw the recovery of France and Great Britain as essential to U.S. interests in Europe – the NAC in May 1946 pressed the Ex-Im to give quick approval to the French

[68] Letter, Martin to Truman, December 20, 1946, "Martin Term" file, Library, Ex-Im.

[69] Minutes, Board of Directors, March 13, 1946, Minutes, Box 6, RG 275.

[70] Minutes, Board of Directors, March 13, 1946; March 27, 1946; quote from March 27, 1946, p. 187, Minutes, Box 6, RG 275; Tirana, p. 12; Semiannual Report for July–December 1946.

request for $650 million. Martin and the board at first resisted because the requested sum sharply limited the Bank's remaining uncommitted lending authority. Then, too, there was insufficient time – at most two weeks – to consider the French appeal. Martin in particular was unhappy about the State Department's pressing the Bank for quick action. Even though the Bank's staff had grown markedly immediately after the war – to 113 at the end of 1947 and to 125 a year later – Martin thought it impossible to review the French proposal thoroughly. While not challenging the authority of the Departments of State and Treasury on political and financial matters, Martin observed that it must be remembered "that the members of the board of the Export-Import Bank are trustees of the money made available to them for loans. Accordingly, the board cannot make a commitment without thorough consideration."[71]

None of these concerns deterred the State Department. Officials there were determined to aid France as major elections approached in which the French communist party might gain ground. On May 15, the Bank's board relented and approved the loan. But, for the record, Martin made clear "that granting a loan of this magnitude would not be in accordance with strict commercial banking principles, but that the political element to the loan was not one for the Bank to judge but was up to the State Department."[72] Even so, in approving the loan the board added the proviso that the "terms and conditions [would] be worked out with the French."[73] Consequently, Bank officials attempted to negotiate strict terms under which the credits would be made available to the French.[74]

In effect, though, the 1946 French loan marked the end of the Bank's emergency reconstruction lending. As the Bank said in its Third Semi-Annual Report to Congress, "the Export-Import Bank has decided that it must bring to an end its program of emergency reconstruction credits

[71] Minutes, Board of Directors, Ex-Im, May 1, 8, 1946, Minutes, Box 6, RG 275; Semiannual Report for January–June 1946; Letter, Martin to Senator Aiken, January 29, 1948, Subject Files, 1933–1975, Box 6, "Budget, 1946–47" folder, RG 275; Martin Interview, pp. 11–12; *FRUS, 1946*, Vol. V, pp. 431–47; *FRUS, 1947*, Vol. III, pp. 756–9, 775, 798–803.

[72] Minutes, Board of Directors, Ex-Im, May 8, 1946, p. 247, Minutes, Box 6, RG 275.

[73] Minutes, Board of Directors, Ex-Im, May 15, 1946, p. 327, Minutes, Box 6, RG 275.

[74] Martin Interview, pp. 11–12; *FRUS, 1946*, Vol. V, pp. 431–47; *FRUS, 1947*, Vol. III, pp. 756–9, 775, 798–803; Tirana, pp. 19–20.

and this decision should apply especially to countries which have access to the facilities of the ... [World] Bank."[75]

Meanwhile, as funding authority was stretched by emergency reconstruction lending, Martin tried to reenergize the Bank's efforts on partnering with commercial financial institutions. The Bank's earlier guarantee arrangements with the private sector had become less necessary following passage of the 1945 act. Once Congress authorized borrowing from the treasury, Ex-Im found it easier to obtain its funds than when it had to sell preferred stock to the RFC. Moreover, the government's need for quick decisions on loans, somewhat unconventional terms, and fast disbursements vitiated the advantages of the guarantee program. Even so, Martin was not about to give up on the private banking sector, even though it showed little interest in postwar lending, especially in Europe. In 1946, the board established a department to promote private sector participation in the Bank's lending. Not too much later, the board authorized a short-term credit to the Netherlands of a two-year $200 million credit, which involved forty-two banks and took $93 million of the loan. This was the first postwar private participation in Europe. In the following year, commercial banks also accepted $18 million of a $50 million four-year loan to Belgium. In both loans, private banks focused on the earlier maturities, leaving the longer, riskier, less traditional credits to the Ex-Im. Martin put the new private sector department in the hands of an experienced investment banker who, nevertheless, according to Martin, had a hard job because of all of the promising lending opportunities in the American economy.[76]

Another way to provide more credits would have been to increase lending authority for the Bank. Despite discussions in June 1946 that the Truman administration would ask Congress for an additional $1.25 billion authority for the Ex-Im, no request was made. Congressional leaders advised Truman against asking for the money, especially if it might be construed that there would be loans to the Soviet Union, whose policies increasingly angered members of Congress.[77]

Under the circumstances, Italy's hopes for assistance on the scale that the French received were unrealistic in view of the limits on the Bank's

[75] Memorandum, Johnson to Kerlin, April 11, 1947, Subject Files 1934–1975, Box 6, "Budget, 1946–1947" folder, RG 275; Semiannual Report for July–December 1946.
[76] Martin Interview, p. 14; Semiannual Report for July–December 1946, pp. 18–19.
[77] *FRUS, 1946*, Vol. I, pp. 1435–6.

available funds. Italian officials came back to the Bank with a more modest and focused request for $100 million in October 1947. Ex-Im sent a mission to Italy to meet with officials of the Istituto Mobiliare Italiano (IMI), a state–private partnership designed to support the rehabilitation of enterprises, large and small, in several industries, including steel, automobiles, rubber, chemicals, and handicrafts. Italian banks, insurance companies, and individual investors owned a majority of IMI's stocks and bonds. The Italian government held a minority of the organization's shares and appointed four of eighteen directors. From the Bank's point of view, IMI's great value was its professional financial and technical staff that both determined which enterprises received credits and later took substantial responsibility in overseeing projects. Because private interests controlled IMI, it minimized political influence over the disposition of reconstruction credits, a problem in Italy and elsewhere in Europe. Using IMI as a model, the Bank subsequently supported a similar, but smaller, developmental organizations in Austria, which received a $13 million credit.[78]

Even though the Italians scaled back their request, the NAC pressed the Bank for large "stop-gap funds" of $600 million to $700 million for both Italy and France in the fall of 1947. Truman administration officials believed that Europe needed urgent financial assistance to make it through the winter of 1947–8. For most of 1947, the White House became more alarmed about the deterioration in relations with the USSR and the continuing political and economic problems in Europe. Truman believed bold steps were necessary. In March 1947, he succeeded in getting a special military and economic aid program for Greece and Turkey, a result in part because the Bank did not believe that lending to Greece could satisfy its standards of reasonable assurance of repayment. A few months later in June, George C. Marshall, by then Truman's secretary of state, proposed that the United States undertake massive assistance to Europe for relief and reconstruction. Ultimately, Congress passed what became known as the Marshall Plan in April 1948 and authorized the first appropriation for the multiyear program in June of that year. By 1951, Congress

78 Edward S. Lynch, "Export-Import Bank Loans Through Foreign Financial Agencies and Development Corporations," Memorandum to the Committee on Banking and Currency of the United States Senate, copy in Subject File, 1934–1975, Box 11, "Capehart Committee, 1953" folder, RG 275.

authorized $12.53 billion – primarily grants not loans – for the Marshall Plan.[79]

But in the fall 1947, Ex-Im responded to the NAC that it did not have several hundreds of millions of dollars in credits to extend to France and Italy. Ex-Im officials believed that the IBRD was the place to go for such assistance. Moreover, Martin argued that neither country could repay, even if the funds were available, and reminded the NAC of the Bank's statutory requirements in regard to "reasonable assurance" of repayment. Still pressed by the NAC, however, Bank officials finally offered to accelerate payments from previously authorized but still unused funds, although they remained opposed to new commitments. But the Truman administration dropped the matter with Ex-Im. Instead, Truman requested a special appropriation from Congress in October 1947 to provide emergency assistance.[80]

Because of Ex-Im's experience in administering complex lending arrangements, the authorities responsible for the Marshall Plan initially contemplated using the Bank to administer loans. Ex-Im officials were not enthusiastic about assuming such a responsibility. They assumed that Marshall Plan aid would require a sharp departure from the Bank's procedures for extending credits. As it turned out, the Bank only played a very limited part in the Marshall Plan, administering a small loan component of the larger program.[81]

THE BANK AS AN INSTITUTION AND THE LESSONS OF THE WAR AND THE EARLY POSTWAR YEARS

During the war and the early years of the postwar period, the Bank faced daunting demands from a government scrambling to meet radically

[79] *FRUS, 1947*, Vol. III, pp. 203–37; *FRUS, 1947*, Vol. V, pp. 11–12, 29–31; a good summary of the Marshall Plan can be found in Diane B. Kunz, *Butter and Guns: America's Cold War Economic Diplomacy* (New York: The Free Press, 1997), chapter 3.

[80] Herbert E. Gaston to Martin, October 3, 1947 and Memorandum for the President (of the Ex-Im) from Herbert Gaston, September 28, 1947, in "Martin Term" file; Tirana ms, pp. 35–6; *FRUS, 1947*, Vol. III, pp. 202–37, 345–51, 473–81.

[81] Letter, Martin to Rep. Frances P. Bolton, February 10, 1948; Memorandum, Rifat Tirana, to Board of Directors, "Eximbank Loans to ECA Countries – the Position of the Executive Branch," November 11, 1948; Letter, Paul G. Hoffman, Administrator, European Cooperation Administration, May 6, 1949, Enclosure: "Memorandum Agreement Defining Agency Relationship Between Economic Cooperation Administration and Export-Import Bank of Washington," Subject Files, 1933–75, Box 37, "International Cooperation Administration, 1940–1954" folder, RG 275.

altered economic, diplomatic, and military circumstances. War-time activities in Latin America honed the Bank's organizational capabilities as it flexibly took on new kinds of project, developmental, and economic stabilization lending. In the immediate postwar years, the government called on the Bank to respond to the emergency lending needed for European reconstruction. President William McChesney Martin was not the only one of the Bank's people who chafed when, in response to the emergency, the Bank's standard loan-making procedures or the terms of its lending had to be compromised. Even so, the Bank proved resilient. It provided what emergency reconstruction lending its resources would allow, while remaining committed to its way of extending credits and managing loans.

The Bank's commitment to its businesslike loan-making culture was not a matter of unthinking attachment to procedure for its own sake. It was the experience of the negative consequences brought on by departure from standard Bank practices that underscored the importance of an orderly way of doing business. In the case of the Rio Doce project in Brazil, the Bank regularly had before it an example of the consequences of not following its own preferences as to terms and guarantees from the borrower.

If Rio Doce was an example of what not to do, the Bank had positive examples to use as a model of how things should be done. Volta Redonda, the national steel company project in Brazil, worked well from the Bank's point of view. It met objectives and followed the Bank's best practices in regard to extending credits and project management. The same could be said for the Italian IMI credits. It was a highly focused effort, where the Bank provided credits for clearly identified, fully worked out projects, which required a minimum of supervision.

As the government in 1947 proposed the dramatic Marshall Plan, Martin articulated a vision for the Bank's role in the future based on his understanding of its history, especially its experience in the war and postwar period. With the end of the Bank's role in reconstruction lending, Martin planned to turn the Bank's credit activities toward programs that would promote a more balanced two-way foreign trade. In 1947, the United States' total imports were $5.7 billion; its exports were $14.4 billion. Martin looked beyond the immediate needs of emergency reconstruction to the longer-term issue of reviving the international trading system. By doing so, in effect, he validated Pierson's earlier emphasis on developmental lending. In 1947, he said that the Bank "has never undertaken to finance exports for their own sake [sic].... [It] is more likely to finance the export of raw materials, such as cotton, and of capital goods, than of finished consumer goods." He believed that the Bank's history, at least in the 1940s, showed that "its credits have served chiefly to promote the export of goods which serve to increase the productive capacity of foreign countries and their capacity to export those products which are desired in the US and elsewhere. In this way the Bank helps to create a steadily growing market for American products of all kinds and at the same time to facilitate the repayment of foreign debts to it and other American creditors."[82]

With the assistance the Marshall Plan and the IBRD ultimately provided to Europe, the Bank turned again toward Latin America as its major field of operations. It was ripe for the kind of lending that Martin and his colleagues believed was best for the United States and the growth of a healthy international trading system.

[82] Martin Testimony, Congress, House Banking and Currency Committee, 1947, 80th Congress, 1st Session, "Martin Term" file.

3

COLD WAR AND THE NEEDS OF A NEW ERA, 1948–1961

INTRODUCTION

In 1948, President William McChesney Martin looked forward to the end of the Bank's role in European reconstruction. One might say that he hoped for normalcy. The Ex-Im's activity in that year focused on agricultural credits and developmental lending, two well-established areas of its business. By the early 1950s, much of the Ex-Im's activities were devoted to developmental lending in Latin America, an area familiar to the institution.[1]

But the year 1948 proved anything but normal for the United States. Already troubled relations with the Soviet Union deteriorated even further with a series of events between 1947 and June 1950 – the start of the Korean War – which froze U.S.–USSR relations in the bitter standoff that came to be known as the Cold War. As a result, the Bank increased lending to promote the production of strategic materials, which in turn opened the Ex-Im to business in the Middle East, Africa, and Asia, places where its role had earlier been either minimal or nonexistent. The increasing scope and volume of the Bank's business required larger budgets for staff and greater attention to the intricacies of managing expanding operations.

The decade following 1947 also witnessed significant changes in the United States' place in the international economy. As Europe's and Japan's industrial base recovered from the damage of World War II, the

[1] "Outline of Testimony: Projected Effect, Eximbank Operations on U.S. Treasury Cash Budget, Fiscal Years 1954–1963," p. 33, Subject Files, 1933–1975, Box 11, "Capehart Committee, 1953" folder, Record Group 275, Records of the Export-Import Bank, National Archives; U.S. Department of State, *Foreign Relations of the United States, 1952–54*, Vol. I, pp. 324–329 (hereafter *FRUS*).

United States lost its unusual postwar preeminence in world markets. The seller's market of the 1940s became a buyer's market in the early 1950s, which resulted in American exporters having a harder time making sales. Consequently, the Bank increased its attention to the needs of exporters coping with these changed economic circumstances. Organized exporter groups welcomed the increased attention to their needs because they had mobilized against a plan early in the Eisenhower administration (1953–4) to limit the Bank's responsibilities. The Bank survived the contentious effort to limit its mission, but there were long-lived consequences to the battle.

By the end of the 1950s, further changes in the international economic situation had an impact on the Bank. In 1958, there was a sharp increase in the United States' balance of payments deficit, a circumstance that worsened in the years ahead. While the Bank's lending was not a major factor in the federal budget deficit, nor in the balance of payments problems, the treasury's broad strategy to combat these problems included pressing the Bank to focus more on private sector participation in loans and the use of its guarantee authority.

OLD BUSINESS/NEW BUSINESS

After the European Recovery Program got underway in 1948, the Bank shied away from extending credits to participating countries in Europe.[2] President Martin and the board instead focused on Latin America and the developmental and emergency foreign trade credits[3] lending the Bank had pioneered in the region. As time went on, however, the United States' Cold War responsibilities increasingly led the Ex-Im in new directions.

Nevertheless, in the spring of 1948, the Bank's attention turned to Latin America in a dramatic fashion. In April, Martin was part of the American delegation attending the month-long Ninth International Conference of American States in Bogota, Colombia. Secretary of State George C. Marshall was the keynote speaker, there to reassure Latin American officials who complained that after the war the United States

[2] Export-Import Bank of Washington, *Sixth Semiannual Report to Congress for the Period January–June 1948*, pp. 1–3 (hereafter Semiannual Report).

[3] Export-Import Bank and other sources also refer to emergency foreign trade credits as balance of payments loans.

Table 3.1 *Export-Import Bank Disbursements by Selected Area (Dollar Amounts in Millions)*

Year	Latin America		Europe		Total
1948	$59.2	14%	$195.0	45%	$428.8
1949	$77.4	42%	$63.9	34.6%	$184.8
1950	$74.0	37%	$61.8	30.9%	$199.9
1951	$128.7	63.1%	$15.4	7.6%	$204.0

Source: "Outline of Testimony on U.S. Treasury Cash Budget, FY 1954–1963," Subject Files 1933–1975, Box 11, "Capehart Committee 1953" folder, RG 275.

had ignored the region. During the meetings, riots broke out following the assassination – not far from where Martin was standing – of one of Colombia's leading opposition politicians. While Martin was trapped overnight in a torched American embassy, he was able to get an urgent message through to the Bank's board in Washington. They approved, on an emergency basis, a pending $10 million loan for Colombia.[4]

Following the sensational events in Bogota, President Truman requested an additional $500 million from Congress for the Bank in large part to assist Latin America. The Senate passed the bill authorizing the increased authority, but the House took no action. Martin and the board were not deterred. They were able to draw on uncommitted lending authority ($627 million as of June 30, 1948) and loan repayments ($109 million between July 1947 and June 1948).[5]

Between 1948 and 1952, Latin America received an increasing proportion of Bank attention (see Table 3.1). The Ex-Im widened its scope of activities to include disaster reconstruction. Following a major earthquake in Ecuador in 1949, for example, the Bank furnished a line of credit to help in rebuilding. There were also credits to complete projects begun during the war, as Ecuador and Bolivia received loans to finish highways. Colombia received additional credits for a flood control and irrigation program begun earlier. There was an expansion of bank-financed projects at the Volta Redonda steel mills in Brazil and in Huachipato, Chile. But there were new projects too. Haiti in 1951

4 Oral History Interview with William McChesney Martin (December 3, 1973), n.p., typescript in Mazo-Mazon files, Library, Export-Import Bank of the United States, Washington, DC (hereafter Martin Interview).

5 President's Message, April 8, 1948, Department of State *Bulletin*, April 25, 1948, p. 548; Semiannual Report for January–June 1948, pp. 2–3.

received financial assistance to purchase the materials and retain the engineering expertise needed to build dams and irrigation systems. Mexico secured substantial credits for highway and rail construction, irrigation systems, electric power generating and transmitting projects, and the joint building with the United States of the Falcon Dam on the Rio Grande. Both Argentina and Brazil secured credits to pay off outstanding obligations to American exporters blocked because of exchange shortages.[6]

Nevertheless, in the late 1940s and early 1950s the Bank also got caught up in the continuing political and economic cross-currents emanating from the end of World War II and the beginnings of the Cold War.[7] The Bank's direct responsibility for postwar European reconstruction assistance ended when the Marshall Plan took effect. But the Ex-Im was not totally disengaged. While much of the plan involved grants, there were also loans, ultimately totally $1.5 billion, which the Bank administered for the Marshall Plan's administrative agency, the Economic Cooperation Administration. Ex-Im acted as agent for the loan credits extended by the ECA, and its successor the Mutual Security Agency (MSA). These administrative agencies were responsible for American foreign aid programs. Bank operations for the ECA were carried independently on its books, as mandated in the Foreign Assistance Act, approved in April 1948. Congress designated the Bank to manage these credits in recognition of the ECA's status as a temporary agency and of the Ex-Im's experience in managing lending programs.[8]

Similarly, the Bank continued to serve the government's interest in coping with other consequences of World War II. Soon after Israel declared its independence in May 1948, President Truman turned to the Bank to aid the new state. The Bank in January 1949 authorized

[6] Semiannual Reports for 1949–1952.

[7] Events that turned official American opinion against the USSR were a March 1946 confrontation with the USSR over troop withdrawals in Iran; a February 1948 communist-inspired coup against a freely elected government in Czechoslovakia; the Russian eleven-month-long blockade of Berlin beginning in June 1948; the USSR's successful test of an atomic bomb in September 1949; the proclamation of a Chinese communist government in October 1949; and finally communist North Korea's attack on South Korea in June 1950, which American officials believed had been approved in, if not inspired from, Moscow.

[8] Semiannual Report for January–June 1949, pp. 13–15; Memorandum of Conversation, Elmer Chase, Ex-Im, and Austin Sullivan, Department of State, April 9, 1951, Central Decimal File (CDF)1950–1954, Box 374 (103-XMB/4-951), Record Group 59, Records of the U.S. Department of State, National Archives.

$100 million in credits as part of a program to promote "a self-sustaining economy" in Israel.[9] At first Martin and other Ex-Im officials resisted the president's request. But Truman pressed the issue for reasons of foreign policy' of domestic politics and because of humanitarian concerns in view of the Holocaust.[10]

As part of a Cold War initiative to support a shaky French government fighting a communist insurgency in Indo-China, Defense and Treasury Department officials requested that the Bank extend a general credit of $200 million to France. The credit was for that country's purchase of military equipment from offshore sources. In this complex transaction, the advances to France would be secured by the assignment of French government claims against the United States, which were expected to arise from the completion of U.S. Defense Department contracts for the purchase of military supplies from France. Board member Gauss unsuccessfully opposed the Bank making such funds available for military purposes. He feared that the credit would set a precedent and that other countries would seek similar loans.[11]

Cold War considerations also influenced the Bank's business after the U.S. government accepted the Soviet Union as a long-term adversary. In 1949, for example, the Bank played a direct role in the jockeying between the alliances that had formed around the United States and USSR. Yugoslavia in September requested assistance from the Ex-Im. Yugoslavia's independent-minded communist leader, Joseph Tito, was distancing his country from the Soviet Union and its satellites in Eastern Europe. Truman administration officials welcomed the apparent breach in the Soviet bloc, and the Bank ultimately authorized $35 million in credits.[12]

Cold War concerns also led to an enlargement of the United States' foreign policy and strategic goals. In his inaugural address in March 1949, President Truman made a case for promoting the economic

[9] Semiannual Report for January–June 1949, pp. 3–4.

[10] Martin Interview (November 20, 1973), pp. 16–17; Memorandum of Conversation, Ex-Im Board, Representatives of Departments of State and Treasury, "Export-Import Bank Meeting of September 26 on Israeli $75 million Loan Application," September 26, 1956, CDF 1955–1959 Box 377 (103-XMB/9-2656), RG 59.

[11] Minutes, Board Meetings, Ex-Im, March 20, 1952 and April 10, 1952; Memorandum, Stenger to Corbett, "Agenda for Meeting of Board of Directors, Eximbank, May 15, 1952," May 13, 1952, CDF 1950–1954, Box 375 (103-XmB/5-1552) RG 59.

[12] Semiannual Report for July–December 1950, p. 1.

development of poor countries. A consensus had formed among policy makers that poverty bred social and political instability that communist insurgents could exploit. In June 1949, Truman followed up with a proposal to Congress that included specific references to the role the Export-Import Bank should play in promoting economic development. He took note of what the Bank had already achieved in its development lending. In the broadest sense, Bank officials believed, such credits would increase the "trade base" of a country through selective projects raising its economic capacity to import American products, or enhancing its ability to earn dollars. Truman proposed expanding the Bank's activities to include encouraging overseas private investment through a guarantee program. The president envisioned Ex-Im's guaranteeing American firms earning profits overseas against blocked exchange and expropriation. Opposition in the House of Representatives doomed the proposal when opponents argued that such guarantees would put those who had already invested abroad at a disadvantage.[13]

In any event, the Bank's lending in these years often linked up with the Cold War objective of restraining the expansionist tendencies of the USSR and Communist China. Such loans included those to Saudi Arabia – a strategically important oil-rich country in the Middle East – for road and harbor improvements. There were credits to the USSR's neighbor Afghanistan for irrigation systems and dams. Iran, a bordering country threatened by a Soviet Union interested in its rich supplies of oil and natural gas, received funds for agricultural and road programs. In Asia, the United States took a particular interest in Indonesia, a former Dutch colony.[14]

Other aspects of the Cold War struggle also drew the Bank close to U.S. foreign policy. In 1949, the USSR tried to use its supplies of manganese – essential to the production of steel – to weaken the United States' steel industry.[15] The United States had very little of its own commercial-grade manganese and had traditionally relied on foreign sources for the needs of the American steel industry. In 1948, the

[13] Semiannual Report for July–December 1949, pp. 2–5.

[14] Semiannual Report for July–December 1950, pp. 1–3.

[15] The principal strategic materials needed for stockpiles were manganese, lead, copper, mica, and zinc. See Memorandum, "Latin American Supplies of Strategic Materials," Assistant Chief of the International Resources Division to Director of the Office of American Republic Affairs, Department of State, March 12, 1948, *FRUS, 1948*, Vol. IX, pp. 233–4.

United States imported 91 percent of its commercial manganese. The major suppliers to the United States were India, South Africa, Brazil, and the Soviet Union. Indeed, the latter was the single largest supplier of manganese to the United States, providing 36 percent of what was used in 1948.[16]

An emergency developed when the USSR announced that it would significantly cut back on its manganese exports to the United States. In fact, at the beginning of 1949, estimates were that the USSR would supply the U.S. steel industry with only about 6 percent of what was needed for the year. Brazil was the most likely place for a significant increase in manganese production. United States Steel Corporation and Bethlehem Steel Corporation approached the Bank in March 1949 about assistance ($5 million of a total investment of $30 million) in developing rich sources of manganese in the Urucum mine in Mato Grosso, Brazil. Bank president Herbert E. Gaston – who had taken over as president and chairman of the board following Martin's resignation in February 1949 – recognized the urgent nature of the situation. The Bank, however, did not make the loan to develop the Urucum mines because the potential borrowers would not meet the Ex-Im's terms. Ex-Im eventually approved a much larger project, which provided credits of $67.5 million to develop manganese resources in the territory of Amapa in Brazil.[17]

Bank lending also assisted in the development of other strategic supplies in the late 1940s and early 1950s.[18] In Peru, in 1950, the

[16] Memorandum, U.S. Steel Corporation, "Original and Revised Plan for the Development of Urucum Mine in Mato Grosso, Brazil," February 28, 1949, CDF 1945–1949, Box 5455 (832.51/2-2849), RG 59.

[17] Memorandum, Hamilton, International Resources Division, to Stenger, Economics Division, Department of State, March 4, 1949, "Interest of American Steel Companies in the Urucum Manganese Deposit in Brazil"; Memorandum, Atterberry, Economics Division to Stenger, Economics Division, Department of State, March 8, 1949, "Manganese Development in Brazil Proposed by U.S. Steel Corporation and Bethlehem Steel," CDF 1945–1949, Box 5455 (832.51/3-849), RG 59; Memorandum, Atterberry to Hamilton, April 6, 1949, "Brazil – Eximbank Credit for Manganese Ore Development," CDF 1945–1949, Box 5456 (832.51/4-649), RG 59; Memorandum, Atterberry to Turnage, September 2, 1952, "Agenda for Meeting of Board of Directors of the Eximbank, September 4, 1954" (topic 3: "Brazil – Amapa Manganese Development,") CDF 1950–1954, Box 375 (103-XMB/9-454), RG 59; Semiannual Report for July–December 1952, pp. 3–4.

[18] Supplies of strategic materials became an important focus of the new national security apparatus that the Truman administration created as relations between the United States and USSR hardened. The new structure revolved around the changes that resulted from the National Security Act of 1947, which joined the military services into a Department

Bank provided $20.8 million in credits to the Cerro de Pasco Copper Corporation, a producer of copper, lead, and zinc, to finance the installation of new zinc production facilities. Originally, Bank officials viewed these credits in terms of development lending, helping Peru to diversify its economy. It was also part of an effort to accommodate a Peruvian government interested in promoting private enterprise and attracting foreign capital. But as the world situation proved more ominous, the loan took on greater significance as a contribution to procuring strategic materials.[19]

Similarly, the same could be said of the development loans to diversify the Liberian economy. By fostering the mining of high-grade iron ore, the Bank hoped to assist this underdeveloped African country; by the time the project was completed, the Bank's attention had turned to aid in procuring strategic materials. Credits of $4 million were extended to a private company, Liberia Mining Company, Ltd., working with Republic Steel Company and other American investors, to develop the mine, a railroad to the port of Monrovia, and improvements to the harbor there.[20]

With the North Korean attack on South Korea in June 1950, the need for strategic materials increased sharply. The Truman administration responded quickly to the advancing armies and sent troops under the auspices of the United Nations. Although Congress did not declare war, the United States became fully engaged in a major military conflict. To be sure, it was not on the scale of World War II, but the government needed

of Defense, created an independent intelligence organization in the Central Intelligence Agency, and established a National Security Council in the White House to coordinate military and foreign policy. In April 1948, there were efforts to coordinate the activities of the agencies and departments interested in strategic materials (the National Security Resources Board, the Department of State, the Munitions Board, and the Bureau of Mines) through a Working Group on Problems of Strategic Material Availabilities and Procurement. See Letter, Robert A. Lovett, Acting Secretary of State, to James Forrestal, Secretary of Defense, April 15, 1948, *FRUS, 1948*, Vol. IX, pp. 240–1.

19 *FRUS, 1951*, Vol. II, p. 1588; Memorandum, "New Degree Favorably Affecting Metal Mining Industry in Peru," August 1949 and Arey to Cerro de Pasco Copper Corporation, August 18, 1950, Credit No. 483, " Cerro Corp.," Credit Case Files, 1954–1967, Box 6, RG 275.

20 Semiannual Report for July–December 1950, pp. 1–2; Semiannual Report for January–June 1949, pp. 4–5; Semiannual Report for July–December 1952, p. 5; Memoranda, "Possible Export-Import Bank Loan to Liberia," August 11, 1949, August 24, 1949, November 1, 1949, November 2, 1949, November 3, 1949, November 10, 1949, November 29, 1949, CDF 1945–1949, Box 5055 (811.516 Export-Import Bank/11-2949), RG 59.

to mobilize. In time, the Bank played a role in the government's efforts to ensure adequate supplies of essential materials. In the three years before June 1950, only about 5 percent of bank lending supported the development of strategic materials ($47.7 million out of $1.05 billion authorized). In the three years following June 1950, credits for essential and strategic materials represented 19 percent of the total authorizations ($288.8 million out of $1.5 billion authorized).[21]

Bank credits for strategic lending between 1950 and 1953 broke down into three basic categories. The largest group of credits ($214.5 million) supported overseas projects producing materials for export to the United States. Another group of credits (totaling $53.8 million) were extended overseas to relieve pressure on supplies of essential materials produced in the United States. Finally, the third group of credits ($20.5 million) supported two projects for facilities to assist in the production and shipment of materials needed for the United States' war effort. These involved improving electric power generating capacity for the expansion of uranium production in South Africa ($19.6 million).[22]

Providing credits for projects that directly and indirectly aided the United States' war effort raised important policy issues for the Bank. During World War II, and the immediate postwar reconstruction effort, the Ex-Im encountered heavy White House pressure to make loans that its officials believed did not always meet the Bank's standards of creditworthiness. This had been particularly a problem in regard to postwar reconstruction loans. The Korean War did not generate the intense demands the Bank faced in the previous conflict; nevertheless, there were pressures for the Ex-Im to relax some of its procedures, if not its statutory requirements, to approve loans with a reasonable assurance of repayment.

In the first year of the war, the administration pressed the Bank to move quickly on requests for loans. Ex-Im succeeded in considerably reducing the time needed to process applications. Helping in this effort

21 A Report to the Committee on Banking and Currency of the U.S. Senate, "Financial Assistance by the Export-Import Bank for the Production Abroad of Essential and Strategic Materials, July 1, 1950, to June 30, 1953," p. 1, Subject Files, 1933–1975, Box 11, "Capehart Committee 1953" folder, RG 275 (hereafter Financial Assistance Report).

22 Financial Assistance Report, pp. 2–3 and Exhibit A, p. 3; on background to uranium lending, see Memorandum, R. Gordon Arneson to Secretary of State, August 6, 1949, "South African Uranium," *FRUS, 1949*, Vol. I, pp. 509–11.

was the NAC's decision early in 1951 that it did not have to approve consideration of loans related to strategic materials. Thus, of the loans for the production of essential and strategic materials, it took on average about 25 weeks from the first contact with the Bank by the applicant to authorization of the credit. In less pressing times, loan approvals could take much longer. Preliminary reviews of proposals might take a few months, and it was not unusual for a major credit to require over a year to consider.[23]

Also speeding up approvals was a system to assign priorities. Because Bank officials were forced by insistent requests to support projects producing essential materials, the Bank realized that it could not make final judgments about the urgency of potential loans on its own. It developed a policy of corroborating requests for assistance in producing essential materials among more than one government agency. Thus, it addressed inquiries to commodity specialists in the Departments of Commerce and Agriculture, as well as the Defense Minerals Administration, the National Security Resources Board, the Munitions Board, and the General Services Administration. In addition, once it made a decision about a loan, it might also need to get assurances about the availability of equipment produced in the United States needed to complete the overseas projects. Hence, the Bank had to work through the agencies – the Defense Minerals Administration and the Defense Production Administration – that by 1952 issued the required priority documents for the equipment.[24]

Inevitably, there were pressures to relax Bank requirements, as well as to speed things up. So the Bank occasionally had to make exceptions to its standard procedures. In producing zinc in Peru, the Ex-Im relaxed its standard requirement that mining projects use generally accepted methods to extract and treat minerals. In this case, it approved the standard process and then six months later sanctioned modifications to encompass new technologies in zinc refining. In addition, the Bank relaxed its policy requiring borrowers to confine themselves to American equipment, materials, and services in the production of tungsten in Peru and manganese in Brazil. Another example of an exception involved uranium being mined in South Africa. At the request of the Atomic

[23] Financial Assistance Report, p. 10.
[24] Ibid., pp. 5–6.

Energy Commission (AEC), the Bank yielded on the engineering and financial information usually required to determine creditworthiness. Because the Bank could not perform its standard technical analysis, the AEC agreed to guarantee the loan.[25]

Overall, even though Gaston and his colleagues were willing to relax some aspects of standard procedures, they did not want to forego the requirement of a reasonable assurance of repayment.[26] Thus, they turned down a number of requests for loans. But in a war situation, some materials were needed regardless of whether the Bank thought them creditworthy. Hence, the Ex-Im cooperated with the Truman administration in coming to a workable solution.

In August 1950, a few months after the war began in Korea, Congress passed the Defense Production Act. This legislation essentially provided the president with the emergency authority over domestic economic activities to prosecute the war. It included provisions for the president to authorize loans to cover the production of essential and strategic materials to private enterprises. "Such loans," the legislation stated, "may be made without regard to the limitations of existing law and on such terms and conditions as the President deems necessary."[27] This act formed the basis upon which the Bank and the administration devised a policy on making loans that did not meet its usual credit standards. Coming to a practicable understanding took until August 1951. Gaston played an active part in the discussions to ensure that the Bank's point of view would be heeded.[28]

In October 1951, Congress increased the Bank's lending authority in large part to address the needs of wartime lending. The increase from $3.5 to $4.5 billion came as part of the Bank's reauthorization for five years through June 30, 1958.[29] Additionally, the government provided separate funds to the Bank for loans that did not meet its usual standards of creditworthiness. On August 28, 1951, President Truman issued an

[25] Ibid., pp. 7–10; Credit No. 498 "Union of South Africa," Credit Case Files, 1954–1967, Box 7, RG 275; Credit No. 483 "Cerro Corp.," Credit Case Files, 1954–1967, Box 6, RG 275.

[26] Quote, Herbert E. Gaston, testimony, hearings, August 28, 1951, before Senate, Subcommittee of the Committee on Banking and Currency, on S. 2006, p. 10 in Financial Assistance Report, p. 5.

[27] Section 302 of the Act of August 8, 1950, quoted in Financial Assistance Report, p. 16.

[28] Ibid., p. 18.

[29] Congress, Senate, Subcommittee of the Committee on Banking and Currency, "Export-Import Bank Act Amendments," 82nd Congress, 1st Session, 1951, pp. 1–21.

executive order that directed that such "loans . . . shall be made upon such terms and conditions as said Bank shall determine . . . and shall be made only upon certificate of essentiality of the loan," by the secretary of agriculture for food and "by the Defense Production Administrator in respect of all other materials and facilities."[30] In the month following, the Bank worked out procedures with the secretary of agriculture and the defense production administrator to administer the new certification-based loan program. In November 1951, the defense production administrator authorized the Bank to borrow funds from the treasury to extend credits for the certified loans. Between November 1951 and February 1953, a series of authorizations provided the Bank with $135 million for certified loans.[31]

By the end of the war in July 1953, the Bank had funded $72.5 million in certified defense loans. The Bank accounted for these funds separately from its other activities. The two largest credits went toward the production of copper and cobalt in Rhodesia and Uganda ($50.9 million) and of manganese in Brazil ($15 million).[32]

Overall, then, the Korean War experience proved less stressful for the Bank than World War II and postwar reconstruction. Its leaders were keenly aware of the difficulties that could ensue in departing substantially from its standards of creditworthiness. Memories of the Ex-Im's experience with Rio Doce in the 1940s stiffened the Bank's resolve to adhere to its standards in extending credits. By 1950, the White House also apparently better understood the Bank's position, perhaps a result of the rapport that Martin had developed earlier with President Truman in disputes over loans for French reconstruction and assistance to Israel.[33] In any event, Gaston was able to make the Bank's strict position on creditworthiness understood in the government. Indeed, the key executive order of August 1951 that established the certification program had been reviewed at a meeting at the Bank before Truman issued it.[34]

30 Executive Order No. 10281, August 28, 1951, quoted in Financial Assistance Report, p. 19.

31 Ibid., pp. 19–21; Memorandum to the Board, R. H. Rowntree, "Critical Materials Financing under the Defense Production Act," September 21, 1951, CDF 1950–1954, Box 375 (103-XMB/9-2651), RG 59.

32 Financial Assistance Report, pp. 20–21, Exhibit B, pp. 1–2.

33 Martin Interview (November 20, 1973) , pp. 11, 16–17.

34 Financial Assistant Report, pp. 17–18; attending that meeting of July 31, 1951, were representatives from the Bureau of the Budget, the Departments of Agriculture, Interior,

While the Bank succeeded in defining how it would contribute to the war effort, the period from the beginnings of the Cold War to the end of the Korean War put enormous demands on the Ex-Im's operations and staff. There was an increase in the geographical scope of its business and in the dollar volume of its lending. By the end of the Truman administration in January 1953, the Bank was administering loans in forty-eight countries.[35]

Generally, both the greater scope and volume of business were related to the Truman administration's commitment to promoting economic development and securing strategic materials. The kind of project lending that resulted from developmental initiatives and promoting essential materials was inherently more complicated than extending credits to exporters, financing commodity exports, and providing emergency foreign trade loans. Authorizing credits for developmental lending routinely required the involvement of many more professionals (examiners, economists, lawyers, engineers, and accountants) working together than in other kinds of lending. Development loans also cost more administratively. In 1949, Gaston estimated that the project loans associated with development lending had administrative costs of $1,000 to $7,000 per year per million dollars of credit as opposed to emergency foreign trade credits which cost $10 to $300 per year per million.[36]

Perhaps the most distinctive aspect of developmental lending was the need for highly specialized engineering expertise. By 1953, a little more than ten years after the Bank retained its first full-time engineer, Ex-Im had eighteen on the staff. Developmental lending did not fundamentally change the way in which the Bank approached a decision about extending a credit. But it became more elaborate, complex, and time-consuming because of the need for the engineers' technical analyses. Engineers were routinely included in the review committees set

State, Treasury, as well as the Defense Production Administration, the Economic Cooperation Administration, the General Services Administration, the Munitions Board, the National Production Authority, the Office of the Assistant to the President, and the Reconstruction Finance Corporation; Memorandum, Gaston to Director, Bureau of Budget, May 11, 1951, Subject Files 1933–1975, "Budget, 1951–52" folder, Box 7, RG 275; Letter, Gaston to Secretary of State, July 26, 1951, CDF 1950–1954, Box 374 (103-XMB/7-2651), RG 59.

35 "Narrative Statement, Program Highlights," n.d., p. 7, Subject Files, 1933–1975, Box 7, "Budget, 1953" folder, RG 275.

36 Letter, Gaston to Director, Bureau of the Budget, September 14, 1949, Subject Files, 1933–1975, Box 7, "Budget, 1949" folder, RG 275.

up to make preliminary and final analyses of applications for credit. In the late 1940s and 1950s, the vice president appointed these review or loan committees. The examiner, economic, legal, engineering, and private financing divisions of the Bank usually each had a representative on the committee. Within the operating divisions, there were geographical specialists who were assigned according to the region in which the loan would be made.[37]

The review process for developmental loans could take more than a year. Examiners in the case of loans to overseas private enterprises made detailed studies of the buyer's financial condition, looking into balance sheets, profit and loss statements, accounting procedures, corporate structure, stock ownership, and so on. Economists studied a country's imports and exports, balance of payments, market structures, and natural resources. The Bank's lawyers had responsibility for ensuring the legality of what might be contracted for and then negotiating and drawing up the contracts. Finally, the engineers – who along with some of the other professionals might travel to the site of a proposed loan – would undertake their analyses. These included an evaluation of the technical requirements of the application. That is, the engineers would make judgments about the availability of raw materials, adequacy of transportation, capacity of power sources, competency of local technical personnel, appropriateness of proposed operating practices, and the state of existing plant. After a favorable decision was made on extending a credit, staff in the private capital participation division determined whether there were prospects for private capital to take some of the maturities.[38]

Thus, in the 1940s and early 1950s, there was a premium on orderly administration. Decision making became more complex, and the

[37] Walter C. Sauer, "Loan Procedures of Export-Import Bank of Washington," for Committee on Banking and Currency, U.S. Senate, September 1953, pp. 6–15, Subject Files, 1933–1975, Box 12, "Capehart Committee, 1953–1954" folder, RG 275 (hereafter "Loan Procedures"); James L. Riddel, "Organization of Export-Import Bank and Expediting Loan Applications," for Committee on Banking and Currency of the U.S. Senate, October 1953, pp. 8–12, Subject Files, 1933–1975, Box 12, "Capehart Committee, 1953–1954" folder, RG 275; "Narrative Statement, Program Highlights," n.d., p. 7, Subject Files, 1933–1975, Box 7, "Budget, 1953" folder, RG 275.

[38] Riddel, pp. 7–9; Memorandum, Hawthorne Arey to Samuel C. Waugh, "Guarantees of foreign loans by U.S. Government agencies," March 3, 1959, p. 7, Subject Files, 1933–1975, Box 32, "Guarantees and Insurance, 1950–1959" folder, RG 275 (hereafter Arey Memorandum).

numbers of transactions multiplied with developmental lending. The numbers of Bank staff steadily increased in the late 1940s and 1950s. Staff positions of 130 in fiscal year 1951 had risen to 234 in fiscal year 1959. But the need for careful, regularized organizational procedures and accurate record keeping did not outweigh the imperative of individual case-by-case consideration of proposed credits. Not until 1957 did the Bank issue a formal set of guidelines or an application form for certain types of credits. Because there were likely to be many variables considered in the Bank's decisions about loans, its leaders preferred to avoid a rigid approach to determining creditworthiness. Thus, by the early 1950s there was in the Bank's organizational culture a built-in tension between the need for order and standardization on the one hand and the imperative to review cases on their individual merits on the other. Ex-Im official Walter C. Sauer perhaps expressed it best when he emphasized that the Ex-Im's procedures for approving loans had *evolved* instead of being "formulated and struck off at any one time." He went on to observe that "the loan procedures of the Bank are by design flexible and in certain respects quite informal. This is not to say that they are haphazard or without pattern. It does mean, however, that the Bank has found by experience . . . that the function in which it is engaged calls for operational procedures which, within an overall uniform framework, are adaptable to the particular needs of the individual loan applications presented to it."[39]

Professional staff employees were an integral part of the Bank's transaction-based culture. The latter was grounded in a loan approval process dependent on deep staff analysis preceding board decisions, and of a board working closely with them in the analysis phases of their work.

But to those whom the Ex-Im denied loans, and to outsiders accustomed to the workings of private sector banks, the Ex-Im's procedures could seem cumbersome and overly complicated.[40] The Bank, of course, defended its careful procedures as being needed to protect the public's

[39] Budget Estimates, Fiscal Year Ending June 30, 1953, Submitted to Congress, January 1952, p. v, Subject Files, 1933–1975, Box 7, "Budget, 1952–53" folder, RG 275; Memorandum, Waugh to Anderson, "Fiscal 1960 Budget Limitation," December 8, 1958, Subject Files, 1933–1975, Box 9, "Budget, 1958–59 folders, RG 275; "Loan Procedures," p. 1.

[40] For such criticisms, see Riddel, p. 12.

funds and to ensure prudent lending.[41] Then, too, unlike private sector institutions, the Bank often had to factor into its loan deliberations the foreign policy interests of the U.S. government.

Criticism of the Bank for the most part remained muted during the Truman years. Gaston was well-connected in Democratic Party circles, and the Bank contributed to the administration's broad foreign policy goals of promoting economic development and ensuring an adequate supply of critical materials. This positive environment, however, did not extend beyond the election of 1952, which brought a Republican president to the White House for the first time in twenty years.

A NEW ADMINISTRATION IN A CHANGING INTERNATIONAL ECONOMY

Republicans took control of the government in the early 1950s. The elections of 1950 returned Republican majorities to Congress, and two years later the party attained the White House with the victory of Dwight D. Eisenhower. The new president did not intend to repeal the New Deal; however, he and his cabinet aimed to rein in a government and budget grown large by twenty years of depression, war, and postwar crises.

The Ex-Im Bank received early scrutiny. On April 30, 1953, only three months after taking office, President Eisenhower sent a sweeping Bank reorganization plan to Congress. Eisenhower's proposal fundamentally changed the Bank's governance structure and mission. It became law on June 30, 1953. Secretary of the Treasury George M. Humphrey was the man in Eisenhower's inner circle of advisers who had convinced him to take such a bold step. The secretary believed that "there should be as little government lending as possible."[42] Humphrey – who had been head of Hanna Mining Company – was one of the most dogged proponents of fiscal conservatism in the cabinet. The new president had made much in his campaign of the need to balance the federal budget, which with promised cuts in taxes would require scaling back government programs.

[41] "Loan Procedures," pp. 8–11.

[42] The president used the Reorganization Act of 1949 as his authority for the plan; Congress, House of Representatives, "Reorganization Plan No. 5 of 1953, Relating to the Export-Import Bank of Washington," 83rd Congress, 1st Session, Document No. 135; "Minutes, NAC, May 18, 1953," in *FRUS, 1952–1954*, Vol. I, p. 321; Semiannual Report for January–June 1953, p. 3.

Humphrey's first impression of the Bank was negative. Soon after taking office, the new secretary – who also served as chairman of the NAC – had to make decisions on business left over from the previous administration. At the time, the Bank had under consideration two of the largest individual credits it had ever considered. Brazil needed $300 million to cover arrears in payments to American exporters in U.S. dollars. The other credit, for approximately $100 million, was to assist Southern Peru Copper Corporation (wholly owned by American Smelting and Refining [ASARCO]) in developing Peruvian copper resources. It was the largest single project loan ever undertaken by the Bank. Humphrey opposed both requests, which seemed to confirm his worst fears about government spending. He saw the credit to Brazil as a "bailout" for U.S. exporters who had foolishly continued to make shipments in the face of blocked exchange. As for lending money to the Peruvian enterprise, Humphrey believed that the private sector could provide the needed capital. Moreover, as a former mining executive he also opposed in principle lending federal funds to one American company that, as a result, might strengthen its position against its competitors.[43]

Eisenhower officials honored the commitment to Brazil, and the Bank extended the credit early in 1953. The Peruvian project was another matter. It was not authorized until late 1954, and only after ASARCO found other equity partners and upped its investment at the urging of the treasury and Ex-Im. Eventually, the Bank's credit was for $90 million.[44]

But Humphrey had other reasons to support the president's reorganization of the Bank. He had sided with the International Bank for Reconstruction and Development in a long-running dispute with the Export-Import Bank. For several years, the IBRD's president, Eugene Black, had maintained that the Ex-Im encroached on its responsibilities in extending credits. The Ex-Im disagreed, arguing that it explicitly served American interests. It could only provide credits for goods purchased in the United States, whereas those of the World Bank could be used for purchases overseas. In any event, the Export-Import Bank continued

[43] Walter Sauer, ms, "Export-Import Bank of the United States, The Years 1953–1969," pp. 1–2, (9), Mazo-Mazon Files, Library, Ex-Im; "Summary of Meeting at the White House," January 21, 1954, CDF 1950–1954 (103-XMB/1-2554), Box 377, RG 59; "Minutes, NAC, May 18, 1953," *FRUS, 1952–1954*, Vol. I, pp. 321–9.

[44] Memorandum, Bennett to Corbett, "Toquepala Copper Project in Peru," and Memorandum, Holland to Under Secretary, "Toquepala Loan," December 31, 1954, CDF 1950–1954, Box 4601 (103-XMB/12-3154), RG 59.

to make loans, despite IBRD objections. In several instances, however, the IBRD thwarted the Bank in the NAC from extending credits it had agreed to; the most notable instance was to an electric power company in Japan. Likewise, the IBRD at times attempted to dissuade governments from doing business with the Bank, even in countries like Mexico with a long relationship with the Ex-Im. The dispute between the two institutions took on personal connotations, as their presidents increasingly saw the disagreement over policy as a bitter contest between themselves.[45]

The dispute abated when Gaston resigned. A partisan Democrat, he left the Bank in January 1953, before Eisenhower's inauguration. In March, the president nominated General Glen E. Edgerton to the board. Upon his Senate confirmation in April, Eisenhower appointed him chairman, and the board followed by electing Edgerton president of the Bank. Edgerton was a retired Major General in the U.S. Army Corps of Engineers, with high-level experience in the lend–lease program and in China as the director of the United Nations' relief and rehabilitation effort.[46]

Eisenhower's reorganization proposal became law on June 30, 1953. It abolished the board of directors and substituted them with a managing director and deputy director. Eisenhower appointed Edgerton managing director and Lynn U. Stambaugh deputy director; Edgerton named Hawthorne Avery assistant director. Stambaugh and Arey were experienced executives, long associated with the Ex-Im. Below this administrative level, however, the Bank staff remained virtually untouched, presumably to follow existing procedures for analyzing applications for credits, administering authorized disbursements, and collecting principle and interest.[47]

Nevertheless, the legislation fully subordinated the Bank to the National Advisory Council, significantly reducing the independence of the managing director and of the institution itself. Edgerton, as managing director, lost his voting membership on the NAC. According to the new law, the NAC "shall from time to time establish general lending and other financial policies which shall govern the Managing Director in the conduct in lending and other financial operations of the Bank."

45 Sauer, pp. 3–4; Memorandum, "More on Eximbank vs. IBRD," February 13, 1951, CDF 1950–1954, Box 374 (103-XMB/2-1351), RG 59; and *FRUS, 1951*, Vol. II, pp. 1520–3.

46 Sauer, p. 1.

47 Riddel, p. 12.

Before that the NAC had authority over what Ex-Im might consider, but the financial decisions were to be the Bank's.[48]

But Humphrey was not done with the Bank. There was still the matter of the Bank's relationship to the IBRD. By the time Edgerton settled into his new post, Black had won over the treasury secretary. Humphrey apparently accepted the IBRD argument that the Ex-Im duplicated its efforts and that the World Bank had the authority to supervise the external borrowing of its member countries.[49]

In September, Humphrey allowed the IBRD to circumscribe the Bank's role in development lending. In a "Statement of Principles" of September 24, 1953 (approved by the NAC in January 1954), Edgerton and Black laid out the roles each institution would take in foreign lending. The IBRD, according to the statement, "should be the normal source of loans for development projects involving direct financial obligations of [an IBRD] member government or government agency or its guarantee of the obligations of the borrowers." It went on to say that "the Export-Import Bank should not make loans within the purview of the International Bank." There were some exceptions that might "warrant departure from the general principle," especially in regard to loans for the development of strategic materials. During the Korean War these had been made to private American firms. The IBRD could only make sovereign loans at the time; the establishment of its International Finance Corporation (IFC) in 1956 changed the World Bank's authority in this regard. Overall, though, the Ex-Im was to confine itself to considering on their merits short- and medium-term commodity loans, exporter credits "involving orders for purchase of United States equipment," and loans "in countries not members of the International Bank."[50]

This weakening of the Bank further troubled the State Department. It was already deeply concerned that the reorganization plan abolished the formal role the department had in the affairs of the Export-Import Bank. By eliminating the Bank's board of directors, the secretary of

48 Quoted in Sauer, p. 2.

49 Ibid., pp. 1–3.

50 "Statement of Principles Governing the United States Position in Respect to Loans by the Export-Import Bank of Washington and the International Bank for Reconstruction and Development," September 24, 1953, attached to Samuel C. Waugh to General (Bedel) Smith, Memorandum, January 25, 1954, "National Advisory Council Meeting on the Export-Import Bank, Friday, January 22, 1954," CDF 1950–1954, Box 377 (103-XMB/1-2554), RG 59.

state lost his statutory position as an ex officio member. Also disturbing to State Department officials was Humphrey's strong opposition to what he saw as economically unsound "political loans." In discussions with State Department representatives within the NAC, he singled out as a prime example the $1.2 billion France owed the Bank, repayment of which looked doubtful in the early 1950s. High-ranking State Department officials feared that Humphrey would make it impossible for the Bank to be used in "special cases of over-riding national interest" and in long-term projects for strategic materials. In addition, American diplomatic specialists on Latin America followed with apprehension the growing concern about the Ex-Im among governments in the region with long-term ties to the Bank.[51]

Despite the Department of State's concerns, in January 1954, the NAC approved limiting the Bank's lending as articulated in the so-called Edgerton-Black statement. NAC Chairman Humphrey accepted that the Bank's primary responsibility was to make short- and medium-term loans and that, as frequently as possible, they be made in participation with private sector lenders. He also believed that in the interest of reducing "charge[s] against the Government's cash budget," the Bank needed to make greater use of "its broad powers of guarantying notes of borrowers [to] permit it to use this device for raising funds from the private capital market."[52]

While Humphrey's new policy toward the Bank triumphed at the White House and in the NAC, opposition built in Congress. Even before the president's reorganization plan became law, key members of Congress opposed what they viewed as a campaign to cripple the Bank. These leaders were responding to the growing concerns of organized export groups and major corporations exporting capital goods, led by Westinghouse. In 1953–4, American exporters faced a rush of competition in foreign markets; there was a changeover from a seller's

[51] Letter, Columbian Ambassador to United States to Thomas Mann, Deputy Assistant Secretary for Inter-American Affairs, March 24, 1953, CDF 1950–1954, Box 376 (103-XMB/3-2453), RG 59; Memorandum Corbett to Waugh, "Eximbank – Your Meeting at the White House January 21, 1954," January 20, 1954 and "Summary of Meeting at White House on January 21, 1954," January 21, 1954, CDF 1950–1954, Box 377 (103-XMB/1-2054), RG 59.

[52] Quoted in Assistant Secretary of State for Inter-American Affairs (Cabot) to Under Secretary of State (Smith), Briefing Memo for White House Meeting, January 20, 1954, *FRUS, 1952–1954*, Vol. IV, pp. 203–5.

to a buyer's market. This was a result primarily of the reconstruction of European and Japanese industry. The apparent suddenness of the changeover, however, was also because hostilities in Korea had formally ended in July 1953. Disrupted trade patterns returned to normal channels just as the Europeans began to experience the delayed positive effect on their exports of currency devaluations in 1949. This turn of events – along with fears of a post–Korean War slump in the United States – increased American exporters' interest in the Export-Import Bank almost coincident with the new administration's initiative to limit its activities.[53]

Opponents to Eisenhower's reorganization of the Bank found a champion in Republican Senator Homer E. Capehart of Indiana. A veteran of 17 years in the Senate, he chaired the Senate Committee on Banking and Currency. Capehart organized a campaign to counter the administration. In the same month the Congress accepted the president's reorganization plan, June 1953, Capehart got Senate authorization for his committee to mount a major study of "The Operations of the Export-Import Bank and the International Bank for Reconstruction and Development and their Relation to Expansion of International Trade." He enlisted bipartisan support for the effort and took the lead in organizing exporters. During the summer, Capehart put together a "citizens advisory committee," made up of nearly 100 prominent industrialists and bankers, which met in Washington in August. From mid October to early December, the Senator led a delegation on a fact-finding mission to fifteen Latin American countries. The delegation included leading members of Congress from both parties, four members of the citizens advisory committee, representatives from the Bank and the State Department, and a contingent of eight professional Senate staff members. The Capehart mission, as it came to be called, visited numerous projects supported by the Bank and by the IBRD, and talked to hundreds of Latin American officials.[54]

[53] Sauer, p. 4; Letter, Arthur Partridge, Assistant to President, Westinghouse Electric International Company, January 26, 1954; W. L. Carroll, Treasurer, Westinghouse..., to Samuel C. Waugh, Assistant Secretary for Economic Affairs, DOS, May 12, 1954; Letter Carroll to Henry F. Holland, Assistant Secretary for Inter-American Relations, DOS, August 4, 1954, CDF 1950–1954, Box 377 (103XMB/8-454), RG 59.

[54] "Capehart Warns of Sharp Inquiry on Export-Import Bank Operation," *New York Times*, July 29, 1953; Congress, Senate, Committee on Banking and Currency, "Interim Report...'A Study of the Operations in Latin American Countries of the Export-Import

The next step in Capehart's campaign were Senate hearings in January and February 1954. In preparing for the hearings, committee staff sent out over 2,000 questionnaires to businesses, bankers, farm organizations, and labor unions interested in foreign trade to determine how it might be of greater service in the future. During the course of the well-orchestrated hearings, a long list of supporters – Capehart scheduled no opponents – of the Bank's programs testified. The upshot of the fact-finding mission and hearings was a report that called for the repeal of Eisenhower's reorganization plan. Capehart and the ranking minority member of his committee introduced a bill in June 1954 to "reaffirm the status of the Export-Import Bank as an independent agency of the United States." In reporting on the bill, the Banking and Currency Committee observed that "your committee finds no legislative limitation upon the loan authority of the Export-Import Bank that would exclude it properly from making long-term, medium-term, or development loans."[55]

Capehart's bill passed in August 1954. Instrumental as a mediator between Capehart and Humphrey was Samuel C. Waugh, assistant secretary of state for economic affairs, and a former Nebraska banker. Waugh, destined to be the next president of the Bank (1955–61), used to good effect ties he had to officials in the White House. Ultimately, Humphrey bowed to the exporter opposition – choreographed by Capehart and Westinghouse – and to the Bank's reorganization, and Eisenhower signed the legislation.[56]

The act of 1954, however, did not fully return the Bank to its former organizational form. It stipulated that the president appoint as officers a president and first vice president of the Bank. The latter two officers would serve as chairman and vice chairman of a bipartisan board of directors, which would include three other members appointed by

Bank and their Relationship to the Expansion of International Trade'...," 83rd Congress, 1st Session, March 16, 1954; "Legislative History – Capehart Committee Hearings," Mazo-Mazon files, Library, Ex-Im; Sauer, pp. 4–7.

55 Congress, Senate, Committee on Banking and Currency, "Report on Export-Import Bank Act Amendments of 1954," 83rd Congress, 2nd Session, 1954, pp. 1–8.

56 Memorandum, Samuel C. Waugh to Secretary Dulles, "Policies With Respect to the Export-Import Bank," October 28, 1954; Memorandum, Waugh to Corbett, "Proposed legislation dealing with the Export-Import Bank – Senator Capehart," May 19, 1954; Memorandum of Telephone Conversation, Waugh and Capehart, May 21, 1954; Memorandum, Waugh to Corbett, "Export-Import Bank," May 21, 1954, CDF 1950–1954, Box 377 (103-XMB/5-2154), RG 59.

the president. All five of these appointees would be subject to Senate confirmation. In the new arrangement, the Bank president served as the chief executive officer. The legislation also created an advisory committee of nine members "broadly representative of production, commerce, finance, agriculture and labor." This committee was to meet at least once a year, to "advise with the Bank on its program." Capehart's successful bill restored the Bank to membership on the NAC, although the legislation left the secretary of state off the board, as had Eisenhower's reorganization plan. Finally, the 1954 act increased the Bank's lending authority by $500 million from $4.5 to $5 billion.[57]

Despite the vindication of the Ex-Im's position in the 1954 legislation, there was unfinished business. The 1953 Edgerton-Black statement, and subsequent NAC action ratifying it, remained a constraint on Bank lending policy. Waugh and others at the Ex-Im managed through patient negotiations over two years to get the NAC to revise its policies. On June 26, 1956, the NAC stated formally that the "activities of the Export-Import Bank and the International Bank are essentially complementary. Borrowers seeking to finance U.S. goods and services normally may look to the Export-Import Bank as a source of financing. Member countries of the International Bank seeking to purchase goods on the basis of international competitive bidding normally may look to that institution."[58]

Nevertheless, the Bank's exposure to the highly politicized jockeying over its organization and responsibilities had other unwanted consequences. The Capehart Committee's staff surveys found a high level of frustration with the Bank's activities since the end of World War II among major corporations and organized exporter groups. A staff report on exporter credit financing characterized the Bank as "a financing institution which has been a responsive instrument in government programs to assist foreign governments, but which has done relatively little export trade financing directly for the U.S. manufacturer." Indeed, the staff report emphasized that between 1945 and 1954 only 3 percent of the Bank's total commitments went toward exporter-initiated

[57] Congress, Senate, Committee on Banking and Currency, "Report on Export-Import Bank Act Amendments of 1954," 83rd Congress, 2nd Session, 1954, pp. 1–8.

[58] Memorandum, Blowers to Waugh, January 13, 1956, Subject Files, 1933–1975, Box 36, "IBRD and Exim" folder, RG 275.

Table 3.2 *Operations of the Export-Import Bank, July 1945 to May 1954*

Commitment	Millions of Dollars	Percent of Total
Exporter Credits	124.0	3.0
Project Credits	603.8	13.0
Strategic Materials Overseas	245.3	5.0
Surplus Commodity Exports	598.7	13.0
Lend–Lease Termination	655.0	14.0
Postwar Reconstruction	1,373.0	28.0
Emergency Foreign Trade Credits	1,150.0	24.0
TOTAL	4,479.8	

Source: R. F. W. Whitcomb, "Exporter Credit Financing by the Export-Import Bank of Washington under the Export-Import Bank Act of 1945," staff report, Committee on Banking and Currency of the U.S. Senate, pp. 1–3, Credit Files, 1933–1975, Box 12, "Capehart Committee, 1953–1954" folder, RG 275.

financing, the smallest of the categories of Bank commitments.[59] (See Table 3.2.)

To be sure, the report recognized that the Bank's developmental lending helped American manufacturers of capital goods. And the committee accepted that emergency foreign trade credits, loans for the export of commodities, and the promotion of strategic materials could have positive effects on exporters' business. But such efforts did not meet the immediate credit needs of capital goods exporters increasingly concerned about the resurgence of competitors in Europe, many of whom had financial assistance from their governments. The staff also reported that exporters complained about the Bank's complex, time-consuming application procedures. The Bank received many more requests than it could fill; consequently, many more exporters failed to get assistance than succeeded. Not surprisingly, unsuccessful applicants harbored negative views of the Ex-Im, which they freely shared with business colleagues who, the report said, were often discouraged in turn from even attempting to gain Bank financing.[60]

Those manufacturers who succeeded in obtaining a loan from the Bank also had criticisms. They disliked the Bank's practice of requiring

[59] R. F. W. Whitcomb, "Exporter Credit Financing by the Export-Import Bank of Washington under the Export-Import Bank Act of 1945," staff report, Committee on Banking and Currency of the United States Senate, pp. 1–3, Credit Files, 1933–1975, Box 12, "Capehart Committee, 1953–1954" folder, RG 275 (hereafter "Financing Export Credits").

[60] "Financing Export Credits," pp. 11–12.

them to participate in the financing of the buyer of their goods. As a rule, the Bank required them to take at least 25 percent of the notes of the foreign buyer, while the Bank took 75 percent of the paper without recourse to the manufacturer. Bank officials justified this distribution of the buyer's debt by arguing that the manufacturer should not expect immediately to receive the profit or margin on the transaction. From the Bank's point of view, the delay assured the manufacturer's continued interest in the transaction. The Capehart staff, however, argued that the Bank's investigation of the buyer's creditworthiness was sufficient to determine the level of risk involved in the credit, especially if the loan was guaranteed by a bank in the purchaser's locality. Requiring assurances from the manufacturer was, according to the report, a secondary condition, one that "appears inappropriate and unduly restrictive." In its report, the committee concluded that the manufacturer should be asked to assume some of the risk only when the Bank had some question about the reliability of the purchaser.[61]

The Capehart staff report ended with a series of recommendations. It was prefaced with the tart observation that there is "no reason for the Bank neglecting its statutory obligation to finance U.S. international trade." To begin with, the committee wanted the Bank to publish guidelines for applying for loans and to provide a standard application form. In addition, because of increasing foreign competition, and the assistance foreign manufacturing exporters often received from their governments, the committee believed that the Bank should assume the major risk in extending credits. Commercial bank participation was desirable, but it was not a substitute for the Bank taking on what the committee saw as one of its prime responsibilities. The Bank, the committee suggested, needed to assist manufacturers competing for specific sales overseas by "agreeing with them in advance that, if they succeed in securing the order, financing will be available for the operation on specified terms."[62] Finally, the committee recommended that the Bank devise a facility for selective export credit insurance. They thought the Bank needed to consider this option "to bridge an important gap in the facilities available to American manufacturing exporters, both for maturities from sight up to about 2 years,

[61] Ibid., pp. 14–15.
[62] Ibid., p. 17.

and for business where the unit of sale is too small for case-by-case consideration."[63]

Bank leaders took the recommendations of the Capehart Committee seriously. Indeed, it would have been foolish to ignore suggestions provided by a natural ally that had rallied to the Bank's defense. These suggestions formed the basis of a new Bank initiative to provide exporter credits expeditiously. Aspects of the staff committee's suggestions, however, were troubling to the Bank, in particular the proposal that the Ex-Im mount a credit insurance program.

In any event, in November 1954 the Bank's leadership announced a new program that provided lines of exporter credits. The $500 million increase in authorization a few months earlier had been intended to support just such a program. According to the Bank, under this new program, individual exporters would be able to finance a series of foreign sales with one credit instead of several separate transactions. This initiative followed Ex-Im discussions with exporter groups and commercial banks.[64] Bank officials devised the line of credit "to enable a particular exporter to know the extent of the credit assistance he might anticipate from the Bank in a given period." As a result, an exporter with such a line of credit "would be able rationally to plan the extension where necessary of credit terms to his foreign dealers... and to plan effectively to supplement and complement his own credit resources and his lines of credit from commercial institutions for this purpose."[65]

In the next two years, the Bank made other adjustments to address the criticisms put forth by the Capehart Committee. By 1956, the Bank reduced the credit information it required from purchasers of American goods, who applied for small loans, that is, those under $50,000. To simplify these procedures, the Bank by then had compiled its own credit files on about 500 foreign importers of American goods. It prepared a

63 Ibid., p. 19.

64 Semiannual Report for July–December 1954, pp. 3–4; Letter, Edgerton to Director, Bureau of the Budget, September 26, 1955, Subject Files, 1933–1975, Box 8, "Budget, 1955" folder, RG 275.

65 "Exporter Credit Lines Announced by Export-Import Bank," Draft Statement for *Foreign Commerce Weekly*, November 12, 1954, Subject Files, 1933–1975, Box 14, "Commerce – Export-Import Bank Correspondence, November 1955 – February 1959" folder, RG 275; Memorandum, Metzger to Atterberry, Department of State, "Eximbank Proposal for Exporter Lines of Credit," November 8, 1954, CDF 1950–1954, Box 377 (103-XMB/11-854), RG 59.

standard application form for small requests (adopted in 1957) and widely publicized its program for exporter credits.[66]

During the 1950s, Ex-Im officials successfully resisted the Capehart Committee's suggestion that the Bank offer export insurance even though the Bank accommodated the interests of exporters in other ways. The only insurance Ex-Im provided in these years involved cotton sales. In 1953, Congress authorized $100 million for cotton insurance, a program run in isolation throughout the years it was in existence. Bank leaders were concerned that short-term insurance would compete with existing private bank financing of short-term export credits. This was the one area in the 1950s in which the private market functioned. There were also staffing issues to the Bank's wariness about short-term insurance, in particular the labor intensive nature of the risk assessment process.[67]

Providing blanket export insurance, Ex-Im thought, would undermine the Bank's careful analysis of potential credits. In addition, Bank officials "questioned the advisability of establishing in the United States a system of export credit insurance which would provide export financing generally without adequate regard to the type of goods sold to a particular market." Ex-Im believed that American interests were better served by the export of capital goods that would contribute to economic development and ultimately lead to better customers for American products.[68]

In any event, over time, the enhanced exporter credit program proved a disappointment. As early as 1956, Ex-Im expressed frustration over the lackluster response to its initiative. Long-time senior executive Walter Sauer attributed the limited interest to a boom in the United States and to the difficulty of obtaining credit information on small foreign borrowers. From the Bank's perspective, the program proved costly, requiring increased staff and staff time. As Edgerton pointed

[66] "Exporter Credit Procedure Amplified," *Foreign Commerce Weekly*, March 11, 1956, "Glassine" files, Library, Ex-Im; Statement of Samuel C. Waugh, President, Ex-Im, before the Appropriations Committee, House of Representatives, 85th Congress, n.d., p. 2, Subject Files, 1933–1974, Box 8, "Budget, 1958" folder, RG 275.

[67] Interview with Warren W. Glick, March 13, 2000, pp. 7–9 Ex-Im Bank Library; Arey Memorandum.

[68] Statement, "Exporter Credits," August 12, 1954, attached to Letter, Hawthorne Arey, Director, Ex-Im, to C. Dillon Glendinning, Department of Treasury, November 2, 1954, CDF 1950–1954, Box 377 (103-XMB/11-254), RG 59; Minutes, NAC, November 5, 1954, *FRUS*, 1952–1954, Vol. I, pp. 380–4.

out in an earlier budget request, the Bank's "more extensive exporter credit program... involving as it does a great number of individual credits, entails much more administrative work than the large-scale government-to-government loans." Then, too, private sector participation in Bank credits dipped in 1957–8 when market interest rates rose, reducing the attractiveness of foreign lending.[69]

The Bank thus considered alternatives to the exporter credit program. It explored the prospects of increased relending through local central banks to foreign borrowers as an option, but postponed a decision.[70] Eventually, the Bank ended the exporter program in 1961 when it expanded its guarantee and insurance operations.

OLD CONCERNS, NEW CONCERNS IN THE LATE 1950s

While the Bank sought to improve its aid to exporters, it continued to be called upon to serve American foreign policy goals. These included contributing to new initiatives devised by Secretary of State John Foster Dulles in prosecuting the Cold War. In addition, late in the 1950s, treasury and White House officials expected the Ex-Im to cooperate in administration efforts to cope with a growing balance of payments problem. Between 1951 and 1957, the country's average payments deficit was $957 million; between 1958 and 1960, the average quadrupled to $3.7 billion.[71]

Overall, Dulles was more supportive of the Bank than the Treasury Department. State weighed in on behalf of the Ex-Im's role in foreign policy at the National Advisory Council. By the late 1950s, it appeared that Latin America was drifting leftward with the growth of radical movements. The United States saw these circumstances as inimical to

69 Letter, Edgerton to Director, Bureau of the Budget, August 29, 1955, Subject Files, 1933–1975, Box 8, "Budget, 1955" folder, RG 275; Memorandum of Conversation, Department of State and Ex-Im officials, January 27, 1956, "Intensification of Activities of Export-Import Bank," CDF 1955–1959, Box 377 (103-XMB/1-2756), RG 59; Letter, Tom Killefer, First Vice President, Ex-Im, to R. J. Thompson, Caterpillar Tractor Company, April 17, 1961, Credit No. 737, "Exporter Credit Line Caterpillar Tractor" folder, Credit Case Files, 1954–1967, Box 14, RG 275; Congress, House, Hearings, Subcommittees of the Committee on Appropriations, "The Supplemental Appropriations Bill, 1958," 85th Congress, 1st Session, 1957.

70 Memorandum of Conservation, "Intensification of Activies of Export-Import Bank," January 27, 1956, CDF 1955–1959, Box 377 (103-XMB/1-2756), RG 59.

71 Harold G. Vatter, *The U.S. Economy in the 1950s: An Economic History* (New York: W. W. Norton & Company, 1963), pp. 259–67.

its interests in freer trade and private enterprise. In particular, Dulles supported the Bank's developmental lending because it promoted private enterprise overseas, especially in Latin America. Moreover, because of the participation of private banking institutions, State Department officials envisioned development lending contributing to the rebuilding of the international capital market. Between 1952 and 1958, the Bank arranged for $880 million in loans and equity investment by commercial banks and other private entities. These commitments were taken on private account concurrent with Bank lending, without an Ex-Im guarantee.[72]

Bank lending also figured into Dulles' calculations about how to cope with other new challenges in the Cold War. Following the Korean War and the death of Stalin, the new Soviet leadership turned to the underdeveloped, or third, world as a new competitive arena with the West. The USSR made the case to developing countries that its model of economic development was less exploitive than that of the capitalist West. The Bank became involved in this aspect of Cold War competition by vigorously promoting lending to neutralist states like India, announcing a $150 million credit in January 1958. Subsequently, the Bank stationed a representative in New Delhi to encourage the Indian government to use the funds.[73]

Officials also saw India as a place to enhance the use of "Cooley loans," named after the congressman who championed this form of lending. Cooley loans, first available in 1957, were designed to utilize American local currency balances generated by purchases of surplus American agricultural products. These balances could be lent to American firms in India or Indian ventures that would increase the demand for American agricultural products. Although such loans were small and in foreign currencies, the Bank hoped that they would promote demand for dollar-denominated direct credits. Until Congress moved the Cooley program to the Agency for International

[72] Memorandum, Holland to Secretary and Under Secretary, Department of State, March 18, 1955, "White House Dinner on March 29 to Discuss Export-Import Bank Lending," CDF 1955–1959, Box 377 (103-XMB/3-2955), RG 59; Memorandum, Henry C. Wallich, DOS, to Presidential Consultant, Randall, April 22, 1955, "Export-Import Bank," *FRUS, 1955–1957*, Vol. IX, pp. 329–33; Arey Memorandum, p. 7.

[73] Export-Import Bank, *Annual Report, Twelve Months Ending June 30, 1960*, p. 13 (hereafter Annual Report; the Bank shifted to annual reports instead of semiannual reports); Dispatch, American Embassy New Dehli to Department of State, "Visit to India ...," March 31, 1958, CDF 1955–59, Box 383 (103-XMB/3-3158), RG 59; and Telegram, Bunker to Dulles, February 13, 1959, CDF 1955–59, Box 385 (103-XMB/2-1259), RG 59.

Development in 1962, the Bank energetically promoted it in many countries like Peru, Israel, Greece, and India.[74]

Other foreign policy interests also influenced Bank lending. Late in 1956, the Bank aided Great Britain when the value of the pound declined after the government's failure in the Suez crisis. British, French, and Israeli forces joined together to retake the Suez Canal following Egypt's nationalization of the waterway. When both the United States and the Soviet Union openly opposed this move in the United Nations, the effort collapsed. Ex-Im, at the behest of the Department of State, joined the IMF in extending a secured credit to Great Britain; the Bank's loan was for $500 million. Great Britain only drew $250 million of the credit, and the United States pressed the British government to repay that quickly.[75]

In the late 1950s, the treasury joined the State Department and encouraged the Bank to serve larger international economic issues. In its last year, the Eisenhower administration drew the Bank into a campaign to cope with increasing payments deficits by enlarging American exports. The president in his 1960 State of the Union address urged that "we must face this situation [of growing payments deficits] by promoting a rising volume of exports and world trade." The Departments of State and Commerce, joined by the Bureau of the Budget, studied how government could help private enterprise sell more abroad. [76]

An upshot of this effort was the Bank's program to provide guarantees to cover noncommercial or political risks in short-term transactions. These included incovertibility of foreign currencies; laws or regulations that prevented delivery of goods; cancellation of import licences; war and rebellion; and expropriation. Ex-Im designed the program to work through the private sector. Commercial banks with foreign departments that financed export transactions received authorization to act for the Bank, as did U.S. insurance companies that offered export credit insurance. At the same time, the Bank began to

[74] Memorandum, NAC Staff Committee to National Advisory Council, July 3, 1958, "Fourth Progress Report on U.S. Private Investment in less Developed Areas," Subject Files, 1933–75, Box 31, "Foreign Economic Policy, Council on, 1956–60" Folder, RG 275.

[75] Letter, Secretary of the Treasury Anderson to President Eisenhower, August 6, 1959, *FRUS, 1958–1960*, Vol. IV, pp. 121–3.

[76] Quoted in "Background Paper Providing Basic Data for Use in Connection With Press Inquiries Regarding the Interagency Export Promotion Study," attached to letter, Philip A. Ray, Under Secretary of Commerce, to Waugh, January 13, 1960, Government Agencies, Commerce Department, Box 5, "National Export Expansion" folder, RG 275.

provide medium-term political risk guarantees (180 days to 5 years and 7 years for aircraft). But these transactions had to be concluded directly with the Bank on an individual basis. Such arrangements could include a comprehensive guarantee against both credit and political risk up to 85 percent of the financed portion of the transaction. Additionally, to increase private participation and hasten transaction arrangements, the Bank would participate in medium-term deals by relying fully on the credit analysis of commercial banks. The latter had to meet several stringent requirements – including terms about the structure of repayment – before the Bank would take part.[77]

But crossing against these tides of foreign and trade policy was a persistent set of domestic economic currents that drove the treasury's relationship with the Bank. From the beginning of the Eisenhower years, Secretary Humphrey strove to balance the budget, routinely searching for opportunities to reduce governmental expenditures. The Bank became one of his targets. From early in his tenure, he had been concerned about the draw that the Bank made against the treasury. The Bank's spending authority showed up as a debit against the treasury whenever the Ex-Im disbursed funds for an approved credit. Humphrey's successor, Robert B. Anderson, who became treasury secretary in 1957, took up where his predecessor left off.

Bank officials responded to the entreaties over the "draw" with several initiatives. One of the easiest things for the Bank to do was to increase its efforts to promote private participation in its lending. This was not by any means a new policy of the Bank; the private participation division had been set up in 1946. But, as the American economy expanded in the 1950s, and foreign trade grew, commercial banks took more interest in overseas business. The Bank capitalized on these developments by encouraging private sector participation in its loans. In 1958, the Bank had its largest level ever of private participation. Of $855.6 million in new credits, $223 million were taken on their own account by twenty-two commercial banks and one insurance company. This represented 26 percent of the Bank's new lending for the year. But levels of private sector involvement through participation varied, often depending on conditions in the domestic economy. When market rates

[77] Press Release, May 10, 1960, Government Agencies, Commerce Department, Box 5, "National Export Expansion" folder, RG 275.

were high, commercial banks were less interested in overseas business. In fiscal year 1960, for example, private participation represented only about 10 percent of new lending, $50.9 million out of $499.6 million in new credits.[78]

Despite these achievements in increasing direct private participation, the treasury kept up pressure on the Bank as the administration failed to balance the budget. As a result, the treasury and the Bureau of the Budget pressed the Bank to rely entirely on the private market to raise its funds. Beginning in 1958, Maurice Stans, the director of the Bureau of the Budget, proposed that the Bank turn to the private sector to raise its funds instead of relying on the treasury. Rather than venturing further into guarantees, Waugh proposed that the Bank issue its own securities.[79]

As it turned out, selling the Bank's own securities would not help the treasury. Because of peculiarities in the Budget Office's definition of receipts, sale of direct Export-Import Bank obligations would not improve the treasury's cash situation. In late 1959 and early 1960, Bank and treasury officials scrambled to find ways to meet the demands of the budget director. Waugh "agreed to explore every possible sound method in order to accomplish the desired results, namely, completing the [1960 budget] year with a zero draw upon the Treasury."[80]

In fact, the Bank did not make a draw on the treasury in fiscal 1960. It had receipts of $629.6 million (from repayments of principle and interest on its large loan portfolio) and disbursements of $398.9 million. This achievement entailed an extraordinary effort, which substantially increased the work demands on staff. The effort to avoid a draw on the treasury involved arranging for prepayments on loans. The Bank also approached insurance companies and pension funds, as well as commercial banks, to take a larger participation in new lending. And the Bank disposed of some of its portfolio paper to commercial banks without recourse.[81]

78 Annual Report for 1958, pp. 1, 8–9; Annual Report for 1960, pp. 12–13.

79 Memorandum to the Files, Walter C. Sauer (Meeting with Secretary of Treasury Anderson), December 16, 1958, Subject Files, 1933–1975, Box 9, "Budget, 1958–60" folder, RG 275.

80 Letter, Waugh to Arthur M. McClauflin, Bureau of the Budget, (Re: "Export-Import Bank Budget – Fiscal Year 1960"), October 26, 1959, Subject File, 1933–1975, Box 9, "Budget, 1959–60" folder, RG 275.

81 Memorandum, Rowntree, Economics Division, to Board of Directors, Ex-Im, April 1, 1959, "Means of avoiding a net draw upon the Treasury in FY 1960," Subject Files, 1933–1975, Box 9, "Budget 1960" folder, RG 275; Memorandum, A. M. Anderson

The Bank's struggle to meet the demands of an administration determined to balance the budget was the beginning of an important change for the Bank. In the future, the Bank would increasingly have to find ways to leverage its lending authority to meet new needs. Thus, an institution that prided itself on flexibility found that quality much in demand as the 1950s ended. It would become an even more important attribute in the decade to come. The increasing interest in guarantees and the persistent discussion of insurance – both inspired by growing exporter and budget pressures – loomed larger in the next decade.

to Waugh, September 22, 1960, "Estimated net draw – Treasury – fiscal year 1961," Subject Files 1933–1975, Box 10, "Budget, 1960" folder, RG 275; Annual Report for 1960, pp. 6–7.

4

BECOMING "TWO INSTITUTIONS"

INTRODUCTION

John F. Kennedy promised to get America moving again in the 1960 presidential election campaign. Despite the youthful energy that Kennedy brought to the White House, problems and issues that had surfaced during the Eisenhower years carried over into the new administration, and that of Lyndon B. Johnson and later Richard M. Nixon. America's balance of payments position continued to erode. Pressures on the federal budget persisted from one administration to the other. And the Cold War became more contentious, especially during the Kennedy years, as an activist administration in the United States faced an opportunistic leadership in the USSR.

These circumstances shaped the Bank's experience in the Kennedy–Johnson, and the first Nixon, administration. Under the leadership of Harold F. Linder (March 1961–July 1968), the Export-Import Bank assiduously followed its established policies of risk assessment and loan management. But the way in which Ex-Im employed its assets changed as the Bank increasingly made use of guarantees and insurance. Indeed, the Bank's 1965 annual report said that it had become two institutions, one focused on direct lending, the other on guarantees and insurance. During the Kennedy and Johnson administrations, the geographic focus of Bank long-term credits shifted away from development projects in Latin America. It also became an important supplier of credits for purchases of the products of the jet aircraft, nuclear power, and new earth satellite industries. Cold War strategy involved the Bank in military-related lending, assistance to countries in Sub-Saharan Africa where the United States wanted to increase its influence, and – in nominally the interest of improved East–West relations – modest support for exports to the Soviet Union and some of its allies. Each of these activities eventually embroiled the Bank in disputes with Congress. Even so, ironically, by the end of Linder's term, some members of Congress also criticized the Bank for not doing enough, for being too conservative in its lending. This charge would not be leveled at the Nixon administration's first appointment to head the Bank, Henry Kearns (March 1969–October 1973).

Overall, though, for most of the 1960s and into the early 1970s the Bank's leadership remained clearly focused on promoting exports. The country's balance of payments problems underscored the importance of this mission. Ex-Im's efforts meshed with the government's larger campaign to increase dollar earnings abroad for the United States. During the 1960s, the gold-dollar fixed exchange rate system established at Bretton Woods came under increasing pressure as dollars accumulated overseas. On the operational side of the Bank, Linder's long Wall Street experience burnished its reputation for prudent – in the thinking of some observers too conservative – behavior. But Linder also understood foreign policy, having served in the State Department in the Truman and Eisenhower years, and he acquiesced when the administration needed the Ex-Im to serve larger administration policy goals.

INSURANCE, GUARANTEES, AND PRIVATE PARTICIPATIONS

Continued concerns about the balance of payments and the cash "draw" the Bank made on the treasury impelled the Ex-Im to innovate in the 1960s. Leaders in the Kennedy and Johnson administrations directed the Bank to enhance support for American exports while also encouraging Ex-Im to finance its operations in private markets. In meeting the need for export expansion, the Bank devised insurance and guarantee programs that ultimately encompassed almost all its support to exporters for short- and medium-term export assistance. Over the course of the 1960s, insurance and guarantees became a larger part of the Bank's business, although the dominant activity of the Bank continued to be its direct long-term lending program.

Within weeks of taking office, President Kennedy sent a special message to Congress on gold and the balance of payments deficit. During the presidential campaign, Kennedy had pledged to defend the dollar at the fixed rate of $35 per ounce of gold. This commitment became a hallmark of the Kennedy–Johnson years. It was, the new president believed, a matter of prestige befitting the country leading the resistance to communist expansionism. Defending the dollar was also a practical matter of the greatest importance. Many American officials held that the fixed exchange rate system buttressed the prosperity and growth of the United States and its allies in Western Europe and Japan.

Exchange rates and balance of payments problems first became acute in 1958. From 1950 to 1958, the United States ran a deficit in its balance of payments, in large part a result of substantial American expenditures for foreign aid and overseas defenses. These deficits elicited little concern for much of the 1950s because the American stock of gold remained relatively stable and there was a surplus in the country's balance of trade. But 1958 proved a turning point. In that year, most Western European countries, by then substantially recovered from the economic damage of World War II, agreed to make their currencies fully convertible. Before their recovery, such a step might have precipitated a flight to hold dollars. Following 1958, however, there was a decline in American gold stocks, as some Europeans opted to trade the dollars they held for gold. The following year, the American balance of payments deficit tripled, which increased pressure on the dollar. Concerns over the stability of the fixed $35 gold-dollar exchange rate heightened when in October 1960 the price of gold went to $40 per ounce on the London market.[1]

Following the 1960 election, the president-elect appointed a task force to study American foreign economic policy. He had its recommendations in hand before the inauguration, and was thus ready to act once in office. In a special message to Congress on February 6, 1961, Kennedy laid out an expansionist approach to the balance of payments and related gold stock problems. His solution included efforts to increase American exports and foreign investment in the United States. Essentially, these were his only alternatives, for he opted not to cut back foreign economic and military aid, nor did he favor restricting American foreign investment or imports of foreign goods. And, clearly, he had no intention of devaluing the dollar.

[1] There is a large literature on this subject. For a succinct discussion, see Diane B. Kunz, "Cold War Dollar Diplomacy: The Other Side of Containment," in Diane B. Kunz, ed., *The Diplomacy of the Crucial Decade: American Foreign Relations During the 1960s* (New York: Columbia University Press, 1994), pp. 81–5.

Kennedy's message identified the Export-Import Bank as a key actor in carrying out his policy. He focused on the Bank's role in a section entitled "export guarantees and financing." Ex-Im must take, he said, "an increasingly important role in our export promotion efforts" by enhancing "the facilities it offers for extending credit to American exporters." Specifically, the president wanted the Bank to build on the start it had made the previous year in offering loan guarantees against political risk. He maintained that American export guarantees and financing were not adequate nor "comparable to those offered by foreign countries, especially those offered to small and medium-sized exporting concerns." His message directed the Bank's president to prepare "a new program . . . to place our exporters on a basis of full equality with their competitors in other countries." He also instructed the secretary of the treasury to undertake "a study of methods through which private financial institutions can participate more broadly in providing export credit facilities."[2]

Thus, the Bank's new president, Harold F. Linder, had his marching orders when the administration announced his appointment on March 2, 1961. Linder came to the Bank with substantial experience in Wall Street at Lehman Brothers and in the government. In fact, as with former Ex-Im president Samuel C. Waugh, Linder had served as assistant secretary of state for economic affairs. He held that office during the Truman administration. Secretary of State Dulles, whom Linder had known through previous business dealings, asked him to stay on briefly in the Eisenhower administration. Linder had gained firsthand experience of the Bank when he sat in on its board of directors' meetings for Secretary of State Acheson, a statutory role secretaries enjoyed until 1953. So Linder knew about the Bank's work when he gladly accepted its presidency. Indeed, from the perspective of a professional banker like himself, he said in a later interview, that he believed that "it was . . . the most important job in the government." He saw Ex-Im, because of its resources and its earnings, as "more important than any bank in the world."[3]

2 "Special Message to the Congress on Gold and the Balance of Payments Deficit," February 6, 1961, in *Public Papers of the Presidents of the United States, John F. Kennedy, Containing the Public Messages, Speeches, and Statements of the President, January 20 to December 31, 1961* (Washington, DC: Government Printing Office, 1962), pp. 57–66.

3 Interview with Harold F. Linder, November 8, 1973, pp. 14–15 (hereafter Linder Interview, November 8, 1973), Mazo-Mazon Files, Library, Export-Import Bank of the United States, Washington, DC (hereafter Mazo-Mazon files).

Once in office, Linder moved quickly to respond to President Kennedy's directive, which required a report by April 1, 1961. Because Bank officials like Walter Sauer began studying the president's request in February, Linder was soon ready with draft proposals on how to proceed in insuring and guaranteeing short- and medium-term credits. These studies also took up the question of how private financial institutions could more fully participate in providing export credits.[4]

On March 20, 1961, the Bank presented the outlines of a program of insurance and guarantees to the National Advisory Council. Ex-Im decided to approach the insurance industry rather than bring the insurance function in-house. Insurance companies, Bank officials believed, had the sales and service forces in place – and access to the credit information generated by their marine, property, and casualty insurance operations or by commercial banks – to take on a new export insurance function. The NAC on March 24 accepted the tentative plans and encouraged the Bank to continue. Linder appointed an intergovernmental committee chaired by the Bank's director and first vice president, Thomas Killefer. It included representatives from the Commerce and Treasury Departments and two private consultants, one each drawn from experts acceptable to organized export groups and leading bankers. In the months following, the committee held numerous meetings with officials of insurance industry trade associations, major companies, and financial institutions. Committee members also, as Linder reported, "informed [themselves] thoroughly as to the methods used by the principal exporting countries abroad."[5]

Killefer took the lead. He worked with a senior official of the Great American Insurance Company who acted as a liaison to other executives

[4] Memorandum to National Advisory Council from Secretary, NAC, March 20, 1961, Re: "Export-Import Bank Proposals for Expanding its Facilities for Financing United States Exports," Department of the Treasury, Assistant Secretary for International Affairs, National Advisory Council, NAC Documents and Supplements, Box 35, Record Group 56, Records of the Department of the Treasury, National Archives; Letter and attachments, Linder to C. Douglas Dillon, March 10, 1961, Subject Files, 1933–1975, Box 32, "Guarantees and Insurance, 1945–1961" folder, RG 275, Records of the Export-Import Bank, National Archives; Congress, House, Committee on Banking and Currency, 87th Congress, 1st Session, Hearing on H.R. 8381, Amend Export-Import Bank Act, 1945; H.R. 7102 and H.R. 7103, Create American Export Credits Guaranty Corporation; H.R. 7266 and H.R. 8249, National Export Policy Act, 1961 (Washington, DC: Government Printing Office, 1961), pp. 34–5.

[5] Letter and attachments, Linder to C. Douglas Dillon, March 10, 1961, Subject Files, 1933–1975, Box 32, "Guarantees and Insurance, 1945–1961" folder, RG 275.

in the industry. In the course of the months that followed they approached almost 75 companies. Assisting Killefer in the effort were Warren W. Glick from the General Counsel's office and R. H. Rowntree, the head of the Economics Division.[6] These endeavors resulted in the creation of an unincorporated association – the Foreign Credit Insurance Association (FCIA) – with an initial membership of fourteen companies. It acted like other insurance syndicates to pool risk but served as an agent of the Export-Import Bank. Ex-Im was formally represented on the FCIA's board to ensure a continuing role in determining and implementing the association's policies. By 1968, FCIA had a membership of over sixty companies, including some of the country's major insurance enterprises. While headquartered in New York City, the association by the 1970s also maintained offices in Atlanta, Chicago, Cleveland, Los Angeles, and Milwaukee.[7]

Linder himself spearheaded the work on the guarantee program. In doing so, he used his close contacts with leading bankers, including Walter Wriston at Citibank and David Rockefeller at Chase Manhattan. Such contacts proved crucial.[8] From Ex-Im's point of view, there were two advantages to private sector participation in encouraging exports through insurance and guarantees. First, private funds obviously would assume some of the financing burden and underscore the Bank's statutory responsibility to avoid competition with private capital. Second, involving commercial banks in financing exports would limit the paperwork burden of exporters coming to the Bank in Washington for credits. Similarly, it would also eliminate the need for the Bank to open branch offices across the country. That is, private sector involvement would allow Ex-Im to decentralize its short- and

6 Memorandum of Meeting, Re: "Participation by Insurance Industry in Short-term Comprehensive Program," April 19, 1961; Memorandum of Meeting, Re: "Export Credit Insurance and Financing," May 11, 1961; Letter, Killefer to R. A. Browning, Independence Marine Services, August 31, 1961; Memorandum of Meeting, Re: "Export Credit Insurance Program," September 21, 1961, Subject Files, 1933–1975, Box 32, "Guarantee and Insurance, 1946–1961" folder, RG 275; Linder Interview, November 15, 1973, pp. 20–1.

7 Interview, Reginald Denton, president, Foreign Credit Insurance Association, November 8, 1973, pp. 3–5 and Thomas H. Bivin, "The Origins and Operation, Under the Law, of Foreign Credit Insurance in the United States," FCIA News Release, February 2, 1979, pp. 4–7, in Mazo-Mazon files.

8 Interview with B. Jenkins Middleton, March 17, 2000, pp. 11–12, Library, Ex-Im (hereafter Middleton Interview, March 17, 2000).

medium-term financing operations, where the Bank anticipated the largest demand.[9]

In the guarantee program the Bank had to address long-standing private sector realities. Ex-Im officials concluded that "we must continue to not only exhort these institutions to do more, but we must seek ways and means of meeting the problems with which they are confronted in lending greater help in the field of foreign financing." U.S. commercial banks were generally reluctant to take on medium- or long-term export financing. There were simply too many other promising opportunities within the American economy. This attitude was reinforced during the economic boom of the mid 1960s, a period in which the United States did not experience a recession between 1960 and 1968. Moreover, other providers of private capital – insurance companies and pension funds – thought export financing too risky. Both also faced legal restrictions on their investments, which further limited interest in export lending.[10]

The Bank had its concerns too. Essential to the Bank was ensuring the acceptance of a sufficient stake by the private sector so that the Ex-Im would not be taking on more risk than it routinely would tolerate as prudent.[11] These changes were undertaken against the backdrop of a culture that had only recently and reluctantly accepted the use of guarantees. Traditionally, Bank officials were hesitant to use guarantees, which they saw as subtly undermining the institution's well-honed practices of rigorous risk assessment. Finally, they were also concerned that accelerated use of guarantees would weaken Ex-Im's control over lending without shifting risk to the private sector.[12]

It took until October to complete negotiations with insurers and discussions with bankers. Meanwhile, Congress passed legislation making it possible for the Bank to insure, reinsure, and co-insure against the risk

[9] Attachment to Letter, Linder to C. Douglas Dillon, March 10, 1961, Memorandum: "Participation by Private Financial Institutions in Export-Import Bank Activities," pp. 1–2, Subject Files, 1934–1975, Box 32, "Guarantees and Insurance, 1945–1961" folder, RG 275.

[10] Ibid., p. 2.

[11] Ibid., pp. 2–6.

[12] Interview with Warren W. Glick, March 13, 2000, pp. 3–8, Library, Ex-Im (hereafter Glick Interview, March 13, 2000); Memorandum, Hawthorne Arey to Samuel C. Waugh, "Guarantees of foreign loans by U.S. Government agencies, March 3, 1959, p. 7, Subject Files, 1933–1975, Box 32, "Guarantees and Insurance, 1950–1959" folder, RG 275.

of loss from defaults in payment for export transactions. The new law also allowed it to secure the face value of insurance and guarantees by reserves of only 25 percent. By backing its insurance and guarantees by these so-called fractional reserves, Ex-Im hoped to increase the numbers of exporters it served, a clear goal of the administration's export expansion initiative.[13]

President Kennedy himself announced the Bank's two new programs on October 27, 1961. His remarks focused on how the dual initiative of insurance and guarantees would help alleviate the country's balance of payments problems and allow American exporters to better meet stiffening foreign competition. It took until February 2, 1962, before all the details were worked out. FCIA soon offered short- and medium-term insurance, and policies provided comprehensive protection against both political and commercial risk. Export credit insurance allowed exporters to extend credit to foreign customers, in the assurance that unexpected circumstances overseas would not subject them to large losses. In addition, exporters who insured their receivables would find it easier to secure financing from commercial banks. The attractiveness of the insurance policies was increased by allowing the proceeds to be assigned to a commercial bank. Short-term credit policies were offered generally for terms up to 180 days; medium-term policies were from 181 days to five years.[14]

FCIA's commercial risk policies essentially covered the insolvency or default of the buyer. Political risk insurance encompassed several contingencies: government interference that in some way prevented payment (the revocation of licenses, expropriation, import restrictions, war and civil disorder, and currency inconvertibility). To obtain a policy, an exporter would have to carry about 15 percent of the commercial risk and between 5 and 15 percent of the political risk. Premium rates depended on conditions in the importer's country and the length of the credit. Ex-Im assumed all the political risk and initially 50 percent of the commercial risk.[15]

13 House, Committee on Banking and Currency, 87th Congress, 1st Session, *Hearing, Promotion of American Exports*, August 31, 1961 (Washington, DC: Government Printing Office, 1961), pp. 34–57.

14 *Export-Import Bank of Washington, Report to the Congress for the twelve months ended June 30, 1962* (Washington, DC: Ex-Im, 1962), pp. 4–5 (hereafter Annual Report).

15 Ibid.

Table 4.1 *Selected Authorizations, FY 1960–1969 (millions of dollars)*

Fiscal Year	Regular Direct Loan and Development Project Credits	Commodity	Emergency F.T.	Guarantees (all types)	Insurance
1960	365.5	70.0	35.0	17.2	–
1961	707.0	63.5	327.2	144	–
1962	555.0	3.5	500.0	–	–
1963	525.0	79.8	35.0	465.0	890.2
1964	570.2	178.0	–	216.8	747.4
1965	435.2	76.3	340.0	282.9	724.6
1966	738.7	76.0	90.0	300.1	692.8
1967	1396.7	76.0	175.0	193.0	690.7
1968	891.4	75.0	525.0	290.1	717.7
1969	730.6	75.0	50.0	396.9	824.6

Source: Appendix B, Summary of Authorizations.

Exporters showed an immediate interest in the insurance program. Within its first four months, FCIA wrote 685 short-term export commercial risk policies with a value of about $360 million. Medium-term commercial risk policies were first offered in July 1961. Short- and medium-term policies covering political risk became available in January 1963. By the end of the 1963 fiscal year, the Bank had issued $524 million of short-term comprehensive insurance; the balance of authorized insurance totaled only $37 million, $20 million of which went for medium-term comprehensive coverage.[16]

In the early 1960s, the insurance program grew dramatically (see Table 4.1). At the same time, both the Bank and FCIA learned as they went along. There was frequent modification of the terms and procedures exporters had to follow to obtain insurance. The most important changes involved the size of policies the Bank routinely would approve on the basis of FCIA's credit analysis. It went from $50,000 to $200,000 in 1964. Another significant change in policy in the 1960s involved the share of risk the Bank accepted. Initially, in 1961, both the Bank and the cooperating insurers assumed that political risk would be more serious than commercial or credit risk. Communist Cuba's refusal in 1960 to honor the debts of its predecessor regime was much on the minds of Bank officials at the time. As it turned out, however, the Bank and FCIA paid out more on defaults resulting from credit than political risk. After

[16] Annual Report for 1963, p. 6.

August 1964, as a result, the Bank no longer shared commercial risk with FCIA, except for policies in excess of $150,000. In the latter case, the Bank totally reinsured medium-term policies and accepted 50 percent on short-term policies.[17]

Ex-Im's guarantee program encouraged commercial banks to take a larger role in financing exporters. The commercial bank guarantee program announced in October 1961 was for medium-term financing. Ex-Im fully guaranteed commercial banks against losses due to political causes on all maturities. It provided guarantees against credit risk on later maturities, although the commercial bank or other financial institution had to carry on its own account the credit risks on the first half of the maturities or on the first 18 months, whichever was shorter. Exporters had to provide 15 percent of the financed portion of the sale and the buyer had to make a cash payment of between 10 and 20 percent.[18]

This program of financial guarantees essentially replaced the Bank's exporter credit effort launched in 1954. By June 1962, the Bank had provided $297 million in medium-term guarantees. Despite the initial interest commercial banks showed in the program, they nevertheless later pressed for changes. They wanted wider discretion in offering credits. Ex-Im announced in June 1963 that it would delegate authority by accepting the commercial banks' independent credit assessments of transactions up to $200,000. In addition, the Bank promised to give advance approval of political risk guarantees. In this way, commercial banks would know early in negotiations whether to proceed with a full credit analysis of potential customers.[19]

In August 1964, the Bank further enhanced the delegated authority of the banks. For exports to countries with the least perceived risk – so-called A countries – the Bank delegated authority to commercial banks to commit it to guarantees of up to $1 million. In riskier B countries, commercial banks could extend guarantees of $500,000. At

[17] Louis G. Guadagnoli, "The Role of Medium-Term Export Credit Guarantees and Insurance in Financing Foreign Trade," *The Southern Economic Journal*, 34 (April 1968) 4: 548–62; David G. Wilson, "The American Export Credit System: An Institutional Analysis," *Harvard International Law Journal*, 8 (Winter 1967) 1: 21–3.

[18] Press Release, "Modifications to Commercial Bank Guarantee Program Announced," June 13, 1963, Subject Files, 1933–1975, Box 33, "Guarantees and Insurance, 1962–1964" folder, RG 275.

[19] Ibid.

the time, the Bank classified countries on perceived credit risk, and set fees accordingly, on a scale from "A to D."[20]

There were further changes in subsequent years. In 1965, the Bank reduced the standard exporter participation needed to secure a guarantee. It declined from 15 to 10 percent. In making the change, Ex-Im officials brought the Bank into line with European and Canadian export credit agency practice. In 1966, the Bank allowed commercial banks to extend its delegated authority to public buyers for revolving or repeating transactions. Ex-Im also would accept credit increases in guarantees from 90 to 100 percent of a longer credit (more than three years), so long as the payment history had been satisfactory. In 1968, delegated authority was further extended to include C markets.[21]

The insurance and guarantee programs thus addressed important issues for the Bank in the 1960s. They enhanced the role of private capital in financing exports, and did so in such a way as to decentralize Bank operations. They represented an important change for the way in which the Bank did its business. For the most part, they did away with the Bank's direct short- and medium-term direct credit lending.

But these programs also had other benefits. Because of "fractional reserve" provisions, the Bank was able to leverage its lending authority. And the use of guarantees helped satisfy the administration's interest in limiting the Bank's draw on the treasury. Fiscal concerns increased during the 1960s because of Lyndon Johnson's "Great Society Programs" and the costs of the Vietnam War. The costs of the Bank's operations were dwarfed by such undertakings, nevertheless, budget officials aimed to minimize Ex-Im demands on the treasury.

The Bank sought other ways to address federal budgetary concerns. As the insurance and guarantee programs were getting under way, the Bank introduced "participation certificates." Beginning in 1962, Ex-Im sold these certificates through two programs. The first involved the sale of pools of loans that the Bank held in its portfolio. There were six such offerings between 1962 and 1966 to American commercial banks that had business with Ex-Im in the past. These offering were known as Eximbank Portfolio Fund sales and later as Eximbank Investment Portfolio sales. By the end of 1966, there had been sales of $2.6 billion

[20] Paper, "Bank Guarantee Program Review," February 28, 1981, p. 6–7, "I.G: RBG: Program Review (1979)" folder, Policy Office Files (POF), Ex-Im.

[21] Ibid.

of such participations. The Bank's second program offered these instruments to overseas investors as a way to assist the U.S. balance of payments. Sales reached $600 million by 1967.[22]

In 1965 and 1966, a tight money situation in the United States worked against the continued sale of participation certificates to those commercial banks that had previously purchased them. Consequently, the Bank planned to reach private investors as well as commercial banks. Ex-Im turned to four major commercial banks and eight investment banks to put together an underwriting syndicate for future issues of participation certificates. These institutions had shown an interest in handling Bank-guaranteed obligations. These lead institutions organized a group of about 100 banks and brokerages to underwrite future sales of certificates.[23]

Tight money also threatened commercial banks' continued lending for exports. When the Federal Reserve raised interest rates in 1966 to cool an overheated economy, commercial bankers used the more limited funds for their best customers and most attractive investments. Export lending was not a high priority in such circumstances. To induce these banks to continue to support exports, Ex-Im in September 1966 introduced a discount loan program that permitted commercial banks to borrow for less than a year from Ex-Im against a portion of their outstanding export loans. In the following year, the Bank agreed to make loans against a larger proportion of export financing extended in the year after the program began. In developing the program, Linder rejected requests from major commercial banks for lower than market rates for these loans. He saw the problem as a short-run phenomenon and accordingly objected to, in effect, subsidizing commercial bank lending for exports. In its first year, the program provided loans to

[22] House, Committee on Banking and Currency, *Hearings to Amend the Export-Import Bank Act of 1945*, 90th Congress, 1st Session, April 1967 (Washington, DC: Government Printing Office, 1967), pp. 69–70 (hereafter 1967 Hearings to Amend the Export-Import Bank Act of 1945). Interview, James Hess, April 3, 2000, pp. 3–5, Library, Ex-Im (hereafter Hess Interview April 3, 2000). Ultimately, as a result of the recommendations in 1968 of the President's Commission on Budget Concepts, participation certificates were treated in subsequent budgets as a means of financing and not as an offset to expenditures. This ended their attractiveness to the Bank. See Comptroller General of the United States, *Report to the Congress: Audit of Export-Import Bank of Washington Fiscal Year 1967* (Washington, DC: General Accounting Office, 1968), pp. 5–9 (hereafter cited as GAO Report 1967).

[23] GAO Report 1967, pp. 69–70, 77, 87–9.

seven commercial banks in the amount of about $70 million. These loans tripled in fiscal year 1968 following a liberalization of terms. Interest rates were lowered, and terms of repayment were extended from a maximum of one year to the remaining term of the underlying export debt obligation. During the Nixon years, in the early 1970s, the program was revamped and became much more active.[24]

THE BANK AND ITS TRADITIONAL BUSINESS IN THE 1960s

Thus, during the 1960s, the Bank became two institutions, as the 1965 Annual Report observed. One engaged in insurance and guarantees, while the other continued the Bank's traditional business of long-term lending, agricultural commodity financing, and emergency credits for countries with balance-of-payments problems. But in its long-term lending, the Bank also moved in new directions. In the early years of the 1960s, there was less long-term lending to Latin America than in the 1950s. Later in the decade, that lending picked up again, in part to serve the interests of American Cold War policy in the hemisphere. But overall, in the 1960s, the Bank's long-term lending moved away from large development projects. Internal Bank studies in the mid 1960s convinced officials that future lending should increasingly focus on assistance to exporters in the capital intensive, high-tech products industries of the day. Thus, while the Bank continued to make loans to mining, manufacturing, and highway-building projects, after mid decade there were more and more long-term credits for the export of jet aircraft, nuclear power plants and equipment, and the ground facilities needed to make communications satellites practicable.

Ex-Im continued in the 1960s to provide agricultural commodity credits and emergency loans or lines of credit. Commodity credits in the 1960s exhibited the same variability as in previous years. The needs for these authorizations varied widely depending on market conditions in

[24] Annual Report for 1968, pp. 5, 12; Memorandum and attachment (Discussion with leading [international] commercial bankers concerning export credit rediscounting, April 18, 1966), Marc C. Feer (Department of Commerce) to Linder, April 22, 1966, and "Notes for Meeting with Chairman Martin of the Federal Reserve," April 6, 1966; Memorandum, Re: "Discount Program, Net Increase Loans and Current Export Loans" to Board of Directors from R. H. Rowntree and W. W. Glick, August 16, 1967, Subject Files, 1933–1975, Box 16, "Discount Program 1966 – 8/29/66" folder, RG 275; GAO Report 1967, pp. 22–3.

the United States and in those countries that purchased American agricultural products. A constant was the credit to Japan for the purchase of American cotton. This one credit usually accounted for the majority of Bank commodity lending.

Much the same could be said about the Ex-Im's emergency foreign trade loans. Demand for these authorizations varied with changing economic conditions in countries importing American goods. These credits were often referred to as balance-of-payments loans, which was not accurate. In fact, they were credits designed to be used during financial crises – in effect, they were of a standby nature – so that a recipient country would be able to maintain its level of imports from the United States while attempting to fulfill its financial obligations. Overall, during the Kennedy and Johnson administrations, credits – totaling almost $2 billion – were authorized twice to Mexico and Canada, as well as to Brazil, Chile, Great Britain, Italy, and Venezuela. In some instances, these funds were made available as part of a syndicate of central banks working with the International Monetary Fund. These credits, and those extended by the Bank on an individual country basis, were often not utilized. They were a transparent effort to calm financial markets, often to halt a crisis. In the second credit extended in 1962 to Canada (for $500 million), for example, the government never drew on it.[25]

There were greater changes in the nature of the Bank's long-term lending for large development projects. Bank officials reduced the institution's interest – and exposure – in Latin America during the first half of the 1960s. This was in part the result of the Bank simply no longer being the only institution aiding the region. In August 1959, the United States joined the Inter-American Development Bank, an institution long under discussion in Latin America. It had two loan programs. The first provided project financing like that of the Ex-Im, without the requirement, however, that goods and services be purchased in the United States. By 1964, the new bank had authorized over $400 million in credits for long-term projects. The second program of the new bank funded "special operations." These were "concessional" – that is, below market rate – loans that provided credits for

[25] Annual Report for 1968, pp. 19–20; Credit No. 2212 – United Kingdom, Credit Case Files, 1954–1967, Box 35, RG 275; Middleton Interview March 17, 2000, pp. 4–7.

loans of longer terms and at lower rates of interest than available from Ex-Im.[26]

There were also other even more ambitious efforts to promote development in Latin America. In August 1961, President Kennedy launched with other American Republics what he called an Alliance for Progress. It held out grandiose goals of economic development, social justice, and political reform. Secretary of the Treasury C. Douglas Dillon pledged the United States to raising $20 billion of public and private funds over a ten-year period for the massive effort. For the first year of the program, Dillon promised $1 billion. Alliance aid included Ex-Im credits and increased foreign assistance consolidated within the newly created Agency for International Development (AID) in the Department of State. This new assistance vehicle directed a variety of programs for both economic and military assistance. At the same time, the World Bank increased its attention to Latin America. During the 1960s, half of that institution's lending was directed to Latin America.[27]

Ex-Im, for its part, was a less than enthusiastic participant in the Alliance in the early 1960s. For one thing, the Bank appeared to Linder as overexposed. It had $800 million on its books to Brazil alone, almost one quarter of its outstanding loans. Moreover, Latin America appeared less stable in the 1960s than before. Radicalism seemed a genuine possibility following the success of the 1959 Cuban Revolution. By 1960, Castro and his associates made no secret of their hope to ignite revolutionary change throughout the hemisphere. However exaggerated these aspirations might have been, lending in Latin America seemed riskier than ever before. In any event, the Bank was directly affected when Cuba acted on its revolutionary pronouncements by defaulting on two outstanding Bank loans. Indeed, Castro's revolutionary compatriot Che Guevarra – in 1960 head of Cuba's national bank – himself bluntly told senior Bank official Walter C. Sauer in January of that year that Cuba would repudiate the $36 million balance of the two loans. One could hardly imagine a meeting of two more incongruous figures.

[26] House, Committee on Foreign Affairs, "Staff Memorandum on International Lending and Guaranty Programs," 88th Congress, 2nd Session (Washington, DC: Government Printing Office, 1964), pp. 25–7.

[27] William O. Walker, III, "Mixing the Sweet with the Sour: Kennedy, Johnson, and Latin America," in Diane B. Kunz, ed., *The Diplomacy of the Crucial Decade: American Foreign Relations During the 1960s* (New York: Columbia University Press, 1994), pp. 49–54.

Guevarra only having recently led a guerilla band meeting with Sauer, a man considered by many of his colleagues to be the consummate professional, reserved, career civil servant. In any event, the original credits had been for projects of the American Foreign Power Company to provide electricity and International Telephone and Telegraph telephone service. Each loan had been extended without recourse to either the former Batista government or the parent companies of the American subsidiaries operating in Cuba. Subsequently, to compound the situation, and demonstrate its commitment to a full-scale campaign against imperialism, the Castro government expropriated the property of the two American firms.[28]

Equally unsettling were events in Chile and Brazil. Marxist politician Salvador Allende gained adherents in Chile with his strong condemnation of foreign economic influence in the country. He made a strong showing in the 1964 presidential election, arguing for the nationalization of the country's American-owned copper mines.[29] Most disturbing was the situation in Brazil. In August 1961, a new government took power after the surprise resignation of a president acceptable to the United States. New President Joao Goulart was, as an advisor to President Kennedy said, a "weak and erratic demagogue." For the next three years, the government followed economic policies that led to a tripling of inflation and rapidly falling rates of growth and foreign investment. As a result, Ex-Im essentially imposed a moratorium on lending to Brazil that lasted until the country's military overthrew the government in April 1964.[30]

These unsettled and unsettling circumstances only served to reenforce Linder's fiscal prudence. He had, for example, firm views about the role of exports in the rapidly expanding American economy of the 1960s.

[28] "Eximbank and Latin America: The 1960's and Beyond," pp. 1–2, Mazo-Mazon files; Linder Interview, November 15, 1973, pp. 24–5.

[29] Walker, pp. 65–6.

[30] Ibid., pp. 54, 55 (quote), 58, 62; "Report from the Inter-Departmental Survey Team on Brazil to President Kennedy," November 3, 1962, *Foreign Relations of the United States, 1961–1963*, Vol. XII, pp. 472–78 (hereafter *FRUS*); "Incoming Telegram," to Secretary of State from Rio de Janeiro, May 18, 1962, Re: AID Export-Import Bank Financing of the Volta Redonda Project, Central Decimal File (CDF) 1960–1963, Box 139 (103-XMB/5-1862), Record Group 59, Records of the Department of State, National Archives; Memorandum of Conversation, Lincoln Gordon, Assistant Secretary of State, Harold F. Linder et al., Subject: Brazil Re-Payments to Export-Import Bank, October 10, 1966, CDF 1960–1963, Box 138 (103-XMB/10-1066), RG 59.

Linder emphasized the Bank's role in improving the country's balance of payments by "facilitating exports... thereby contributing to the rising merchandise surplus which helps offset the deficit in our international accounts." As he said to a 1966 meeting of the Bankers' Association for Foreign Trade, "domestic stimulation is *not* what our economy needs today... the interests of our nation are best served by the promotion – not of exports for exports' sake – but of exports for which we can reasonably expect to receive payment as promptly as possible from the foreign purchaser."[31]

Moreover, the Bank's own studies in the mid 1960s extolled the promise of new technologies. In particular, the Bank staff championed the export possibilities of commercial jet aircraft, nuclear power generation, and the on-the-ground facilities needed to make satellite communications feasible. In fiscal year 1957, the Bank began to provide credits for overseas purchasers of jet aircraft. In fact, because of their commercial promise, Ex-Im had first set up a special committee in 1958–9 to focus staff attention on the business. In subsequent years, lending increased for jet aircraft. During fiscal year 1967, the Bank provided $748.0 million in credits for commercial jet aircraft. For the other heavy-capital goods growth area of nuclear power, it was $145.3 million in that year.[32] Continued technological advances in jet propulsion and aerodynamics led to the industry's adding new models of commercial jetliners to their fleets throughout the 1960s. These developments culminated in 1969 with the commercial introduction of the Boeing 747 jumbo jet. In Congressional testimony in 1967, Linder estimated that in the next five years that the Bank would be called upon to extend credits from $2.5 billion to $3.5 billion for aircraft and about $1 billion for nuclear power.[33]

These were not the only "big ticket" items that Ex-Im financed in the 1960s. Indeed, for the Bank, the most portentous decision to seek new kinds of long-term lending involved funding military procurement for American allies. Such credits appeared to be an easy way to assist in

[31] Address, Harold F. Linder, to Bankers' Association for Foreign Trade, Boca Raton, FL, April 26, 1966, p. 5, 1962–1966 Press Releases, Library, Ex-Im.

[32] Appendix B, Summary of Authorizations.

[33] On the aircraft committee, see William Balderston Interview, November 6, 1973, p. 10, in Mazo-Mazon files; House, *1967 Hearings to Amend the Export-Import Bank Act of 1945*, pp. 42–4.

alleviating the country's balance of payments problems. In 1962, Linder agreed to extend credits for the purchase of military equipment. Whatever reservations he might have had – to say nothing of those of some other Bank officials – were overcome by reassurances from Treasury Secretary Dillon, an old and trusted friend from Wall Street.[34]

Earlier Congress had authorized the Bank to make loans either for foreign economic or military assistance in the 1955 Mutual Security Act, which combined previous economic and military aid programs. Even so, as Linder knew, his predecessors, Edgerton and Waugh, had refused to involve the Bank in significant military lending. Be that as it may, Italy received the first such military procurement loan in 1963, and there were large credits for Great Britain and Australia in 1965. Subsequently, the Department of Defense (DOD) guaranteed other credits, on the basis of authority Congress granted in 1965 as part of a Foreign Assistance Act to advance military sales through commercial banks or government agencies. In making the guaranteed loans, the Bank relied on the advice and analysis of the DOD, which was after all assuming the risk. [35]

In 1966, the Bank broadened the military procurement lending activities through the so-called Country-X program directed at less-developed countries (LDCs). Ex-Im acquired from the Defense Department its obligations resulting from sales to LDCs. Under the arrangement with DOD, the Bank did not deal with the purchaser, nor indeed did it know who the borrower countries were. The Defense Department fully guaranteed these obligations. Both the Ex-Im and DOD hoped that these government-guaranteed loans would be placed with commercial banks. When money market conditions made that impossible, the Bank simply held onto the obligations as part of its portfolio. By mid 1967, the Bank had acquired about $600 million of these DOD guaranteed loans. Its direct military lending to American allies came to $1,210.5 million between 1962 and 1967. When military lending reached its peak in 1966–8, about 37 percent of the net loans authorized by the Bank were

34 Interview with Ray Albright, April 6, 2000, pp. 6–8, Library, Ex-Im (hereafter Albright Interview April 6, 2000).

35 "Legislative History – E – Military, 1967 uproar," pp. 1–2, in Mazo-Mazon files; House, Committee on Banking and Currency, "Export-Import Bank and Credit Sales of Defense Articles," 90th Congress, 1st Session (Washington, DC: Government Printing Office, 1967), pp. 3–5, 65–6.

for military equipment and about 15 percent of all outstanding Bank loans also were for such procurement.[36]

Even though the Bank saw these loans in strictly financial terms, Congress interpreted them differently. They caused the Ex-Im considerable difficulties during its 1968 reauthorization. Nevertheless, Linder defended the military procurement loans as an acceptable kind of long-term lending, even though, of course, they involved the Bank in the country's national security strategy. In any event, broadening exposure to foreign policy concerns more generally began to influence the Bank's lending again in the mid 1960s. The Kennedy and Johnson administrations were deeply committed to warding off revolution in Latin America. One aspect of that effort was the considerable attention both administrations paid to development assistance.[37]

Foreign policy considerations forced the Bank to expand its exposure in Latin America later in the second half of the 1960s. Once the Brazilian military overthrew the Goulart government in 1964, the administration looked for ways to bolster the new anticommunist regime. Despite the new government's authoritarian antidemocratic methods, which invited widespread criticism and left open the possibility of further instability, the United States pushed ahead with assistance. The Bank did its part by renegotiating credits and extending new ones beginning in 1965. In fiscal year 1967–8, for example, Ex-Im provided Brazil with almost $51 million in credits and $59 million in guarantees.[38]

Similarly, the administration involved the Bank in the American government's efforts to influence events in Chile. The United States provided assistance to the government of the Christian Democratic Party's Eduardo Frei who won the 1964 presidential election. Following his election, Frei continued to be challenged by the growing leftist movement led by Salvadore Allende. To counter Allende's charge that previous governments had sold the country's patrimony to foreign investors, Frei espoused a policy of "Chileanization," essentially partial Chilean ownership of the copper mines. In 1967, the Bank contributed to this effort by providing $110 million in credits to a joint venture between the

[36] Ibid., pp. 1–3, 2a; Press Release, "Statement of Harold F. Linder, . . . before the Committee on Banking and Currency of the United States Senate," July 25, 1967, in Mazo-Mazon files; Albright Interview, April 6, 2000, pp. 10–12; GAO Report 1967, p. 1.

[37] Walker, pp. 58–63.

[38] Annual Report for 1968, p. 30; Linder Interview, November 15, 1973, pp. 29–30.

Chilean government and Kennecott Copper to expand the El Teniente copper mine – in the transaction the government took a 51 percent interest in the new facility. Similarly, in the same year, Ex-Im approved a credit that amounted to $145 million to the Cerro de Pasco mine, a subsidiary of Kennecott, with the understanding that it would offer 40 percent of the subsidiary's stock to the Chilean public.[39]

These were not the only instances where the Bank, as many times before, served the foreign policy interests of the United States. Africa became a Cold War arena in the late 1950s and early 1960s, as former European colonies received their independence. Kennedy and his national security advisers saw Africa as a new and important front in the struggle against international communism. They were determined that newly independent African countries be enlisted on the side of the West.[40]

Before the 1960s, Ex-Im lending in Africa had been, for the most part, confined to the white South African government and to Liberia, the African country whose elite traced its ancestry to freed American slaves in the nineteenth century, and where American steel and rubber firms had substantial interests. But discussions about assistance to Ghana began during the last years of the Eisenhower administration. Following its independence in 1957, Ghana's president Kwame Nkrumah assigned a high priority to building a dam on the Volta River to produce electricity and a smelter to process bauxite into aluminum. In 1958, the Eisenhower administration, under attack from Democrats for ignoring Africa, took an interest in the Volta project. A year later, Kaiser Industries put together a consortium (VALCO), including ALCAN, the Aluminum Company of America (ALCOA), Reynolds Metals Company, and Olin Mathieson, which signed an agreement with Nkrumah to participate in the proposed undertaking.[41]

That's where matters stood at the end of the Eisenhower administration. JFK took a personal interest in Ghana, which his administration saw as a pivotal state in the Cold War battle for the future of Africa. After

39 *1967 Hearings to Amend the Export-Import Bank Act of 1945*, p. 71; 2 letters, Joseph H. Regan, Secretary, Ex Im, to Charles R. Harley, Secretary, NAC, November 16, 1966 (NAC Docs. 66-450, 66-451), Records, Assistant Secretary of Treasury for International Affairs, NAC/Docs and Supplements, Box 45, RG 56; Walker, pp. 63–5.

40 Thomas J. Noer, "The New Frontier and African Neutralism: Kennedy, Nkrumah, and the Volta River Project," *Diplomatic History*, 8 (Winter 1984): 61–79.

41 Ibid., pp. 63–5.

contentious policy debates within the administration Kennedy decided to go ahead with financial assistance to Ghana for the Volta project, despite concerns about Nkrumah's reliability. He had set up an authoritarian government, established warm relations with the USSR, and had a propensity to give anti-American speeches. Moreover, Kennedy was haunted by the negative image the United States and its allies got in the developing world by pulling out of the Aswan Dam project in 1956. Thus, the administration prevailed on the Bank for assistance. Ultimately, Ex-Im provided a $110 million credit for the project in February 1962. Half of that was transferred to AID, for later reimbursement to the Bank.[42]

So, despite Linder's predilections, the Bank's role in meeting certain foreign policy goals increased. As the policies of the Kennedy and Johnson years became more controversial, the Bank found itself the subject of greater congressional scrutiny.

CONGRESS, THE BANK, AND THE COLD WAR

During the 1960s, Congress intensified its oversight of Bank activities. Ex-Im received high marks from the Senate and House Banking and Currency Committees, which handled its periodic reauthorizations. And generally the Bank enjoyed the good opinion of members of Congress because it earned a profit for the U.S. government. Beginning in 1961, however, the Bank became a symbol of practices that some members of Congress opposed. In that year, determined opponents of foreign aid attacked the Bank's annual level of direct lending (i.e., its annual obligational authority). Much to its chagrin, in 1963 the Bank found itself in a political crossfire over its reauthorization. Congress and the White House, the Senate and the House, and committees of the House were the protagonists in numerous disputes over congressional and executive branch authority in regard to foreign policy and budgeting. Later in the decade, the Bank became a direct target – in 1968 because of its lending for military procurement and in 1965 because of loans to communist

[42] Ibid., pp. 67–77; Linder Interview, November 8, 1973, pp. 18–20; "The Outlook for Ghana," October 17, 1962, *FRUS, 1961–1963*, Vol. XXI, pp. 378–9; Memorandum, NAC Staff Committee to National Advisory Council, Re: "Aluminum Company Request for United States Guarantees and Loans – Ghana and Guinea," January 31, 1961, Records of the Assistant Secretary of the Treasury for International Affairs – NAC, NAC documents/Supplement 1, Box 35, RG 56.

countries. Again, the controversy revolved around issues larger than the mission of Ex-Im – in particular, Congress' effort to reassert itself in the making of foreign policy during the Vietnam War. But, to be sure, some of the Bank's practices made it vulnerable to criticism. Consequently, the 1968 reauthorization somewhat circumscribed to whom the Bank might lend, and for what purposes. Later that same year, in response to persistent criticism of Linder's conservative lending practices, Congress mandated that Ex-Im set aside $500 million for an export expansion facility that slightly relaxed its statutory requirements of "reasonable assurance of repayment" for loans and to only require "sufficient likelihood of payment." As it turned out, the facility was not aggressively used in future years.

Signs of trouble in Congress first emerged in 1961. Legislation in that year amended the basic Export-Import Bank Act of 1945, articulating Ex-Im's powers with respect to guarantees and insurance, as well as authorizing fractional reserves. Congress, however, failed to extend the life of the Bank for the five years the administration requested in the 1961 legislative proposal, from June 1963 to June 1968. Instead, the charter was extended only to June 1963. Key members of the House were unsure about the new authority given to the Bank – some preferred a private sector, government-supported corporation to provide guarantees separate from Ex-Im – and wanted to keep open an opportunity to review the Bank again in the following year.[43]

While nothing came of the idea of a separate government guarantee corporation, the Bank's increased visibility made it something of a target in 1961. It ended up in the sights of Congressman Otto E. Passman, chairman of the Subcommittee on Foreign Operations, Committee on Appropriations. Each year, as part of the budget process, Congress included Ex-Im's annual administrative expense allocation in the Foreign Assistance and Related Agencies Bill. Since the 1930s, Congress had established annual limitations on these relatively small administrative expenses of the Bank. Budget submissions had included the administration's much larger figure of the funds that the Bank obligated annually to provide direct credits, but Congress never specifically legislated limits on loan obligations.

43 Jordan Jay Hillman, *The Export-Import Bank at Work: Promotional Financing in the Public Sector* (Westport, CT: Quorum Books, 1982), pp. 40–1.

A small, but resolute group of senior House members, long ideologically opposed to foreign aid, took aim at Kennedy's proposed large increases in spending on foreign assistance. As one committee member observed, "We are discussing billions of dollars through an aid program, and through new programs previously unheard of, *even for foreign aid*" (emphasis added). Some of the shots fired in this battle hit the Bank. Leading the attack on the Ex-Im's loans was Congressman Passman. That the Bank was not providing foreign aid, which Linder pointed out in testimony, was to no avail. Passman's subcommittee in 1961 capped the Bank's annual obligational authority (funding loans to foreign buyers and their local banks). The Senate accepted the new principle of setting such a limit, although some Senators thought that the House cap was set too low. In the subsequent legislative conference compromise with the Senate, the House increased the proposed obligational authority to $1.3 billion, bringing the figure close to what the administration had proposed for the Bank in the first place. Thus, these congressionally mandated limitations were added to those already existing statutory ceilings on outstanding loans, guarantees, insurance, as well as the debt at any one time owed the treasury.[44]

Linder and other Bank officials hoped that these limitations were a short-term aberration. They saw these annual ceilings as potentially limiting the Bank's ability to cope with unanticipated emergency foreign trade lending, which was at times significant in the 1960s. Even so, by the end of Lyndon Johnson's term, the ceilings had become an accepted feature of budget proposals, although the Bank was able to convince Congress to set them at generous levels. Ultimately, the battle over these ceilings contributed to the Bank's changing rhetoric about its mission. Following the Kennedy administration's championing trade over aid, Ex-Im began talking more in terms of trade. "Developmental loans" were increasingly referred to as "long-term project and equipment loans," and later more simply as "equipment and services loans."[45]

In any case, during 1962, the Bank prepared for its five-year reauthorization. Early in 1963, the Kennedy administration sponsored legislation to extend the Bank's charter beyond its June 30, 1963,

[44] Hillman, pp. 44–5; quote from House, *Hearing Before a Subcommittee of the Committee on Appropriations: Foreign Operations Appropriations for 1963*, 87th Congress, 2nd Session, (March 14, 1962), p. 92.

[45] Hillman, pp. 44–5.

expiration. In February 1963, the House Banking and Currency Committee approved the administration's bill. In the proposed legislation, Ex-Im received a five-year extension, authority to increase its lending and borrowing ceilings by $2 billion, and approval to double its guarantee and insurance authority.

The committee's Republicans, however, issued a minority report, which lobbed the Bank's reauthorization into a roiling battle on Capitol Hill. The committee's minority approved of the Bank and its work, but they questioned authorizing it to borrow more funds from the treasury. Such borrowing, they maintained, would, in effect, raise the national debt when the treasury sold obligations to raise funds for Ex-Im's activities. This, of course, was not a new concern. Beginning late in the 1950s, the Bank faced pressure to reduce its treasury borrowings. Since the legislation of 1945, the Ex-Im had authority to borrow funds from the treasury, after it made an initial $1 billion purchase of Ex-Im's stock.[46] Thus, each of the subsequent increases in borrowing authority in 1951, 1954, and 1958 in effect raised the public debt when treasury sold obligations to cover the Bank's increased authorizations.[47]

But it was not only the committee's Republican minority that questioned the reauthorization. Democrat Passman challenged the bill by raising jurisdictional issues. He questioned the appropriateness of the Banking and Currency Committee, chaired by Wright Patman, making determinations about the levels of the Bank's expenditures. Such judgments, he believed, were the prerogatives of the Appropriations Committee. Passman's objections attracted the support of those who believed the House abdicated its constitutional authority when it allowed financing outside of the appropriation process. Such practices weakened the House's role in policy making, especially in regard to foreign relations.

In regard to the Bank, Passman complained about what was called at the time backdoor financing. This involved the Bank's practice of borrowing funds from the treasury as needed on a revolving basis up to its authorized lending ceilings. The Bank was not the only government agency to utilize this practice. But whenever backdoor financing came up

46 Before 1945, the Bank sold preferred stock to the Reconstruction Finance Corporation. The latter used funds that came from its annual appropriation.

47 "Legislative History – 1963 Extension of Eximbank Authority, and hiatus in Authority," in Mazon-Mazo files, pp. 1–4.

in the first session of the Eighty-Eighth Congress, powerful committee chairmen battled each other, and in effect the House challenged the administration. Consequently, Ex-Im found itself in the middle of the debate. A result of the House debate over the Bank's reauthorization was an amendment, passed in May 1963, to require the Bank to seek the additional funding authority it needed through direct congressional appropriations from treasury's funds.[48]

The administration and the Ex-Im strongly opposed these changes. If the Bank had to rely on yearly appropriations, they argued, the new legislation would inevitably narrow the long-term focus that was necessary in making loans. Annual appropriations, they added, would provide perverse incentives to spend all the funds allocated within a fiscal year, lest future budget requests be reduced. It would also, many feared, make the Bank more prone to congressional political pressure and reduce its ability to respond quickly to emergency balance of payment lending.[49]

Meanwhile, the Senate's version of the original administration reauthorization bill received approval. It included the $2 billion more in borrowing authority from the treasury to complement the $2 billion increase in authorized ceilings. Conference committees considering the two bills took until August to come to agreement. These labored deliberations left the Bank for almost two months without statutory authority to contract new loans. Ex-Im's General Counsel determined that without enabling legislation the Bank could not continue to make loan commitments. This turn of events energized the Bank's constituencies among exporters and commercial bankers. They were unhappy with the House bill and pressed sympathetic members hard for a settlement when the Bank's authority expired at the end of June 1963 without definitive legislation. Ultimately, the bill Congress passed increased the Bank's authorized lending ceilings by $2 billion without prohibiting the authority to borrow the funds from the treasury.[50]

[48] Hillman, p. 42; "Legislative History – 1963 Extension of Eximbank Authority, and hiatus in Authority," pp. 1–2.

[49] "Legislative History – 1963 Extension of Eximbank Authority, and hiatus in Authority," pp. 3–4.

[50] Ibid., pp. 1–4; Senate, Committee on Banking and Currency, *Report on Export-Import Bank Act Extension,* June 19, 1963, 88th Congress, 1st Session (hereafter *Report on Export-Import Bank Act Extension*; Hillman), pp. 41–3.

Reauthorization in 1963 had thus been a difficult experience. If anything, the bruising battle served to press the Bank's leadership to move forward with alternative measures of raising capital, in particular, the program to issue certificates of participation.[51] But that, as it turned out, was not enough to save it from a more difficult time in 1967–8, when Congress considered Ex-Im's next scheduled reauthorization.

The Export-Import Bank also suffered some wounds in the congressional and administration crossfire of 1967–8. None of them proved life threatening, but for the first time the Bank came in for sustained criticism in Congress. As a result, the 1968 reauthorization legislation put more limits on to whom and for what the Bank could lend.[52]

In anticipation of the Bank's statutory expiration on June 30, 1968, the administration in spring 1967 sponsored bills in both houses of Congress to extend the Bank for five years, increase its lending authority by $4.5 billion (from $9 to $13.5 billion), and boost its guaranty and insurance authority from $2 to $3.5 billion. The Bank and the White House hoped that, by starting early, there would be ample time to get the reauthorization approved before June 1968. By the time the bills were introduced, however, Congress was focused on the Vietnam War, as opposition to the conflict increased on Capital Hill. Opponents and proponents of the war clashed on issues – like that of the Bank's reauthorization – that at first glance seemed unrelated to the conflict and the passions it generated. Also stoking the feelings about the war – on both sides of the issues – was a general congressional unease that the conflict began and was being prosecuted without sufficient attention to the legislative branch. So it was that the Bank's reauthorization became enmeshed in two emotional disputes – one about Ex-Im's funding the classified acquisition of military equipment and the other the provision of credits

[51] Legislative History – 1963 Extension of Eximbank Authority, and hiatus in Authority," pp. 2–3; "'Backdoor' Financing for the Export-Import Bank: A Brief History," Congressional and External Affairs Bureau, Records (no box), Legislative History Folder, 1976–1978, Archives, Ex-Im. *Report on Export-Import Bank Act Extension*, pp. 13–15; Memorandum of Conversation, Harold Linder with Robert V. Roosa, January 8, 1962, Subject Files, 1933–1975, Box 10, "Budget 1960–1964" folder, RG 275.

[52] Middleton Interview, March 17, 2000, pp. 19–23; Albright Interview, April 6, 2000, pp. 13–14; Glick Interview, March 13, 2000, pp. 33–4.

to communist countries, powers aiding the United States' enemies in Southeast Asia.

The reauthorization process began smoothly enough. By May 1967, the House Banking and Currency Committee gave the administration's bill a favorable report. Its one addition to the original proposal was in regard to the Bank's name. The administration proposed dropping "of Washington" – thus it would be the Export-Import Bank. Instead, the committee added "of the United States," making the name of the institution, the Export-Import Bank of the United States.[53]

These changes prompted no opposition. That could not be said for other parts of the bill reported out of committee. The committee's Republican minority issued its own report advocating a prohibition of lending to communist countries. This was becoming a hot issue, as the Vietnam War intensified, in large part because of the feeling that communist countries were assisting North Vietnam and the Vietcong. It was part of a larger critique of the "hypocrisy" of the Johnson administration, which was fighting communists in Southeast Asia while trying to increase trade with them in Eastern Europe. These concerns involved the Bank because of its visible role in the administration's efforts to promote East–West trade. As early as 1963, for example, Congress debated the advisability of Ex-Im providing credits for the purchases of wheat destined for the Eastern bloc. The upshot that year was a prohibition on such lending, unless the president determined that it was in the national interest for the Bank to do so.[54]

Despite such earlier Congressional concerns, in October 1966, President Johnson introduced a program of "building bridges" to Eastern Europe and the USSR by expanding trade. One of the most prominent efforts involved the Ex-Im. Fiat, the Italian automobile manufacturer, had contracted in 1966 to build a small passenger car facility in the Soviet Union. When the contract negotiations were completed, the Italian development agency, Istituto Mobiliare Italiano, approached

53 "Legislative History – F – Extension of Eximbank Authority, 1968," in Mazo-Mazon files, pp. 1–2; Hillman, pp. 54–6.

54 Memorandum: "Loans, Guarantees, and Insurance for Exports to Communist Countries, July 1, 1962, to September 30, 1967," December 6, 1967, Subject Files 1933–75, Box 33, "Guarantees and Insurance, 1965–68" folder, RG 275.

the Bank about a loan to cover Fiat's purchase of machine tools in the United States for its new plant in the Soviet Union.[55]

By this time, though, attitudes in Congress about East–West trade had changed. In August 1967 when the Senate Committee on Banking and Currency reported on the administration's reauthorization bill, the Democratic majority included a prohibition against the Bank lending to communist countries, without a presidential determination that the country's national interest would be served by such funding. When the bill went to the floor for debate, it was further amended to include a direct prohibition against the Fiat loan.[56]

Injected into the Senate debate over reauthorization for the first time was direct, sharp criticism of the Bank. Leading the attack were Florida's senators who had been upset with the Bank since it made a loan to Morocco in 1965 to improve its phosphate production. Florida was a major producer of phosphate, about a third of which it exported. Senators Spessard Holland and George Smathers questioned the wisdom of the Bank increasing the capacity of the state's overseas competitors. They argued that the Bank in the future should explicitly consider whether its funding would have an adverse effect on the U.S. economy. Holland also complained that the Bank had not consulted with him before making the loan. Linder opposed the amendment, arguing that it would significantly increase the complexity of the Bank's review process. Ultimately, a compromise on the amendment was reached that Ex-Im accepted. It included watered-down language requiring that the Bank take into consideration the possibility of adverse affects when making its decisions. Whether Holland was mollified by this compromise was unclear, but he did observe that the whole episode demonstrated that the Bank "does not seem to develop greatly its relations with Congress."[57]

That Ex-Im's handling of Congress left much to be desired became abundantly clear in the summer of 1967. The Bank's lending for military procurement became an explosive issue. As it played out in

55 Memorandum: B. Jenkins Middleton, "FIAT – Soviet Automobile Plant," July 1, 1967, in Mazo-Mazon files; House, Banking and Currency Commitee, Report, *The FIAT–Soviet Auto Plant and Communist Economic Reforms*, March 1, 1967 (Washington, DC: Government Printing Office, 1967), pp. 1–8.

56 "Legislative History – F – Extension of Eximbank Authority, 1968," in Mazo-Mazon files, p. 3.

57 Ibid., pp. 4–5; Hillman, pp. 56–8.

congressional hearings, and the press, Linder appeared to have deliberately misled Congress and cooperated with the Department of Defense in an effort to circumvent explicit congressional restrictions on military spending. In the tense atmosphere of summer 1967, as opposition to the Vietnam War mounted, the issue took on a large significance. Ex-Im's lending for military purposes seemed to demonstrate to key members of Congress – both liberals and conservatives – yet again the need to rein in the administration.[58]

What caused so much trouble was Linder's failure to inform the ranking minority members of key committees about the secret military lending. From the beginning of such activity in 1962, he cleared the program in general terms with the Democratic chairman of the relevant congressional committees. Members of Congress sharply criticized the Bank for expending so much money (almost $2 billion) without full knowledge of the terms of its loans; this was the case with lending to LDCs. That the Bank was able to rely on Defense Department guarantees did not mollify Congress. Matters became worse when it also appeared that the Bank's lending helped the Defense Department violate several congressional spending caps on foreign military aid. A number of the Vietnam War's leading congressional opponents took particular exception to the Bank's lack of actual knowledge that loans were going to both sides of long-standing disputes among LDCs – India and Pakistan, as well as Israel, Jordan, and Saudi Arabia. After all, they believed, it was the government's increasing military assistance to South Vietnam that got the United States involved in Southeast Asia in the first place.[59]

As a result of these controversies, the legislation approving the Bank's 1968 reauthorization included some restrictions. In the final debate on the bill, the ranking member of the House Committee on Banking and Currency observed that the experience with Ex-Im's lending for military procurement demonstrated that "there was [a] real need for the Congress to ride herd more closely on the activities of the Bank." Thus, the bill that became law in March 1968 included language that prohibited the Bank from extending credit to any country that directly

[58] "Legislative History – E – Military, 1967 uproar," in Mazo-Mazon files, pp. 2–3; Press Release, "Statement of Harold F. Linder... before the Committee on Banking and Currency of the United States Senate, July 25, 1967," in Mazo-Mazon files.

[59] "Legislative History – E – Military, 1967 uproar," pp. 1–4.

provided assistance to North Vietnam. This in effect eliminated lending to all communist countries, except Yugoslavia. Congress also constrained the Bank in the kind of military lending it could undertake to LDCs. The act prohibited credits to LDCs for military procurement, unless the president determined it was in the national interest. In any event, the legislation limited to 7.5 percent of "outstanding loans" Ex-Im funds that could be used for financing military sales to LDCs.[60]

Criticism of Linder and the Bank did not end with approval of the reauthorization. During the spring of 1968, the Banking and Currency Committees in both the House and Senate took up a bill to create an "export expansion facility" within the Bank. In June, Congress approved legislation authorizing the Bank to use up to $500 million of its $13.5 billion obligational authority for transactions that included a higher degree of risk than permitted under the Bank's basic statutes. Congress justified this step as helping increase exports to deal with the country's persistent balance of payments deficit. Congressional supporters of the legislation also hoped that it would induce the Bank to increase its lending to countries like Indonesia, with potentially large markets, but without the credit to fully develop them. The hearings on the bill also revealed that the congressional proponents of the facility, as well as representatives of industry, saw it as an instrument to relax the real, or certainly perceived, tightfisted approach of Linder. As the House committee said in its report, the Bank took "an overly conservative view of its present authority."[61]

Linder and his colleagues were strongly opposed to the legislation. But in the spring of 1968, he had little choice but gamely to go along. Ultimately, the Bank in most years did not make use of the facility. But it was another sign that the Bank needed to nurture its relationship with Congress.

[60] Ibid., pp. 6–7 (quote); Memorandum, Judith F. Mazo to Walter Sauer, "Legislative History, Presidential 'National Interest' Determination in Connection with Eximbank Credit for Communist Countries," February 13, 1974, in Mazo-Mazon files.

[61] Senate, Committee on Banking and Currency, *Hearings on S. 3218, Extend Authority of Export-Import Bank in Order to Improve the Balance of Payments*, April 5, 1968, 90th Congress, 2nd Session (Washington, DC: Government Printing Office, 1968), pp. 15–24; House, Committee on Banking and Currency, *Report on Export-Import Bank Loans*, May 27, 1968, 90th Congress, 2nd Session. Rept No. 1476, pp. 1–7; Announcement, "Eximbank Given More Liberal Export Financing Authority," *FRUS, 1964–1968*, Vol. VIII, pp. 568–9.

Clearly, improving relations with Congress would have to be one of the primary tasks of the next president of the Bank. Nevertheless, despite all the Bank's problems with Congress, it succeeded in having its administrative budget increased, so that it had the staff needed to meet the increased demands put on the Bank by its new insurance and guarantee programs. The Bank's staff increased 30 percent between 1960 and 1967, as it went from 250 to 325 people.[62]

Nevertheless, there was little that Linder could do in the last months of the troubled Johnson administration to improve relations with Congress. One can argue, of course, that Linder and the Bank were often pitched into the middle of congressional battles driven by large issues of principle, as well as petty personality differences between powerful committee chairmen. It was also true that much of the criticism on military lending was unfair. Linder had provided information about the Bank's military lending, not only to key committee chairmen but also before committees.[63]

Overstated too might be the more general criticism that the Bank under Linder had been too conservative. Linder, to be sure, prided himself on being a "hard-boiled" banker. But he also tried to see the Bank's role in the context of the prosperous 1960s. He surely understood the political imperative of promoting exports to assist in the government's efforts to cope with balance-of-payments problems. In this context, the Bank was perhaps not sensitive enough to the growing concern among exporters about foreign competition. There were persistent criticisms among exporters that the Bank was too rigid in its procedures. Even so, Linder's "conservatism" was also responsive to congressional concerns about the quality of the loans the Bank made. Cuba's defaults and expropriations frightened members of Congress who regularly thereafter questioned the Bank on

[62] House, Subcommittee of Committee on Appropriations, *Hearing, Mutual Security Appropriations for 1961 (and Related Agencies)*, 86th Congress, 2nd Session, March 17, 1960 (Washington, DC: Government Printing Office, 1960), p. 1; House, Subcommittee of Committee on Appropriations, *Hearing, Foreign Assistance and Related Agencies Appropriations for* 1967, 89th Congress, 2nd Session, March 24, 1966 (Printed for the Committee), p. 245.

[63] See, for example, Linder's testimony at hearings before the Senate Subcommittee on Foreign Assistance and Related Agencies Appropriations, Fiscal Year 1967, 89th Congress, 2nd Session, pp. 197–8; Press Release, "Statement of Harold F. Linder...before the Committee on Banking and Currency of the United States Senate, July 25, 1967," in Mazo-Mazon files.

the safety of its lending. Moreover, Linder and the Bank did not get credit from Congressman Passman and others concerned with back-door financing for reducing Ex-Im's borrowings from the treasury. "At the beginning of the 1960 fiscal year," according to Linder, "the Bank was borrowing $2 billion from the Treasury. Today, it is borrowing $300 million from the Treasury," while also raising funds from private markets.[64]

Linder left the Bank on July 31, 1968. He had served the longest tenure of any postwar Bank president. It is not surprising that, working with Sauer as his vice chairman, he set his imprint on Ex-Im. Long-time Bank official Warren W. Glick believed that Linder established a high "intellectual tone" for the institution and referred to him "as the best or one of the best financial chairmen the Bank ever had." As Glick went on to say, both Sauer and Linder were extremely demanding. These thoughts were echoed by B. Jenkins Middleton, who thought Linder could "read a balance sheet like nobody I have ever seen." Despite Middleton's own favorable view of Linder, he was certainly not greatly liked by a number of staff members.[65]

The incoming Nixon administration was going to have to face up to issues that Linder had confronted, and then some. For one thing, the United States late in the 1960s and early 1970s experienced an acceleration of "dollar crises," as the fixed-rate exchange system established at Bretton Woods collapsed. A system of floating exchange rates, which ultimately followed, fundamentally changed the international economic system, with consequences for both its public and private players. But Nixon's choice for Bank president, entrepreneur Henry Kearns, came into office determined to do a better job in addressing the problems that Linder faced. Ultimately, though, the Bank in the 1970s faced a very different world, something that was not entirely clear to Kearns in the early Nixon years.

64 House, Subcommittee of Committee on Appropriations, *Hearing, Foreign Assistance and Related Agencies Appropriations for 1967*, 89th Congress, 2nd Session, March 24, 1966 (printed for the committee), pp. 250–4; Report, Doering and Wrigley, "Financing of Railway Equipment Exports," International Finance Division, Bureau of International Commerce, Department of Commerce, Government Agencies Files, Box 4, "Commerce Department" folder, RG 275; Glick Interview, March 13, 2000, pp. 17–18.

65 Glick Interview, March 13, 2000, pp. 17–18, 21–2; Middleton Interview, March 17, 2000, pp. 7–8.

HENRY KEARNS AND THE LESSONS OF THE 1960S

Richard M. Nixon appointed a long-time California political associate to head the Bank. Henry Kearns was in many ways an unusual choice. For one thing, he was better acquainted with the president who appointed him than his predecessors were with those who selected them. For another, Kearns was not from Wall Street, nor indeed was he a banker. He was a wealthy businessman from southern California, with an interest in a range of enterprises and a long-term commitment to Nixon and the Republican Party. He had held offices in the California party and had been vice-chairman of the national Republican Party finance committee. He had also served as assistant secretary of commerce for international affairs in the Eisenhower administration. In his three years in that post (1957–60), Kearns mastered international trade issues as chairman of the International Trade Fair Committee, the Trade Missions Committee, the Committee on Export Expansion of the Inter-Agency Committee for the Reciprocal Trade Agreements Act, and the cabinet-level Trade Policy Committee.[66]

Nevertheless, Kearns' appointment raised disparaging comments. Unfriendly commentators fixated on his one-time ownership of a car dealership. They disdained him merely as "a used-car salesman," a job in fact he held early in his working career. Clearly, such comments underestimated the entrepreneurship and ambition of a man who had made a fortune and who traveled easily in high-ranking political circles. But Kearns himself was a self-described salesman, and proud of it. Fundamentally, he believed that his task at the Ex-Im was to change attitudes, to "sell" domestic manufacturers on export markets and foreign purchasers on American goods.[67]

Kearns believed that an energetic boosting of American exports would help address the country's serious foreign and domestic economic problems.[68] By the time he took office, U.S. trade and payments had deteriorated further. The year before, in 1968, the country had weathered

[66] Obituary, "Henry Kearns, 1911–1985," *Exim News*, n.d., Library, Ex-Im.

[67] Kearns, Remarks to World Trade Week Luncheon of the Foreign Trade Association of Southern California, May 21, 1970, "The Foreign Trade Challenge of the 70's and How to Meet It," Press Release, Library, Ex-Im (hereafter "The Foreign Trade Challenge of the 70's and How to Meet It").

[68] "The Foreign Trade Challenge of the 70's and How to Meet It"; Remarks, Kearns, November 19, 1969, to National Foreign Trade Convention, New York, Press Release, Library, Ex-Im (hereafter Remarks, 1969 NFTC).

the most serious of the so-called dollar crises of that decade, one of the periodic international scares that finally forced the overvalued dollar to be devalued in 1971. Moreover, it was clear that the boom of the 1960s had come to an end. Instead, the domestic economy was marked by stagflation, an unusual mix of growing unemployment and slowing growth rates accompanied by rising inflation. None of these problems was solved by the Nixon administration's domestic economic policy. At first, the government raised interest rates and tightened the money supply. When that failed to deal with any of the aspects of stagflation, the administration lowered interest rates and increased spending. Nixon, more obsessed than most first-term presidents about his reelection, concluded that, for political purposes, it was better to lower unemployment than inflation.[69]

Kearns took office (March 20, 1969) as the new Nixon administration first confronted the difficult foreign and economic problems the country faced. The United States' balance-of-trade position showed clear signs of continued deterioration. Fiscal 1969 was to have a trade surplus of only $700 million, when on average it had been about $4 billion a year in the postwar years. Concern turned to alarm in 1971 when the country ran a trade deficit for the first time since 1893. An eroding trade situation contributed to a worsening balance-of-payments position which increased pressure on an already-overvalued dollar. In fiscal year 1969, the payments balance slipped into a deficit of $2.9 billion.[70]

Kearns was determined that the Ex-Im would help solve some of these problems and zealously attacked his new job. His goal was to finance exports, lots of them and quickly. He placed in high-level positions new people who shared his views, made a point of promoting younger people already at the Bank, and reorganized it to concentrate on a high volume of business. He also met with the Advisory Board several times in his first year to discuss his promotional ideas.[71] Under Kearns, Bank board meetings were no longer decorous exercises to consider carefully the financial aspects of proposed loans. Decisions were taken quickly,

[69] Allen J. Matusow, *Nixon's Economy: Booms, Busts, Dollars, and Votes* (Lawrence, KS: University Press of Kansas, 1998), pp. 115–16.

[70] Ibid. p. 117.

[71] *Annual Report for 1970*, p. 15 (hereafter Annual Report); Joint Interview with John D. Bierman and Delio E. Gianturco, May 31, 2000, pp. 15–20, Library, Ex-Im.

often with little discussion, in an almost fevered atmosphere. Kearns wanted to energize the staff, some of whom were frankly skeptical about whether he knew what he was doing. But he talked to staff regularly after he returned from trips – not a practice of his predecessors – where he spoke enthusiastically about what was at stake in promoting exports.[72]

Kearns frequently traveled abroad. He observed that in his first year in office he had "talked with several hundreds of buyers [of American goods] in dozens of countries."[73] At the same time, Kearns assigned Bank officials and staff to better "listen to the heartbeat of America's export trade." This was accomplished by "continually exchanging views and information with exporters, customers and sources of export credit through a series of planned seminars, symposia, consultations, correspondence, and through the advice of our Advisory Committee." Kearns also sponsored what he called a self-analysis program. "In my private business experience," he said in congressional testimony, "I always found that I learned more from sales I lost than the sales that I made if I would talk to customers." The program involved sending out questionnaires to applicants asking them about their experience with the Bank.[74]

In the midst of this whirlwind of promotional activity, Kearns nevertheless kept his eye focused on Washington. He used his political skills and contacts to get the administration and Congress to change the Bank's budget status. It helped that he was an old friend of fellow Californian Casper Weinberger, then head of Office of Management and Budget.[75] Under budget concepts in effect at the time, Bank loan disbursements were considered budget outlays (expenditures). Repayments of principal and interest were treated as receipts. Under this system, the Bank had a deficit in terms of the federal budget in both 1969 and 1970. This resulted from the timing of the Bank's activities and the budget's failure to take account of receivables as assets – scheduled repayments,

[72] Glick Interview, March 13, 2000, pp. 28, 37–8, 66–7: Interview with John F. Corette, April 19, 2000, pp. 4–6, Library, Ex-Im (hereafter Corette Interview, April 19, 2000); Albright Interview, April 6, 2000, pp. 20–1.

[73] "The Foreign Trade Challenge of the 70's and How to Meet It," p. 3.

[74] Ibid., p. 6; Statement, Kearns, Senate, *Hearings to Amend The Export-Import Bank Act of 1945 . . .*, Subcommittee on International Finance, Committee of Banking, Housing, and Urban Affairs, 93rd Congress, 1st Session, October 29, 1973 (Washington, DC: Government Printing Office, 1974), p. 14 (hereafter Kearns Statement, October 29, 1973).

[75] Hess Interview, April 3, 2000, pp. 9–11.

of course, followed by many years' authorizations and disbursements. Kearns brushed aside such budget concepts and reemphasized that, under generally accepted accounting standards, the Bank made a substantial profit in 1969 and 1970.[76]

Kearns prevailed. Congress had authorized the unified budget for essentially political reasons. By placing ceilings on the activities of agencies such as the Bank, Congress and the White House could be seen as exercising restraint in order to balance the budget. Kearns' emphasis on the Bank's profitability trumped, for the time being, concern over balancing the budget. Thus, in 1971, when Congress reauthorized the Bank and increased its loan authority from $13.5 to $20 billion, it also removed Ex-Im from the unified budget put in place in fiscal year 1969. Kearns extolled the reauthorization as assuring the Bank greater flexibility.[77]

But loosening the Bank's budgetary and political bounds was only one of Kearns' goals. From the beginning of his term, he also emphasized increasing private capital's role in export financing. He developed some of his own initiatives, but also built on what he found when he took office, in particular some programs put in place during the Linder years. Implicitly, in taking up where Linder left off, Kearns seemed to accept the criticisms leveled at his predecessor at the end of his term – that he had made the Bank too cautious.

Early on in his tenure, Kearns had the Bank restructure its Discount Loan Facility. Originally established in 1966, it provided loans to commercial banks of up to 50 percent against their export debt obligations. The Commercial Bank Export Credit Loan program, as it was officially known, languished because its approval procedures were complicated and unwieldy. Ex-Im substantially revised the discount facility in July 1969, with further refinements in December 1971. Essentially, the Bank redesigned the program to offer full liquidity for commercial banks holding medium-term export debt obligations. Under the reorganized plan, Ex-Im offered commercial banks an advance commitment for a

76 Ibid., pp. 8–11; Senate, Report, *Export-Import Bank Amendments of 1971*, Committee on Banking, Housing and Urban Affairs, 92nd Congress, 1st Session (Washington, DC: Government Printing Office, 1971), pp. 3–4 (hereafter *Export-Import Bank Act Amendments of 1971*).

77 Statement by Henry Kearns Regarding Final Passage of the Eximbank Finance Act of 1971 (S. 581), n.d., Library, Ex-Im.

discount loan against 100 percent of its export obligations. Banks could obtain these discount loans any time during the life of the obligation, and they could prepay without penalty.[78]

Private sector interest in the program increased dramatically under Kearns. The number of commercial banks using the facility rose from 83 to 189 by the end of 1973, although most of the business originated with a few big money-center banks. Commitments, however, jumped from 45 in fiscal year 1969 to 2008 in fiscal year 1973.[79] In essence, Ex-Im redesigned the facility to encourage private sector lending for export financing at favorable market rates. The commercial banks found the program attractive in times of rising market rates, since Ex-Im pegged its rates at between 5 and 6.75 percent in the early 1970s. Thus, commercial banks could use the Ex-Im Discount Loan Facility to ensure themselves low-cost funds when necessary. Whether the facility specifically increased exports was a question raised by OMB after Kearns' term in office. In the mid-1970s, the Bank tightened the program and raised rates in response to OMB. Later in the decade, despite these changes, interest in the program exploded when market rates increased markedly. Indeed, in fiscal years 1978 and 1979, the program exhausted its budgetary authority before the end of the budget year. Nevertheless, OMB never overcame its skepticism, and the program was terminated in 1983.[80]

In any case, by the end of Kearns' tenure, he listed the discount loan program as an important success.[81] He had an equally positive view of the Cooperative Financing Facility (CFF), a program derived from the Relending Credits Program begun in the late 1950s. The program had extended credit to banks (development, agricultural, and commercial)

78 Memorandum, to William Casey from Richard D. Crafton and James C. Cruse, Subj: "Review and Highlights of the Medium-Term Discount Loan Program," October 21, 1974, Subject Files, Box 16, "Discount Program 9/3/69–12/8/75" folder, RG 275.

79 Additional Statement, Henry Kearns, October 31, 1973, attached to Statement Before Senate, Subcommittee on International Finance, Committee on Banking, Housing and Urban Affairs, 93rd Congress, 1st Session, October 29, 1973, Library, Ex-Im.

80 Memorandum, to William Casey from Richard D. Crafton and James C. Cruse, Subj: "Review and Highlights of the Medium-Term Discount Loan Program," October 21, 1974, Subject Files, Box 16, "Discount Program 9/3/69–12/8/75" folder, RG 275; "Review of Eximbank's Export Credit Discount Loan Program, From Inception to December 31, 1980," February 28, 1981, pp. 1–8, "Discount Program Review" folder, POF, Archives, Ex-Im.

81 Kearns Statement, October 29, 1973, p. 5.

in developing countries. Ex-Im covered 90 percent of financing, with a 10 percent cash payment. Bank officials shaped CFF to expand the scope of the languishing relending program. Under the new program, Ex-Im lent 45 percent of the contract value of a sale to a foreign purchaser. A foreign bank would provide another 45 percent credit. If an American bank loaned this second part of the credit, the Bank provided a financial guarantee.[82]

Kearns was enthusiastic. "This program," he said in 1972, "has caught fire."[83] CFF not only contributed to the export side of the trade balance but also encouraged small businesses to export. He saw CFF assisting small and medium-sized foreign firms to acquire U.S. products, often from small American enterprises. By the end of fiscal year 1972, there were CFFs in 42 different countries, and the program continued to grow until the end of 1974. OMB questioned whether CFF was generating new sales or simply syphoning business away from guarantees and insurance. In reality, the program was not particularly cost-effective because it involved numerous small transactions. OMB substantially cut its budget in the late 1970s, and the program was ended in 1981.[84]

Among the first of Kearns' own initiatives was a program to provide preliminary commitments (PCs) to borrowers begun in 1970. He prided himself on learning from his travels and the dialogues he initiated with the Bank's constituencies (exporters, commercial bankers, and foreign purchasers). To make the Bank more responsive to exporter needs – there was persistent criticism that the Bank's approval procedures were cumbersome – he championed a program for advance or preliminary commitments. After providing the Bank with essential information about a proposed transaction, buyers, suppliers, and financial institutions could secure a PC. It is a contingent, nonbinding assurance that Ex-Im financing would be available subject to a detailed application and subsequent approval. Their value as a sales tool was supplemented by the ability of foreign buyers or governments to use PCs to establish

82 "Review of Eximbank's Cooperative Financing Facility, From Inception to December 31, 1980," pp. 1–5, "CFF Review" folder, POF (hereafter "Review of Eximbank's Cooperative Financing Facility").

83 Annual Report for 1972, p. 5.

84 "Review of Eximbank's Cooperative Financing Facility," pp. 5–6; Interview with James C. Cruse, April 3, 2000, pp. 15–17, Library, Ex-Im (hereafter Cruse Interview April 3, 2000); Glick Interview, March 13, 2000, pp. 49–51.

priorities for projects with their countries and to order these demands on foreign exchange.[85]

In the midst of a busy first year in office, Kearns also embraced the concept of a Private Export Funding Corporation (PEFCO). Interest in creating a consortium of private lenders for long-term export finance of capital goods had taken shape in 1967–8, at the end of the Linder years. Walter Sauer, acting chairman between Linder and Kearns, kept the Bank involved in efforts to establish PEFCO. Generally, it was a response to a huge anticipated demand for jet aircraft finance between 1968 and 1978. At the end of the 1960s, the commercial jet aircraft manufacturers planned to introduce a new generation of commercial jet aircraft, especially Boeing's "jumbo" 747. In April 1968, the investment banking house of Dillon, Reed & Company issued a confidential study on aircraft financing commissioned in October 1967 by the Jet Aircraft Export Financing Committee for the Bankers' Association for Foreign Trade (BAFT). The report estimated that during the next decade about $13 billion would be spent on aircraft purchases. About $7 billion of that, the study suggested, would need to come from the Ex-Im or private banks.[86] Concern about aircraft finance heightened when, in fiscal year 1968–9, the Office of Management and Budget placed a $200 million restriction – later removed through Kearns' efforts – on Bank lending for aircraft. Officials at Ex-Im, NAC, and treasury believed that the private sector alone would be unable to provide the necessary financing.[87]

Operational details for PEFCO were worked out during the fall and winter of 1968. Because there was to be a change in administration in January 1969, the NAC postponed until after then final approval of the new arrangement.[88] The expansion-minded Kearns, along with the new

85 "Summary and Conclusions," p. 3, Documents on "Interest Rate History," 1976, POF; Jordan Jay Hillman, *The Export-Import Bank at Work: Promotional Financing in the Public Sector* (Westport, CT: Quorum Books, 1982), pp. 125–6; Annual Report for 1971, p. 36; Corette Interview, April 19, 2000, pp. 7–8.

86 "Feasibility Study for Jet Aircraft Export Financing Committee of the Bankers' Association for Foreign Trade," Dillon, Read & Company, Inc., April 1, 1968, POF; Minutes, E-Staff Meeting, May 14, 1968 (Bureau of Economic Affairs), 1960–1969, RG 59.

87 Glick Interview, March 13, 2000, pp. 21–4; Hess Interview, April 3, 2000, pp. 60–5; Letter, to John C. Colman, Department Assistant Secretary of Treasury, January 17, 1969, Records of Assistant Secretary of Treasury for International Affairs – NAC, NAC Doc/Suppl., Box 51, RG 56.

88 Memorandum, Treasury Department to NAC, Subj.: PEFCO, May 2, 1969, Records of Assistant Secretary Treasury for International Affairs, NAC Docs/Suppl., Box 51, RG 56.

administration's treasury officials, readily approved. Ultimately, PEFCO received its corporate charter in April 1970 and opened for business the following May.[89]

PEFCO's stockholders initially represented a consortium of fifty-five commercial banks, seven industrial exporting corporations, and an investment banking enterprise. Together they endeavored to assemble private capital to finance American exports of heavy capital goods, although they provided little capital of their own. PEFCO made funds available at fixed rates and for longer terms than commercial banks were willing to provide. It purchased the obligations of foreign importers, for which Ex-Im had guaranteed the principal and interest. These obligations were then used as security for PEFCO's long-term notes, which were to be sold in the United States and abroad. The Bank's guarantee minimized the risks for purchasers of PEFCO's debt and encouraged its marketing in large quantities and at favorable terms, matters of prime importance because initially PEFCO was thinly capitalized by its owners.[90]

The Bank had a substantial role in PEFCO's conduct of business. Ex-Im was heavily involved in the corporation's most significant money management decisions. The Bank approved each of PEFCO's financings, issuances of long-term debt, and investment of surplus funds. PEFCO was flexible in its lending. Generally, the early loans involved PEFCO's shareholders with the Ex-Im, which kept the Bank's exposure to 50 percent or less. Ex-Im accepted the longer maturities, while the participating commercial banks took the short- and medium-term securities. Maturities varied, but in its first two years PEFCO did arrange a loan for fourteen years. In its first two years of operation, PEFCO financed – in addition to commercial jet aircraft – nuclear power plants and equipment for mining, steel mills, petroleum refining, petrochemical operations, and oceanographic surveys.[91]

PEFCO got off to a relatively slow start. In 1972 it only funded $88 million of loans out of requests for quotations on about $1 billion of business. But it was a year in which credit from other sources was

89 Hillman, pp. 127–8.

90 Ibid., p. 128; *Second Annual Report*, Private Export Funding Corporation, 1972 (New York: PEFCO, 1973), pp. 5–6.

91 *Second Annual Report*, PEFCO, 1972, pp. 5–6, 15.

readily available, even for export lending.[92] PEFCO's business picked up in the later 1970s, as credit circumstances changed. By then PEFCO was participating in lending for major purchases, and in 1980 Ex-Im used it to meet loan demand when it surged above the Bank's budgeted legislative limitations.

PEFCO was not the only new Bank program to leverage its assets by working with the private sector. From early in his term, Kearns championed what became known as a participation program, an initiative to reduce the Bank's authorization of direct credits by using financial guarantees. In June 1969, only three months after he took office, the NAC approved a participation financing program. Ex-Im's board followed suit in July. The country's trade and payments problems prompted insistent political rhetoric about the need to enlarge American exports. Privately, treasury officials made similar arguments to Bank officials and pressed them to devise some new approaches. Commercial interest rates for export financing had risen to between 8 and 10 percent. Because the Bank was laboring under the consequences of the unified budget concepts adopted in fiscal 1969, its funds for direct lending were constrained. So, meeting the goals of export expansion required innovative activity on the part of the Bank.[93]

Kearns' first public speech as Ex-Im president hinted at the approach to the problem. "Cooperation between Exim and the financial community must be improved." He went on to say that "undoubtedly ways can be found to make greater use of the Bank's guarantee program so that funds of the Export-Import Bank can gain leverage." Under the participating financing program approved by the Bank in the summer of 1969, an equal division of loan financing between the Export-Import Bank and a commercial bank was standard. Typically, after a cash payment of 10 percent of the contract value of the purchase, the Bank and commercial lender each took responsibility for 45 percent of the remaining 90 percent. Often the Bank supported the commercial bank's loan with its guarantee.[94]

[92] Ibid., p. 3.

[93] Paper, "A Review of EXIMBANK's Participation Financing Program, FY 1970 through 1972," pp. 1–3, September 26, 1972, "Participation Program" folder, POF (hereafter "A Review of EXIMBANK's Participation Financing Program"); Memorandum (Walter Sauer), October 22, 1976, "Evolution of Financial Guarantees," "Evolution Financial Guarantees – 1976," folder, POF.

[94] Ibid., pp. 4(quote)–5; Hess Interview, April 3, 2000, pp. 11–12.

Table 4.2 *Selected Authorizations, Fiscal 1969–1973 (millions of dollars)*

Fiscal Year	Total Loans	Direct Loans	Guarantees (Long Term)	Insurance
1969	1295.2	730.6	112.3	824.6
1970	2208.8	1187.6	335.5	1147.9
1971	2362.1	1451.7	1076.7	1615.9
1972	3284.6	1951.7	1190.5	2202.3
1973	4053.5	2046.5	1490.1	2472.8

Source: Appendix B, Summary of Authorizations.

During Kearns' term, long-term financial guarantees rose markedly, from $112.3 million in 1969 to $1,490.1 million in 1973 (see Table 4.2). Most of the transactions in the participation finance program were for amounts above $1 million and for terms beyond five years.[95]

These changing participation percentages further leveraged the Bank's assets. In offering guarantees, Ex-Im only drew 25 percent – because of accepted policy toward fractional reserves – against its lending authority. Kearns also encouraged an increase in the Bank's offering of insurance through the Foreign Credit Insurance Association to exporters (for the most part small- and medium-sized businesses) engaged in short- and medium-term transactions. Insurance authorizations rose sharply between fiscal year 1969 and fiscal year 1973, from $824.6 million to $2,472.8 million.[96]

Participation program financing proved successful because it met the major concerns of commercial banks engaged in financing exporters. For one thing, they did not have to get into long-term financing; they were able to keep to the medium-term, five-year maximum maturities that they preferred. Ex-Im accepted the later maturities in the financing jointly offered with commercial banks that took the earlier maturities. Also, the Bank's program allowed the commercial banks to finance their part of the loans at market rates. Ex-Im's provision of financial guarantees also addressed commercial bankers' long-standing concerns about the higher risk and, because of the Bank's administrative role in the loans, greater costs for underwriting and

95 Kearns Statement, October 29, 1973, pp. 7, 10; "A Review of EXIMBANK's Participation Financing Program," pp. 6–10.

96 Appendix B, Summary of Authorizations.

administering credits that they believed were inherently higher in overseas lending.[97]

Kearns and his colleagues appreciated the participation program because it benefitted the Bank in a number of ways. It reduced private sector criticism that Ex-Im took business away from commercial banks. To be sure, this criticism seemed misplaced in view initially of the small number of such financial institutions that cooperated with the Bank. Nevertheless, criticism that the Bank appeared to be competing with those who would be willing to provide export credits was not something that the politically attuned Kearns wanted to hear. In fact, as it turned out, the participation financing program contributed to the number of banks cooperating in some form with Ex-Im. By the end of 1972, 139 commercial banks were involved in export financing, up from 27 in 1969.[98]

The participation program was important to the Bank for other reasons too. It allowed Bank officials to demonstrate attentiveness to the growing concerns among American exporters about foreign government's export credit agencies subsidizing their exporters. Indeed, these concerns manifested themselves in Congress' consideration of the Bank's reauthorization in 1971. Congress specifically mandated that the Bank produce a semiannual report on competitiveness, and directed the Ex-Im "in the exercise of its functions to provide guarantees, insurance, and extensions of credit at rates and on terms and conditions which are competitive with the Government-supported rates and terms and other conditions available for the financing of exports from the principal countries whose exporters compete with United States exporters."[99] The addition of this change to the Bank's longstanding mandate to seek reasonable assurance of repayment and financial security would create tension that would not be finally resolved until the passage of legislation in 1983.

In any event, Kearns justified the Bank's financial participation program in terms of the competitiveness of American exporters. In particular, he defended Ex-Im's adherence to a fixed 6 percent rate for its part of a participation loan. When commercial banks had to raise their rates because of higher costs for money in private markets, the Bank's fixed rate provided for a loan that overall was at below market rates. Kearns

97 "A Review of EXIMBANK's Participation Financing Program," pp. 9–10.

98 Ibid., pp. 6–10; Kearns Statement, October 29, 1973, p. 10.

99 PL 92–126. The semiannual reports became annual reports in fiscal year 1981.

Table 4.3 *Government Rates and Ex-Im Lending Rates*

Year	10-Year Government Bond	Ex-Im Rate	Spread
1969	6.67	6	−0.67
1970	7.35	6	−1.35
1971	–	6	−0.16
1972	6.21	6	−0.21
1973	6.84	6	−0.84
1974	7.56	7.42	−0.14
1975	7.99	8.13	0.14
1976	7.61	8.5	0.89
1977	7.42	8.43	1.01
1978	8.41	8.2	−0.21
1979	9.44	8.2	−1.24
1980	11.46	8.61	−2.85
1981	13.91	9.79	−4.12

Source: Rita M. Rodriguez, "Exim's Mission and Accomplishments, 1934–1984," in Rita M. Rodriguez, ed., *The Export-Import Bank at Fifty: International Environment and the Institution's Role* (Lexington, MA: Lexington Books, 1987), p. 33.

believed that this would strengthen American exporters in competing with those overseas who received benefits from ECAs.[100]

Ultimately, adhering to a fixed rate in a time of rising commercial and government lending rates later created enormous problems for the Bank. Such a gap ("spread" in the Bank's parlance) became the starting point for much of the pointed criticism that mounted during the middle 1970s (see Table 4.3).

But Kearns in the early 1970s was not so concerned, even as market rates began to rise in 1973. To be sure, rates fluctuated, and the gap opened and closed. Long-term government bonds declined from 6.59 percent in 1970 to 5.63 in 1972. Similarly, the prime rate gyrated as the Nixon administration tried to cope with inflation – and secure the president's reelection. It went from 8.5 percent in 1970 to 5.8 in 1972.[101]

Under the circumstances, Kearns believed the Bank needed to be consistent and predictable. Stable relations with exporters were important, in his view, to firmly establish the Ex-Im as an aid to American exports. "Just as the Bank did not reduce its rate when private funds fell below

100 Kearns Statement, October 29, 1973, p. 7.
101 Matusow, pp. 186–90.

6 percent," he said in his last testimony before Congress, "it would be shortsighted today and possibly disastrous to our long-range needs, to lose the stabilizing and encouraging effects of known dependable financing support in the future."[102]

Nevertheless, during the five-month interim between Kearns' departure and William J. Casey's arrival (March 14, 1974), the Bank's board increased its lending rate from 6 to 7 percent. Within a year, most of the Bank's credits were at 8 percent. But the consequences of rapid expansion, and below market rates, hallmarks of the Kearns administration, began to be felt in the Casey years. Indeed, between fiscal year 1972 and fiscal year 1973, the Bank's net income declined from $148 million to $140 million, presaging further decreases under Casey. In fiscal year 1974, net income was $110 million; in fiscal year 1975, $81 million.[103] Declining income, though, proved to be only one of the problems that the Bank faced in the mid 1970s. By that time, the international economy was experiencing tectonic changes with far-reaching ramifications for the Bank.

[102] Kearns Statement, October 29, 1973, p. 7.
[103] Annual Report for 1974, pp. 32–3; Annual Report for 1975, pp. 18–20.

Export-Import Bank Officers

Fig. 1 Jesse H. Jones was director of the Reconstruction Finance Corporation (RFC) and secretary of Commerce during the Roosevelt administration. He was chairman of the Export-Import Bank 1941–1943.

Fig. 2 Five chairmen of the Export-Import Bank at the celebration of its 50th anniversary in 1984. From left to right William J. Casey (1974–76), John L. Moore, Jr. (1977–1981), William McChesney Martin, Jr. (1946–1949), William H. Draper III (1981–86), and Henry Kearns (1969–1973).

Fig. 3 President Dwight D. Eisenhower (right) cuts a cake at the Bank's celebration marking its 25th anniversary on February 12, 1959, with Chairman Samuel C. Waugh (1955–61).

Fig. 4 President Dwight D. Eisenhower addresses the staff of the Export-Import Bank at its 25th anniversary celebration at the Bank on February 12, 1959. Chairman Samuel C. Waugh (1955–61) (far left) looks on.

Fig. 5 Vice President Al Gore (center), Chairman James A. Harmon (1997–2001) (right), and Director Rita M. Rodriguez (1982–1999) (left) and staff gather following Vice President Gore's congratulatory remarks marking the 65th anniversary of the Export-Import Bank in 1999.

Fig. 6 The Board of Directors of the Export-Import Bank in 1966. (Seated from left to right) Vice Chairman Walter C. Sauer (1962–76), Chairman Harold F. Linder (1961–1968) and Director Elizabeth S. May (1964–69). (Standing left to right) Director Hobart Taylor (1965–68) and Director Tom Lilley (1965–72).

Fig. 7 Chairman Stephen M. DuBrul, Jr., 1976–77.

Fig. 8 Chairman John A. Bohn, 1986–89. He was also Vice Chairman, 1984–86.

Fig. 9 Chairman John D. Macomber, 1989–92 (right) and Vice Chairman Eugene K. Lawson, 1989–93 (left).

Fig. 10 The Board of Directors of the Export-Import Bank in 1994. (From left to right) Director Rita M. Rodriguez (1982–99), Director Marie Lusia Haley (1994–99), Chairman Kenneth D. Brody (1993–95), Vice Chairman (1993–96) and later Chairman (1996–97) Martin A. Kamarck and Julie Belaga (1994–99).

5

NEW MANDATES AND NEW LIMITS

INTRODUCTION

There were momentous changes in the international economy in the 1970s, an altered environment that heavily impacted the Bank. The institutional arrangements and the "rules of the game" that had structured international economic activity since the end of World War II were undone in the 1970s. U.S. trade and payments surpluses turned into deficits, which among other things accelerated pressures to devalue the dollar. Consequently, in August 1971, President Richard M. Nixon abandoned the gold-backed, dollar-based fixed exchange rate system established at Bretton Woods in 1944. Its demise was followed by a depreciation of the dollar against major currencies, and ultimately a system of floating exchange rates. In 1973–4, the Organization of Petroleum Exporting Countries (OPEC) delivered the first of its oil shocks by quadrupling per barrel petroleum prices. One immediate consequence was increasing inflation and higher interest rates in the industrialized world and hardship in the developing countries. Most countries importing oil believed they needed to stimulate exports to counter the negative impact of OPEC prices on their balance of payments. Over the longer term, the recycling of "petrodollars" distorted international capital flows, which set the stage for the debt crisis of the 1980s.

These changes helped end the favorable economic conditions in the United States in the 1960s. The American economy gave way to slower growth, lower profits, and higher levels of inflation and unemployment in the 1970s. Each of the administrations of the 1970s – those of Nixon, Ford, and Carter – struggled with the problems of stagflation, the unusual combination of growing inflation *and* unemployment.

For the most part, the Ford and Carter administrations focused on inflation, and in turn the need to tighten the government's budget, restrain spending, and raise interest rates. Under these circumstances, increasing foreign competition became both a domestic and a foreign policy concern. As for the former, increasing imports challenged the market share of major firms in key industries, igniting a debate over the country's competitiveness. In regard to the latter, the export policy practices of the United States' major industrial competitors became a significant issue, as competition in state-sponsored export finance intensified. The Bank took part in long-term negotiations within the Organization for Economic Cooperation and Development on the terms of export support provided by the major industrial powers' export credit agencies.

Within the Bank, the mid 1970s were marked by a high level of introspection about the consequences of the altered international and domestic economies. Moreover, by the time Kearns left in 1973, some in Congress focused more critically on the Bank than ever before. Serious criticisms first clearly manifested themselves during William J. Casey's term (March 1974 to January 1976), fostered in large part by probing critiques of Bank operations by the General Accounting Office (GAO) and the Office of Management and Budget. Casey defended the Bank's promotional policies, while reining in its operations somewhat. But his successor, Stephen M. DuBrul, Jr., president from January 1976 to May 1977, took the criticisms seriously. He scaled back lending significantly, while entertaining fundamental questions about Ex-Im and its operations in the face of changed circumstances – the troubled economic picture in the United States and new international realities centered on floating exchange rates and skyrocketing commodity prices.

Congress, for its part, also struggled to cope with the new economic environment. While a few prominent members criticized the Bank, others reflected the widespread concern about the country's ability to compete in the new international economic environment. One consequence was new mandates for the Ex-Im in 1971 and 1974. They charged the Bank with responsibility to help American exporters cope with increased foreign competition in overseas markets. As a result, the Bank worked jointly with other members of the OECD to find common ground on government-sponsored export assistance. After much discussion, the first of a series of relatively weak understandings was reached in 1976.

The Bank also found itself a target for critics as it sought to fulfill its traditional role as an instrument of foreign policy. The results were not always good. In Zaire, to help the United States promote "state building," the Bank extended large credits for a complex project that quickly went into default. To support the Nixon administration's policy of detente with the USSR, Ex-Im helped finance East–West trade. Prominent members of Congress, however, opposed assisting the USSR and other communist countries. Congressional critics also raised questions about trading with noncommunist countries that had poor human rights records (South Africa and Chile). These disputes, as a result, led Congress to legislate constraints on some Bank activities.

DuBrul was followed by John L. Moore, Jr. (May 1977 to March 1981) who refocused the Bank on export promotion. Enthusiastically promoting exports proved to be a popular policy because the country was running large trade deficits. Moore approached this goal with an enthusiasm akin to, if not fully matching, that of Kearns. One consequence – unintended to be sure – of the promotional policies of both these presidents was ultimately to make the Bank financially vulnerable. "Subsidies" became a source of criticism in the Moore years, as the Bank lent money below prevailing market rates, even though Ex-Im had to continue to acquire its capital at higher rates. Critics in Congress, academia, OMB, and GAO referred to the spread between these two rates as the Bank's subsidy, and questioned the wisdom and necessity of such a policy.

Ultimately, critics were asking whether the Bank's traditional role was appropriate to the circumstances of the economically troubled 1970s. Economic conditions did not improve in the early 1980s, opening the Bank to more searching criticism, this time emanating from the Reagan administration. But overall, Ex-Im also had to face some new realities beginning midway through the 1970s. Congress increased its responsibilities and mandate, especially in regard to American exporters' competitiveness, while regulating more tightly the scope of its activities and limiting its access to federal budget resources.

ADJUSTING TO NEW REALITIES

President Nixon replaced Kearns with William J. Casey. These two chairmen had very different personalities and backgrounds. Casey had a career in Wall Street before turning to public service. And like several earlier Bank presidents he came to the presidency after a brief stint as under secretary of state for economic affairs (1973–4). In terms of personality, Casey had a much more reserved approach to his colleagues and the Bank's customers than the gregarious Kearns.[1] Aside from matters of personal style, Casey's Bank was very different from that of his predecessor. The new president and chairman came in with almost a billion dollars in preliminary commitments outstanding – $700 million beyond the Bank's congressional loan authorization. Casey saw tightening procedures and operations as one of his primary tasks. In this regard, he focused closely on PCs, which he thought had been too easily available under Kearns. He also believed that the Bank needed to be more selective in the kinds of goods it supported for export. He preferred capital goods, such as mining or petroleum drilling equipment, that might help produce materials – such as ores and petroleum – needed in the United States.[2]

Even so, Casey accepted Kearns' analysis of the Bank's financial situation and its mission to promote exports vigorously. Like Kearns he believed that once the Bank began to collect on loans made at high interest rates, revenues would rise. Moreover, Casey did not abandon the Bank's prevailing rhetoric. He too argued that it was not only advancing the interests of the export community but also helping to solve the country's serious domestic and foreign economic problems.[3]

Nevertheless, not everyone applauded Kearns' policies. In particular, the Bank gained an intractable antagonist in Wisconsin's Democratic Senator William Proxmire after Kearns succeeded in having the Bank removed from the unified federal budget in 1971. Proxmire prided himself on ferreting out waste and what he considered unjustified spending, making himself unpopular with both his Democratic and Republican colleagues in Congress. "Waste" was, of course, very much a subjective

[1] Interview with John F. Corette, April 19, 2000, pp. 19, 23–4, Library, Ex-Im (hereafter Corette Interview, April 19, 2000).

[2] Interview with William J. Casey, May 4, 1974, p. 12, Mazo-Mazon Files, Library, Ex-Im (hereafter Casey Interview, May 4, 1974); Draft, "William J. Casey, March, 1974 to January, 1976," p. 1, Mazo-Mazon Files, Library, Ex-Im.

[3] Casey Interview, May 4, 1974, pp. 4–8; Jordan Jay Hillman, *The Export-Import Bank at Work: Promotional Financing in the Public Sector* (Westport, CT: Quorum Books, 1982), pp. 131–2; Export-Import Bank of the United States Annual Report for 1974 (Washington, DC: Export-Import Bank of the United States, 1974), pp. 7–12; Annual Report for 1975, pp. 2–8.

judgment in a legislative body convinced of the rightness of supporting programs to benefit constituents. But the senator gained significant public approval during the 1970s through adept use of the media. He became famous for his "golden fleece awards," given to hapless government programs that the senator believed to be wasteful. As such, Proxmire's interest in the Bank was not the kind of congressional attention to be desired. While the Bank was never the major target of Proxmire's fire, he proved a dogged critic.

But trouble with Senator Proxmire was only the beginning of growing criticism that marked the 1970s. Ex-Im's leadership had to adjust to a more contentious atmosphere, as critics appeared not only in Congress but also in the executive branch and academia. Most of the antagonists recognized a need to promote exports and conceded some role for the Ex-Im. But they came to question both the Bank's justifications for, and methods of, promoting exports. In essence, the critics were making the case that the Bank had not adjusted itself to new realities, both in the domestic and international economies. The Bank, they believed, rolled on, especially under Kearns and later Moore, accelerating its lending and programs without sufficient attention to whether rationales and policies developed in the 1950s and 1960s fit the actualities of the 1970s.

Ex-Im, of course, was not defenseless in the face of a critical assault on its basic assumptions. Many in Congress accepted the Bank's still-powerful argument that it made a profit and paid dividends to the treasury. Leaders of organized exporter groups, as well as top officials of major corporations financing sales through the Bank, defended the Ex-Im's unabashed commitment to promoting exports, and honed their skills at making such arguments. And important members of Congress also continued to defend the Bank as an institution that helped create American jobs.

Most of the criticisms in the 1970s did not result in the kind of negative publicity it received in the 1960s over secret financing of military purchases. But the questions raised about the Ex-Im in these years persisted for much of the 1970s, and beyond. They had a staying power precisely because they were not sensational – they were not the kind of issues that grabbed media attention and then fizzled. Politics, of course, was not absent from the debates over the Bank in the 1970s, and there was a large heated political controversy over aircraft financing in 1980 (the Ansett case).

Many times in the 1970s the Ex-Im's sharpest critics were public sector analysts. They saw it as their responsibility to track the Bank's finances and also to square its leaders' rhetoric with its accomplishments. Critics were also academics – usually economists – trained to weigh costs and benefits or to test the utility and welfare benefits of long-standing policies. Thus, these critics questioned the Bank's financial soundness, whether it was receiving and providing unwarranted subsidies, and the extent to which its policies contributed to exports that would not have occurred without its assistance ("additionality").

Cost-cutting also gained the attention of members of Congress interested in reducing federal spending. More generally, in the aftermath of the Vietnam War and then the Watergate scandal, many legislators were looking to reassert congressional authority against the executive branch.

Bank officials replied to the substantive issues as best they could. Clearly, the days of "benign estrangement," as one Bank document characterized previous relations with Congress, were over.[4] One tangible result of all the criticism was the creation in January 1975 of a policy planning office to provide analytical background material needed to address the kinds of questions underlying the criticisms of the Bank.

In essence, though, the questions of the 1970s stemmed from a need to understand the implications of the rapidly changing environments in which the Bank operated. There were transformations in the world and domestic economies, in international relations after the Vietnam War in 1975, and in American politics and government following the Watergate scandal. These circumstances undermined public trust in the federal government, especially the executive branch. During the late 1960s and the 1970s, the latter seemed to have abandoned American leadership in the institutions of the international economy, followed inconsistent policies to cope with serious domestic economic problems (growing inflation and unemployment, falling rates of productivity and corporate profits), and failed to maintain a bipartisan foreign policy.

These changing circumstances affected the way in which all the Bank's constituencies – Congress, exporters, the GAO, OMB – viewed its work. A changed setting led to altered perceptions by which to judge its effectiveness. Altered conditions also enhanced Congress' expectations

4 Export-Import Bank, Introductory Briefing Book, n.d. (1975?), "Relations With Congress," Policy Office Files, Archives, Ex-Im (hereafter POF).

of the Bank. In what Congress saw as a more competitive world environment, it expected the Bank to help ensure the competitiveness of American exporters.

For much of the 1970s, then, the Bank found itself justifying its mission, adjusting policies and programs to critiques when necessary, and meeting heightened expectations. The decade was a time of tension, as old ways came up against new realities, and critics with power demanded that attention be paid to the need to adjust. Much of the required change resulted from altering economic circumstances rather than the demands of policy. Nevertheless, the Bank still had its statutory responsibilities and ardent constituencies to support, and in presidents Kearns and Moore, leaders who believed that the Bank despite the critics needed aggressively to promote exports. The three reauthorizations in the decade often brought issues to a head, forcing the Bank each time not only to come to terms with its critics but also to reexamine how rapid change in its environment might in fact require it to alter or abandon some aspect of its programs.

Exempting the Bank from the unified federal budget in 1971 caused the first set of criticisms. Senator Proxmire argued that the step dislodged the Ex-Im from "the discipline of the budget process," from "budgetary restraints or ceilings."[5] Fundamentally, he objected to privileging Ex-Im over other federal loan programs designed to help farmers, small business, and low- and moderate-income purchasers of homes, all of which remained subject to spending constraints in the unified budget. Proxmire also seized on the issue because he was a strong proponent of congressional prerogative. He believed it was compromised – especially that of the congressional appropriations committees – by exempting the Bank from limitations on annual loan commitments.[6]

In making his criticisms, Proxmire raised fundamental questions about the Bank's mission and accomplishments. He challenged its claims about assisting exports and the balance of payments. For one thing, because exports were "booming" – there had been a 25 percent increase between 1968 and 1970 – he disputed the linear connection between Ex-Im activity and exports that Kearns and others claimed

5 "Individual Views of Mr. Proxmire," *Export-Import Bank Act Amendments of 1971*, Report of the Committee of the Committee on Banking, Housing and Urban Affairs, United States Senate, 92nd Congress, 1st Session, 1971, p. 13.

6 Ibid., pp. 13–14.

for the Bank's policies. For another, Proxmire seized on what he called the "phony" arguments about the balance of payments. Because Ex-Im loans took so long to be paid, he argued that whatever effect the Bank's lending had on the balance of payments would take time. And, even if the Bank contributed to assisting the balance of payments, he did not want its ability to lend for exports to take precedence over federal loans to groups he thought socially as important as exporters.[7]

Proxmire also raised a question about what he called the Bank's back-door subsidies from the treasury. Subsidies was one of the most dogged issues the Ex-Im faced in the 1970s, and after. Critics meant two different things when they talked about the Bank's subsidies: what Ex-Im provided to borrowers and what the Bank received from the government. In Proxmire's case, he was referring to subsidies the treasury provided to the Bank. To Proxmire the Bank's backdoor subsidy resulted from its use of the government's capital ($1 billion in original capital stock and $1.2 billion in retained earnings) at a "ridiculously low rate." During 1970, he pointed out, the yield on treasury obligations was 7.4 percent. Hence, in his calculation, the interest it cost the federal government in financing the Bank for the year was $162 million (7.4 percent of $2.2 billion). Because the Bank only paid $50 million in dividends to the government, the senator maintained that the Ex-Im in effect was only paying 2.5 percent on the government's investment in the Bank. The situation was compounded because the Bank retained earnings of $60 million in 1970. The difference between what the Bank paid in dividends against what the treasury could have earned from the Ex-Im's capital was what the senator referred to "as a hidden subsidy paid by the taxpayer." Moreover, Proxmire maintained, there was another hidden subsidy because the Bank could borrow from the treasury at rates below that department's own cost of funds.[8]

In 1971, Proxmire's critique made little impression outside of Congress. And, in any event, it did not stop the legislation conferring the Bank off-budget status. But Proxmire continued to keep the Bank in his sights. What got more attention than Proxmire's criticisms was a GAO report – "Essentiality of Export-Import Bank Capital Loan Financing in Expanding United States Exports" – issued in the spring

[7] Ibid., pp. 14–17.
[8] Ibid., pp. 17–18.

1972. By law, the GAO annually audited the Bank's financial statements and made a report upon which the comptroller general issued an opinion. The Bank responded vigorously to a draft copy of the highly critical report – Bank Executive Vice President Don Bostwick publically called it a "hatchet job" – nevertheless, it raised questions the Bank would hear again and again. The most significant was perhaps the questions GAO raised about the criteria the Bank used in selecting what loans to authorize. GAO's report focused on $10 million – out of loans of $387 million – to Japan for the purchase of aircraft and thermal and nuclear power plants. GAO also criticized the Bank for being a lender of "first resort" instead of "last resort." Because of its below-market lending rates, the report maintained, the Bank probably took business away from commercial banks. The report came down hard on Ex-Im officials for not determining fully whether private financing was available before authorizing its own loans. GAO also concluded that the Bank probably hurt rather than helped the country's balance-of-payments position. Since Japan had ample dollar reserves, its purchasers most likely could have financed the export transactions fully on their own. As such, the funds would have been paid immediately to the American companies rather than through a long-term repayment to the Ex-Im. If the Bank was to be involved in concessional financing, the report concluded, its lending should be directed at less-developed countries.[9]

Kearns responded vigorously to the draft GAO report. Balance-of-payments problems and growing competition for exporters justified moving quickly, Kearns pointed out in a lengthy (38-page) letter to Elmer B. Staats, comptroller general. To back him up, Kearns collected numerous letters from leading manufacturers selling aircraft and power equipment to Japan – Boeing, McDonnell Douglas, United Aircraft, General Electric, and Westinghouse. They too were highly critical of the GAO report and supported the work of the Bank in getting business in Japan.[10]

Kearns was defensive about the critique's focus on Bank procedures in selecting customers and determining whether commercial financing was available. Bank officials contended that it would be a "waste of time" to take every loan proposal it received to commercial banks to

9 "Eximbank Abused Low-Rate Lending Power, GAO Says," *American Banker* (n.d., probably February 1972), p. 1, c. r., Library, Ex-Im (hereafter "Eximbank Abused Low-Rate Lending Power, GAO Says").

10 Kearns to Staats, March 10, 1972, "GAO Loan Program, 1973" folder, POF.

determine whether they might be interested.[11] Certainly, from the Bank's perspective, such a time-consuming process was not always possible, especially in a time of a fast-growing loan portfolio. Ultimately, however, under Casey, the Bank went through a reorganization designed, among other things, to provide more careful case-by-case analysis of the need for Bank financing.[12]

The arguments over the 1972 GAO report eventually passed. But two issues the report raised were eventually taken up by others in the 1970s. One was concern about the consequences of the spread between the Bank's loan and market rates. The other issue was what later came to be called additionality, that is, the question of what kind of Ex-Im activity made possible exports that might not otherwise have occurred in the absence of Bank financing.

The appearance of spreads and subsidized lending brought the Bank to the attention of academics, especially economists. Indeed, Senator Proxmire commissioned an analysis of export-credit subsidies and exports. Conducted by a professional economist, the study concluded – in support of a point Proxmire made earlier – that there was not a correlation between Bank activity and U.S. export levels. Other early academic studies focused on the consequences of below-market financing. As such, they provided a body of analysis later utilized by other critics of Ex-Im.[13]

Criticism of the Bank picked up in the mid-1970s prompted by declining income and the interest rate spread between its borrowing and lending. The Bank's 1974 reauthorization became the occasion for its antagonists to insist on changes in policies and operations. Soon after the White House announced that the government would seek reauthorization, OMB argued that the Bank be put back into the unified federal budget. This request was an element of the Ford administration's campaign to cope with inflation by reducing government spending.

Bank officials vigorously objected to OMB's position. Casey argued strenuously against restricting the Bank's flexibility, but to no avail.

[11] "Eximbank Abused Low-Rate Lending Power, GAO Says," p. 1.

[12] Annual Report for 1975, p. 3.

[13] "Chronological Log of Significant Publicly Available External/Academic Studies on Ex-Im Bank Programs, Policies, and Economics (As of May 15, 1997)," POF; Interview with James C. Cruse, April 3, 2000, pp. 9–17, Library, Ex-Im (hereafter Cruse Interview, April 3, 2000).

President Ford's attempts to rein in the federal budget had widespread support in Congress, as inflation was becoming a source of growing public anxiety in the United States. The Bank also had little support for staying outside the budget elsewhere within the government. Indeed, at the treasury the controversy over OMB's suggestions provided the opportunity to raise other questions about the Bank. In particular, the treasury's international economic specialists doubted the Bank's claims about promoting an overall increase in the country's exports. The dollar's devaluation following Nixon's abandonment of the Bretton Woods system in August 1971, and especially the international acceptance of floating exchange rates in 1973, convinced many economists that ultimately the country's balance-of-payments problems would take care of themselves. In short, they believed that a devalued dollar – its value routinely adjusted to supply and demand in open currency markets – would do more to spur American exports than the Bank. This view held sway among many believers in the mid 1970s.[14]

Proxmire's arguments would probably have not carried the day alone. But they came in the midst of other criticism and controversies involving the Bank. As a result, Congress removed Ex-Im's special budget status, effective FY 1977.[15] Casey saw the Bank's return to the unified budget as a defeat, especially in regard to the 1971 mandate on competitiveness. Personally, Casey – who never enjoyed nor particularly sought good relations with Congress – believed that short-term political gamesmanship won out over the longer-term national interest in promoting exports. Then, too, Senator Proxmire succeeded in having an amendment added to the 1974 legislation, which demanded that the Bank pay greater attention to its cost of money.[16]

Even so, not everything in the 1974 reauthorization proved negative and restrictive. Indeed, Congress mandated an important new responsibility for the Bank, one that enlarged its responsibilities and henceforth

14 Casey Interview, May 4, 1973, p. 12, Mazo-Mazon Files, Library, Ex-Im. The United States in effect, devalued the dollar when President Richard Nixon abandoned the fixed-exchange rate (Bretton Woods) system on August 15, 1971. In the two years following, the major industrial powers accepted a floating system of exchange rates in a series of international understandings. David Held et al., *Global Transformations: Politics, Economics, and Culture* (Stanford, CA: Stanford University Press, 1999), pp. 199–202.

15 Interview with James K. Hess, April 3, 2000, pp. 17–18, Library, Ex-Im (hereafter Hess Interview, April 3, 2000).

16 Casey Interview, May 4, 1973, pp. 22–3; Corette Interview, April 19, 2000, pp. 17–23.

reshaped how the Bank defined its mission. In particular, Congress required the Bank to address the increased competition American exporters faced from their European and Japanese counterparts. The 1974 reauthorization mandated the Bank to undertake "in cooperation with the export financing instrumentalities of other governments, [to] seek to minimize competition in government-supported export financing [and to] reach international agreements to reduce government-subsidized export financing."[17] These other ECAs were receiving subsidized low-cost financing to promote exports. Ever since OPEC's quadrupling of oil prices in 1973–4, high import costs for petroleum disrupted many countries' balance of payments. Consequently, export promotion became an important public policy goal of the governments of the United States' traditional export competitors. Indeed, throughout the 1970s, countries all over the world increased their efforts to promote exports.

Ensuring a fair competitive environment for American exporters became an increasingly important justification for the Bank's work in the decades to follow. It allowed the Bank to identify itself as contributing to efforts to improve the country's competitive position and to promote trade liberalization. Congress' new requirement reflected more than an acknowledgment of the needs of the well-organized exporter constituency. There was a widespread concern over the general competitiveness of the American economy in the 1970s and 1980s.

Competitiveness as a major public issue got its initial boost from the White House in 1971. With much fanfare, in December of that year, President Nixon released the first official – and truly alarmist – study of the United States' increasing competitiveness problems. It emphasized the impact on American industries and workers of growing imports from Western Europe and especially Japan.[18] Indeed, Nixon had used these countries' restrictive policies toward American exports – which he characterized as "unfair" – to justify the draconian measures announced August 1971 in connection with the end of the Bretton Woods system. In addition to the wage and price controls promulgated at the time, Nixon imposed a temporary 10 percent surcharge on imports.[19]

[17] PL 93-646, Export-Import Bank Amendments of 1974.

[18] Peter G. Peterson, *The United States in the Changing World Economy* (2 vols.; Washington, DC: Government Printing Office, 1971).

[19] Allen J. Matusow, *Nixon's Economy: Booms, Busts, Dollars, and Votes* (Lawrence, KS: University Press of Kansas, 1998), pp. 136–9.

In any event, within months of President Ford's signing of the 1974 reauthorization in January 1975, the Bank had to confront another critical report from the GAO. In the summer, the GAO criticized the Bank's finances in a report, "Need to Improve Financing Practices of the Export-Import Bank of the United States." In the fall, the comptroller general bluntly reported to Congress that the "Eximbank is in financial difficulty."[20] This conclusion rested on the Bank's having expanded its operations without increasing its income. Reserves remained fairly stable, but the exposure on loans, guarantees, and insurance had doubled since 1969. In the future, the report believed that risk would increase because prospects for improving income were not good. GAO and the comptroller traced the Bank's problems to the interest rate spreads, between borrowing funds at rates of interest higher than it expected to earn on loans made with the borrowed funds. Making the problem even more serious was that the Bank financed these long-term loans with short-term borrowings. So the Bank would have to borrow short-term again at undetermined rates of interest to cover future disbursements on long-term loans at fixed rates of interest. The result was an inability to predict what future income would be. GAO bluntly questioned the Bank's ability to remain self-sustaining.[21]

The GAO singled out aircraft loans as illustrating the reasons for the Bank's potential difficulties. Ex-Im had made a heavy commitment to financing commercial aircraft, which accounted for almost 25 percent of the Bank's loans in the previous fiscal year. In particular, the report questioned the wisdom of below-market financing for aircraft sales, especially since the U.S. manufacturers dominated the market. It concluded that "unfortunately, clear guidelines do not always exist for determining whether Eximbank support is needed to promote exports." The report also suggested that "another course of action available to Eximbank would be to reduce its participation in export financing and to examine more closely the need for its financing to ensure the export."[22]

As he had done earlier in regard to the unified budget, Casey took the report's criticisms personally. He saw it as a poor reflection on his

20 Quote from cover page, Comptroller General of the United States, Report to the Congress, *Weakened Financial Condition of The Export-Import Bank of the United States* (Washington, DC: GAO, 1975) (hereafter *Weakened Financial Condition*).

21 Hess Interview, April 3, 2000, pp. 29–30, 56; *Weakened Financial Condition*, pp. 2–4.

22 *Weakened Financial Condition*, p. 7.

financial management of the Bank.[23] For the record, he responded that many of the GAO's recommendations were already being undertaken. Interest rates had been raised, for instance, on aircraft financing in the first half of 1975, and the Bank reduced the percentage of a purchase it would finance – its "cover." The new rates were based on a band between 7 and 9 percent. Guarantee and commitment fees were also increased to augment income. But Casey defended the Bank's borrowing short term at variable rates and lending long term at below market fixed interest rates. It was a way to meet overseas competition. Foreign governments, he asserted, made annual appropriations to provide subsidized below-market interest rates for their exporters. Overall, Casey argued that the GAO was, in effect, overreacting to the potential risks to the Bank's reserves by not giving enough credence to the Bank's loss history. Up until June 1969, Ex-Im had only written off $3.7 million in loans and paid $4.7 million in guarantee and insurance claims. Since that time, an additional $6 million in loans had been written off and $26.2 million in claims paid. Even though these sums were considerably higher than before, the Bank's reserves were, in his opinion, more than adequate to meet any likely eventuality.[24]

These critiques were not the only source of controversy in the mid 1970s. During the Kearns and Casey years, the Bank found itself deeply embedded in disputes over foreign policy. These controversies did as much as any of the critical reports emerging from OMB or GAO to give the Bank a sense of working in a much more contentious atmosphere.

FOREIGN POLICY AND THE BANK

Neither Kearns nor Casey viewed the foreign policy demands placed on the Bank in the 1970s as onerous. Indeed, both expected that satisfying

[23] Hess Interview, April 3, 2000, pp. 29–30.

[24] *Weakened Financial Condition*, Appendix I, Letter, William J. Casey, to Frank M. Zappacosta, Assistant Director, International Division, August 18, 1975. Also see the internal Bank studies prompted by the GAO report: Memorandum, Roy Shrobe to Warren Glick, Subj.: "Net Earnings of Bank After Reasonable Provision for Possible Losses," May 21, 1975 and Report, "Adequacy of the Retained Income Reserve for Contingencies and Defaults," July 1975, both in Introductory Briefing Book, Export-Import Bank of the United States Policy Analysis Staff, POF.

these interests was compatible with the larger Bank goals of expanding exports. As it turned out, Kearns' zeal in promoting business overcame caution in funding a large project in Zaire, a country with substantial political and economic problems. For his part, Casey was also a good soldier in supporting the Nixon and Ford administrations' efforts to increase East–West trade, which the prevailing foreign policy wisdom thought would contribute to detente, that is, normalized relations with communist countries.

Zaire's Inga-Shaba project was a 1,100-mile transmission line from a giant hydroelectric dam at Inga to rich copper mines in Shaba province. Kearns drove the project in the Bank. In Ex-Im's review process in 1972–3, the separate pieces of the project each seemed feasible. Both the U.S. Department of State and the Central Intelligence Agency (CIA) pressed the Bank to take part in the funding. U.S. officials anticipated that the project would contribute to "state building in Zaire" by linking two different parts of the country together in an endeavor with significant economic potential. Moreover, Zaire promised to provide a sovereign guarantee. The worth of such an assurance, however, eventually depended on the price of copper. It was high in 1972–3, but considerably less so later in the decade.[25]

In any event, Ex-Im provided direct credits of $102 million, which represented 45 percent of the initial financing of the project. The Bank guaranteed commercial bank loans of another $102 million, the other 45 percent of the transaction. Because of exploding costs, the Bank extended another $69 million in credits in 1976.[26] Within a year, though, there were repayment problems. In September 1977, the Bank purchased almost $20 million of private bank loans guaranteed by Ex-Im. At that time, the Bank had an additional $186 million of commercial bank guarantees, "some or all of which the Bank may be requested to purchase," according to the 1977 Annual Report. By the end of the

[25] Cruse Interview, April 3, 2000, pp. 25–8; Advance Release, "Eximbank Supports $227.2 Million Sale of U.S. Goods and Services for Transmission Line Project in Zaire," Janaury 14, 1974, Library, Ex-Im.

[26] Advance Release, "Eximbank Supports $227.2 Million Sale of U.S. Goods and Services for Transmission Line Project in Zaire," January 14, 1974, Library, Ex-Im; Hearing, "U.S. Loans to Zaire," Senate, Subcommittee on International Finance, Committee on Banking, Housing, and Urban Affairs, 96th Congress, 1st Session, May 24, 1979 (Washington, DC: Government Printing Office, 1979), pp. 1–2.

1970s, Zaire represented the largest default to that point in the Bank's history. [27]

Troublesome as Zaire proved to be, the major foreign policy problem for the Bank in the 1970s was its provision of credits to finance East–West trade. Its policies became part of a roiling debate over detente with the USSR, which in turn was part of the continuing disputes between the executive and Congress over the making of foreign policy that emerged in the Vietnam War era and its aftermath. Because of its role in promoting East–West trade, the Bank became a target of congressional opponents of such dealings, in particular Senator Adlai E. Stevenson III, who took a special interest in the Soviet Union. Eventually, critics succeeded in prohibiting Ex-Im from such lending. Much to the chagrin of Bank officials, this battle was not an isolated occurrence. Congress also constricted the Bank's activities in an effort to increase policy makers' attention to violations of human rights. Concern over the proliferation of nuclear material prompted Congress similarly to restrict Bank support of such exports.

Increasing East–West trade in the early 1970s initially gained fairly widespread support in Congress, and with the public. It was part of President Nixon's determination to reorient the United States' Cold War policies. He took steps to normalize relations with the People's Republic of China in 1971–2 to gain leverage with that country's erstwhile ally, the Soviet Union. At the same time, he wanted to relax tensions with the USSR. As part of this so-called detente policy, he issued national interest determinations in 1971–2, as required by the Export-Import Act of 1964, which allowed the Bank to finance export sales to the Soviet Union, Poland, and Romania. This followed repeal in mid 1971 of the 1968 prohibition against sales of goods to countries aiding North Vietnam. During 1972, President Nixon made state visits to the USSR and Poland. In the Soviet Union, still-outstanding World War II lend–lease debts were finally settled, opening the way to further trade between the two countries.

Subsequently, in 1973, the Bank concluded agreements for direct loans, guarantees, and insurance with the Soviet Union, Poland, and Romania. The largest single credit in the agreements was $86 million

[27] Annual Report for 1977, p. 18; Hess Interview, April 3, 2000, pp. 27–30.

for the Kama River project, a truck and engine plant in the Soviet Union. In 1974, the Bank authorized a $180 million credit to support the production in the USSR of two nitrogen fertilizers (ammonia and urea) scarce in the United States at the time, using natural gas resources in the production that were abundant there.[28]

Kearns and Casey approved the possibilities of trade opened up by Nixon's detente policy. Casey believed that the United States had been missing opportunities for export sales to the communist bloc for some time. In the 1960s, both the Soviet Union and its Eastern European satellites began to borrow in the West to support the purchase of technologically advanced capital goods. Because of Congress' restrictions on trading with countries supplying the North Vietnamese, Casey believed that the Japanese and West Europeans had established new export markets while the United States remained on the sidelines.[29]

The optimism of 1973–4 did not last. For its part, the Bank found that the Soviet Union was not easy to deal with. The Soviets proved tenacious negotiators questioning the necessity of much of the initial loan documentation.[30] They refused, for example, to provide the financial data that the Bank required for its analyses of the Kama River project. Chase Manhattan Bank, which had 45 percent of the financing, was frustrated in dealing with the Soviet bureaucracy. It syndicated its loan to other commercial banks, and requested Bank guarantees, which at first it had passed up. More generally, as the business community became aware of such problems and frustrations, interest in doing business in the East waned.[31]

In addition, the political situation between the White House and Congress deteriorated late in 1973 and 1974, as the Watergate scandal

[28] Background Paper, "East-West Trade," 1976, POF; Advance Release, "Eximbank and USSR Reach Agreements for U.S. Export Sales Totaling $225 Million," March 21, 1973, Library, Ex-Im; Advance Release, "U.S. Export Sales of $400 Million Plus Energy and Fertilizer Benefits Promised by Eximbank Credit of $180 Million to the U.S.S.R.," May 21, 1974, Library, Ex-Im; "Eximbank and East-West Trade Chronology," Mazo-Mazon file, Library, Ex-Im.

[29] "Eximbank Role in East-West Trade," and Draft Speech, William J. Casey, "Statement of William J. Casey . . . Before the Committee on Commerce, United States Senate," July 15, 1975 in Background Book, Vol. II (n.d., 1975?), POF.

[30] Interview with Stephen G. Glazer, August 7, 2000, pp. 7–10, Library, Ex-Im.

[31] Interview with Karnig Ekizian, Ex-Im Loan Officer, February 22, 1974, Mazo-Mazon files, Library, Ex-Im.

unfolded. Years of frustration over the executive's prosecution of the Vietnam War were exacerbated by evidence of wrongdoing in the White House. Members of Congress were in a mood to assert the institution's authority in foreign affairs. In such an atmosphere, those with special complaints were able to get the support of their colleagues for positions on a host of issues so long as the result would be to strengthen the hand of the legislature as a branch of government.

It was in such a context that the Bank's support of East–West trade became an issue in the long drawn-out consideration of the 1974 Ex-Im reauthorization. It was also a source of dispute in consideration of what became the Trade Act of 1974. Sharp restrictions on Ex-Im financing of trade with the Soviet Union and other communist countries came out of these pieces of legislation. Congressional debate in 1974 was long and at times dramatic. Issues related to the USSR's domestic policies, especially its treatment of Jewish emigrants, became highly emotional. The terms of the Bank's reauthorization reflected these and other concerns, especially about the Soviet Union's petroleum industry. In any event, the legislation limited Ex-Im credits to $300 million for new credits or financial guarantees. In addition, no more than $40 million of that could be used for goods or services needed for research and exploration of fossil fuel energy resources. Furthermore, any loan of $50 million or more to a communist country needed a presidential determination that it was in the United States' national interest.[32]

These restrictions became moot soon after when Congress passed the 1974 Trade Act. That legislation, in effect, precluded Bank financing of exports to the Soviet Union. Before any credits could be extended to a communist country, Congress continued to require that the president had to make a national interest determination. Poland and Yugoslavia were exempted from the provisions of the act, and Nixon successfully pressed the national interest considerations of providing credits for exports to Romania. But the Soviet Union was not included, which put an end to the hopes of those like Kearns and Casey who saw such promise in that aspect of East–West trade.[33]

32 "Eximbank Legislation 1978: Position Paper on East-West Trade," "1976–1978 Position Papers – 1978" folder, Congressional/External Relations Records, Archives, Ex-Im.

33 "Eximbank Legislation 1978: Position Paper on East-West Trade," "1976–1978 Position Papers – 1978" folder, Congressional/External Relations Records, Archives, Ex-Im.

A more assertive Congress affected the Bank in other ways. In October 1977, legislation required that the Ex-Im consider the human rights records of countries where the Bank financed American exports. Since 1964, the U.S. government prohibited Export-Import Bank direct credits to finance exports to South Africa, although there had been some liberalization in the 1970s in regard to the use of guarantees and insurance. On the basis of the 1977 legislation, however, the Bank refused credits for projects in Chile, Brazil, and Uruguay. That refusal, however, upset Rhode Island's Republican Senator John Chafee. Consequently, he included in the reauthorization legislation passed in November 1978 an amendment that deleted the previous restriction in regard to human rights. This Chafee amendment specified that the Ex-Im could not deny a transaction for nonfinancial or noncommercial reasons. Only the president was given the authority to withhold support on such a basis, but he had to determine that to do so was in the national interest. In December 1979, President Carter delegated his authority to make such determinations under the statute to the secretary of state.[34]

Thus, the foreign policy battles of the 1970s brought the Bank into the forefront of some of the most contentious issues of the time. Unpleasant as it was to be in the middle of some of these battles, the Bank as an institution was never the target of congressional displeasure, only some of its policies in support of the administration's foreign policy came under fire. But the Bank did not remain unscathed in the more assertive congressional atmosphere that developed during the 1970s.

Casey left the Bank in January 1976. He made no secret of his frustration over the battles he fought with Congress, OMB, and the treasury. He departed as convinced as when he arrived that the Ex-Im performed important work in the interest of the United States. But he had lost patience with its critics who "want to clip our wings." He had preferred his job at the Department of State, he told interviewers in the 1970s, better than his time at the Bank.[35]

34 Ibid.; Senate, Hearings, "Export-Impact Bank Programs and Budget," Subcommittee on International Finance, Committee on Banking Housing, and Urban Affairs, 96th Congress, 2nd Session, February 22, 1980 (Washington, DC: U.S. Government Printing Office, 1980), p. 38; Briefing Book: Export-Import Bank of the United States, December 1980, Attachment 17, "Countries in Which Eximbank Financing is Restricted for Statutory Reasons," POF.

35 Draft, "William J. Casey, March, 1974 to January, 1976," pp. 2–3, Mazo-Mazon Files, Library, Ex-Im.

A TIME OF RETRENCHMENT AND RETHINKING

The next president exhibited more skepticism about the Bank than either Kearns or Casey. While Stephen M. DuBrul, Jr. (January 1976 to May 1977) did not buy into all the critics, complaints about the Bank, he gave them more credence than his two predecessors. DuBrul had spent his career on Wall Street at Lehman Brothers and Lazard Freres, where he developed a conservative investment banker's belief in markets and skepticism toward government. During his time at Ex-Im, DuBrul developed close ties to the treasury. And he took seriously OMB's concerns about the Bank's finances and some of Senator Proxmire's criticisms. He was the first Bank president to come to terms with critics' attention to additionality.[36]

DuBrul was predisposed to ask fundamental questions – in almost an academic approach – about Ex-Im's policy objectives and the way it went about its business. He spent much of his short tenure at the Bank examining in detail internal operations.[37] Soon after arriving at the Bank, DuBrul reorganized senior staff to streamline policy coordination. He also championed a new records management system and fostered numerous changes in operating procedures. Indeed, many of these changes resulted from DuBrul's "suggestion box"; those who came up with usable suggestions received a financial award. According to DuBrul, during his short tenure, the Bank paid out $42,000 for these ideas, dwarfing the $2,500 paid for suggestions since the founding of the Bank.[38]

In public forums, DuBrul toned down the promotional rhetoric of his two predecessors. Toward that end, he observed in the 1976 Annual Report, that "most exports do not require Eximbank support." He acknowledged that a "significant share" – approximately 16 percent of nonagricultural exports – needed Bank assistance, but he was striving to

[36] Interview with Ray Albright, April 6, 2000, p. 23; Interview with Stephen M. DuBrul, Jr., May 18, 2000, pp. 3–5, 17–18, Library, Ex-Im (hereafter DuBrul Interview, May 18, 2000); Interview with Warren W. Glick, March 13, 2000, p. 29, Library, Ex-Im (hereafter Glick Interview March 13, 2000).

[37] Hess Interview, April 3, 2000, pp. 55–6; Cruse Interview, April 3, 2000, pp. 49–51; Glick Interview, March 13, 2000, p. 29; Interview with John L. Moore, Jr., May 8, 2000, p. 5, Library, Ex-Im (hereafter Moore Interview, May 8, 2000).

[38] Annual Report for 1976, p. 4; DuBrul Interview, May 18, 2000, pp. 7–11.

put some proportion back into discussions of the institution's work.[39] DuBrul also deemphasized the tendency to equate the Bank's activity with growing exports and improved levels of employment.[40]

DuBrul was critical of below-market, subsidized lending. He wanted to bring the Bank back to what he saw as its essential responsibilities. As a matter of routine, he believed that the Bank should set customers' interest rates and maturities close to those of the market. Exceptional or "concessional" rates were to be determined on a case-by-case basis related to the terms provided by overseas competitors.[41] As he said at a House subcommittee hearing in May 1976, "Eximbank's policy is to provide as little support as possible, but as much as required. This policy, which is reflected in all of the Bank's programs, is dictated by the free-market principle that whatever government does unnecessarily is ineffective."[42]

During DuBrul's tenure, the Bank's net income increased 43 percent. Prospects for the Bank also appeared better because government interest rates were for the time being below the Bank's loan rates. So the negative spread disappeared for fiscal 1976 and fiscal 1977. Authorizations for loans, guarantees, and insurance in fiscal year 1976 were only slightly below those of fiscal year 1975. But in fiscal year 1977, the only full fiscal year over which DuBrul had responsibility for the Bank's activities, there was a substantial decline in loan authorizations. Guarantees and insurance also declined, although less sharply than direct credits. Part of these changes could be explained by a worldwide recession, as the international economy continued to adjust to the oil price shocks of 1973–4, and to the downside of an aircraft purchase cycle.

In part, though, these figures – and the relative increase in guarantees and insurance in the mix of authorizations – reflected the chairman's views about the Bank's role in coping with risk. He believed that there would always be political and commercial risk that exporters and commercial banks would not be able to assess or undertake. In fact, in the troubled years of the 1970s, risk in international lending was increasing. In the aftermath of the oil price shock of 1973–4, developing

39 Annual Report for 1976, p. 2.
40 Hillman, p. 135–6.
41 Ibid., p. 135–6.
42 Quoted in Hillman, p. 135.

countries became heavily dependent on private sector borrowing to cover the increased costs of importing petroleum. Consequently, a growing burden of debt service increased the perception of risk in international lending. DuBrul thought that the Bank would have a larger role to play in coping with the uncertainty and risk the private sector could not handle. Thus, the Bank's greatest contribution in this regard would come "primarily through its insurance and guarantee programs."[43]

Overall, DuBrul aimed to adjust the Bank to his perception of growing risks in international lending. But he and others at the Bank and in the administration also understood another emerging challenge stemming from OPEC's 1973–4 price increase. Because oil prices had dramatically increased the cost of imports among both developed and developing countries, governments attempted to stimulate exports through substantial increases in subsidized export credit. The United States' major competitors – Japan, France, and Great Britain – increased authorizations for both credit and insurance to cover a higher percentage of their exports than did the United States. The United States continued to support a larger percentage of its manufactured exports than Canada, Germany, and Italy, but each of these countries provided direct subsidies to exporters.[44]

To meet the increased credit competition, the Bank took two steps. It looked at the impact of foreign official export competition on American exporters on a case-by-case basis. But the Bank also engaged in an international effort to set parameters on the terms governments offered for export credit assistance. In July 1976, DuBrul had the Ex-Im issue a "unilateral declaration" to move export credit practices closer to market terms. This step was part of on-going international negotiations under the auspices of the Organization for Economic Cooperation and Development to ward off a competitive war in the provision of official support for exports. The Bank played a role in these discussions under the mandate handed it by Congress in the 1974 amendments. Ex-Im's 1976 declaration was only one step in what proved to be a long drawn-out, still on-going process. But DuBrul's step established the Bank's place in the commercial negotiations aimed at leveling one part of the playing field in international trade.

[43] Annual Report for 1976, pp. 3, 7.
[44] Ibid., p. 8.

THE BANK AND THE OECD

When the Bank joined the discussions about the policies of public export credit agencies in the 1970s, concern about their behavior was already decades old. Indeed, in 1934, in the same year Congress established the Ex-Im, representatives of three private insurance companies in France, Italy, and Spain, along with Great Britain's official Export Credits Guarantee Department, set up the International Union of Credit and Investment Insurers. The Berne Union (BU), as this voluntary group came to be known, coordinated the insurance and guarantee practices of export credit agencies. In organizing such a group, the BU's founders recognized the pitfalls of an unregulated extension of credit in international trade. Without some common rules among insurers, there might be no restraint on what could turn into a highly destructive export credit race.[45]

In the 1930s and 1940s, governments in most European countries created export guaranty agencies. After World War II, other governments in Europe, and Asia as well, set up export credit agencies. Initially, they were responding to the limited availability of capital in domestic markets and the lack of currency convertibility. By the 1960s, most of these organizations, like the Ex-Im, extended direct loans, loan guarantees, and insurance. At the end of that decade, there was a renewed recognition of the hazards that government-sponsored subsidized export credit posed to orderly export markets. Late in the decade, U.S. officials, increasingly concerned about their own balance of payments problems, looked askance at subsidized export credit policies overseas. Concern turned to alarm as the industrialized countries embarked on a highly competitive export credit race following the 1973 OPEC price increase.[46]

The United States' willingness to cooperate with the OECD in the 1970s represented a reversal of position. Up until that time, both the United States and Canada resisted efforts at cooperation on export credits. With well-developed capital markets, both countries could offer longer-term maturities than the Western Europeans and Japanese, which gave the two North American nations a competitive advantage. Other OECD members preferred a standard of shorter-term credits, not

45 John E. Ray, *Managing Official Export Credits: The Quest for a Global Regime* (Washington, DC: Institute for International Economics, 1995), pp. ix–x, 33–4.

46 Ibid., pp. ix–x.

to exceed five years, or at least prior notification of loans exceeding that limit.[47]

In any event, since its organization in 1960, the OECD had monitored developments in member countries' policies toward export credits. These efforts built on the activities of its predecessor agency, the Organization for European Economic Cooperation (OEEC). In 1963, OECD established an export credit group (ECG) to produce guidelines for export credit agencies. ECG focused on articulating procedures for consultation among OECD members about individual transactions. The long-term goal was to prevent destructive competition by creating a more orderly and disciplined environment for the provision of export credit, as well as guarantees and insurance.[48]

As promoting exports became a more urgent goal of U.S. policy in the early 1970s, the work of the OECD and its ECG looked more promising to American officials. The Bank sent a representative to meetings of the ECG as early as 1970. In that year it was R. H. Rowntree, the economic adviser to the board.[49] In July 1972, the United States joined an OECD-sponsored "exchange of information system" in which members pledged to answer requests for information about on-going or proposed export transactions. The ECG was particularly interested in finding common ground in technologically advanced new fields, such as ground satellite communications systems, nuclear power plants, and aircraft. These areas proved particularly difficult because of the complexity of the technology, the costs of the goods, and the advantages that countries like the United States had in having led in many aspects of the development of these goods. Discussions were slow and tedious.[50]

Contacts at the Berne Union were also important as the Bank saw a need to have a presence in the international community devoted to export issues. The Ex-Im had been a member of the Berne Union since the founding of the FCIA. Indeed, late in the 1970s, John L. Moore became the first Bank president to head the Berne Union.[51] But it was only in the Bank's 1974 annual report that there was mention of OECD

47 Ibid., pp. 45–6.
48 Ibid., p. 45.
49 Annual Report for 1970, p. 14.
50 Ray, pp. 47–8.
51 "Status of Negotiations – Arrangements on Guidelines for Officially Supported Export Credits," Attachment 12 in "Briefing Book: Export-Import Bank of the United States," December 1980, POF (hereafter "Status of Negotiations").

negotiations for the first time.[52] As a rule, a treasury official took the lead in OECD discussions, although he was usually accompanied by a representative from the Ex-Im. President DuBrul, however, followed developments closely during his tenure. After 1977, John Duff, the Bank's deputy general counsel, represented the Bank, and he took an active role in negotiations.[53]

In May 1974 there was an informal consensus on credits for nuclear fuel, which fixed minimum down payments and rates of interest, as well as maximum limits on the duration of credits. Two months later in July, the ECG members reached a similar informal understanding on down payments, interest rates, and maturities for ground satellite communications stations.[54]

In May 1975, so-called standstill understandings were reached on commercial aircraft and nuclear power plants. In effect, they reflected the inability of the participants to agree to more comprehensive or binding terms. More fully developed understandings on the terms of government-supported export financing in these two critical sectors were not reached until the 1980s. In 1975, the understandings simply froze export credit terms. In the future, then, none of the terms were to be more advantageous than those in effect at the time. They set maximum durations for credits for aircraft and nuclear power plants, as well as minimum down payments for the latter. These understandings were quite informal, as one of treasury's negotiators observed. Indeed they were little more than a couple of pages.[55]

But these were not the only discussions about export credit at the time. At higher levels of government, the danger of an all-out export credit war received more and more attention. At the annual meetings of the International Monetary Fund and World Bank in October 1973 in Nairobi, Kenya, officials of the leading industrial countries – United States, France, Germany, Italy, Japan, and Great Britain – got together

52 Annual Report for 1974, p. 12.

53 Interview with John Duff, June 20, 2000, pp. 4–8, 12–14, Library, Ex-Im. (hereafter Duff Interview, June 20, 2000); DuBrul Interview, May 18, 2000, pp. 21–3; Statement, John L. Moore, Jr., March 20, 1978, Senate, Subcommittee on International Finance, Committee on Banking and Urban Affairs, 95th Congress, 2nd Session, Typescript Copy of Statement, p. 8, POF (hereafter Moore Statement, March 20, 1978).

54 Ray, pp. 47–8.

55 Ray, p. 47; Interview with Gary C. Hufbauer, May 31, 2000, pp. 3–6, Library, Ex-Im (hereafter Hufbauer Interview, May 31, 2000); "Status of Negotiations."

to discuss export credits.[56] In June 1974, OECD ministers pledged that they would not respond to the alarming 1973 OPEC challenge in a mercantilist way by limiting imports or artificially stimulating exports. They avowed not to engage in "destructive competition in official support of export credits" and to take part in "appropriate cooperative actions to this effect in the immediate future."[57] In October, at the IMF–World Bank meetings, industrial country leaders again gathered outside the official meetings. They adopted a preliminary agreement on government export credit policies that set a minimum 7.5 percent interest rate for maturities over five years.[58]

But the momentum for some kind of understanding slowed at a special meeting of the European Community Commission in Belgium in May 1975. Matters stalled at these meetings when there was a push for a comprehensive understanding that would cover most aspects of official export credits: down payments, interest rates, levels of government support, mixed credits, and so forth. France and Belgium in particular resisted efforts to lower subsidies.[59] Nevertheless, heads of state reenergized the effort to reach a common understanding of terms at the first economic summit at Rambouillet, France, in November 1975. At any event, in France the leaders of the six major industrial members of OECD pledged an intensified effort to reach agreement on export credits.[60]

Buoyed by the high-level support, the six countries plus Canada came to a "Consensus on Converging Export Credit Policies" in the spring of 1976. DuBrul took an active part in the discussions leading up to the final document. The consensus provided for targets on the duration of credits (10 years to developing countries; 8.5 years to others), as well as minimum down payments (15 percent) and minimum interest rates (7.5–8 percent for credits over five years; 0.25 percent less on credits from two to five years). There were provisions for prior notification among those participating, should one country plan to deviate – or "derogate" in the parlance of the negotiations – from the terms of the consensus agreement. Terms were also included for guidelines

[56] Ray, pp. 50–1.
[57] "1974 OECD Trade Pledge," quoted in Ray, p. 51.
[58] Ibid., p. 51.
[59] Hufbauer Interview, May 31, 2000, pp. 4–7.
[60] Ray, p. 52.

relating to mixed credits, that is, where aid and commercial credits were linked.[61]

Nevertheless, the seven countries failed to agree on how to implement what they agreed to, and they excluded the high-tech sectors still subject to the 1975 standstill agreements. Consequently, instead of a multilateral agreement, what emerged were unilateral declarations among the various countries, negotiated in parallel by OECD members.[62]

Initially, the understandings were secret. But at the initiative of Ex-Im's DuBrul, the United States made the understandings public in June 1976. In its "declaration," the Bank pledged to adhere to policies similar to those laid out in the consensus in regard to interest rates, repayment terms, and mixed credits. Other countries, initially with the exception of France, soon followed with similar public statements. Although DuBrul limited the Bank's adherence to a year, the United States succeeded in forcing most of the other signatories to accept some jointly agreed terms on export credits. In addition, at the Bank's urging, the ECG arranged to continue exchanging information on transactions providing export credit for terms of five years or more. DuBrul's goal was to bring official export credit policies closer to the realities of market norms, at least for one year.[63]

By going public with the understandings, the Bank also succeeded in putting some pressure on the other signatories. To depart from the terms of the consensus would have had to be done publicly, resulting in bad publicity and strained relations with allies. This was, to be sure, a weak understanding because serious disagreements remained among the signatories. So moral suasion was all that underpinned the understanding, but it was more than would have been available had the terms remained secret.[64]

In the next two years, the 1976 consensus understanding received further support among OECD members. OECD ministers approved the "progress" that had been made, as did heads of state meeting at

[61] Ibid., p. 53.

[62] Ibid., p. 53; Hillman, p. 136.

[63] Ray, pp. 52–3; Appendix W, "United States Declaration on Official Support for Export Credits, 9 July 1975," pp. 309–10, "International Negotiations (1978)" folder, POF; Export-Import Bank of the United States, "Report to the U.S. Congress on Export Credit Competition and the Export-Import Bank of the United States, for the period January 1, 1976 through June 30, 1976 . . . ," December 1976, pp. 38–47.

[64] Hillman, pp. 136–7.

economic summits in San Juan, Puerto Rico, in 1976 and London in 1977. At the latter meetings, participants agreed as part of their concluding joint declaration that "efforts be made this year to improve and extend the present consensus" in order "to reduce counter-productive competition in officially supported export credits."[65]

High-level support induced almost all the OECD countries to accede to the consensus statement. By the end of 1977, only Austria and New Zealand had failed to publicly support it. At that time, through the fall and winter 1977–8, the ECG worked on turning the unilateral proclamations into a unified document. By February 1978, all twenty-two participants had signed a draft, which went into effect in April 1978. The Arrangement on Guidelines for Officially Supported Export Credits (Arrangement) did not include agreements on agriculture, aircraft, nuclear power plants, new oceangoing vessels, and military equipment. There had been a previous sector understanding on ships, and agreements were later hammered out in the early 1980s on nuclear power plants and commercial aircraft.[66]

Like the earlier 1976 consensus understanding, the 1978 Arrangement depended heavily on transparency and moral suasion.[67] The Bank advocated continuing efforts to strengthen the Arrangement, in particular setting higher minimum interest rates for export credits. France, while not alone in its views, was the most outspoken naysayer to limiting subsidized interest rates for exports. Within two years of the Arrangement's taking effect, the United States had become thoroughly frustrated by a lack of progress in strengthening its terms. Consequently, in November 1980, the United States announced that the Ex-Im would offer credits for longer than ten years. Bank officials targeted these loans to markets of significance to France.[68]

The Bank's derogation had the desired effect. OECD negotiations intensified on a number of outstanding issues. These included fuller definitions of official support, which before had been vague as to whether insurance and guarantees (so-called pure cover) were to be included in the Arrangement. Derogation, or the circumstances under which participants could depart from understandings, was another issue that

65 Quoted in Ray, p. 53.
66 Ibid., p. 53; "Status of Negotiations."
67 Hufbauer Interview, May 31, 2000, pp. 4–8.
68 Ray, pp. 53–4.

received attention. A major source of discussion was how to set minimum interest rates for exports in a world where the value of currencies fluctuated, at times dramatically. Intense discussions eventually led to an OECD understanding on this matter in 1982.[69]

Thus, from the mid 1970s forward, the Bank accepted an important new responsibility. As part of the mandate Congress gave it in the 1974 reauthorization, Ex-Im began to address the increasing competition faced by American exports by taking part in the OECD negotiations toward leveling the international playing field for export credit finance. It was a role the Bank was to play throughout the next decades into the twenty-first century.

EXPORT PROMOTION AGAIN

After the inauguration of President Jimmy Carter in 1976, the new administration again emphasized assisting exporters in making deals. But it also continued to focus on creating a uniform international regime to govern the provision of export credits. The administration accepted the precept that the more active the United States was in supporting its exporters, the greater the pressure on competing ECAs to come to the table at the OECD.

President Carter replaced DuBrul with John L. Moore, Jr. (May 1977 to March 1981). Moore was an Atlanta attorney who had worked for Carter when he was governor of Georgia and with Roslyn Carter on mental health issues. He served on the president-elect's transition team where he reviewed the financial reports of potential appointees in the new administration.[70]

Moore had no previous experience with the Bank. But Moore saw himself as a pragmatist and an activist, with little appetite for what he characterized as the academic approach to issues favored by his predecessor.[71] He saw his job as addressing the finance needs of exporters, while also helping the country's balance-of-payments problems and combating aggressive foreign export credit agencies. He understood that revising DuBrul's policies would be costly, but he believed that living up to the Bank's competitiveness mandate was more important than

[69] Ibid., pp. 54–5.
[70] Moore Interview, May 8, 2000, pp. 1–4.
[71] Ibid., pp. 4–7.

the financial losses that might ensue from interest rate spreads. For one thing, neither he nor anyone else in the Bank anticipated that such spreads would remain so wide for so long. For another, he averred that the Bank's reserves were sufficient to meet them.[72]

In the troubled times of the late 1970s, Moore accepted that the Bank had a critical role to play in the administration's economic campaign. Carter identified the Ex-Im as an important element in a national export policy (announced in September 1978), which was itself part of a macroeconomic strategy designed to reinvigorate exports of the United States' capital goods sector, essentially through dollar depreciation.[73] Interest rates, inflation, and unemployment were high. There was concern over the balance of payments, as the trade deficit widened to $27 billion in 1977, a sum that caused considerable worry in Congress and the White House, as well as among the interested public. In 1977, imports grew by 22 percent (much of this attributable to imported oil), while exports expanded only by 5 percent. In the Moore years, the Bank thus revived arguments about the importance of promoting exports to offset growing imports, themes last so loudly trumpeted in the Kearns years.[74] Moreover, beginning in January 1979, OPEC began raising prices again so that by the end of 1980 per barrel costs had tripled, exacerbating economic problems in the United States and the rest of the world. This turn of events led to further U.S. trade deficits and lent greater credence to Bank arguments about the importance of promoting exports.

To raise support for American exporters, the Bank moved dramatically during Moore's first full year in office. It increased authorizations for loans, guarantees, and insurance 31 percent, from $5,599.6 million in fiscal year 1977 to $7,376.4 million for fiscal year 1978. This included a more than 300 percent increase in authorizations for fixed-rate direct lending, from $700 million to $2,872.4 million.[75] These expansionist efforts intensified for the rest of Moore's term. By fiscal 1980, such authorizations for direct credits reached $4,045 million.

[72] Hess Interview, April 3, 2000, pp. 56–7; Moore Interview, May 8, 2000, pp. 4–7; Duff Interview, June 20, 2000, pp. 14–15; Moore Statement, March 20, 1978, p. 12.

[73] Memorandum, James Cruse to Warren Glick, November 25, 1980, Subj.: "1977–80: Outline," "1977–1980 outline" folder, POF.

[74] Moore Statement, March 20, 1978, p. 2; Annual Report for 1978, p. 2.

[75] Annual Report for 1978, p. 3.

Moore also attempted to broaden the United States' export base. He traveled extensively both in the United States and overseas to stimulate interest in American exports. This included a well-publicized trip to Sub-Saharan Africa in September 1979 with America's United Nations Ambassador Andrew Young and executives from twenty-five American companies.[76] Overall, the Bank's lending to less-developed countries increased to 66 percent of its business by 1978, from 50 percent in 1972.[77]

Moore's prime goal was to have the Bank meet the competition of foreign export credit agencies, "often at significant costs to their national treasuries." "This support," as Moore went on to state in the 1978 annual report, "severely tested the Bank's ability to offer competitive financing for U.S. exporters."[78] While he took a great interest in subsequent OECD negotiations to strengthen the 1978 Arrangement, he and Carter were disappointed in their lack of progress.[79] Carter was a strong proponent of "fostering a fairer and more secure world trading system," and of confronting forcefully nontariff barriers to trade, one of the prime subjects in the Multi-Lateral Trade Negotiations (the Tokyo Round, 1974–9) being conducted at the time. But he and Moore were not willing to rely solely on negotiations.[80]

Moore aggressively countered the foreign competitive challenge to American exporters. Because foreign ECA's provided credits at fixed interest rates to their exporters, the Bank adjusted its participation program. Ex-Im took a larger percentage of loans, in large part because unlike commercial banks at the time it offered fixed interest rates, and in particular fixed rates that were competitive with other ECA rates. Between fiscal 1977 and the end of 1980, Ex-Im drastically increased its loan cover from 30–45 percent to 65–70 percent. Larger provisions of direct credit lending pressed the Bank's resources, which was one of the reasons the Ex-Im requested Congress to increase its lending authority from $25 billion to $40 billion in the 1978 reauthorization.[81]

76 Annual Report for 1979, p. 2; Moore Interview, pp. 24–6.

77 Export-Import Bank of the United States: Policy Analysis Staff, Introductory Briefing Book, Background Book, "NAC Study of Eximbank Lending Policies, Report of the Subgroup on Eximbank Lending Patterns," August, 1975, p. 2, POF.

78 Annual Report for 1978, p. 2; Moore Interview, pp. 5, 19–22.

79 Annual Report for 1979, p. 5–6.

80 Ibid., quoted on p. 2.

81 Moore Statement, March 20, 1978, pp. 1–2; Annual Report for 1978, p. 3; Memorandum: "Major Factors in the Demand for Eximbank Credits," June 4, 1981, "Direct Credit: Demand Influences" folder, POF.

In addition, Ex-Im met foreign ECA competition on a case-by-case basis. It responded forcefully to what it considered particularly egregious examples of highly subsidized credits. Thus, in 1978, the Bank authorized nineteen credits below its scheduled rate. Moore targeted a French credit offered to Cyprus as a mixed credit (i.e., tied aid, which included both concessional financing and commercial export credits) for an earth satellite system. Ex-Im beat out the French with a rate of 6.00 percent, which was below the Bank's 7.75 to 8.50 scheduled rate. Late in 1978, the Bank successfully offered 5.5 percent to match a mixed credit provided by France, Germany, and Japan to Tunisia.[82]

Ex-Im followed its aggressive policy of providing its own subsidized credits as market and government rates climbed. So, as the cost of capital increased, the Bank was offering rates below its own schedule for direct loans, which in 1979 averaged 8.35 percent. Consequently, for the latter years of Moore's term (from 1978 to 1981) negative spreads again appeared. Even though the yearly average for ten-year government bond rates in 1980 was 11.46 percent, the Bank's borrowing costs for medium and long-term lending were in fact higher. In 1980, the Bank obtained funds from the Federal Financing Bank (FFB) whose interest rates fluctuated sharply that year. When in March 1980, for example, the Ex-Im borrowed $714 million, the FFB rate was 13.2 percent. Consequently, the Bank faced such large interest charges in fiscal 1980 that it applied its total net income (which was down from the previous year) to reserves, not paying a dividend to the treasury that year.[83] By then, the GAO had questioned the adequacy of the Bank's reserves, and indeed its ability to remain self-sustaining. In fact, fiscal 1980 was the beginning of a difficult period financially for the Bank that extended throughout the 1980s. Ultimately, both its reserves and capital were undermined and liquidated. At the time, Moore and his colleagues did not believe that the subsidies would last as long – or have as negative an impact – as they in fact did.[84]

[82] Annual Report for 1979, p. 9; "Eximbank Matches French Offer: U.S. Exporter Wins Contract," *EXIM News*, December 19, 1978; "Eximbank Extends Availability of Special Credit Line to Tunisia . . . ," *EXIM News*, November 3, 1980, Library, Ex-Im.; Moore Interview, May 8, 2000, pp. 19–22.

[83] Annual Report for 1980, pp. 4–5, 14–15, 16–17.

[84] Hess Interview, April 3, 2000, pp. 39–40; Duff Interview, June 20, 2000, pp. 14–15; Hufbauer Interview, May 31, 2000, pp. 18–19; Comptroller General, Report to the

Requests for Bank loans soared as market rates shot up in the late 1970s. Attractive interest rates played their part. But purchasers of aircraft also wanted to lock in sales agreements well in advance of the delivery date of new models of planes. As a result, Ex-Im staff were swamped by fast-rising demand. Aircraft manufacturing was the United States' leading manufactured export in the 1970s. By the end of the decade, 45 percent of the Bank's direct loans supported aircraft sales. Between 1969 and 1980, this important capital goods sector had represented the largest proportion of Bank direct lending for eight out of eleven years. In the three years when aircraft financing came in second, manufacturers producing nuclear power equipment placed first. Such a reversal in the top two spots occurred in 1978 with the Bank's largest single financing to that date – $936 million to South Korea for the construction of two nuclear power plants.[85]

In any event, Bank financing for aircraft became even more important to manufacturers when in the mid 1970s the European Airbus Industries consortium began producing competitive planes. To manage the increased demand for aircraft financing in a time when the Bank was pressed for capital, Ex-Im developed restrictive policies on aircraft lending. As a result, direct credit support was available only for medium-range, wide-bodied aircraft and new generations of planes in direct competition with Airbus. Support for other types of aircraft were generally limited to financial guarantees.[86]

Aircraft financing also led to the most embarrassing incident for the Bank during the late 1970s. It involved the terms the Bank offered in a PC for the sale of Boeing 767s, 727s, and 737s to Ansett Airlines, an Australian domestic air carrier controlled by Rupert Murdoch. The latter had numerous financial interests in a number of industries, including publishing. He was the owner of the New York *Post.* Critics of President Carter charged that the Bank issued a PC to Annsett on particularly favorable terms to curry favor with Murdoch and to gain his support in presidential primaries against Senator Edward Kennedy.

Congress of the United States, *Financial and Other Restraints Prevent Eximbank from Consistently Offering Competitive Financing for U.S. Exports*, April 30, 1980, pp. 12–13, Appendix III (Letter, Moore to Fasick, GAO, January 18, 1980), POF.

85 Annual Report for 1979, p. 9; "Aircraft" Attachment 7 in "Briefing Book: Export-Import Bank of the United States," December 1980, POF.

86 "Aircraft" Attachment 7 in "Briefing Book: Export-Import Bank of the United States," December 1980, POF.

Following Murdoch's discussions at the Bank and White House in February 1980, the Ex-Im issued a PC. Soon thereafter, Murdoch's newspaper endorsed Carter for renomination. Supporters of Kennedy raised questions about the generous terms of sale to Ansett. Congressional hearings followed. Ultimately, Carter and the Bank were exonerated, and the potential scandal evaporated, but not before prominent senators – including two of the Bank's most faithful supporters – scolded the Bank for "sloppy" procedures. They also raised questions about the high level of direct credits devoted to aircraft sales, "including a disproportionate share for Boeing – one of the largest corporations in the country."[87]

Thus, by the end of the Moore years, the Bank was hard pressed to provide the kind of assistance that key export industries believed they needed. Ex-Im, to be sure, had vastly increased its lending activity. Moore strenuously made the case that the Bank had met the competitive challenges posed by foreign ECAs.[88] But the slippage in its financial performance was the kind of vulnerability that exposed the Bank to a new set of critics in the 1980s. Many of the criticisms leveled at the Bank in the 1980s, to be sure, were an echo of those heard earlier in the 1970s. But the incoming administration of President Ronald Reagan had an acutely different view of the role of government in the economy. Unlike earlier critics, such as DuBrul, Reagan's people were not necessarily interested in making the Ex-Im more efficient. In fact, the Bank became a target of those on the right who were ideologically opposed to large government, and its costs, especially government credit programs. Thus, the Bank found itself under attack by an administration initially unsympathetic to the Ex-Im on both ideological and practical grounds. It also had to face a new set of criticisms. From both the left and right of the political spectrum critiques focused on the Bank's supposed favoritism toward large corporations, a theme highlighted in the Ansett case.

Overall, the 1970s proved a difficult time for the Bank. It entered the 1980s in a financially much weaker position than it faced a decade earlier. While foreign policy considerations were less pressing than

[87] Letter, Senators Jake Garn, William Proxmire, John Heinz, and Adlai E. Stevenson, May 22, 1980, "Ansett" folder, POF; Hillman, pp. 165–6; Senate, Hearings, "Ansett Loan and Export-Import Aircraft Financing Policies," Committee on Banking, Housing, and Urban Affairs, 9th Congress, 2nd Session, May 12, 13, 1980 (Washington, DC: Government Printing Office, 1980).

[88] Annual Report for 1980, p. 2.

they had been before, Congress' interest in the Bank's activities had increased enormously. On the one hand, some of its members wanted the Bank to expand its mandate to cope with a much more competitive international economic environment. On the other hand, the troubled domestic economic conditions of the decade focused greater congressional attention on the efficient use of government resources. So, in trying to meet an expanded mandate, the Bank's financial performance suffered and its resources were constrained. At the same time, however, the Bank became embedded in congressional efforts to assert its authority following the excesses of the executive branch in both the Vietnam War and the Watergate scandal. In the coming years, the nature of the criticism would become more ideologically driven, and the challenges to the Bank in many ways would become more demanding.

6

TURMOIL AND TURNING POINTS

INTRODUCTION

Much of the decade of the 1980s proved a difficult period for financial institutions. The Export-Import Bank was not immune to the consequences of the unusual macroeconomic developments of the period. For the Bank, the 1980s, especially after 1983, created a time of turmoil and important turning points.

At the beginning of the decade, domestic inflation reached unprecedented peacetime levels. To cope with these problems, the Reagan administration slowed the economy by raising interest rates, which resulted in the deepest recession since the depression of the 1930s. At the same time, large tax cuts and increased military spending led to record deficits. Compounding the decade's economic problems were the first signs of trouble in the domestic savings and loan industry, a consequence of banking deregulation in the late 1970s.

Internationally, a serious debt crisis occurred among less-developed countries unable to service debts incurred in the 1970s. One consequence of these difficulties was a sharp decline in the demand for imports in affected areas. An unusually strong dollar, at least until agreements between 1985 and 1987 to drive its value down, further contributed to a growing trade deficit as American exporters were priced out of many markets.

Together these domestic and international economic developments contributed to a serious reduction in the levels of the Ex-Im's lending activity and the quality of its loan portfolio. In 1983, the Ex-Im's direct lending plunged. It would never again reach the levels of 1978–82. Huge spreads in interest rates from 1979 to 1982 also created a stream of staggering financial losses that essentially eliminated the Bank's capital, undermining its financial health. Large claims paid as a result of the LDC debt crisis also caused a realignment of Ex-Im's relationship with the Foreign Credit Insurance Association. Aside from these problems, implementation of Organization of Economic Cooperation and Development understandings lessened ECA competition and set the stage for the shift from direct credits/loans that would characterize the activity of the Bank in the 1990s.

Compounding the Bank's difficulties was the new Reagan administration's distrust of what it saw as the excessive size and scope of the federal government. The Bank, along with many other federal civilian agencies, was under pressure to cut its budget. Administration officials were particularly skeptical of the government's credit programs, which brought Bank activities under intense scrutiny by treasury and Office of Management and Budget officials. These circumstances profoundly altered the Bank's working environment and put great pressure on its chairmen during the 1980s, William H. Draper III (1981–6) and John A. Bohn (1986–9).

Nevertheless, the Bank's champions in Congress, and industry boosters, continued their support, despite the skepticism shown by the Reagan administration. Indeed, the Bank's congressional supporters succeeded in strengthening and expanding its mission, at a time the administration was reducing its budget. In the reauthorizations of 1983 and 1986, Congress enlarged the Bank's mandate. Its supporters defined the Ex-Im as the main bulwark against official, subsidized foreign competition and also expected it to devote time and resources to the reinvigoration of private foreign lending and assistance to small business exporters.

Even so, Ex-Im only began the difficult process of adjusting its organization and processes to the changed domestic and international economic environment after 1986. These were tumultuous years as the Bank faced budget problems and sharp external criticism of its operations. Key Bank constituencies distrusted the leadership of Chairman Draper – his approach to the Bank's problems and commitment to their interests. While budget problems remained severe from 1986 to 1989, Chairman Bohn began the work of remaking the institution to cope with the new domestic and international environment, a process that would continue under his successor, John D. Macomber (1989–92).

The mid 1980s appeared so difficult, in part, because the Bank began the decade at a high tide of activity. Indeed, there were times in the early 1980s when Ex-Im officials believed that it would be literally swamped with demands for financing. Pending cases in 1980 mirrored the Bank's activity during the late 1970s. Almost 55 percent of the projected financing was for aircraft.[1] Nuclear power represented 20 percent of the demand, and three large project development cases took an additional 10 percent.[2] Pressure on the Bank budget had increased exponentially because the typical financing package for a direct credit had changed dramatically from 1977 to 1981. During this period, the Bank had altered its degree of long-term support (cover) for direct credits. They moved from 30 to 45 percent of an export at essentially market rates in 1977, to 65 to 75 percent at highly subsidized rates in 1981.[3]

Fiscal year 1981 marked a historical peak of Bank activity. It authorized $12.854 billion in loans, guarantees, and insurance, which included $5.431 billion in loans (direct credits). The latter figure has not been reached since, and the levels of all Bank activity (loans, guarantees, and insurance) would not be surpassed until 1993.[4] By fiscal year 1986, direct loan activity had declined sharply, to approximately $577.4 million, barely one-tenth of the figure of five years earlier. Loans, guarantees, and insurance were $6.085 billion, less than half of its total activity in 1981.[5] In early 1987, the House Committee on Foreign Affairs observed that the "value of nonagricultural United States exports supported [by direct loans, guarantees, and insurance] by the Export-Import Bank in relation to all such exports, has ... declined consistently during the last five years, from approximately 13 percent in 1980 to approximately 5 percent in 1986."[6]

[1] Memorandum, "Aircraft Policy Overview," October 18, 1984, "Aircraft Finance Agreement, 1983–84" folder, Policy Office Files, Archives, Ex-Im (hereafter POF).

[2] Memorandum, "FY 1980 Budget: Balancing Supply and Demand, February 14, 1980," "1980 Budget" folder, POF.

[3] Memorandum, "Major Factors in the Demand for Eximbank Credits," June 4, 1981, "Direct Credit: Demand Influences" folder, POF.

[4] "Eximbank Briefing Book," December 1988, Section F, pp. 1–2, POF; Export-Import of the United States, Annual Report for 1981 (Washington, DC: Export-Import Bank of the United States, 1981), pp. 16–17; Export-Import Bank of the United States, Annual Report for 1993 (Washington, DC: Export-Import Bank of the United States, 1993), pp. 16–17 (hereafter Annual Report).

[5] Annual Report for 1986, p. 16.

[6] House, Committee on Foreign Affairs, 100th Congress, 1st Session, Report, *Trade and International Economic Policy Reform Act of 1987*, Report 100-40, p. 15; John E. Ray,

CHANGING CIRCUMSTANCES: THE BANK AND INSURANCE

In the early 1980s, the Bank's relationship with the Foreign Credit Insurance Association became strained. Until October 1983, Ex-Im had assumed the political risk under policies written by FCIA, while the association's member companies accepted a small amount of the commercial risk. Ex-Im also acted as a reinsurer of FCIA commercial risk above specified levels. The introduction of multibuyer policies in the mid 1970s, where insurance was underwritten for an exporter's entire book of business under one policy, greatly increased insurance written by FCIA.[7]

FCIA participants increasingly wanted to be more involved in the country's risk evaluation process and to enlarge their ability to influence premium levels.[8] In an effort to increase underwriting authority from the Bank, the FCIA companies expanded their level of risk participation on an annual basis from $8.4 million in 1977 to $15 million in 1981. From 1978 through 1981, policies written by the members of FCIA increased, from $3.363 billion to $5.910 billion.[9] Member companies shifted their business into traditional markets like Latin America, especially to major construction and industrial equipment companies, who extended credit in local currency. Additionally, American insurance companies in this period of high interest rates were willing to take on more risk relative to premium income because of the attractiveness of investing at high interest rates. Since 1975, several American insurance companies had entered the export insurance market, though some subsequently withdrew when difficulties arose because of the Latin American debt crisis.[10] In 1981–2, the new Reagan administration's OMB pressed the Bank seriously to examine options for privatization of all insurance

Managing Export Credits: The Quest for a Global Regime (Washington, DC: Institute for International Economics, 1995), pp. 55–8.

7 Interview with Jack Bierman and Delio Gianturco, May 31, 2000, pp. 22–5, Library, Ex-Im (hereafter Bierman and Gianturco Interview May 31, 2000).

8 Interview with Joseph Williams, June 12, 2000, pp. 5–7, Library, Ex-Im (hereafter Williams Interview, June 12, 2000).

9 Rita M. Rodriguez, "Exim's Mission and Accomplishments: 1934–84," in Rita M. Rodriguez, ed., *The Export-Import Bank at Fifty: The International Environment and the Institution's Role* (Lexington, MA: Lexington Books, 1987), pp. 26–7.

10 *Assessment of Export-Import Bank's Role*, September 1987, pp. 1–19; Report, Exim's Guarantee and Insurance Program Objectives, September 20, 1984, "Guarantee and Insurance Program" folder, POF; See also Bierman and Gianturco Interview, May 31 pp. 53–5.

functions. Events of the next few years, however, would short circuit these efforts.[11]

Trouble began in 1981, in Costa Rica and Venezuela, and subsequently spread to other Latin American countries. They abandoned or substantially modified long-standing schemes to pay foreign-currency-denominated debts and established long deferrals for payment of such obligations. Several governments coupled these actions with major devaluations of their currencies. This resulted in significant defaults. Insurance claims mounted.[12] Ex-Im's board ultimately determined that the major losses in Venezuela were commercial and that those in Mexico were primarily political.[13] The Bank had always acted as the reinsurer of commercial coverage above certain limits for FCIA, and the claims paid in Costa Rica alone triggered the "stop-loss" or maximum FCIA participant limitations on claims paid as contained in FCIA's master agreement with Ex-Im.[14] But the claims paid by FCIA were substantial. In 1982, FCIA reported its share of these paid claims at $44 million. Foreign credit insurance had never been a major money maker for the participants in FCIA. The association had not been consistently profitable until the early 1970s, and only $11.3 million in association earnings had been distributed to member firms through 1980.[15]

Under these circumstance, most of the participants in FCIA (51 in 1981) declined to continue their risk participation in the association. A small number of firms were willing to continue their role at the reduced rate of $2 million. Ex-Im rejected this proposal as too small. Consequently, all the member companies withdrew their risk participation in FCIA effective the end of September 1983.[16] At that time, FCIA and the Bank agreed to continue the association on a nonrisk participation basis for the companies. Ex-Im agreed to reinsure 100 percent of FCIA transactions, cover all of its expenses in excess of revenues, and hold

[11] Interview with James Cruse, August 15, 2000, p. 16, Library, Ex-Im (hereafter Cruse Interview, August 15, 2000).

[12] Memorandum, Origin of FCIA, 1988, Mazon-Mazo Files, Library, Ex-Im.

[13] Interview with Warren C. Glick, March 13, 2000, pp. 15–16, Library, Ex-Im (hereafter Glick Interview, March 13, 2000).

[14] Interview with Rita Rodriguez, June 15, 2000, pp. 23–4, Library, Ex-Im (hereafter Rodriguez Interview, June 15, 2000).

[15] General Accounting Office, Report, *Export Credit Insurance: Assessment of Export-Import Bank's Role*, September 1987, p. 19.

[16] Ibid.

members harmless for any FCIA operations after September 1983. In exchange, Ex-Im made a final settlement with FCIA's member companies for all prior years' business, and the companies returned all prior years' earnings. Ten firms agreed to continue to participate as nonrisk-bearing members; by 1986 only four remained. As part of the restructuring, FCIA adopted a new constitution and by-laws that gave the Bank the primary role in management and policymaking. An Ex-Im officer chaired FCIA's board of directors, the Bank had a majority of members of the board, and it controlled all committee, rate-setting, claims, and major underwriting decisions.[17]

During the height of the debt crisis in 1982 and 1983, the Bank participated in the United States' financial rescue packages for Mexico and Brazil. In both instances, the primary mechanism was an insurance facility of $500 million for Mexico and $1.5 billion for Brazil. The latter did not make use of the facility, but Mexico did so extensively. Indeed, Mexico used the Bank's facility, while Ex-Im was processing millions of dollars of insurance claims of American exporters to Mexico.[18]

Congress circumscribed such "rescue" activity in its 1983 reauthorization of Ex-Im's charter. The legislation expressly authorized these facilities through March 31, 1985. It also extended existing congressional notification requirements to include any general guarantee and insurance facility, like the ones for Mexico and Brazil. Congress prohibited the Bank from providing balance-of-payments lending or assisting any country (as the primary purpose of such assistance) in the management of its international debt, other than Ex-Im debts. Such financing would be permissible only if its primary purpose were to support American exports, which in fact the Bank believed it was doing.[19]

The Export-Import Act amendments of 1986 directed the GAO to undertake a study of the need for government involvement in export credit insurance, the value of employing an agent (FCIA), and the efficiency and effectiveness of FCIA in the postdebt crisis environment. GAO's 1987 report found that private insurers remained unwilling to insure the smaller exporters, which accounted for much of the insurance written in 1986. Its survey established that most insurers were satisfied with

[17] *Export Credit Insurance,* pp. 19–21.

[18] Rodriquez Interview, June 15, 2000, pp. 17–21.

[19] "Summary of Major Provisions of Export-Import Amendments of 1983," no date, "Congress: 1983" folder, POF.

the level of FCIA's service, its expertise, and its post-1983 role. Even though GAO questioned the need for Ex-Im to continue to employ an agent to administer the program, it concluded that "FCIA's overall performance and its special expertise support a continuation of the agency relationship at the present time."[20]

GAO also took note that FCIA insured a much higher proportion of exports to certain areas. About 34 percent of the exports insured during 1982–6 went to countries in Latin America and Africa, while the portion of all U.S. exports to these countries was just 17 percent. This was especially the case in riskier markets, where FCIA insured 6 percent of the exports to Mexico and Brazil, 12 percent to El Salvador, and 42 percent to Nigeria. The GAO also noted that small businesses were holders of a substantial number of credit insurance policies.[21]

Thus, the shocks of the 1981–6 period had a profound effect on FCIA and the insurance program. Insurance authorization declined significantly from $6.085 billion in fiscal year 1982, to a low of $4.380 billion in fiscal year 1986. Estimates were that through fiscal year 1986 FCIA had net claim payments of about $360 million, the overwhelming amount (approximately $317 million) absorbed by the Bank.[22] Ultimately, the Bank and FCIA ended their relationship in 1992, when the higher-risk portions of the insurance business were brought in-house and private sector firms took over the balance.[23]

OECD ARRANGEMENTS

Inflation, rising interest rates, and the international debt crisis affected ECAs and the OECD Arrangements that had been worked out in the late 1970s. New OECD Arrangements negotiated in response to these changing circumstances also had a major impact on the level of Bank business during the Draper years (1981–6).

Between 1979 and 1982, the OECD Arrangement on Export Credits, formalized in early 1978, proved of little help in addressing competition

[20] Export-Import Bank and the Office of Management and Budget, *Report on U.S. Government Involvement in Export Credit Insurance* (Washington, DC: Government Printing Office, 1987), pp. 2–5, 18–19. Hereafter *Government Involvement in Export Credit Insurance.*

[21] Ibid., pp. 10–12.

[22] Ibid., p. 8; Annual Report for 1984, pp. 26–7; Annual Report for 1986, p. 16.

[23] Williams Interview, June 12, 2000, pp. 26–30.

in export finance. Fixed minimum rates were set at levels that prevailed in the mid 1970s, which were below the market rates of the late 1970s and early 1980s. Hence, the minimums were a source of the intense competition between ECAs during this period. Below market rate financing could be, and was, aggressively pursued. Earlier arrangements – the so-called stand-still arrangements of 1975 covering the important aircraft and nuclear power sectors – were even weaker. They did not address the question of minimum rates of interest and were limited as to duration and/or down payment.[24]

Participants saw the 1978 Arrangement as a compromise between the interest of the aggressive French in limiting the duration of the credits (a strength of the American capital markets) and the American interest in limiting interest rate subsidies. But, in fact, the 1978 Arrangement favored countries such as France that had high interest rates and extensive trade with developing countries because it set interest rates in nominal terms and at lower rates for trade with developing countries.[25]

France, Japan, and other parties to the 1978 Arrangement proved unwilling to make adjustments in minimum rates or take into account differences in interest rate levels in various countries. To avoid the prospect of a complete deadlock and possible collapse of the Arrangement, the parties in 1979 directed OECD vice chair (later chair) Axel Wallen of Sweden to conduct a study of the issues. His efforts resulted in proposals the following year on adjustable rates, which were not approved and effective until 1983. In the interim, the United States derogated the agreement as to term, that is, went beyond Arrangement-specified maximums for certain credits directed at competitive French offers.[26]

When the Bank's new chairman, William H. Draper, III, took office in July 1981, he changed directions.[27] Draper subsequently characterized his approach as a "three fold strategy of targeting resources, negotiating

[24] "Standstill Declarations on Export Credit Terms for Aircraft and Nuclear Power States," attached to Memorandum, "Possible Accord on Export Credit Subsidies for Nuclear Power Plant," n.d., "Nuclear Power Station Regulation – 1984" folder, POF.

[25] John E. Ray, *Managing Official Export Credits: The Quest for a Global Regime* (Washington, DC: Institute for International Economics, 1995), pp. 50–4.

[26] Ibid., pp. 55–7. The ability to make such derogations would be restricted by the 1982 changes to the Arrangement.

[27] Draper had been a venture capitalist, primarily raising capital for high-technology companies in California. Interview, William Draper, June 20, 2000, pp. 2–3, Library, Ex-Im (hereafter Draper Interview, June 20, 2000).

to reduce export credit subsidies and maintaining [the Bank's] financial condition to meet the challenge."[28] The most important elements of the strategy were to address deteriorating Bank finances through rate and fee increases – and to accelerate the pace of the OECD negotiations – all of these were designed to end costly subsidies.

In July 1981, the Bank unilaterally raised its lending rate for nonaircraft loans from 8.75 to 10.75 percent to close the gap between Ex-Im Bank rates and market rates. Such a decision would not have any sudden impact on the Bank's financial condition because of the several years of lag time that existed between the authorization of a typical credit and the disbursement of the funds. Draper hoped, however, that an immediate boost to income could be achieved by introducing a one-time, 2 percent application fee for each credit authorized. The latter would have the effect of increasing interest rates over the length of the loan an average of 0.5 percent.[29] Not surprisingly, both actions proved exceedingly unpopular with exporters.

Soon after, in August, OECD negotiators reached an understanding concerning lending rates for large aircraft. Instrumental in bringing the Europeans to an agreement in the all-important aircraft sector was their concerns about the ability of American capital markets to go beyond the ten-year term maximum in the existing standstill agreement on aircraft finance.[30] Then, too, according to the Treasury Department's John Lange, who participated in the OECD negotiations, the extent of the subsidy for Airbus loans was so large that "even the French choked," especially when pressed by their partners Great Britain and West Germany.[31]

On August 3, 1981, the United States, France, West Germany, and the United Kingdom each unilaterally increased their rates for competing aircraft. They harmonized their aircraft lending policies through an exchange of letters. The Bank then announced that it would charge a minimum rate of 12 percent on aircraft loans and the one-time fee of 2 percent on exports of commercial jet aircraft that were competitive

[28] Speech, William Draper, Bankers' Association for Foreign Trade, Boca Raton, FL, April 26, 1982; Ex-Im, Press Release, July 16, 1981, Library, Ex-Im.

[29] Ibid.; Interview with James Hess, August 15, 2000, pp. 3–4, Library, Ex-Im (hereafter Hess Interview, August 15, 2000).

[30] Interview with John Lange, April 10, 2000, pp. 16–21, Library, Ex-Im (hereafter Lange Interview, April 10, 2000).

[31] Ibid., pp. 14–16.

with Airbus – the Boeing 757 and 767 series. The same rate would apply to officially supported export credits made in U.S. dollars for exports of Airbus. It was not until July 1985 that the United States and the European Community (EC) reached a comprehensive agreement on large aircraft (over seventy seats), referred to as the Large Aircraft Sector Understanding, or LASU. This arrangement provided for an optional twelve-year term, a commitment to avoid distortion of competition in each other's home markets, a prohibition against mixing developmental and commercial (tied aid) credits for aircraft, and biweekly adjustments in interest rates on new credits connected to changes in government bond rates in respective currencies.[32]

These 1981 and 1985 agreements had a marked effect on the Bank's financial guarantees and direct credits. As the agreements raised minimum lending rates for aircraft, and subsequently tied them to quickly adjusting market rates, the effect was to push financing into financial guarantees and to reduce the incentives for loans (direct credits). This, of course, had been a long-term goal of U.S. negotiators at the OECD. Additionally, during the recession of 1981–3, and the onset of the debt crisis in 1982, many of the LDCs were simply unable to borrow to supplement or upgrade airline fleets. Ex-Im loans for aircraft dropped from in excess of $2 billion in fiscal years 1980 and 1981 to approximately $200 million in 1982 and $400 million in 1984. With a subsequent decline in interest rates, commercial financing became more attractive than the 12 percent minimums agreed to in the 1981 exchange of letters. Hence demand for the Bank's direct credits (loans) was reduced further. In fiscal year 1985–6, Ex-Im authorized just $46 million in direct credits (loans) to support aircraft sales, barely 2 percent of 1980 levels.[33]

Ex-Im's unilateral increase in the minimum rates for nonaircraft loans in July 1981 was followed three months later by the other twenty-one OECD countries, with the exception only of Japan. They raised the minimum rates for long-term credit for the "relatively poor" countries to 10 percent.[34] This took effect November 16, 1981. The parties to

32 "Eximbank Briefing Book," December 1988, Section D, pp. 2–3, POF.

33 Memorandum, "Influence on Exim's Credit Utilization," February 5, 1987, "Credit Utilization (1987)" folder, POF. See also, Memorandum, Chapman to Sharpe, January 16, 1987, "LASU 1986" folder, POF.

34 Ray, p. 57; the OECD Arrangement had provided for three categories. They were "relatively rich," "intermediate," and "relatively poor." The minimum lending rates for the latter were the lowest, and therefore the most subsidized.

the OECD Arrangement agreed to meet six months hence to assess the situation.[35] Meanwhile, the Bank continued to press its strategy of unilaterally raising rates, in hopes of breaking the cycle of ECA subsidization, bringing OECD minimums to market rates as quickly as possible, and then establishing a mechanism to link automatically changes in Arrangement minimum rates to changes in market rates.[36]

Soon after the November 1981 announcement, the Bank again unilaterally raised its minimum rates on nonaircraft loans to 12 percent. Ex-Im had, according to Draper, "well-founded hopes that the other OECD countries will again follow us.... I think they have added up the true costs of their export credit policies and they too see the folly in the unwarranted subsidies of the past." In addressing the Bankers' Association for Foreign Trade in April 1982, Draper observed that OECD countries paid more than $7 billion in subsidy in 1981 and "it is time for all of us to stop squandering so much money."[37] Subsequently, participating countries agreed to raise the OECD minimums to 12 percent.

OECD participants achieved a more comprehensive system of periodic adjustments in minimum rates in 1982. It became effective in October 1983. The new system involved a so-called uniform moving matrix (UMM). It established a single matrix of interest rates that would move automatically (in six-month adjustments) as market rates moved. It applied to all currencies used by the adherents to the OECD Arrangement to extend export credit. Ironically, just as OECD minimums rose dramatically in 1981–2, market rates began to decline. Countries that had long opposed automatic adjustment of OECD minimum interest rates through mechanisms like the UMM, now found them much more attractive. Additionally, the 1982 Arrangement provided flexibility for countries whose market rates of interest fell below the matrix minimums. In these circumstances, such countries could use what the OECD called a commercial interest referenced rate (CIRR). The net effect of the new system was that countries with high interest rates could continue to provide subsidies down to the matrix minimum rates, while countries with low market interest rates used the CIRR rates

[35] Press Release, "Eximbank Program Changes," December 10, 1981, Library, Ex-Im.

[36] Transcript, Interview with William Draper, Bureau of National Affairs, Special Report (No. 373), September 8, 1981, "Draper" folder, POF.

[37] Speech, William Draper, Bankers' Association for Foreign Trade, Boca Raton, FL, April 26, 1982, Library, Ex-Im.

at close to market rates without subsidies.[38] Further changes in this system of adjustable, minimum rates were not made until late 1986. Indeed, the problems with the various formulas were not comprehensively settled until the OECD Helsinki Package of 1991 went into effect in early 1992, followed by the Schaerer Package in 1994.[39]

The 1982 changes in the OECD Arrangement and its implementation seriously influenced the amounts of subsidies extended by ECAs. By early 1985, the OECD stated, in a view echoed by the Reagan administration, that about 80 percent of the subsidies extended by ECAs had been eliminated.[40] Draper's strategy of coupling lending rate increases with success at the OECD negotiations resulted in rapid reductions in the negative spreads in Ex-Im lending. In fiscal year 1982, the average negative spread was reduced to 1 percent; and it was approximately that figure in fiscal year 1984 (0.95 percent). There was actually an average positive spread in fiscal year 1983 of 0.39 percent.[41] In 1987, Bank Chairman Bohn observed that the 1982 OECD Arrangement that tied adjustment of OECD minimum lending rates to a market basket of currencies ensured that a negative spread could exist only for a short period of time, and that it would not be large.[42]

38 Ray, pp. 55–8. Ray also notes that the 1982 changes to the OECD Arrangement addressed another issue of particular interest to the United States. That was the impact of ECA subsidies on the USSR and other Soviet bloc countries. The Soviet Union had been classified as a Category II "intermediate" country, receiving lower credit rates than Category I "relatively rich" countries. A subsequent 1985 Department of Defense study indicated that "direct and indirect subsidies accounted for 21 percent of officially supported credits to centrally planned economies, or about $3 billion in 1981." In 1982, OECD revised national categories so that all countries with per capita incomes of $4,000 or more were considered Category I. This subsequently included the USSR, the German Democratic Republic, and Czechoslovakia.

39 Ray, p. 58. The OECD's 'Schaerer Package' (agreed to in 1994 and which took effect in 1995) made the application of the CIRR universal and eliminated the use of matrix rates. Thus, in effect, it squeezed much of the last subsidy out of the funding element of commercial export credit activities.

40 Congress, Senate, Committee on Banking, Housing, and Urban Affairs, *Oversight Activities of the Export-Import Bank*, 99th Congress, 1st Session, February 5, 1985, pp. 28–30.

41 Rodriguez, p. 33. In this piece, Rodriguez used statistics that had average, annual spreads. It should also be noted that the lower or positive spreads of the period 1982–5 were done on a much lower volume. Direct credits authorized for the period were $3.516 billion (1982); $845 million (1983); $1.465 billion (1984); and $659 billion (1985).

42 Congress, House, Committee on Banking, Finance and Urban Affairs, Subcommittee on International Finance, Trade and Monetary Policy, *Export-Import Bank*, 100th Congress, 1st Session, 1987, pp. 21–2.

Thus, the 1982 changes (effective in 1983) to the OECD Arrangement substantially reduced competition in officially supported export credits extended by ECAs. Still, the reduction in Bank business at the time must be kept in perspective. The early 1980s, for example, saw a complete collapse in demand for U.S. exports of nuclear power plants. The latter had been second only to aircraft during the 1970s in terms of Bank activity. Many of the same concerns about safety and cost that had eliminated the domestic United States' orders for nuclear plants in the 1970s were replicated worldwide. Mushrooming LDC debt problems also hastened the decline in demand in developing countries. In 1984 negotiators reached an OECD sector understanding on export credits for nuclear plants. It was little used. By 1987–8, the industry was experiencing a deepening recession that showed no real prospects of improving.[43]

Despite changes in demand over which the Bank had little control, Draper believed Ex-Im had an important role to play as a lender of last resort to countries injured by debt problems. The Latin American debt crisis impaired LDC demand for commercial export credits. It had also seriously reduced the availability of credit from commercial banks, which had greatly expanded their foreign lending during the 1970s. Many LDCs had to restructure their debts in the wake of the 1980–2 recession and financial crisis. They found that ECAs were unwilling to lend or guarantee debt under any circumstances for considerable periods of time. Overall, ECA lending, including that of the Ex-Im, declined precipitously and remained at low levels for much of the 1980s. Between 1982 and 1987, official ECA support for export credits with a duration of more than one year declined 43 percent; for long-term credits (more than five years), the figure declined by two thirds.[44]

Yet, about two thirds of the Bank's prevailing loan, guarantee, and insurance activity was focused on the developing world. Ex-Im remained "open for business," or in the lexicon of ECAs "on cover," during these periods of financial crisis and deteriorating financial conditions when many other foreign ECAs had gone "off cover." Near the end of his tenure at the Bank – February 1986 – Chairman Draper told a Senate committee: "It is particularly in the area of risk taking where

43 Memorandum, "Nuclear Power Sector Agreement," August 22, 1984, "Nuclear Power Sector Agreement" folder, POF.

44 Ray, pp. 63–5.

the Eximbank has led all other nations. We have supported American exporters in country after country where our competition has bowed out. During the international crisis of confidence, we stayed open in Mexico, when such nations as Japan, Germany, and France stopped doing business at all and are still cautious. In Brazil, the world's largest heavily indebted nation, Eximbank stayed open in all its programs while Japan, Britain, and Canada all closed down." Resonating 50 years of Eximbank policy, especially with respect to its Latin American activities, Draper added, "We have been able to take the leadership role in risk assumption during this period because Eximbank takes the long-term view of the resource-rich debtor nations. We view their problems as those of illiquidity rather than insolvency."[45]

THE REAGAN AGENDA AND THE BANK

When Ronald Reagan took office in January 1981, the new president vowed to sharply reduce the size and cost of the federal government, while increasing defense spending and reducing taxes. Federal credit subsidies became a particular target. As federal budget deficits more than doubled between 1981 and 1983, the Bank budget provided an attractive opportunity for budget cutters.

Of course, critiques of Bank policy had been a feature of the 1970s. The appearance of negative spreads (subsidies) between Bank lending and borrowing rates had fueled a probing debate. OMB's 1975 questioning of the philosophical rationales for Bank activities had set the tone for serious criticism of the institution during the decade. OMB (and its predecessor agency, the Bureau of the Budget) and the Department of the Treasury had since 1953–4 exhibited varying degrees of skepticism about the direct lending activities of Ex-Im. Critiques of the Bank's activities also arose because of the intensified conflicts over the Bank's budget in the Carter administration, as large budget deficits became a standard feature of federal finance.

Criticisms of the Ex-Im intensified with the arrival of Reagan's free market conservatism, part of a larger ideological stance in Great Britain

[45] Congress, Senate, Committee on Banking, Housing, and Urban Affairs, Subcommittee on International Finance and Monetary Policy, *Renewal of the Export-Import Bank Act of 1945*, 99th Congress, 2nd Session, 1986 (Washington, DC: Government Printing Office, 1986), p. 6.

and the United States that questioned much of the postwar commitment to government as the instrument of economic progress. Typical of such criticisms was an analysis provided by the Heritage Foundation, a relatively new, but well-funded conservative Washington-based think tank. Its early 1981 *Mandate for Leadership* addressed the incoming administration. The document recommended policy options consistent with conservative philosophy and the premises of neoclassical theoretical economics. The Heritage chapter on treasury discussed Ex-Im policies and recommended elimination of subsidized credit. It revived the argument that floating exchange rates would solve the United States' balance-of-payments problems, a position that had been radically deemphasized by the Carter administration when the facts did not bear out economic theory. The treasury chapter also took on Bank activities to assist American exporters facing foreign competition. Heritage authors maintained that export subsidies reduced productivity in the overall U.S. economy, offsetting any export gains generated through the subsidy.

Such arguments were also the core of OMB arguments against the Bank's direct lending program; they served as the rationale for planned major reductions in overall Ex-Im activity.[46] David Stockman, the Director of the Office of Management and Budget, took aim at Ex-Im's direct lending program. Typical of Stockman's attacks was his 1985 position on the Bank's loan program. He pointed to the impact of the Bank's $15.624 billion in direct lending between 1980 and 1984. About 43 percent – $6.7 billion – went to assist the exports from five firms (Boeing, McDonald Douglas, Westinghouse, General Electric, and Lockheed). Boeing alone received $4.3 billion, or more than 27 percent of all direct loans. Stockman argued that "in an era of prospective quarter-trillion dollar budget deficits, the federal government simply

[46] Memorandum, Cruse to Directors and Senior Staff, "Eximbank and Recent Policy/Budget Studies," February 12, 1981, "Heritage/Hoover Policy/Budget Studies 1981" folder, POF. The Heritage Foundation's chapter in *Mandate for Leadership* on the Department of Commerce (by a different author) rejected a broad Bank effort to meet officially foreign competition. It did advocate meeting it in situations involving the "worst" offending nations, in effect to enhance the negotiating value to reduce export credit competition. Cruse's memorandum notes, however, that "the section ends . . . right at the point of real debate, i.e., 'in the long-term, if we are unsuccessful in substantially reducing foreign credit subsidies for exports, the Bank will either have to be funded at mass levels, or we will see long-term drop in our exports.'"

cannot afford to maintain a subsidized credit boutique for a handful of multi-billion dollar U.S. companies." He maintained that the "present value of [the] Eximbank credit subsidy" to these firms for 1980–4 was $1.6 billion, though he acknowledged that the extent of the "subsidy" element would diminish because of recent changes in the OECD Arrangements. Stockman buttressed his attack on the Bank as a haven for a privileged few by comparing the Ex-Im's lending activity with all U.S. merchandise exports during the same five-year period. Bank activity in this context was truly de minimus – the United States exported $1.1 trillion in merchandise (during 1980–4), and the Bank's direct lending program supported just $15.6 billion, or 1.4 percent of this trade.[47]

Early in his term, Draper futilely attempted to assuage some of the leaders of the Heritage Foundation. But the latter's arguments remained consistent and indeed intensified through 1987, when it published *Slashing the Deficit Fiscal Year 1987*. This study relied on a Federal Reserve analysis using 1976–80 Bank activity to measure the extent of Bank subsidies. In fact, subsequent changes to the OECD Arrangement and declines in Bank business in the 1980s made projections using such levels of Ex-Im activity irrelevant at best. *Slashing the Deficit* also maintained that many of the Bank's loans would have been made by private banks in the absence of Ex-Im. From the Bank's perspective these essentially polemical critiques failed to focus on the continued existence of foreign, subsidized competition and the decline in international lending of most commercial banks in the wake of the debt crisis.[48]

In coping with this mind set, Draper sought to balance the dual mandates in Ex-Im's charter. [49] He addressed the issues raised by the competition of ECAs, while remaining attentive to the concerns about the Bank's financial condition.[50] To the external world, Draper was a loyal Reagan appointee. As former Ex-Im General Counsel Warren Glick observed, Draper asked "can't the market do this without us, and he wanted to push that envelope as far as he could." Yet Draper was an aggressive

[47] Transmittal Memorandum and Attachments, Cruse to Others, "Stockman's View of Exim," April 22, 1985, "(1985) Stockman/Bandow Report on Exim Subsidies" folder, POF.

[48] Memorandum, Cruse to Bohn and others, "The Latest Heritage Views on Exim," and attachments, December 1986, "Heritage 1986" folder, POF.

[49] Draper Interview, June 20, 2000, p. 4.

[50] Rodriguez Interview, June 15, 2000, pp. 12–13.

defender of the Bank when the administration sought to cut both its administrative budget for personnel and resources for credit operations.[51]

Nonetheless, the administration's approach to Bank policy distressed large exporters of capital goods, the major beneficiaries of the Ex-Im's direct lending program. As their dismay with the administration's approach to the Bank grew, they turned to supporters in Congress for assistance. One of the most willing of their congressional allies was Pennsylvania Republican Senator John Heinz. Indeed, as early as 1981–2, Heinz began to counter the administration's attempts to circumscribe Bank operations. As chair of the Senate Subcommittee on International Finance and Monetary Policy of the Committee on Banking, Housing, and Urban Affairs, he refused, for example, to confirm new directors for the Bank unless they were politically neutral professionals.[52]

A few major exporters took the lead in garnering congressional support for the Bank. They had always been instrumental in arguing the case for a viable Ex-Im (especially a viable direct credit-loan program) before Congress. As early as 1953–4, major users of Bank programs, organized by Westinghouse Electric, led the fight to thwart efforts by Eisenhower's Treasury Department to curtail the scope of bank lending radically. Such exporter activism had increased in the 1970s, as the Bank became a much more visible agency. Indeed, in response to Reagan administration attacks on the Bank's direct lending in 1981–3, exporters mobilized a vigorous defense of Ex-Im when the Bank's charter was up for reauthorization in 1983.

In the ensuing battle, Stockman and others in the administration dismissed the importance of the Bank. They were quick to point out the obvious self-interest of the few companies leading the campaign to build congressional support for Ex-Im. Moreover, they argued that in macroeconomic terms the activities of the Ex-Im did not amount to much in 1983. Exports accounted for only 7 percent of gross national product (GNP), and the Bank only supported 8 percent of exports, or simply 0.6 percent of all U.S. economic activity. Its direct credits (loan)

[51] Glick Interview, March 13, 2000, p. 55. The Reagan administration's virtually government-wide cuts in administrative budgets posed a major strain on an agency like Ex-Im whose administrative expenses were largely composed of salaries for personnel. Draper's use of attrition (rather than layoffs) had a salutary impact on staff morale but, according to one former director (Rita Rodriguez), may have augmented executive staff complacency. Rodriguez Interview, June 15, 2000, pp. 59–60.

[52] Rodriguez Interview, June 15, 2000, pp. 59–60.

program represented only 2 percent of all exports, and even that figure was declining rapidly.[53]

Internal Bank studies, however, took a different view. They showed that in certain critical sectors, such as capital goods, exports accounted for 30 percent of output, and Ex-Im supported 20 percent of the exports. Thus, the argument went, Bank support was ten times more important in this sector than in the U.S. economy as a whole. Moreover, these exports provided significant contributions to capacity utilization and productivity enhancement in certain industries.[54]

Even so, the major capital goods exporters faced serious political problems. For one thing, their allies among major business advocacy groups, such as the National Association of Manufacturers, generally supported the proposed Reagan budget cuts.[55] For another, because social expenditures were reduced in the early Reagan administration, liberal political defenders of such spending focused on, and attacked, assistance to business, especially that to a few very large enterprises. The combination of the small and decreasing macro economic impact of the Bank's operations with the concentration of its importance in a few industries (and firms) fueled these arguments about "corporate welfare." Such challenges to the Bank's programs would be a feature of attacks from the political right and left for the next two decades.

In any event, major exporters like Boeing and Westinghouse launched public defenses of the role of the Ex-Im in financing their exports. T. A. Wilson, Boeing's chairman of the board and chief executive officer, made a fairly typical defense of the Bank before a House budget hearing in 1981. He told the committee that his company was losing orders to Airbus' "subsidized export financing that U.S. private industry cannot

[53] Memorandum, Cruse to Draper, "Uneven Distribution of Export/Exim Importance Throughout the U.S. Economy," July 5, 1983, "Exim Importance – 1983" folder, POF. Total loans had reached a peak of $5.5 billion (1981); they were $3.5 billion in 1982 and $845 million in 1983. See Annual Report for 1983, pp. 12–13.

[54] Transmittal Memorandum and Attachments, Cruse to Others, "Stockman's View of Exim," April 22, 1985, "(1985) Stockman/Bandow Report on Exim Subsidies" folder, POF; Memorandum, Cruse to Draper, "Uneven Distribution of Export/Exim Importance throughout the U.S. Economy," July 5, 1983, "Exim Importance – 1983" folder, POF; Memorandum, "A Strategy for Defending Exim Subsidies – 1985 Context," February 6, 1985, "1985 Defense of Exim" folder, POF.

[55] Interview with Elizabeth Schwartz, April 24, 2000, pp. 3–5, Library, Ex-Im (hereafter Schwartz Interview, April 24, 2000).

meet without Eximbank help." He expressed special concern about the loss of important first orders, which had long-term ramifications because airlines generally standardized later purchases on the basis of their initial choices. Wilson also emphasized the complex relationship Boeing had with its suppliers, what he termed its "invisible exporters." Boeing, he pointed out, subcontracted 53 percent of each 747 aircraft. The firm had a supplier and subcontractor network of 1,306 major and 2,247 small business firms in forty-four states; their sales to Boeing were more than $6 billion in 1979. He estimated that, in addition to these first-level suppliers, there "are an estimated 50,000 second and third-tier firms that provide parts and services for our programs." According to Wilson, any change in Bank policy that affected major exporters like Boeing would also have an impact on its extensive supplier network around the nation.[56] Westinghouse – another major Bank customer – made similar arguments. It based its position on two commissioned studies by Wharton Econometric Forecasting Associates of its economy-wide benefits.[57]

To increase their clout, the major exporters tried to widen the base of support for the Bank. Thus, in 1981, Westinghouse, Boeing, and General Electric combined their efforts to form the Coalition for Employment Through Exports (CEE). It opposed the substantial reductions in the Bank's lending programs championed by the Reagan administration. By June 1982, it had grown to forty firms. In the following year, CEE leaders expanded beyond its corporate base to include fourteen unions and three governors.[58] Despite past instances of tense management–union relations in some firms, labor leaders cooperated with CEE because of its contention that Ex-Im's financing was crucial to the creation and retention of quality jobs. CEE was exceedingly active in the shaping of legislation reauthorizing the Bank in 1983, as it joined forces with

56 Congress, House, Committee on Banking, Finance and Urban Affairs, Subcommittee on International Trade, Investment, and Monetary Policy, *Export-Import Bank Budget Authorization*, 97th Congress, 1st Session, 1981, pp. 2–6.

57 Memorandum, "Critique of Westinghouse/Wharton Cost/Benefit Analysis of Eximbank Credit Support," August 13, 1982, POF; Memorandum, Cruse to Directors and Senior Staff, "View on latest Westinghouse/Wharton Study," December 16, 1982, "Westinghouse/Wharton Study – 1982" folder, POF; Schwartz Interview, April 24, 2000, pp. 8–9.

58 Schwartz Interview, April 24, 2000, pp. 4–6; Carole M. P. Neves, "The Export-Import Bank of the United States: Decay and Renewal" (Ph.D. diss., Virginia Polytechnic Institute, 1985), pp. 161–3.

such organizations as the Banker's Association for Foreign Trade and the National Foreign Trade Council.[59]

On November 21, 1983, Congress approved a short (three-year) charter extension, through September 30, 1986. The most important amendment to the Bank's charter was the clarification of the dual mandate that emanated from the 1970s. In those years, Congress directed Ex-Im to be fully competitive with foreign ECA financing (1971) and to take into account the cost of borrowed money (1974). The Draper administration had focused on this dual mandate to, in the opinion of many exporters and their supporters in Congress, circumscribe Ex-Im's direct lending program. In any event, the new legislation gave the Bank a primary mission of expanding American exports through fully competitive financing. But the terms and conditions of that financing did not need to be equivalent to those offered by foreign ECAs, so long as the effect of those terms and conditions was to neutralize financing offered by foreign ECAs.[60]

The legislation also mandated that the Bank set aside authorizations for loans, guarantees, and insurance for small business. These sums were to be at least 6 percent for fiscal 1984; 8 percent in fiscal 1985; and 10 percent in fiscal 1986, and thereafter. It also stipulated that at least one bank director would represent the interests of small business. The effect of this provision was muted, however, because Ex-Im could count subsuppliers of companies receiving Bank financing to meet the percentage requirements. This was not changed until 1992. In addition, the amendments to the Export-Import Bank Act also established staggered, four-year terms for newly appointed directors and reconstituted the Bank's advisory board.[61]

Just one week before Congress passed the Bank's reauthorization, it also approved the Bank's budget for fiscal year 1984. The latter gave the Ex-Im authority to extend $3.9 billion in loans and $10 billion in guarantees and insurance in fiscal 1984. In fiscal year 1982, the Bank had

[59] Schwartz Interview, April 24, 2000, pp. 4–6.

[60] Hearings, House, "Eximbank Reauthorization," Subcommittee on International Trade, Investment and Monetary Policy, Committee on Banking, Finance and Urban Affairs, 98th Congress, 1st Session, April 19–20, 1983.

[61] Ibid. For a discussion of the impact of the pre-1983 "dual" mandate on the Bank, see Interview with Allan Mendelowitz, February 13, 2001, pp. 8–10, Library, Ex-Im (hereafter Mendelowitz Interview, February 13, 2000); Rodriguez Interview, June 15, 2000, pp. 4–6.

made \$3.516 billion in loans. These numbers declined to \$845 million in fiscal year 1983, increased to \$1.465 billion in fiscal year 1984, only to decline to \$659 million in fiscal year 1985. Direct lending remained below \$1 billion until fiscal 1993, reflecting the impact of the LDC debt crisis and the general international economic slowdown. In fact, the Bank would substantially spend less than its committed loan authorization limit each year between 1983 and 1986. Ironically, several members of Congress criticized Ex-Im because it was not "doing enough." Others chafed at this shortfall that created problems because it reduced Congress' ability to appropriate that money for other federal needs in a period of tight budgets.[62]

BUDGETARY PRESSURES: INTEREST RATE MATCHING PROGRAM (I-MATCH)

Ex-Im was subject to the budgetary rules that applied to all U.S. government credit agencies. These directives had resulted from a report issued by a bipartisan commission on budget concepts in 1968. The rules provided that, at the time cash disbursements occurred on direct credits, those disbursements were counted as outlays (expenditures) in the calculation of the government surplus or deficit. If and when the loan was repaid, the inflow of principal and interest paid counted as receipts in the surplus or deficit calculation. Thus, direct loans had a large negative budget impact in the early years of the loan as it disbursed, and only in the later years as it was repaid, generally beyond the horizon for budget decision making, did the offsetting receipts counter the earlier disbursements. Since guaranteed loans did not count against the deficit, unless and until a claim was paid, guarantees were essentially "free" for budget decision-making purposes.

In early 1985, under the aegis of OMB and the Treasury Department, Draper submitted an unusual budget proposal to Congress for fiscal year 1986. It advanced the elimination of all the Bank's direct credit/lending programs, both medium term (two to five years) and long term (more than five years). In its place, Ex-Im would substitute an Interest Rate Matching Program (I-Match). This was essentially an interest rate

[62] Office of the Chief Financial Officer (Eximbank), *Export-Import Bank of the United States: Financial and Budgetary Aspects, 1970–2000*, April 1993, pp. 29–30; Hess Interview, August 15, 2000, pp. 39, 48.

buy-down. The program, as initially proposed, was put forward to counter officially subsidized foreign competition. A commercial lender would make a fixed rate loan for the term appropriate to the transaction at the minimum interest rate established in the OECD Arrangement. The same commitment and application fees that applied to Ex-Im direct lending would apply – 0.5 percent and 2 percent. The Bank would fully guarantee repayment of the principal and interest on the loan. If the OECD Arrangement rate was below the market rate, Ex-Im would enter into a funding agreement with the commercial lender. The Bank would pay the commercial lender an additional amount of interest to ensure that it earned a market rate on the loan. Ex-Im and OMB hoped that, because OECD Arrangement rates were then linked to market rates, the overall cost of the program would be kept at acceptable levels.[63]

According to the Bank, such a program was possible because of the on-going convergence of market and OECD Arrangement rates. It also anticipated that the same factors in recent OECD sector understandings on large aircraft and nuclear power would enable any financing of such big ticket items to be accomplished under the Bank's existing financial guarantee programs. Furthermore, the I-Match proposals would not affect existing Bank financial guarantee or insurance programs.[64] Financial support for the I-Match program would be limited to $136 million in fiscal year 1986; when adjusted for the receipt of the Bank's application fees, this amount would be $100 million. Ex-Im stated that the amount of loans funded under I-Match for fiscal year 1986 would be limited to $1.8 billion. No funds would be appropriated for I-Match, according to the Bank, since "it would make use of its borrowing authority and usual sources of funding."[65]

Draper believed that the substitution of such an interest rate buy-down program would have an immediate positive impact on the computation of the Bank's budget cost. It would also make transparent the subsidy element in its direct lending. Draper highlighted the historic incongruity of budget treatment of the Bank's loans to the Senate Committee on Banking, Housing, and Urban Affairs in early 1985.

63 Memorandum, "Eximbank's FY 1986 Budget," January 28, 1986, and Memorandum, "Interest Matching Program (IMP)," January 28, 1986, both in "I-Match Program Options" folder, POF.

64 Ibid.

65 Ibid.

"I come out of business [he said] and I cannot believe anybody would run a business on a cash basis, and that's exactly the way the budget works today – our loans are counted on a cash basis. We make an investment in a loan that collects interest and that's counted against the budget as if we had spent the money for food, or on salaries, or whatever. This program corrects that. The loans will not be counted on the budget anymore, but we will spell out our subsidy which will be counted."[66]

Besides the transparency of subsidies under I-Match, it had the short-term impact of substantially reducing Ex-Im's effect on the federal budget deficit. Bank officials estimated that the elimination of the direct loan program and the substitution of the I-Match would result in deficit reductions of $329 million in fiscal year 1986 and $3.4 billion for the fiscal period 1986–8, largely because only interest rate buy-down payments and not loan disbursements would be counted against the budget. As it turned out, this would be a relatively short-term phenomenon. And in later years the I-Match would increase the Bank's contribution to projected deficits because there would be no repayments to the Bank as there would have been under a direct loan.[67]

Within the Ex-Im there were serious concerns about the implications of the scheme and how it would work. The most obvious was that the program would entail higher interest expenses because the government's cost of borrowing would always be less than that of the private sector. Thus, the Bank would be subsidizing a higher cost of funds. Bank staff estimated that the extra expense would be substantial on medium and long-term loans. Draper told the Senate Appropriations Committee that such costs would be $40 million more than the equivalent direct loan program (based on a loan volume of $1.8 billion).[68] These costs would be incurred in delivering essentially the same amount of capital toward export financing. It was also assumed that I-Match would require more administrative costs to calculate and track the disbursements of the subsidy. Finally, there was concern that an overall limitation on the amount of subsidy disbursed by Ex-Im could distort its decisions concerning the types of cases that the Bank assisted with direct credits.

[66] Congress, Senate, Committee on Banking, Housing, and Urban Affairs, *Oversight Activities of the Export-Import Bank,* 99th Congress, 1st Session, 1985, pp. 48–9.

[67] Memorandum, "Eximbank's FY 1986 Budget," January 28, 1986, "I-Match Program Options" folder, POF.

[68] Draper quoted in Letter, Jasinowski to Gray, June 12, 1985, "1986 Budget" folder, POF.

OECD Arrangement rates were the lowest (and the most subsidized) in the poorest countries, and these were often the most competitive cases. And the Bank's rationale, reinforced in the 1983 reauthorization, was to assist in such cases. Limitations on subsidies would discourage its use in just such cases, and instead encourage its use in more prosperous markets where OECD rates were higher and less subsidized.[69]

Bank officials supporting I-Match envisioned from the start that the Private Export Finance Corporation would play a major part in the implementation of the program. Bank staff assumed that only on large, short disbursement cases (like aircraft) would it be possible for any other institution to be competitive with PEFCO's pricing model. Early Ex-Im surveys of the private sector banks (investment and commercial) indicated a mixed reception at best for I-Match. Investment banks were negative on the medium-term approach but felt that they might be interested in the long-term program, if the Bank's guarantee was made more marketable.[70]

I-Match faced vigorous opposition from major exporters and business groups and within Congress. Coming little more than a year after Congress had amended the Bank's charter to ensure that the Ex-Im's primary focus was to provide facilities for American exporters facing subsidized foreign competition, I-Match looked like a deficit-reduction gimmick. Indeed, Draper had said that it "will enable us to make a significant contribution to the number one problem facing our nation today – reducing the massive Federal Budget deficit."[71]

Making the battle over I-Match particularly bitter was the distrust Chairman Draper had engendered among certain members of the export community. To be sure, at key junctures Draper had been a partisan of the Bank's programs within the administration. Yet the existing reservoir of suspicion spilled over in regard to I-Match. CEE argued that the

69 Memorandum, "Eximbank Subsidies – A Brief on the Appropriate Form and Substance," February 11, 1985, POF.

70 Memorandum, "Findings of Discussions with Major Commercial and Investment Banks, Regional Banks, and PEFCO on Aspects on the I-Match Proposals," February 28, 1985, "I-Match Program Options" folder, POF.

71 "Eximbank Seeks Charter Amendment for Operation of New Program," *Exim News*, March 6, 1985, Library, Ex-Im, Congress, House, Committee on Banking, Finance and Urban Affairs, Subcommittee on International Finance, Trade and Monetary Policy, *To Extend and Amend the Export-Import Bank Act of 1945*, 99th Congress, 1st Session, 1985, pp. 76–95, 119–29.

program was contrary to the intent of the Bank's 1983 reauthorization.[72] Many exporters feared that commercial banks would not make such loans. Broad business organizations such as the NAM and the U.S. Chamber of Commerce thought that the program relied too heavily on PEFCO and provided a poor substitute for the Bank's direct lending program. Finally, exporters and commercial banks with substantial Ex-Im business feared the prospects of getting a clearly identified, and presumably more politically vulnerable, subsidy.[73]

These exporter and business concerns reinforced congressional opposition among key Bank supporters. Typical were the initial comments of Senator Heinz in February 1985. He was, he stated, "mystified" how the I-Match would replace the direct lending program since commercial banks would be unwilling to extend terms beyond six years, while standard terms under the OECD Arrangement were eight to ten years. He too believed that the I-Match Program violated the 1983 amendments to the Bank's charter. The senator questioned a direct transfer payment "from the Treasury to U.S. banks, particularly when better methods of defending U.S. exports are available and have been used successfully for years." Finally, he queried how the program could provide an adequate response to foreign mixed credits offers.[74] Heinz's views resonated among interested colleagues, and Draper and Bank staff were put through several "rough" hearings in 1985.[75]

The relevant legislative committees rejected I-Match in 1985. For fiscal year 1987, the Bank submitted (in early 1986) a revised I-Match that attempted to streamline guarantee and funding procedures for both the medium- and long-term program.[76] Draper continued to try to convince critics in Congress and elsewhere that the program was workable.[77] But he was near the end of his tumultuous tenure as Bank chairman, and left in February 1986 for a United Nations post.

72 For the opposition of exporters see Congress, House, Committee on Appropriations, *Foreign Assistance and Related Programs Appropriations for Fiscal Year 1986*, 99th Congress, 1st Session, 1985, pp. 728–9.

73 Ibid., pp. 730–1; Hess Interview, August 15, 2000, pp. 41–5.

74 Congress, Senate, Committee on Banking, Housing, and Urban Affairs, *Oversight Activities of the Export-Import Bank*, 99th Congress, 1st Session, 1985, pp. 1–5.

75 See, for example, Congress, Senate, Committee on Appropriations, *Foreign Assistance and Related Programs Appropriations for Fiscal Year 1986*, 99th Congress, 1st Session, 1985, pp. 707–53.

76 Memorandum, "I-Match II," n.d., "I-Match II" folder, POF.

77 Hess Interview, August 15, 2000, pp. 44–5.

Ultimately, exporter opposition to I-Match lessened, if for no other reason than that the program was the best attainable alternative from the Reagan administration. That was certainly the view of Iowa's Republican James Leach, an important member of the House Subcommittee on International Finance, Trade and Monetary Affairs.[78] Others like Boeing's treasurer, Jack Pierce, believed that the revised I-Match was an improvement.[79] Senator Heinz continued to view I-Match as a budget gimmick, a cumbersome and untested program that he thought would bleed the financial life out of the Ex-Im. He wanted to consider other budget options, including removing the Bank from the budget, only considering for budget purposes (or "scoring") the subsidy component of Bank loans, or continuing the direct loan program and only authorizing I-Match as a back-up or pilot program.[80]

Finally, the Congressional Budget Office (CBO) sealed the fate of I-Match. For purposes of the budget deficit reduction figures, I-Match was "scored" as a direct loan for the amount of the loan – in other words treated as similar to the existing direct lending program. With the allure of budget reduction gone, the other problems and costs associated with I-Match doomed the program.[81] Nonetheless, the Bank's 1986 reauthorization allowed for a two-year pilot program for I-Match, although subject to stringent conditions.[82]

Other budget-induced programs also created problems. In 1986, OMB required Ex-Im to sell sufficient loans from its portfolio to reduce new budget outlays by $1.5 billion in fiscal year 1987. The Bank identified three large borrowers as the most viable loans to sell (Japan, Korea,

[78] Congress, House, Committee on Banking, Finance, and Urban Affairs, Subcommittee on International Finance, Trade, and Monetary Policy, *The Charter Renewal of the Export-Import Bank*, 99th Congress, 2nd Session, 1986, pp. 90–1; Memorandum, JW, WA, & SW to Heinz, "Strategy for Eximbank Hearing on February 7, 1986," January 31, 1986, "1986 Reauthorization" folder, POF.

[79] Congress, House, Committee on Banking, Finance, and Urban Affairs, Subcommittee on International Finance, Trade, and Monetary Policy, *The Charter Renewal of the Export-Import Bank*, 99th Congress, 2nd Session, 1986, pp. 64–79.

[80] Memorandum, JW, WA, & SW to Heinz, "Strategy for Eximbank Hearing on February 7, 1986," January 31, 1986, "1986 Reauthorization" folder, POF; and JW, WA, & SW to Heinz, "Eximbank's I-Match Proposal," January 28, 1986, POF.

[81] Hess Interview, August 15, 2000, pp. 43–5; Congress, House, Committee on Appropriations, Subcommittee on Foreign Operations and Related Agencies, *Foreign Assistance and Related Programs Appropriations for 1987*, 99th Congress, 1st Session, 1986, pp. 692–3.

[82] Congress, Committee of Conference, *Export-Import Bank Act Amendments of 1986*, 99th Congress, 2nd Session, 1986, pp. 4–8.

and Taiwan) and gave those borrowers the option of prepaying the loans in lieu of the Bank's selling them. All three chose to prepay the loans rather than have them sold in the market. Although the loans were all prepaid at the full outstanding amount plus accrued interest, the Bank had to use the proceeds to prepay high-interest-rate borrowings from the FFB, which charged a premium to the Bank on the prepayment.[83] This increased somewhat the Bank's reported loss for the years of the sales. Additionally, because the Bank sold some of the highest-rated credits in its portfolio, the portfolio remaining after the sale had a higher overall risk.[84]

The I-Match proposals and the debates that surrounded them reflected just how important federal budget considerations were for the Bank during the Reagan administration. They determined the future and shape of the Bank's direct lending program. I-Match was among the major issues in the Ex-Im's reauthorization in 1986, which extended the charter of the Bank through 1992. In many respects, the 1986 reauthorization was a congressional response to the accumulated grievances of exporters to the Draper administration. Additionally, it sought to streamline Bank programs to coax the private sector back into trade finance. In this vein, the legislation prohibited restrictions on the transferability of new medium- and long-term obligations insured or guaranteed by the Bank.[85] The 1986 reauthorization also addressed the hated application fee instituted by Draper. It prohibited the Bank from imposing such credit application fees unless competitive with fees of other ECAs. It also afforded the borrower the option of paying the fee up-front or over the life of the loan. Additional sections directed Ex-Im to improve the competitiveness of its midterm financing (two to five years).[86]

The budget battles over the future funding levels of the Bank's direct lending had extended from 1981 through 1986. Beginning in 1983, however, the LDC crisis and factors peculiar to the aircraft and nuclear

[83] Interview with Raymond Albright, April 6, 2000, pp. 47–9, Library, Ex-Im (hereafter Albright Interview, April 6, 2000).

[84] Annual Report for 1987, p. 34.

[85] Memorandum, JW, WA & SW to Heinz, "Exim Charter Reauthorization Issues," January 30, 1986, POF; Summary of H.R. 5548 Export-Import Bank Act Amendments of 1986 Enacted October 15, 1986, no date, both in "1986 Reauthorization" folder, POF.

[86] Summary of H.R. 5548 Export-Import Bank Act Amendments of 1986 Enacted October 15, 1986, n.d., "1986 Reauthorization" folder, POF.

Table 6.1 *Budgeted Levels Versus Authorizations (Direct Credits), 1983–1986 (millions of dollars)*

Year	Budget	Authorizations
1983	3,775	845
1984	3,840	1,465
1985	3,830	659
1986	800	577

Source: Memorandum, "Influence on Exim's Credit Utilization," February 5, 1987, "Credit Utilization – 1987" folder, POF.

industries resulted in dramatic gaps between levels budgeted for direct lending and amounts actually used. For the years 1983–6, budgeted levels were considerably more than actually used. (See Table 6.1.)

In late 1986, Senator Heinz sharply criticized these trends noting that "since 1981 the bank's use of credit authority has plunged faster than shrinking credit ceilings in the Budget." In a letter to the Bank's new chairman, John A. Bohn, he essentially laid the blame for much of this at the door of the Bank and his predecessor. He prodded Bohn, stating that the Ex-Im needed to do more to match the aggressiveness of foreign ECAs and to use authority in the reauthorization to "develop export financial linkages with capital markets."[87]

Bohn responded that Bank credit policies were a relatively minor factor in its inability to fully use its authorized resources. He noted that the value of long-term export credits extended by other official ECAs (Germany, Japan, France, and the United Kingdom) fell by more than 80 percent during the period. Rather Bohn and the staff pointed to the impacts of the LDC debt crisis (cancellation or deferred major projects), the strong dollar, and the successful operation of the OECD Arrangement (including aircraft).[88]

OECD AND TIED AID

John A. Bohn had already been the Bank's vice chairman for two years when he succeeded William H. Draper in April 1986. Before coming

[87] Letter, Heinz to Bohn, October 17, 1986, "1986 Reauthorization" folder, POF.

[88] Letter, Bohn to Heinz, February 5, 1987, "1986 Reauthorization" folder, POF; Memorandum, "Influence on Exim's Credit Utilization," February 5, 1987, "Credit Utilization – 1987" folder, POF.

to the Bank, he had been the American ambassador to and executive director of the Asian Development Bank in Manila, Philippines, between 1981 and 1984. Before that he had been with Wells Fargo for fourteen years.[89] Many users of Ex-Im services welcomed the change in leadership. Typical was Westinghouse's representative Stuart Eizenstat who, in a congressional hearing, referred to Bohn as "a breath of fresh air at Eximbank."[90]

Bohn would need such goodwill. He faced major challenges in the Bank's international environment. He had to continue to refine OECD export credit formulas and push ahead negotiations on the OECD Arrangement, especially concerning what was referred to as tied aid. The latter issue, he later described as one of the "thorniest" of his tenure as chairman.[91]

The 1980s witnessed a substantial rise in the use of so-called tied aid as a mechanism for ECAs to subsidize exports. Simply stated, tied aid is the practice of linking concessional foreign aid grants to procurement in the donor country, where the balance of the export's cost is linked to commercial export credits supported by ECAs. France in the late 1950s had pioneered in the process of tying concessional assistance to commercial export credits, a practice imitated by others – especially Japan – by the early 1970s. Ironically, the tied aid programs of some OECD countries were originally prompted by the United States. In the late 1950s and early 1960s, the United States pressed its Cold War allies to assume some of the aid burden to reduce American foreign assistance expenditures, an area of the budget that often faced opposition in Congress. The programs of these countries were smaller, more focused, and more closely linked to national economic policies than those of the United States.[92]

The relationship between export credit and developmental aid had long been a matter of discussion within the OECD. Participants recognized rather early that mixed credits – the combination of concessional

89 BAFT Update, "John Bohn and his Priorities at the Export-Import Bank," March 31, 1986, "Bohn" folder, POF.

90 Congress, House, Committee on Banking, Finance and Urban Affairs, Subcommittee on International Finance, Trade and Monetary Policy, *U.S. Export-Import Bank: On Recapitalization and Other Issues*, 100th Congress, 2nd Session, 1988, pp. 18–19.

91 Interview with John Bohn, November 16, 2000, pp. 8–9, Library, Ex-Im.

92 Report, "Financing of Railway Equipment Exports," by W. F. Doering and A. Rigley, n.d., Box 4, "Commerce Department" folder, Government Agencies file, RG 275.

aid and commercial export assistance – created market distortions. It was entirely possible that small amounts of concessional financing could be combined to make more attractive projects that were primarily of a commercial nature. One consequence was that legitimate developmental projects could be starved for funds. The original 1976 unilateral declarations, which became the 1978 OECD Arrangement, contained statements that all mixed credits with a combined grant element of under 15 percent could be subject to prior notification.[93]

There was a dramatic increase in the use of tied aid in the period from 1978 to 1981. Totals for concession and commercial financing in tied aid offers, reported to the OECD, increased from $969 million in 1978 to more than $2.3 billion in 1981.[94] The 1982 OECD Arrangement also contained provisions related to the minimum concessional levels that could be extended in either single-source or mixed tied aid packages. No such aid packages would be extended that had a grant element of less than 20 percent. The hope was, according to a leading student of export credit practices, "to separate true commercial credits, which in principle have no grant element, from true development, which should generally have a higher grant element."[95] Thus, increasing the attractiveness of a commercial package by including a sliver of concessional aid would be more expensive, and presumably less attractive to the grantor nation.

Even so, tied aid offers by OECD countries exploded to $6.4 billion in 1982. Reagan administration officials seemed to disregard the intensified pressures on American exporters created by the heightened use of tied aid by other parties to the 1982 OECD Arrangement, especially France, Belgium, Italy, and Japan. Domestic institutional impediments also hindered a coordinated U.S. response to the tied aid efforts of others. Since 1961, the American aid program had been run by a separate agency, the Agency for International Development. The American program of concessionary assistance had been large enough to support its own goals and culture, separate from the commercial lending operations of the Bank. Furthermore, AID did not finance capital projects, often the focal point of foreign ECA competition.

[93] Ray, pp. 58–61.

[94] Congress, House, Committee on Foreign Affairs, Report to Accompany H.R. 3667, *Mixed Credits* (Washington, DC: Government Printing Office, 1986), pp. 5–6 (hereafter *Mixed Credits*).

[95] Ray, pp. 60–1.

Congress was not so hesitant as the administration. Increased competition from tied aid offers of OECD participants, accompanied by the pressure on American exporters created by a strong dollar in the early 1980s, prompted legislation. In 1983 Congress passed the Trade and Development Enhancement Act (TDEA). The legislation established what it characterized as a "defensive" mixed credits program. It set aside funds for the Ex-Im and AID together to assist American exporters in responding to specific mixed credit offers initiated by foreign ECAs. Neither agency could initiate mixed credit offers under the legislation. The program mandated them to "neutralize predatory financing by foreign governments" and "to encourage them to enter into effective and comprehensive agreements with the U.S. to end the use of tied aid."[96]

The Reagan administration initially opposed these programs, and American exporters were skeptical whether aggressive action would be taken. Moreover, AID was exceedingly reluctant to enter into the arena, reflecting its strong developmental orientation and institutional culture.[97] During the first eighteen months of the mixed credits program, it participated with Ex-Im in matching just two foreign offers.[98]

The Bank was more aggressive. Between January 1984 and June 1985, it matched ten foreign, mixed credit offers. It also drew public attention to the incongruous nature of the use of tied aid by France, its most refined practitioner. In a September 1984 press release, Draper applauded legitimate use of low-interest aid loans for humanitarian and developmental purposes. But he severely criticized French offers of aid funds to finance the sale of computerized machine tools to the Indonesian aircraft industry and digital switching telecommunications equipment to Cyprus. Draper publicly likened the French use of aid funds to support the sale of a satellite communication station "to using famine relief funds to buy pate de fois gras and champagne." Ex-Im matched both the Indonesian and Cypriot loans.[99] The chairman also attacked

96 *Mixed Credits*, pp. 5–6.

97 Congress, House, Committee on Foreign Affairs, Report to Accompany H.R. 3, *Trade and Internaitonal Policy and Reform Act of 1987* (Washington, DC: Government Printing Office, 1987), pp. 107–9; Albright Interview, April 6, 2000, pp. 42–3.

98 *Mixed Credits*, pp. 5–6.

99 "Eximbank President Attacks Misuse of Aid Funds by Foreign Governments" and "Eximbank's Concessionary Financing Wins U.S. Machine Tool Export Sale," *Exim News*, September 27, 1984; "Eximbank Counters Mixed Credit for Cyprus," *Exim News*, November 15, 1984, Library, Ex-Im.

Japan's tied aid offer to sell satellite communications equipment to Algeria, noting that "the financing of a sophisticated telecommunications project in an oil and gas rich country is not an appropriate use of aid money."[100]

Tied aid nonetheless continued to have a negative impact on American exporters. Exporters and interested members of Congress considered the Bank's few victories at confronting tied aid offers as at best unusual. Criticism mounted. By the end of 1985, business groups, especially the U.S. Chamber of Commerce, wanted the TDEA mixed credit program amended to force AID to use its funds to respond more aggressively to the specific mixed credit offers of Japan and France.[101] In early 1986, the House Committee on Foreign Affairs noted that, according to OECD figures, mixed credit offers nearly doubled from $3.4 billion in 1983 to $6.5 billion in 1985.[102]

Nevertheless, Chairman Draper continued a broad instead of targeted tied aid strategy. He and the administration simply did not view tied aid as seriously as the export credit competition that prevailed when they took office. Testifying before Congress in early 1985, Draper articulated the point that "the tied aid problem is significant, but quantitatively, it is not on a scale with the overall export credit problems which we have already solved, as a matter of priority." He questioned the use of large figures in the billions to assess the magnitude of the tied aid problem. Speaking for calendar year 1984, he added, "only about 15 or 20 cases of really problematic or commercial foreign aid credit cases amounting to between $300 million and $400 million were brought to our attention and confirmed during the last year [1984]."[103]

100 "Exim President Attacks Misuse of Aid Funds by Foreign Government," *Exim News*, September 27, 1984.

101 Memorandum, JW, WA & SW to John Heinz, "Exim Charter Reauthorization Issues," January 30, 1986, "1986 Reauthorization" folder, POF.

102 *Mixed Credits*, pp. 5–6.

103 Congress, House, Committee on Banking, Finance and Urban Affairs, Subcommittee on International Finance, Trade and Monetary Policy, Hearings on H.R. 120, *To Extend and Amend the Export-Import Bank Act of 1945*, 99th Congress, 1st Session, 1985. In fact, a 1989 Ex-Im Bank report estimated that U.S. capital goods exporters lost between $400 million and $800 million a year in export orders because of the tied aid practices of foreign ECAs. See General Accounting Office, Report, *Export Finance: The Role of the U.S. Export-Import Bank*, (Washington, DC: Government Printing Office, 1992), p. 46.

Draper preferred that the United States focus on OECD negotiations on tied aid. Since 1983, American representatives at the OECD in Paris had introduced proposals that would make mixed credits and other forms of tied aid more costly by increasing the proportion and concessionality of the aid element in tied aid offers. The objective was to widen the distinction between development assistance and export credits.[104] Ultimately, the United States proposed a ban on all tied aid credits with a concessional element of less than 50 percent. But successes at the OECD, through 1985, were small. In 1985, OECD participants increased the minimum grant element in tied aid offers to 25 percent and accepted procedures for transparency, that is, notification of tied credits. And OECD sector arrangements for large aircraft and nuclear power excluded the use of tied aid.[105]

Even so, exporter frustration with the Reagan administration grew. If anything, annoyance increased as the value of the dollar increased, heightening worries about the country's competitive position that might fuel protectionist sentiments. Eventually, on September 23, 1985, the administration proposed a $300 million fund (tied aid credit fund or "War Chest") to address foreign mixed credits. Doubts abounded both within the Ex-Im and the exporter community that this amount, to be administered in consultation with the Treasury Department, would be sufficient to address the problem.[106]

Prominent exporters continued to think that the Bank's response to tied aid competition remained slow and inadequate. It was hindered, they thought, by the conservative influence of the Department of the Treasury, which promoted negotiations and questioned aggressive Ex-Im matching of foreign ECA offers. Exporter complaints found fertile ground in Congress. Because of such opinion, and with legislation imminent on the tied aid fund, the pace at the Bank quickened. On October 23, 1985, Ex-Im announced over $250 million in offers of highly concessionary financing in six transactions (including one in conjunction with AID – $27 million for computers to India). Bank officials directed these offers primarily at the French whom they saw as the most recalcitrant at the ongoing OECD

104 "Eximbank Briefing Book," December 1988, Section D-1, pp. 7–8, POF.

105 Ray, pp. 73–4.

106 "Eximbank Chairman Pledges More Aggressive Tied-Aid Program," *Exim News*, October 2, 1985, Library, Ex-Im.

negotiations.[107] Not all these efforts succeeded, and additional offers were made the next year. For fiscal year 1986, exporters secured six orders totaling $171.4 million with high concessionary financing provided by the Bank. All the transactions involved normal terms for the direct credit/guarantee portion of the loan and a heavily subsidized direct credit with interest rates of 2 percent for the rest.[108]

Congress approved the Tied Aid War Chest as part of a six-year extension of the Bank's charter (the Export-Import Bank Amendments Act of 1986) on October 15, 1986. This legislation established funding levels for the program at $300 million for fiscal years 1987 and 1988, as well as for any tied aid matching credits Ex-Im authorized in fiscal year 1986.[109] Subsequently, the Bank used $78.1 million of the appropriation for six mixed credits authorized in fiscal 1987.[110]

The more aggressive stance of the administration and the targeted actions of the Bank produced movement in Paris at the OECD. In early 1986, France in part as a response to its own domestic budgetary problems, changed its position. Consequently, the European Community in early 1986 presented a unified position on tied aid. It accepted increases in the minimum concessionary element of loans and a calculation of the existing uniform discount factor for concessionary aid, that is, to allow for different countries' costs of money.[111]

Though the United States applauded the new EC position, others such as the Swiss, and especially the Japanese, were not supportive.[112] Consequently, the Bank went ahead and used the War Chest to increase pressure on Japan, among others. In November 1986, it offered three highly concessionary lines of credit to Thailand, the Phillippines, and Indonesia to assist American exporters in high-technology sectors, such as telecommunications, electronics, and power generation and its transmission. The Bank publicly targeted the widespread activities of

107 "Eximbank Implements Aggressive Program to Combat Tied-Aid Credit," *Exim News*, October 23, 1985, Library, Ex-Im.

108 Congress, House, Committee on Appropriations, Subcommittee on Foreign Operations and Related Agencies, *Foreign Assistance and Related Agencies Appropriations for 1988*, 100th Congress, 1st Session, 1987, pp. 1665–70.

109 Summary of H.R. 5548, "Export-Import Bank Act Amendments of 1986 Enacted October 15, 1986," n.d., "Congress: 1986" folder, POF.

110 Annual Report for 1987, pp. 1, 34.

111 "Eximbank Briefing Book," December 1988, Section D-1, pp. 8–10, POF; Ray, pp. 77–82.

112 "Japan Must Consider Tied-Aid Stance," *Japan Times*, May 13, 1986, POF.

Japan's tied aid programs in these countries, as well as activities of Switzerland and France.[113]

Ultimately, the participants struck a compromise. The so-called Wallen Package (for Axel Wallen, chairman of the OECD participants) included a reluctant Japan. The package – which became effective on March 15, 1987 – increased to 50 percent the minimum concessionary levels for mixed credits for the least-developed countries. For other developing countries, the increase was to 30 percent (from 25 percent) in July 1987. A year later, in July 1988, the latter rose to 35 percent. Additionally, the deal modified the formula to calculate the concessionary elements in mixed credit offers to eliminate the standard 10 percent discount rate and to rely on market rates, but with some formula modifications to reduce the impact on lower-interest-rate countries.[114]

Although the Ex-Im and the administration applauded the new understanding on tied aid/mixed credits, its limitations were soon apparent. John Lange, treasury's negotiator at the OECD, observed that "everyone recognized that [we] were just establishing a groundwork." He added that it was "as weak as the initial OECD Arrangement [1978]."[115] Fundamentally, American officials soon realized that the Wallen package did not act as a significant brake on tied aid. After July 1987, many OECD countries paid the increased cost of tied aid assistance by financing more projects with low concessionality credits (between 35 and 50 percent). Projects that before would have been financed by grants or high concessionality aid were now being financed by loans with lower levels of concessionality, but above the new, higher OECD minimums. Average concessionality had fallen, but the potential for trade distortions had increased, as had the number of tied aid offers.[116] The OECD reported a 30 percent increase in offers of tied aid credits between 1986 and 1987 and 1987 and 1988. In 1989, Acting Bank Chairman William F. Ryan noted that "In addition to increases in offers from countries

[113] "Eximbank to Offer Southeast Asian Concessionary Credit Lines," *Exim News*, November 26, 1986, Library, Ex-Im; Albright Interview, April 6, 2000, pp. 40–2.

[114] "Eximbank Briefing Book," December 1988, Section D-1, pp. 8–10, POF; Ray, pp 77–82.

[115] Lange Interview, April 10, 2000, pp. 38–9.

[116] Ray, pp. 85–6; Congress, House, Committee on Banking, Finance and Urban Affairs, Subcommittee on International Finance, Trade and Monetary Policy, *U.S. Export-Import Bank: On Recapitalization and Other Issues*, 100th Congress, 2nd Session, 1988, pp. 7–8, 31–2.

Table 6.2 *Authorizations (millions of dollars)*

Year	Loans	Guarantees	Insurance	Total
1985	659.4	1,320.1	6,529.5	8,509.0
1986	577.4	1,127.9	4,379.9	6,085.2
1987	598.9	1505.5	6,444.0	8,548.4
1988	685.3	601.0	5,133.6	6,419.9
1989	718.8	1,292.2	4,344.8	6,355.8

Source: Appendix B, Summary of Authorizations.

traditionally active in mixed credits, such as Japan and France, we're seeing increases in new players. Offers from Spain, for example, have increased 80 percent since 1984."[117] It would take a new round of protracted OECD negotiations, and fresh approaches to the issue, to achieve new, improved tied aid rules in the so-called Helsinki Package of 1991.

REORGANIZATION

Overall, Bohn's tenure focused on adapting the programs and people of the Ex-Im to the radically changed environment of the 1980s, and to the 1986 congressional mandates. To begin with, it was obvious that a sea change in the Bank's external environment worked a fundamental change in the nature and volume of its business. Ex-Im activity, especially direct credits/loans, were at very low levels throughout the middle and late 1980s. Its structure and processes would have to be changed or reworked to fit a changed world in which demand for its services had declined and where the private sector grew more reluctant in the mid-1980s to provide foreign trade finance. Bohn established a trade finance task force to review Ex-Im's loan and guarantee programs in late 1986; the Bank instituted an overhaul of its loan and guarantee programs in May 1987. Coupled with the implementation of provisions mandated by the 1986 reauthorization, these brought major changes to the Bank.[118] (See Table 6.2.)

117 Congress, House, Committee on Appropriations, Subcommittee on Foreign Operations, Export Financing, and Related Programs, *Foreign Operations, Export Financing, and Related Programs Appropriations for 1990*, 101st Congress, 1st Session, 1989, pp. 128–9.

118 "Eximbank Briefing Book," December 1988, C-1, p. 1, POF; Congress, House, Committee on Banking, Finance and Urban Affairs, Subcommittee on International Trade and Monetary Affairs, *Export-Import Bank*, 100th Congress, 1st Session, 1987, pp. 4–12.

Organizational changes were necessary to harmonize the operation of the medium- and long-term loan and guarantee programs. For decades long-term direct credits/loans had been the cornerstone and the most prestigious part of the Bank's work. Throughout much of the 1970s and until 1986, the Ex-Im divided itself essentially into two organizational units, each under a senior vice president. Direct Credits and Financial Guarantees dealt with long-term (five years or more) buyer credits for capital equipment or capital intensive projects. Export Credits, Medium-Term Guarantees and Insurance was a supplier credit program designed to support smaller transactions where repayment terms were short term (generally under one year) or medium term (generally more than one but less than five years). It also dealt with insurance issues. Until the mid 1970s, comparable positions in the latter unit were in many cases a pay grade lower in terms of rank and salary scale than in Direct Credits and Financial Guarantees.

Bohn's reorganization of 1986–7 led to fundamental changes. It placed all lending and insurance activity (regardless of size) in the Export Finance Group under an executive vice president. This executive also had responsibility for overseas regional divisions (Africa/Middle East, Asia, Europe and Canada, and Latin America), engineering, insurance, claims and recoveries, and a United States division. The reorganization separated Country Risk Analysis from the Export Finance Group and put it directly under the chairman as an independent staff function. Under the older organization, country risk analysis had been a line function under the regional divisions. Similar managerial structural changes were occurring within the banking industry. The LDC debt crisis, and the Bank's experience with an increasing number of nonperforming loans in the 1980s, required that it hone its risk analysis function.[119] Access to preliminary commitment procedures was expanded to all loans.[120]

The unpopular 2 percent application fee was replaced with a consistent risk and term-based, flat front-end exposure fee on all loans and guarantees, eliminating earlier disparate fees for various programs. In conjunction with this more risk-adjusted fee structure, the Bank

119 "Eximbank Briefing Book," December 1988, pp. A-1 and B-1, POF; Rodriguez Interview, June 15, 2000, pp. 7–9; "Eximbank Reorganizes to Provide Better Service," *Exim News*, June 9, 1986.

120 Annual Report for 1987, p. 4.

liberalized its cover policies in more than sixty-five markets.[121] This "price-to-risk" policy, however, also had the effect of increasing fees in markets with higher risks.[122] Ex-Im's sharpening of its risk differentiation skills, as well as other ECA's increasing risk awareness in the post-debt-crisis environment, provided the impetus for OECD discussions on risk primia. Ultimately, the result was an OECD Arrangement on risk primia in 1997.

There were other measures to address the collapse of demand and the private sector's flight from foreign trade finance in the 1980s. Congress in 1986 directed the Bank to improve the transferability of its guarantee in an effort to attract investment bankers to guaranteed loans. Generally, treasury officials had opposed making government-guaranteed obligations of any federal credit-issuing agency transferable. They feared that to do so would heighten the possibility of competition with the private sector. Be that as it may, the congressionally mandated transferable Ex-Im guarantee provided an attractive inducement to the private sector. The downside of this change was, in the view of some Bank officials, the creation of a labor-intensive mode of operation for guarantee transactions that would have future consequences by increasing processing times.[123]

Additionally, in 1986 the Bank substantially liberalized its foreign content rules in response to changing patterns of global manufacture and pressure from multinational exporters. Until that time, the Bank only supported transactions involving 100 percent U.S. goods and services, and occasionally permitted limited foreign content on a case-by-case basis. Other ECAs provided their exporters much greater flexibility. The new rules allowed Bank support for American-made items containing foreign-made components provided they were incorporated into the item in the United States. Under such circumstances, Ex-Im would finance or guarantee (medium- or long-term financing) up to 100 percent of the American content provided that the total amount financed or guaranteed did not exceed 85 percent of the contract price and that the total American content was not less than 50 percent of the contract price. In projects, however, which involved export of a number of what

[121] Ibid.; Eximbank Briefing Book, December 1988, Section C-1, pp. 4–5, POF.

[122] Cruse Interview, August 15, 2000, pp. 3–6.

[123] Ibid., pp. 6–10; Memorandum, "Credits and Guarantees – Costs to the Budget and Rates Provided to Borrowers," July 18, 1991, "CR/Credits vs. Guarantees" folder, POF.

the Bank considered "contract line items," the Ex-Im's content rules applied to each item individually. Bank support would be available for the American-made items in projects, even though they might aggregate less than 50 percent of the cost of the project.[124]

The major changes in Bank practices would have to be accomplished with a much smaller staff. During fiscal year 1980, Ex-Im averaged 392 full-time employees. Between 1975 and 1980, the Bank ordinarily had 400 to 450 employees. By 1987, the number was only 320.[125] These reductions had been accomplished through attrition, which contributed to Draper's reputation of being "staff friendly."[126] In addition, Bohn tried to address staff issues with a human resources task force and changes in personnel policies. But personnel problems facing the Bank (and to a large extent federal service) in the 1980s were much deeper. They resulted from the Reagan administration's (and to a lesser extent its predecessor's) institutionalized denigration of the federal service and the increasing disparities between the compensation available in the private sector compared to that in the public sector. Finally, the nature of the Bank's work changed in the post-debt-crisis 1980s. Business declined, big projects disappeared, and what remained was usually done on a sovereign guarantee basis, a significant contrast to the 1970s. One former director observed that the cases that remained were probably just not very exciting for Ex-Im loan processors.[127]

In addition to reorganization, Bohn also attempted to address mounting concern about the deteriorating financial health of the Bank. The problem had two dimensions – net operating losses regularly incurred after 1981 and concerns about the quality of the Bank's outstanding loan portfolio as defaults and underperforming loans accelerated in the wake of the LDC debt crisis. Of course, the issue of Ex-Im's financial viability was in many ways an artificial one. The Bank had authority to borrow from the U.S. treasury (Federal Financing Bank or FFB) to support its on-going operations. It also, however, had always been able to point to a steady stream of income, despite the existence of average

[124] "Eximbank Briefing Book," December 1988, Section C-1, p. 6, POF.

[125] Ibid., Section E-2, p. 1; "Eximbank Briefing Book," December 1980, Attachment 16, POF; Office of the Chief Financial Officer (Eximbank), *Export-Import Bank of the United States: Financial and Budgetary Aspects 1970–2000*, April 1993, pp. 23–4.

[126] Interview with James Hess, April 3, 2000, p. 60, Library, Ex-Im (hereafter Hess Interview, April 3, 2000).

[127] Rodriguez Interview, June 15, 2000, p. 61.

Table 6.3 *Export-Import Bank Losses, 1982–1989 (millions of dollars)*

Year	Loss	Year	Loss
1982	159.8	1986	332.9
1983	247.3	1987	460.9
1984	342.6	1988	847.9
1985	344.2	1989	1948.6

Source: Annual Reports for 1982–1989.

negative spreads between its average borrowing and lending rates (with a few years' exceptions) since 1966. Ex-Im also had "capital and reserves" that peaked at $3.2 billion in 1981.

In 1981, the Bank's net income declined precipitously to just $12.1 million (from $109.7 million the year before) and presaged the huge losses of the 1980s. The dramatic decline in income in 1981, however, was only the beginning of the effect of the large spreads and huge volume of loans in the late1970s/early 1980s. The OECD Arrangements that lifted ECA lending to approximately market rates had come too late to prevent substantial losses. Furthermore, though rates later rose to approximate market levels, the volume of Bank activity fell drastically below previous levels. Consequently, the Bank had large financing losses through the rest of the decade. By the mid 1980s, the Bank's credit losses also increasingly reflected the approximately 20 percent of its loan portfolio, which was not performing in the wake of the LDC debt crisis and which did not contribute to income.

These large losses resulted in dramatic declines in the Bank's balance sheet reserves for contingencies. At the end of fiscal 1987, they stood at just $312 million and were declining.[128] As early as 1975, the GAO had refused to certify the adequacy of the Bank's reserves for contingencies in light of its then declining income and large loan portfolio.[129] In 1981, GAO warned that the Bank's reserves were inadequate to cover possible losses on loans and guarantees that had not matured. The LDC debt crisis focused more attention on the quality of the Ex-Im's outstanding loan portfolio. And in 1985 the GAO suggested that the Bank's reserve for contingencies and defaults may have already been depleted (based

[128] Annual Report for 1987, p. 37.

[129] Annual Report for 1975, p. 25.

on nonperforming loans), and that the Bank was probably consuming its original $1 billion in capital.[130]

In the wake of the debt crisis, loan rescheduling under the "Paris Club"[131] accelerated dramatically. In 1988, the GAO noted that "the bank's reported assets included loans and accrued interest receivable of $11.8 billion to foreign countries, of which $6.7 billion in principal and accrued interest is delinquent or has been rescheduled. These assets also include $1 billion in estimated recoveries on claims the bank paid because of defaults under its insurance and guarantee programs." It estimated that the Bank's assets and reserves for contingencies would have been decreased by an amount of between $3.3 billion and $5.0 billion as of September 30, 1987.[132]

The Bank had always maintained that such a loss reserve was unnecessary. Officials routinely recited Ex-Im's high historic repayment rate for its loans, sovereign guarantees, and the negative diplomatic consequences of setting up such loss reserves for sovereign loans. The Department of the Treasury opposed such a reserve, as did the Federal Reserve and the State Department. Such a policy, they thought, might compromise the rescheduling of defaults. And until spring 1987, no commercial banks had established reserves for sovereign loans in response to the debt crisis.[133] At that time, however, Citicorp established a $3 billion loss reserve for such debt. Nevertheless, the Bank continued to oppose establishing such a reserve. Bohn also questioned the need to recapitalize the Bank.[134]

[130] Congress, Senate, Committee on Banking, Housing and Urban Affairs, Subcommittee on International Finance and Monetary Policy, *Renewal of the Export-Import Bank Act of 1945*, 99th Congress, 2nd Session, 1986, p. 23.

[131] Government-to-government discussions of debt renegotiations and restructurings, hosted by French officials in Paris.

[132] Annual Report for 1987, p. 37.

[133] Hess Interview, April 3, 2000, Library, Ex-Im, pp. 32–4.

[134] Congress, House, Committee on Banking, Finance and Urban Affairs, Subcommittee on International Finance, Trade and Monetary Policy, *Export-Import Bank*, 100th Congress, 1st Session, 1987, pp. 4–12. A high-profile example of Ex-Im's arguments that it ultimately recovered on virtually all of its nonperforming loans was illustrated by Credit No. 6771 between 1980 and 1985. In 1980, the bank loaned transatlantic low-fare pioneer Laker Airways funds to purchase five DC-10s. The Bank took possession of them when Laker declared bankruptcy in 1982. The planes were parked in the Arizona desert, and the Bank waited for the aircraft market to improve. The planes were ultimately sold in 1984. The liquidator for Laker Airways filed an antitrust suit against McDonnell Douglas and ten airlines that flew transatlantic routes and competed with Laker. As part of a complex settlement of that lawsuit, Ex-Im was able to recover the balance

Ultimately, the Bank's position provoked intense congressional criticism. Representative David Obey, chairman of the Foreign Operations Subcommittee of the House Appropriations Committee, wanted the Bank to establish a loss reserve. At the end of 1987, he threatened that his committee would not appropriate any administrative expenses for the operations of the Bank unless it established such a fund. Paul Volcker, chairman of the Federal Reserve, had to convince Obey that such action was not conducive to an orderly resolution of the LDC debt crisis. Other powerful representatives, such as Henry Gonzalez of the House Banking and Currency Committee, were more outspoken, accusing the Bank of "phoney accounting" in regard to the extent of its losses.[135] Resolution of the loss reserve and recapitalization issues would await Bohn's successor.

These issues were not the only ones to face John D. Macomber (1989–92), who took over as chairman in July 1989. As so often in the past, the external environment changed forcing on the Ex-Im the need to adjust its thinking and operations yet again. Congress, for one thing, changed the way in which the federal government accounted for the public extension of credit. Externally, by the 1990s, the Cold War was history – the Soviet Union and its Eastern European allies were no longer communist countries. The remaining major communist power, the Peoples Republic of China, was in the midst of a market revolution. Equally dramatic changes in the realm of information technology – the linking of high-speed networked computers to advanced means of communications – transformed capital markets. What followed was a vast increase in the volume and velocity of private capital flows, which in turn prompted the development of new kinds of capital instruments. The Bank's capital market milieu was transformed. Together, these changes, and the beginnings of an unprecedented period of economic growth for the United States, forced the Bank in the 1990s to cope with a new set of needs and demands.

owed on the original Laker credit. See Albright Interview, April 16, 2000, pp. 30–2; Draper Interview, June 20, 2000, pp. 39–45; and Memorandum, Albright and others to Board of Directors, "Settlement of Eximbank Claim Against Laker Airways Ltd. Exim Credit No. 6771/Gtee. No. 6772," July 25, 1985, Mazon-Mazo files, Library, Ex-Im.

135 Hess Interview, April 3, 2000, pp. 34–7; Hess Interview, August 15, 2000, pp. 27–8; Interview with William Ryan, October 14, 2000, pp. 32–5, Library, Ex-Im.

7

A NEW ERA AND ITS CHALLENGES, THE 1990S

INTRODUCTION

Following the unprecedented international and domestic economic problems the United States faced in the 1980s and early 1990s, circumstances during the rest of the last decade of the twentieth century improved markedly. These changes influenced the Bank and its work. By 1992, recession gave way to the beginnings of a lengthy domestic economic boom, highlighted by an expanding export sector. Internationally, conditions also brightened. The Latin American debt crisis had abated following the substantial rescheduling of debt championed by U.S. Secretary of the Treasury Nicholas F. Brady in 1989.

In 1993, the Clinton administration embarked on an effort to stem the growth of the country's very large budget deficits. Spurred on by a Republican victory in the 1994 congressional elections, the White House and Congress both sought deficit reduction. By 1999, the federal government accumulated its first surplus since 1969. These conditions accelerated foreign capital flows to the United States, which fueled not only the stock market but also private business investment. The latter helped drive new network computer and telecommunications technologies that together fostered a revolution in "information technology" (IT). The latter made possible the commercialization of the Internet, perhaps the most important technological breakthrough of the 1990s. The United States became the leader in the new technologies, which were attractive candidates for export, despite the strong dollar. Additionally, in its first years in office, the Clinton administration embarked on an expansive export drive. Secretary of Commerce Ron Brown wanted the United States to expand exports of "big" sectors – that is, the high-technology capital goods that had traditionally been the strongest of the country's exports.

While the macroeconomic environment improved, there were important microeconomic changes in the 1990s that also contributed to the longest economic expansion in the country's history. Stimulating the growth was fast-paced business spending for IT, the computer equipment and software that linked computers within enterprises and to customers and suppliers. These developments led to lower costs in transmitting information as well as increases in the volume and velocity of communications.

Also contributing to the expansion in microeconomic terms was the corporate restructuring begun in the 1980s that continued into the 1990s. Major companies – in manufacturing, services, and finance – reorganized their operations by cutting employees, flattening hierarchies, and selling divisions. The result was more flexible and innovative enterprises, which often helped improve their competitiveness in overseas markets. IT and falling communications costs linked multinational enterprises more closely than ever to the international market. Multinationals increased the integration of their overseas supply, manufacturing, and distribution operations. Companies adept at working in global markets could emphasize operations in countries that offered them the most favorable conditions. Cross-border mergers further loosened corporate identity within a particular country during the 1990s. They occurred in key sectors, such as equipment manufacturing, pharmaceuticals, telecommunications, automobiles, and finance.

Improved information technology also facilitated an increase in the velocity and volume of capital flows sent to a growing number of developing countries. In the 1990s, private capital outpaced public sources of funds to emerging markets in Asia, Latin America, the Middle East, Africa, and the former USSR and its allies. Rapidly improving IT also helped transform the structuring of financial transactions. As a result, lenders were better able to identify component risks and levels of return so as to more creatively and efficiently fund transactions.[1]

[1] William R. Cline, "Ex-Im, Exports, and Private Capital: Will Financial Markets Squeeze the Bank?" in Gary Clyde Hufbauer and Rita M. Rodriguez, eds., *The Ex-Im Bank in the 21st Century: A New Approach* (Special Report 14; Washington, DC: Institute for International Economics, 2001), pp. 103–10.

But the collapse of the Mexican peso in 1994–5, and the Asian financial crisis beginning in 1997, stemmed the flow of private funds in international markets. They also altered the structure of lending by reducing the role of commercial bank credit to developing countries. Subsequent improvements in 1998 and 1999 in the economies hardest hit by the Asian collapse, however, did not by 2000 stimulate a return to pre-crisis levels of private commercial lending.[2]

The 1997 crisis and its aftermath, as in the international debt problems of the 1980s, demonstrated the continued relevance of the Bank in providing export credits, guarantees, and insurance. Following the 1997 Asian crisis, private capital pulled out of emerging markets and was slow to return. Other opportunities for the Bank existed in the Newly Independent States (NIS) and Africa, although lending there involved higher levels of risk. The Bank also found itself challenged by a departure from the OECD understandings worked out to equalize the terms offered by export credit agencies. The German, Canadian, and other smaller ECAs began or expanded governmental programs for lending on allegedly market terms, through what has been called market windows instead of the traditional government financing.

Nevertheless, at the end of the 1980s, no one anticipated the remarkable changes about to occur in the global economy. Nor were there many who foresaw in the last years of the Reagan administration that in the 1990s the United States would soon begin the longest period of economic growth in its history, that the vaunted Japanese economy would falter, and that many American firms would establish themselves again as formidable international competitors. All these changes were to impact the Ex-Im, which as so many times before had to adjust to a constantly changing environment, while continuing to operate within parameters set by Congress and the White House.

LOSS RESERVES, RECAPITALIZATION, AND CREDIT REFORM

In late 1988 the outgoing Reagan administration "zeroed out," or provided no appropriation for, Ex-Im's direct credits/loans in the fiscal year 1990 budget. In many respects, this was the parting shot of the Office

[2] Ibid.

of Management and Budget in a battle that had raged through the eight Reagan years. Of course, OMB had proposed such cuts three times in the previous eight years (twice in conjunction with the ill-starred I-Match Program). Congress overwhelmingly rejected such drastic budget proposals. In fact, during a period of several years in the mid 1980s, legislators approved considerably more direct credit/loan authority than Ex-Im could use in the weak demand environment of the 1980s. For its part, political battling aside, the Reagan administration took its position because of significant successes since 1980 in negotiating OECD understandings to lower export credit subsidies offered by the other ECAs. Such an approach followed the practice of Germany and Switzerland to provide only guarantees. Reagan budget officials believed that a broad range of loan guarantee and insurance programs could provide the needed comprehensive financial support for U.S. exporters and supported a substantial increase in authority for guarantees and insurance.

The incoming Bush administration stepped back a bit. It announced, according to the Bank's Vice Chairman William Ryan,[3] that it was "beginning with a 'predisposition' that a direct loan program is needed and is important as far as exports are concerned." The new administration lived up to its promise. It stated its preference for guarantees because they "generally have a lower subsidy component and entail private sector participation," but it did not dismiss out of hand the principle of direct loans.[4] Relations between the Bank and Bush's OMB assumed a more businesslike tone. OMB's supervision of the Bank's budget remained vigorous, but gone were the ideological attacks (often based on irrelevant or outdated facts), which were part of a general campaign against government credit subsidies. This is not to say that the Bush years were uneventful. The savings and loan/credit guarantee crisis that had developed late in the second Reagan administration exploded early in the Bush years. The resulting Credit Reform Act of 1990 altered the budgetary and political landscape of the operation of

[3] Ryan had been brought to the Bank as Bohn's vice chairman. Before taking that post, Ryan had served for the previous twelve years as a vice president at Gulf and Western Industries. As vice chairman, he oversaw the Bank's activities following Bohn's departure and before Macomber's arrival.

[4] Letter, Richard Darman to Robert Michel, February 16, 1989, "1989 Direct Loan" folder, Policy Office Files, Archives, Export-Import Bank of the United States, Washington, DC (hereafter POF). Interview, William Ryan, October 14, 2000, pp. 45–7, Library, Ex-Im (hereafter Ryan Interview, October 14, 2000).

federal loan/guarantee institutions, including that of the Export-Import Bank.

The new Bush administration and Ex-Im had to address an issue that had become exceedingly contentious with Congress during John Bohn's chairmanship (1986–9). It involved provision of loss reserves for delinquent and defaulted loans. A subsidiary question arose out of the dispute over the loss reserves and the necessity of Bank recapitalization. These were issues addressed by Bohn's successor, John D. Macomber (1989–92).[5]

At his Senate confirmation hearing in July 1989, senators quizzed him on deliquent and nonperforming loans and reserves. Macomber put the extent of Ex-Im's nonperforming or delinquent loans at $2.5 billion, while the General Accounting Office placed the figure at $3.5 billion to $6 billion. In any event, Macomber argued that the Bank's financial position in no way compromised its ability to continue to function, which essentially involved borrowing from the Federal Financing Bank.[6]

Macomber and his new vice chairman Eugene Lawson[7] determined to end the escalating impasse over the issue. They decided that Ex-Im should establish loss reserves for the delinquent and nonperforming loans. According to Macomber, despite Ex-Im's long successful record of ultimately collecting on its loans, guarantees, and insurance, "it was clear that the so-called balance sheet of the Export-Import Bank was not really reflective of the assets that we had, in that an awful lot of the assets were [to] put it mildly seriously impaired. And of course people in Congress and others knew that as well as we did."[8] But considerable opposition to such a course existed within the administration, from Treasury, State, and OMB, and persistently at the professional staff level at the Departments of State and Treasury. Macomber and Lawson, however, believed that the Bank had to address the loss reserve issue in

[5] Congress, Senate, Committee on Banking, Housing, and Urban Affairs, *Nomination of John D. Macomber*, 101st Congress, 1st Session, 1989, pp. 10–15 (hereafter Macomber Nomination). He had spent much of his career at McKinsey and Company, the high-powered management consultant group, and was instrumental in building its European operations. He had also served as chairman and CEO of Celanese, the chemical manufacturer, until it was taken over by Hoechst AG.

[6] Ibid.; see also Congress, Congressional Budget Office, "Budgeting for Eximbank: A Case Study of Credit Reform," 1990, pp. 22–3.

[7] Lawson was a former deputy assistant secretary of state for Asia.

[8] Interview with John Macomber, August 26, 2000, pp. 4–5, Library, Ex-Im (hereafter Macomber Interview, August 26, 2000).

order to show good faith and to establish a harmonious relationship with Congress. According to Lawson, Macomber's previous long-term experience as chairman of the audit committee of the Chase Manhattan Bank helped him overcome opposition to the Bank's proposed course of action.[9] Within Macomber's first five months at the Bank, he also garnered the support of James A. Baker, secretary of state, and Treasury Secretary Nicholas F. Brady, who ultimately overruled staff opposition.[10]

On January 4, 1990, the Bank formally announced that it had changed its accounting practices. It did not write off any specific obligation. Instead, it established a non-country-specific loss reserve of \$4.79 billion that was approximately 40 percent of its \$12.1 billion portfolio of loans and claims receivables. The reserve slated \$2.78 billion for loans and \$1.56 billion for guarantees. The Bank noted that the "accounting change does not mean that any loans or guarantees will be written off, but that, because of current economic conditions, the prospects for full collection of some loans and guarantees is sufficiently far into the future that the value of the loan portfolio and estimated recoveries on guarantee claims should be reduced for financial reporting purposes." Furthermore, Ex-Im also modified its past practice of reporting as interest income accrued interest receivable on loans more than 90 days overdue. As a result, interest income for fiscal year 1989 was reduced by over \$271 million, increasing the Bank's loss by a similar amount.[11]

These actions had the effect of eliminating the remaining capital of the Bank, creating a negative shareholder equity in excess of \$4 billion. But setting up the loss reserve enabled Ex-Im to get a "clean" opinion from the GAO. As such, Macomber defused an escalating political problem with key Republican and Democratic committee and subcommittee members who had oversight responsibility for the Bank. It set the stage for a cooperative, rather than an adversarial,

[9] Interview with Eugene Lawson, September 21, 2000, pp. 3–5, Library, Ex-Im (hereafter Lawson Interview, September 21, 2000); Macomber Interview, August 26, 2000, pp. 4–6; Interview with James Hess, April 3, 2000, pp. 32–4, Library, Ex-Im (hereafter Hess Interview April 3, 2000).

[10] Hess Interview, April 3, 2000, pp. 36–7; Interview with James Hess, August 15, 2000, pp. 27–30, Library, Ex-Im (hereafter Hess Interview, August 15, 2000); Lawson Interview, September 21, 2000, pp. 5–6.

[11] Export-Import Bank of the United States, Annual Report for 1989 (Washington, DC: Export Import Bank, 1989) pp. 14, 38–41 (hereafter Annual Report).

relationship with Congress, the tone that characterized Macomber's tenure.[12]

Nonetheless, the Bank was destined to operate in an entirely different fiscal environment for other reasons as well. Congress in 1990 passed sweeping changes in accounting for how the federal government provided credit. The Federal Credit Reform Act of 1990 addressed past costs of various federal credit, guarantee, and insurance programs. Many such programs generated large losses and required compensatory payments from the federal treasury. Losses related to indirect (guaranteed) credit operations were huge, especially in the savings and loan industry. The problems of federal credit operations were two: (1) how to address the existing loss/underperforming assets of past federal credit and insurance activities and (2) how to ensure that the future cost of federal credit operations was reflected in annual appropriations.

The Federal Credit Reform Act applied to the Bank (and other federal agencies) at the beginning of fiscal year 1992 (October 1, 1991). Congress would appropriate funds to finance the cost, including potential credit losses, of providing direct loans, guarantees, and insurance, as well as the costs of administering these programs. The legislation required that Ex-Im (and other governmental entities) provide a calculation of the cost of providing such credit on all commitments made during and after fiscal year 1992.[13]

Credit reform had the potential of altering the way the Bank did business. Decades of escalating budget pressures had increased the Bank's reliance on guarantees, as opposed to direct credits. Under the precredit reform budget rules, guarantees were not "counted" for purposes of calculating annual appropriations. In addition, Congress directed Ex-Im in the 1986 reauthorization to enhance its guarantees by making them more transferable. The goal was to reengage the reluctant commercial banking sector in export finance. In adding the mandate, Congress

[12] Lawson Interview, September 21, 2000, pp. 5–6; "Export-Import Bank Transition Book," 1992, Section F-2, POF. See also Interview with Allan Mendelowitz, February 13, 2001, pp. 19–20, Library, Ex-Im (hereafter Mendelowitz Interview, February 13, 2001).

[13] Following its 1986 reauthorization and the implications of the international debt crisis, Ex-Im restructured its fee structure, as discussed in the last chapter. See Congress, Congressional Budget Office, *Budgeting for Eximbank: A Case Study of Credit Reform* (Washington, DC: Government Printing Office, 1990), pp. 9–12.

expected to provide foreign trade finance cheaper and in larger volumes than commercial banks had been able to do in the past. As one Bank official summed up the situation in 1990: "Eximbank has spent 20 years developing ways a guarantee can achieve as many of the characteristics of a credit as possible.... Starting in FY 92, however, new budget rules will 'count' both credits and guarantees. In fact, guarantees are showing up under credit reform with a *higher* [emphasis in original] cost than credits." Using the existing OMB model for credit subsidy rates, loans were 3.45 percent and guarantees were 6.15 percent for similar transactions in terms of markets and risks. Thus, under the new budget rules a $100 million subsidy appropriation would support almost $3.0 billion in direct credits, but only $1.7 billion in loan guarantees.[14]

Traditional wisdom at Ex-Im held that engagement of commercial banks through loan guarantees was exceedingly valuable. Commercial banks provided services – marketing, advisory services, loan packaging, and debt collection – which Ex-Im could not by itself offer on the scale needed. Ex-Im thinking also emphasized that banks using its guarantee programs would be more willing to extend a larger number of other non-Ex-Im finance-related services, such as trade credit lines and letters of credit, than they would have otherwise provided.[15]

The reason these factors had been turned on their head was simple. Under credit reform budgeting, the current "cost" of Ex-Im credit activity was a combination of (1) the discounted present value of the estimated loss due to the activity over the duration of the credit/guarantee and (2) the funding loss/profit from the same transactions. The credit risk in (1) would be the same for either a loan or a guarantee for a similar transaction/risk. The Bank, however, made a "profit" on the funding of a credit because its direct credits carried an interest rate of 1 percent above its cost of funds from the treasury. Consequently, loans generally were less expensive than identical guarantees for the same typical transaction; additionally, a different commitment fee structure existed for direct credits and guarantees.[16]

[14] Memorandum, James Cruse, "Credits and Guarantees – Costs to the Budget and Rates Provided to Borrowers," July 18, 1991, "CR Review/Credit vs Guarantee" folder, POF.

[15] Memorandum, "Benefits to Exporters of Guarantee Use," July 23, 1991, "Credit Reform Review/Guarantee Benefits" folder, POF.

[16] Memorandum, Jim Cruse, "Credits and Guarantees – Costs to the Budget and Rates Provided to Borrowers," July 18, 1991, "CR Review/Credit vs. Guarantee" folder, POF; Hess Interview, August 15, 2000, pp. 5–8; Memorandum, "Benefits to Exporters of

The commercial banking sector, the primary user of the Bank's guarantee facilities, feared that their reviving foreign trade business would be lost if, in light of the new budget realities, the Ex-Im were to favor direct credits over guarantees. The Bank, following the implementation of credit reform, could shift the emphasis in its credit operations. In past appropriation acts, Congress established maximum levels for direct credits, and loan guarantees and insurance as *individual* line items. Administrative expenses had a separate limitation. For fiscal year 1992 and after, however, *Ex-Im would be given a fixed appropriation to cover the cost of all direct credit, guarantee, and insurance operations which it could use for any of them.*[17] Administrative expenses would have a separate appropriation. Commercial banks pressed their concerns upon Ex-Im officials but took little solace in their assurances that the Bank would not dramatically alter its established policy.[18]

In fact, the Bank essentially maintained its policy direction regarding the relationship between direct credits and loan guarantees. It did not abandon guarantees and remained "agnostic" with regard to the type of financing sought by applicants. Commercial banks, however, remained concerned that Ex-Im might favor direct lending operations if confronted with a severe budget crisis, and Bank officials were unwilling or unable to make categorical assurances to the contrary.[19]

Guarantee Use," July 31, 1991, "Credit Reform Review/Guarantee Benefits" folder, POF. See also Hess Interview, August 15, 2000, pp. 5–8.

17 Hess Interview, August 15, 2000, pp. 4–8; "Transition Briefing Book," 1992, p. F-3, POF.

18 Hess Interview, August 15, 2000, pp. 8–10, 12–13; Interview with Rita Rodriguez, August 15, 2000, pp. 1–3, Library, Ex-Im (hereafter Rodriguez Interview, August 15, 2000).

19 Rodriguez Interview, August 15, 2000, pp. 1–3. This continues to be a matter of some concern. In fiscal 1997 there was a program budget shortfall and in the competitiveness report for that year the Bank's Advisory Committee raised just such concerns. The Advisory Committee bemoaned the draconian remedies proposed such as the Bank exiting high-risk countries, increasing bank fees, and deferring loan approvals until the next fiscal year. It also specifically noted that credit reform, based on the OMB, guidelines, "may induce Ex-Im Bank to shift emphasis, in times of budget constraints, to direct lending mode and thus compete with, rather than support, the commercial suppliers of trade finance." The chair of the Advisory Committee went on to suggest that the components of the subsidy calculation formula should be reviewed so that the cost difference between these two mechanisms "are more accurately reflected." See "Alert–Alert–Alert," July 22, 1997, and the Advisory Committee Statement in Export-Import Bank, *Report to the U.S. Congress on Export Credit Competition and the Export-Import Bank of the United States, January 1, 1996 through December 31, 1996*, 1997 (hereafter Competitiveness Report).

Credit reform not only prompted concern and extensive analysis of the possible directions that the Bank's credit policy could take, it also had implications for the Private Export Finance Corporation and its traditional role as a supplementary lender. Ex-Im's long-standing policy of encouraging the role of private capital and its enhanced guarantee facilitated a "broad-based and steadily expanding use of securitization techniques to access fixed rate capital markets," according to Bank officials. Securitization involved assembling obligations into a package for sale to commercial banks, insurance companies, and institutional investors. The fear was that if such practices became routine, PEFCO's traditional role as a supplementary lender would be compromised. PEFCO's existence had been premised on there being a gap between what Ex-Im could do with a credit and what private institutions could do with a guaranteed loan. Such premises were now in question.[20]

Concerns about PEFCO's future coincided with discussions about the Ex-Im–PEFCO agreement set to expire in 1995. In late 1992, the Bank's board believed that the exporter and banking communities appreciated PEFCO's uniqueness and value. So, the Bank continued to explore ways for PEFCO to advance its traditional work.[21] Ultimately, PEFCO found a role, for the process of taking the enhanced Bank loan guarantees to market was not cheap. Because only the major banks could manage securitization on their own, PEFCO continued to exist largely as a securitization mechanism for others in the industry to bring guarantees to market.[22]

The 1990 Federal Credit Reform Act also resolved the contentious issue of defaulted, underperforming loans, guarantee claims, and the loss reserve addressed in January 1990. The legislation provided for a permanent, indefinite appropriation to cover the repayment of obligations outstanding as of September 30, 1991, to the extent that the new cash flows from commitments (loans, guarantees, and insurance) made prior to that date were insufficient to meet the payment of those obligations.[23]

[20] Memorandum, "Credit Reform and PEFCO: New Directions," August 9, 1991, "Credit Reform/AEF Status" folder, POF; Memorandum, "PEFCO – Board Decisions," November 25, 1992, "PEFCO Long-Run Role 1992" folder, POF.

[21] Memorandum, "PEFCO – Board Decisions," November 25, 1992, "PEFCO Long-Run Role 1992" folder, POF.

[22] Interview with James Cruse, August 15, 2000, pp. 13–15, Library, Ex-Im (hereafter Cruse Interview, August 15, 2000).

[23] Annual Report for 1992, p. 28.

The legislation had the effect of mooting the question of the need for a formal recapitalization of the Bank because all its past and future losses would be covered by these future appropriations.[24]

INSURANCE

By 1987, as the effects of the debt crisis abated, Bank officials sought to reengage the private sector in export credit insurance. In the next few years, the private companies again showed interest in foreign credit insurance. In the efforts to reengage them, Ex-Im assumed that a contractual relationship would be the most beneficial for exporters, while providing the Bank with a needed degree of control over the operation. It hoped that contracting out the "government book" of insurance would stimulate private export credit insurance to provide services to underserved exporters.[25]

Effective October 1, 1991, Foreign Credit Insurance Association member firms began assuming risks under some of the export credit insurance policies they wrote, while Ex-Im continued to assume all risks under the remaining FCIA policies – the "government book." At that time, however, Ex-Im entered into a two-year $10 million contract with FCIA Management Company (FCIAM), a privately owned firm, for it to issue and service this government book of insurance policies. FCIAM also provided similar services for polices underwritten by FCIA – the "private book." Ex-Im terminated its control over FCIA's operation and its board of directors before the contract was signed. According to the GAO, the only mechanisms that the Bank retained to monitor and control administration of its insurance programs by FCIAM were participation in its quarterly meetings and monitoring and receiving reports required by the contract.[26]

[24] "Transition Briefing Book," 1992, p. F-3, POF.

[25] Memorandum, Crafton, "Federalization Option: Variables Known and Unknown," April 30, 1992, "Insurance Federalization (1992)" folder, POF; Memorandum, Fessenden to files, "Eximbank's Insurance Program Competitive Bidding," April 6, 1992, "Insurance Federalization (1992)" folder, POF; *Government Involvement in Export Credit Insurance*, pp. iv–v; "Transition Briefing Book," 1992, Section D-13, POF.

[26] The majority owner of FCIAM was a private insurance company (Great American Insurance) that underwrote its own private export credit insurance policies. Another insurance company (Enhance Reinsurance) owned the remainder of the FCIAM shares. See General Accounting Office, Report, *Export Finance: The Role of the U.S. Export-Import Bank* (Washington, DC: Government Printing Office, 1992), pp. 31–6 (hereafter *Export Finance*); Annual Report for 1991, p. 38.

By early 1992, however, it was clear that there were problems with the new arrangement with FCIAM. The Bank's original assumption that contracting would encourage a proliferation of additional insurance (increased capacity and new services) proved wrong. Exporters concluded that the products offered were largely similar, though some new coverage was made available. Those submitting applications and information to FCIAM would be eligible for premium quotations under either portfolio. There was also a perception of unfairness in that FCIA gained an advantage by its access to additional information derived from managing the Ex-Im contract.[27]

An Ex-Im in-house insurance task force delineated this and other issues in a spring 1992 report. The costs of contracting were greater than expected. It required a substantial commitment on the part of Bank staff, while FCIAM also incurred considerable management expenses. Bank staff estimated that FCIAM's cost of operating the "government book" exceeded 25 percent of the estimated expenses of administering such business in-house. Under these circumstances, Ex-Im essentially abandoned its historic preference for private sector engagement and supported a "federalization option."[28]

Federalization was a hard political sell. Chairman Macomber recalled that many in the administration thought federalization inappropriate. But it was clear to him, Vice Chairman Lawson, other directors, and senior staff that the government book (approximately 60 percent of the insurance written by FCIA) could be written and serviced "less expensively and probably better" by the Bank itself. Simply, the private sector was not doing the job, and the contract cost too much. At least in the view of the Bank leadership, there were sufficient reasons to "take the heat" on a decision that ran contrary to the political rhetoric of the administration and both political parties at the time.[29]

[27] Memorandum, Crafton, "Federalization Option: Variables Known and Unknown," April 30, 1992, "Insurance Federalization (1992)" folder, POF; Memorandum, Crafton to Macomber, "Proposed Talking Points...," May 12, 1992, "Insurance Federalization (1992)" folder, POF; Cruse Interview, August 15, 2000, pp. 16–17; Lawson Interview, September 21, 2000, pp. 21–2.

[28] Cruse Interview, August 15, 2000, pp. 16–17; Interview with Hart Fessenden, November 9, 2000, pp. 20–3, Library, Ex-Im; Lawson Interview, September 21, 2000, pp. 21–3.

[29] Macomber Interview, August 26, 2000, pp. 24–6; Lawson Interview, September 21, 2000, pp. 21–3.

But serious opposition within the administration and in Congress did not materialize.[30] On September 14, 1992, the Bank terminated its contractual relationship with FCIAM, effective September 30, 1992. The Bank also paid a termination fee of $1.5 million to FCIAM and assumed responsibility for certain liabilities of approximately $1.2 million.[31] The Bank put every policy up for sale, with the ultimate result that approximately one third of the outstanding insurance was privatized. These policies were generally with experienced exporters who generated at least $25,000 in annual premiums. What essentially had been the unprofitable government book policies were handled by the Bank's insurance division, under a senior vice president.[32] Simultaneously, the Bank began to operate five branch offices of FCIA (in Los Angles, Chicago, Houston, Miami, and New York). The Bank also brought in-house approximately 100 FCIA employees to staff the insurance program.[33]

After 1991, the dollar levels of insurance written by the Bank declined by approximately 8 percent, as private sector insurers became more aggressive in seeking business. Consequently, Ex-Im's posture was that of an "insurer of last resort," with its business characterized by riskier markets, many small buyers, and numerous new exporters.[34] A 1995 staff review of the Bank's insurance function concluded that Ex-Im continued to perform an important role in short-term markets. During this period the Bank's standard multibuyer insurance program had shown very few claims, which indicated that the Bank had been conservative in the underwriting business that the private sector was unwilling to serve.[35] (Table 7.1.)

THE 1992 REAUTHORIZATION AND SMALL BUSINESS

The goodwill Macomber had built up in Congress paved the way for a relatively uncontroversial reauthorization of the Bank in 1992. It had

30 Macomber Interview, August 26, 2000, pp. 25–6.

31 Annual Report for 1992, p. 33.

32 Cruse Interview, August 15, 2000, pp. 18–19. See also Memorandum, Cruse to Cabe, "Transition Issues," February 21, 1997, "Transition Issues – 1997" folder, POF.

33 FCIA figures from Memorandum, Crafton to Board of Directors, "FCIA Management Company, Inc. and Eximbank Credit Insurance," April 9, 1992, "Insurance Federalization (1992)" folder, POF.

34 Cruse Interview, August 15, 2000, pp. 18–20.

35 Memorandum, Cruse to Cabe, "Transition Issues," February 21, 1997, "Transition Issues – 1997" folder, POF.

Table 7.1 *Insurance Authorizations (millions of dollars)*

Fiscal Year	Authorization
1989	4,344.8
1990	4,841.1
1991	4,553.5
1992	4,220.2
1993	4,229.0
1994	4,261.4
1995	4,555.0
1996	3,868.1
1997	2,848.8
1998	4,296.3
1999	3,865.9
2000	3,291.1

Source: Appendix B, Summary of Authorizations.

none of the contentious elements that had prevailed in the 1983 and 1986 reauthorization efforts. As in the past, however, Congress increased the Bank's responsibilities in addressing certain issues. In 1992, the continued needs of small business exporters received an extra boost from the legislation that enlarged the requirements of the mandate first laid down in 1983.

In regard to other matters, the legislation substantially increased the Bank's aggregate loan, guarantee, and insurance authority from $40 billion to $75 billion and, at the same time, ended the concept of "fractional reserves." It allowed for the cancellation of Bank debt for several Latin American and Caribbean countries, authorized a tied aid war chest for three years at $500 million per year,[36] required that the Bank take into account potential environmental effects of goods and services for which it had extended long-term support of $10 million or more, encouraged Ex-Im to use its programs to promote environmental exports, and prohibited financing the export of defense articles to less developed and developed countries, except when they were to be used for antinarcotic purposes.[37]

36 Congress, in fact, never appropriated the full amounts.

37 Memorandum, Cruse to Staff, "New Charter" and attached "Statement of Managers," October 6, 1992, "Congressional Charter 1992" folder, POF.

In focusing on the needs of small business exporters, Congress in 1992 mandated that the Bank do more than it had been doing. At the same time, however, the legislation eliminated the ability of Ex-Im to use subcontractors under contracts held by larger exporters to count for the 10 percent minimum of its authorizations earmarked for small business. This change increased the demands on the Bank's efforts to provide services to small business. As it was, serving their needs had large administrative costs.[38] In terms of time, money, and effort, it was, according to Macomber, "terribly uneconomic."[39] But Macomber and Lawson thought that the Bank ultimately could make small business operations profitable, even though it was going to take hard work. They also envisioned significant political benefits in assisting small business, in that it might offset the growing congressional criticism of the Bank as a provider of "corporate welfare" for some of the country's largest enterprises.[40] Indeed, Macomber's successors, Chairmen Kenneth D. Brody (1993–5) and Martin A. Kamarck (1996–7), saw the cultivation of small business as a "win–win" situation in budget terms. Small business exporters typically sold in less-risky markets, and they were not supplying big ticket items. As a result, under the terms of credit reform, the subsidy and budget cost was less.[41]

At the end of the decade, Chairman James A. Harmon (1997–2001), like his immediate predecessors, saw small business as an important area for the Bank, too. He emphasized the need for small business exports in terms of the larger issue of continued U.S. economic growth. In reflecting on the Bank's assistance to small business, he observed that at the end of the twentieth century only 5 percent of all American businesses exported.[42]

Nonetheless, when Congress enhanced the Bank's mandate in 1992, Ex-Im's efforts on behalf of small businesses were dispersed throughout a number of programs. The overwhelming amount of Bank assistance to small business was in the form of export credit insurance.

38 Ibid.

39 Macomber Interview, August 26, 2000, pp. 12–14.

40 Lawson Interview, September 21, 2000, pp. 7–9; Mendelowitz Interview, February 13, 2001, pp. 23–6.

41 Interview with Martin Kamarck, September 14, 2000, pp. 54–5, Library, Ex-Im (hereafter Kamarck Interview, September 14, 2000).

42 James A. Harmon, "A Chairman's Perspective on the Future of Ex-Im Bank," in Hufbauer and Rodriguez, p. 41.

Of $1,716.7 million small business authorizations in fiscal year 1989, some $1,490.3 million were export credit insurance. For fiscal year 1990, the figures were $1,569.7 million of $2,054.6 million.[43]

One of the Bank's other primary efforts for delivering services to small business was the working capital guarantee program. The latter had originated in the 1982 legislation (the Export Trading Company Act) Congress designed to encourage commercial lenders to make loans to small firms that needed funds to market goods or services for export. The number of authorizations in the program expanded dramatically after 1992. In 1995, the Bank introduced two new working capital guarantee programs fashioned to further address small business needs. One was a liquidity facility to lenders where PEFCO was available to purchase their Bank working capital guaranteed and originated loans. Another allowed an exporter with a working capital guarantee, but unable to find a lender, to fund a transaction directly from PEFCO.[44] The number of working capital program authorizations increased from 130 in 1992, to 330 in 1999. Authorizations increased from $143.4 million in 1992 to $443.3 million in 1997; in 1999 they leveled off to $415.9 million. (See Appendix B.) The use of delegated authority to commercial banks was instrumental in the program's growth, for in fiscal year 1995 about 50 percent of the transactions were under delegated authority. This rose to about 80 percent of transactions by summer 1997.[45]

After 1992, the Bank also sought to assist small business exporters by building on other earlier programs. In 1987, Ex-Im had introduced a program to improve the delivery of its services to small- and medium-sized businesses through cooperation with state and city export finance and development agencies. Bank officials anticipated that this so-called city/state program would provide a conduit for information about and wider use of Ex-Im's services.[46] Assistance to small business had been disproportionately impacted by the withdrawal of commercial banks from international lending during the 1980s debt crisis. Historically, the Bank had relied on commercial banks to provide the outlets for its services. Efforts such as the city/state program were early attempts

[43] Annual Report for 1990, p. 13.
[44] Competitiveness Report 1996, p. C3.
[45] Ibid., p. 10.
[46] *Export Finance*, pp. 25–6.

to provide alternatives to delivery of services through commercial banks.[47]

Bank chairmen, starting with Macomber, focused on Bank procedures in dealing with small business exporters. Macomber had a small business task force evaluate Bank services. He believed that such attention to its own activities was especially needed because the Small Business Administration (SBA) had been weakened by scandal during the Reagan administration.[48] Later, in 1993, Congress required the Bank to coordinate its small business programs with the SBA. The latter handled requests under $750,000 and Ex-Im handled those over that sum. SBA utilized its own offices and lending specialists, while Ex-Im relied primarily on delegated authority to financial institutions.[49] Ex-Im extended its delegated lender authority to $2 million and then raised this to $5 million in 1996.[50]

In addition, Macomber supported formation of a small business group, headed by a senior vice president. This official was to centralize, coordinate, and integrate the Bank's small business activities. The group included the Bank's marketing and U.S. divisions. The branch offices of FCIA, following its absorption by the Ex-Im in 1992, became Bank regional offices and were used to assist small business exporters. These offices of the Bank were placed under a new Bank division – the Business Development Division – in 1994.[51]

During the later 1990s, the Bank's leadership addressed speeding up the processing of small business requests for working capital guarantees. The chairman delegated authority from the Loan Committee to the vice president for small business to approve such financing up to $2.5 million. Additionally, Ex-Im also increased loan guarantee and insurance coverage for small business.[52] Ex-Im support for small business, as a percentage of its dollar authorizations, increased dramatically after 1992.[53] In 1997 approximately 21 percent of Bank financing

47 *Export Finance*, p. 24.

48 Macomber Interview, August 26, 2000, pp. 12–14; *Export Finance*, pp. 29–30.

49 GAO, Report, *Export Finance: Federal Efforts to Support Working Capital Needs of Small Business*, 1997, pp. 1–6 (hereafter *Working Capital Needs*).

50 Competitiveness Report 1996, pp. C1–C2.

51 *Working Capital Needs*, p. 5.

52 Ibid., pp. 29–30.

53 Annual Report for 1996, p. 25.

supported small business. This was a 60 percent increase from fiscal year 1992.[54]

NEW INTERNATIONAL ENVIRONMENT/PROJECT FINANCE

It was not only Congress that affected the way the Bank operated in the 1990s but also striking international changes. Commercial and investment banks were exceedingly cautious at the beginning of the new decade because of the overseas debt crisis in the 1980s and the failure of the savings and loan industry in the United States early in the 1990s.

At the same time, profound changes were reshaping the international economic and financial environment. Both industrial and developing countries opened their financial markets by easing restrictions on financial activity, especially in regard to cross-border capital transactions. These changes were part of a larger metamorphosis in the international economy as governments privatized public enterprises, deregulated markets, liberalized trade, and pursued stable macroeconomic policies. In areas that had suffered the worst aspects of the debt crisis – Latin America in particular – these changes were often induced by the conditions set by the International Monetary Fund and World Bank in return for their assistance.

Elsewhere, in Southeast Asia especially, the 1990s witnessed extraordinary growth. Several countries in the region – Taiwan, South Korea, Malaysia, Thailand, Indonesia, Hong Kong, Singapore – had adapted to varying degrees the Japanese or Asian model of export-led economic development some years before. They emerged in the 1990s as highly desirable, fast-growing markets for foreign capital as well as provided attractive business opportunities for exporters in many of the major developed countries.

Despite these positive developments in the 1990s, it had taken international institutions time to recover from the debt crisis of the 1980s. Ex-Im lending and guarantee activity hit rock bottom in fiscal year 1988. In that year, the Bank only authorized $685.3 million in direct credits and just $601.0 million in loan guarantees. This represented

[54] Testimony, James A. Harmon, Congress, Senate Committee on Banking, Subcommittee on International Finance, July 17, 1997, 105th Congress, 1st Session, pp. 3–4 (hereafter Harmon Senate Testimony).

100 mid- and long-term guarantees and eighty-five working capital guarantees. (See Appendix B.)

Commercial banks had much to do with these changes as they pulled back from providing capital in developing countries. In 1989, Macomber portrayed their behavior as "running away from the willingness to provide financing for capital and trade investments outside of the United States."[55] In the 1970s, commercial banks had represented about two thirds of flows to developing countries; by the end of 1997 – the beginning year of a currency and financial crisis in southeast Asia – they represented only 16 percent of net flows (about $41 billion).[56] This affected Ex-Im because commercial banks had been the traditional vehicles used by the Bank to deliver financial services for foreign trade finance.

In fact, commercial and investment banking was undergoing major changes in the 1980s and 1990s. These developments – and not just the fallout from the international debt crisis of the 1980s – contributed to their behavior in overseas markets. Restructuring and realignment of all sectors of the industry in the 1980s and early 1990s also resulted from losses in domestic junk bond and real estate investments. In addition, more stringent capital adequacy standards in the United States had an effect on the major commercial banks. Banks with a higher percentage of nonperforming assets generally sought large volume, high-quality/risk-free assets for securitization. And investment banks, having been stung by large losses in the 1980s, preferred to acquire assets through securitization.[57]

In any event, following the sluggish activity of the late 1980s, the Bank experienced a surge in business between 1990 and 1993. The number of medium- and long-term guarantees authorized increased from 212 (1990) to 326 (1993); the dollar amounts increased from $3,332.7 million (1990) to a record $9,094.5 million (1993).[58] Even though the country's overall economic performance was torpid in these years (the real gross domestic product [GDP] grew only at 1.0 percent annually

[55] Macomber Nomination, pp. 4–5.

[56] *1999 Economic Report of the President of the United States* (Washington, DC: Government Printing Office, 2000), pp. 1–3.

[57] Memorandum, "Banking Industry and Export Finance: Perspectives and Conflicts," July 24, 1991, "Credit Reform Enhancements" folder, POF.

[58] See Appendix B. Some of the guarantee facilities, although authorized, were never or poorly utilized.

during 1990–2, down from 3.1 percent during 1981–8), the export sector, fueled by a devalued dollar and the easing of the debt crisis, was one of the few bright spots. The dollar fell by nearly 60 percent between 1985 and 1995; it had risen by 63 percent between 1981 and 1984.[59] American exports as a percentage of GDP had been in a long-term upward trend since the 1950s, but that trend had slowed during the high-dollar, debt crisis period of the mid to late 1980s. In the early 1990s, however, exports continued their rapid acceleration. In 1986, exports were only 7.5 percent of GDP, but by 1991 they were 10.5 percent.[60]

During this revival of business, the Ex-Im firmly supported the traditional business of its exporter constituency among capital goods manufacturers. Capital goods exports were increasing. Bank support (either through medium- or long-term loans or guarantees) increased from just 1 percent of capital goods exports in 1990 to 6 percent in 1993.[61] The latter year represented the peak for the number of mid- and long-term loan guarantee authorizations. The same was true for the dollar volume of loan guarantees ($9,094.5 million). For the subsequent years, they varied from a high of $8,299.0 million in fiscal year 1999 to a low of $5,711.6 million in fiscal year 1995.[62]

But there was also increasing business for capital goods exporters because of the "market revolution" underway in the last two decades of the twentieth century. During the 1980s, the government-directed, import-substitution, development model weakened and was replaced by a growing trend toward the privatization of state industries, or the use of private enterprise to reinvigorate state-directed energy industries and related activities. Consequently, the universe for such potential projects increased, as did the need for project financings, repayment of which would depend on the revenue stream of the projects, rather than sovereign guarantees.

Analysis of the improved opportunities for project finance/limited recourse lending began under Macomber in 1991. In that year, Ex-Im

[59] *1999 Economic Report of the President of the United States* (Washington, DC: Government Printing Office, 2000).

[60] Competitiveness Report 1996, pp. 1–3; *Export Finance*, p. 12.

[61] Competitiveness Report 1996, pp. 2–3. Note that this 6 percent figure decreased to 5 percent in 1994 and to 3 percent in 1995. Of course, Ex-Im supported crucial sectors (telecommunications, major construction projects, and power) in high-growth developing markets. These exports ran from 10 to 40 percent of all U.S. capital goods exports.

[62] Appendix B.

established a project finance/limited recourse lending program. Commercial banks, notably JP Morgan, had been active in project finance in the recent past, and Ex-Im wanted to avoid competition with private sector efforts. So the Bank proposed cooperation with other lenders. Among the earliest projects Ex-Im supported were Mobil Producing Nigeria and Oso Gas Condensate. Here the Bank was able to pull in JP Morgan and the World Bank Group's International Finance Corporation, with its $95 million guaranteed financing without a sovereign guarantee.[63]

Project finance expanded substantially under Macomber's successor.[64] In 1993, the Clinton administration's new Bank chairman, Kenneth D. Brody (1993–5), created a new Project Finance Division (along with a new Business Development Division) and in June 1994 an Aircraft Division.[65] In its 1995 competitiveness report to Congress, Ex-Im estimated that it would do approximately $2.7 billion in project finance authorizations in fiscal year 1995 and another $2 to $3 billion in fiscal year 1996. Other ECAs introduced some form of project finance program by 1995. They characterized their project finance programs as case-by-case risk analysis. The 1995 competitiveness report pointed to the Bank's leadership position in project finance, although subsequently other ECAs offered more comprehensive coverage of risks.[66]

Project finance business continued to increase into 1997. From 1993 to 1997, the Bank provided almost $7 billion in export credit support for twenty-seven project finance transactions, with an average amount of support per project of $255 million. Ex-Im supplied about 28 percent of all ECA-supported projects, even though private sources of funds, such as the bond market, increasingly moved into project financing and dwarfed ECA activity. Total project financing, from all sources, outside of North America and Western Europe, topped $138 billion in 1996. Overall, at the Bank, project finance activity accounted for an increasingly large part of its volume of business. In 1993, such activity had

[63] Macomber Interview, August 26, 2000, pp. 15–17.

[64] Lawson Interview, September 21, 2000, pp. 32–4.

[65] Interview with Kenneth Brody, October 3, 2000, pp. 13–16, Library, Ex-Im (hereafter Brody Interview, October 3, 2000). When Brody set up the Project Finance Division in 1994, he brought in two private sector people to run it and, according to the Annual Report for 1994 (pp. 4–5), "hired five leading project finance firms to assist in project evaluation."

[66] Competitiveness Report 1995, p. 45; Competitiveness Report 1996, pp. 35–7.

accounted for just 3 percent of the Bank's medium- and long-term authorizations; by 1997 the figure had risen to 22 percent.[67]

By early 1997, the Bank also observed a maturation of the business. Earlier financing had been overwhelmingly for power projects (thirteen of twenty-two projects financed between 1993 and 1996). In fiscal year 1997, Ex-Im funded nine projects valued at $2.6 billion, which included a liquid natural gas (LNG), a mining, and two telecommunications projects.[68]

The dramatic increases in project finance business presented the Bank with several challenges. Project financing was susceptible to sudden shifts in international economic conditions. This was true, of course, for other ECAs as well. In fact, the Asian financial crisis that began in Thailand in July 1997 contributed to the sharp decline of the project finance business for ECAs, including that of the Bank. It also severely curtailed private (bond) financing of such activities. In 1999, the Bank reported that, "although Ex-Im Bank vigorously pursued potential projects, no transactions were authorized in 1998."[69]

Project finance also typically involved transactions in countries where risks were significant. Risk abatement strategies, such as off-shore hard currency escrow accounts, and careful analysis of project risks could mitigate risk and reduce subsidy costs.[70] But the new environment of greater risk in project finance transformed the demands on many of the Bank's staff. Risk analysis became a much more complex task. In the risk averse 1980s, the Bank had relied on sovereign guarantees for much of its lending. In 1990, just 22 percent of its credits were private sector/nonsovereign-based. By 1999 the figure had increased to 55 percent.[71] Risk analysis had to be tailored to the changing "book" of the Bank's business. Project finance required more, *new* sophisticated techniques. But the complexity and changing nature (and increasing volatility) of the Bank's customer base, which now included a wide

[67] Competitiveness Report 1998, p. 39; Competitiveness Report 1997, p. 41.

[68] Competitiveness Report 1998, p. 39.

[69] Competitiveness Report 1999, p. 33.

[70] Statement, Martin A. Kamarck, House of Representatives, Committee on Appropriations, Subcommittee on Foreign Operations, March 28, 1996, 104th Congress, 2nd Session, p. 11 (hereafter Kamarck Statement).

[71] Testimony, James A. Harmon, House of Representatives Small Business Subcommittee on Tax, Finance, and Exports, July 15, 1997, 105th Congress, 1st Session, p. 10 (hereafter Harmon House Testimony).

array of both public institutions and private entities, also required more sophistication in risk assessment, as did the new disciplines brought about by federal credit reform. Before the 1990s, Ex-Im could produce country ratings with relative ease. But it was a much more complex task to rate (price to risk) private or diverse enterprises within a country.[72]

By 1995, the Bank had switched to a system of "transaction pricing" to determine the exposure fee for each foreign buyer transaction.[73] In lieu of the sovereign guarantee, in an increasing number of cases, Ex-Im resorted to a wide range of market-based risk mitigation techniques. These included liens, standby credits, covenants, hard currency sales assignments, escrow accounts, and direct exporter participation in the risk associated with the transaction.[74]

In the past, the Bank had relied on geographic divisions to distribute its work. With the deemphasis on sovereign guarantees and the proliferation of the numbers and variety of individual transactions, flexible analysis increased in importance. Thus, by 1999 the Bank eliminated geographic divisions and substituted function or product organizational units in their place.[75]

NEW INTERNATIONAL ENVIRONMENT/THE FORMER USSR

The growth of project finance during the 1990s was occurring alongside one of the major events of the century, the collapse of the Soviet Union. That tectonic occurrence fundamentally altered the relations among the world's great powers, but it also impacted international finance. In that regard, it certainly affected the Bank's business. Through the 1970s, Ex-Im had financed extensive mineral development projects without the sovereign guarantee of the host country. Instead, these projects had relied on the creditworthiness of the firms responsible for the undertaking and the viability of the project revenue streams. But these projects were unusual. Most of the more recent development projects receiving Bank support were secured by a sovereign guarantee, which was also the practice of the other ECAs. In the risk-sensitive 1980s, the

72 Rodriguez Interview, August 15, 2000, pp. 47–9.
73 Harmon Senate Testimony, pp. 19–21.
74 Kamarck Statement, pp. 7–9.
75 Annual Report for 1999, p. 5.

necessity of a sovereign guarantee seemed axiomatic. In retrospect, the experience of the debt crisis, of course, seemed to point to another lesson: even a sovereign guarantee provided no absolute assurance of repayment.

Be that as it may, energy projects in the Russian Federation and the other republics of the former Soviet Union looked particularly promising.[76] By the end of 1992, the Bank had received twenty-one applications from that region with a value of $4.1 billion, although few of them had been approved. The Bank noted that "the complex characteristics, considerations and basic nature of project lending require[d] considerable amounts of staff time involving project evaluations and financial structuring."[77] But larger projects would come later because the Ex-Im generally laid the groundwork for a subsequent increase in business.[78]

Much of the foundation for future transactions with the NIS, including the Russian Federation, was put in place in July 1991. Clearly, lending to the NIS was going to be expensive. Macomber believed that subsidy rates on some Russian loans would exceed 35 percent.[79] The potential for business, however, was large. Vice Chairman Lawson remembered that in 1991, over one quarter of the oil wells in the Russian Federation were idle because of a lack of spare parts. He and Macomber believed that targeted loans to the lagging Russian oil sector could jump start its troubled economy.[80]

76 Interview with Stephen Glazer, August 7, 2000, pp. 33, 37–9, Library, Ex-Im (hereafter Glazer Interview, August 7, 2000). The Bank had not offered financing to the Soviet Union since 1974. The USSR had made all payments on its pre-1974 loans on schedule. In December 1990, President Bush waived the Jackson-Vanik Amendment to the Trade Act of 1974 that, among other things, prohibited these countries engaged in certain emigration restriction practices, from participating in U.S. government credit or guarantee programs. On January 10, 1991, the Bank announced that it would begin taking loan guarantee applications for the Soviet Union. With the collapse of the USSR, the Bank opened its programs to the Russian Federation on February 27, 1992, for sovereign risk transactions. And the Bank subsequently opened for business in other successor states. Other restrictions on trade with the USSR/former USSR existed in the form of the Stevenson-Byrd amendments to the Export-Import Bank Act, passed in 1974, which imposed a $300 million ceiling on Bank credits to the Soviet Union and prohibited loans to the Soviet energy sector. These were repealed in 1992. *Export Finance*, pp. 39–40.

77 "Transition Briefing Book 1992," Section A-2, p. 5, POF.

78 Macomber Interview, August 26, 2000, pp. 34–5.

79 Glazer Interview, August 7, 2000, pp. 39–41; Lawson Interview, September 21, 2000, pp. 11–14.

80 Lawson Interview, September 21, 2000, pp. 11–14.

In May 1992, the Ex-Im approached the Russian Ministry of Fuel and Energy about purchasing exports to assist in modernizing the Russian oil sector. The problem was, though the NIS countries (especially the Russian Federation) were rich in resources, their financial condition was precarious. Financial activity in these states, even with a sovereign guarantee, might not meet the Bank's statutory standard of "reasonable assurance of repayment." The resulting agreement reflected the risks of doing business in the former USSR. In lieu of government/sovereign guarantees, the Bank agreed to look to assurance of payment from the assignment of revenues generated from exports of existing production under long-term hard currency contracts, the revenues from which were to be deposited in offshore (from Russia) escrow accounts. According to Lawson, negotiations with the Russians were lengthy and sometimes acrimonious, including an allegation by the Russians that the Bank was treating the country "like Nigeria because of the Bank's insistence on escrows."[81] Nevertheless, negotiations were nearly completed when Macomber and Lawson left their positions. The incoming Clinton administration's Bank Chairman Brody signed the Oil and Gas Framework Agreement (OGFA) in July 1993. Ex-Im approved the first transactions one year later. After three years, the Bank had approved twelve transactions under the OGFA totaling approximately $2 billion. And the OGFA served as a model for arrangements within other, smaller Russian sectors.[82]

At first, however, the Bank had opened in Russia and several of the other countries of the former USSR on a sovereign risk basis. These included the Russian Federation in March 1992 and then later in the year in the Baltic countries, Kazakhstan, Uzbekistan, Turkmenistan, Belarus, and Ukraine. By early 1997, the Bank's sovereign risk exposure in these countries was Russia ($896 million), Ukraine ($183 million), Uzbekistan ($411 million), Turkmenistan ($194 million), and Kazakhstan ($126 million).[83]

The loss of confidence in Asia beginning in July 1997 spread to Russia and the NIS in August 1998. As a result, during fiscal year 1999, Ex-Im

[81] Lawson Interview, September 21, 2000, pp. 11–14.

[82] Harmon Senate Testimony. There appears to have been a significant "pipeline" of projects for the OGFA, since over $1 billion in loans and guarantees was approved in fiscal 1994. See Annual Report for 1994, pp. 30–1.

[83] Harmon Senate Testimony, pp. 19–21.

authorized no new loans to Russia, Ukraine, and most other of the NIS. Ex-Im's activity in the NIS was almost exclusively limited to $256.2 million in sovereign guaranteed loans for farm, mining, and aircraft to Uzbekistan.[84] Also contributing to an unfavorable atmosphere was official U.S. disenchantment with political developments in Russia, as well as reports of rampant corruption there. Despite these difficulties, later in the 1990s, Bank business with the Russian Federation resumed, a subject treated in the epilogue.

OECD AND INCREASED EXPORT COMPETITION

Other overseas developments affected the Bank in the late 1980s and early 1990s. In particular, concerns about tied aid increased in the late 1980s. Tied aid was only one manifestation at the time of the more competitive international environment faced by American exporters. In the early 1990s, there was also the issue of risk premiums or exposure fees.

Most worrisome in the late 1980s was the apparent inability of the Wallen Package, which raised the minimum concessionality to 35 percent on projects, to arrest the expansion of tied aid use by other ECAs, especially the Japanese. Coming at a time when the Japanese economic model appeared triumphant, and while the United States was mired in a period of slow growth in the late 1980s and early 1990s, exporter complaints increased about the assistance available to them to meet foreign competitors. The exporters found a receptive audience in Congress. Additionally, the demise of the USSR gradually had the effect of focusing the foreign policy establishment and Department of the Treasury on the need for enhanced tools to address foreign ECA competition.

Discussions on tied aid, beginning in the summer 1989, took a new direction. They focused on not necessarily raising the minimum level of concessionality that had characterized past efforts, but instead on the clear separation of commercial and concessional finance and on the interest rates for official export credit. After two years of negotiations, the OECD participants agreed to modifications of the earlier Arrangement.

84 Annual Report for 1999, pp. 16–27. The same report indicated that at the end of fiscal year 1999 approximately $3.6 billion in Bank obligations was outstanding to the former USSR: Russia ($1.94 billion); Uzbekistan ($969 million); Turkmenistan ($313 million); Ukraine ($222 million); and Kazakhstan ($86 million). The remainder was accounted for by three other smaller countries.

On December 16, 1991, they assented to what was called the Helsinki Package.[85]

The Helsinki Package restricted the use of tied aid in relatively well-off developing countries, that is, countries whose per capita GDP made them ineligible for seventeen- or twenty-year loans from the World Bank. In 1990, this amount was $2,465. The majority of tied aid financing had gone to middle income countries such as China, Indonesia, Thailand, Philippines, India, and Pakistan. The OECD participants agreed that in these countries tied aid and partial untied concessional or aid credits should not be extended to public or private projects that normally could be commercially financed at market or OECD Arrangement rates. The tests for commercially viable projects included "whether the project lacks the capacity to generate cash flow sufficient to cover the project's operating costs and to service the capital employed and whether (based on communication with other OECD participants) it is unlikely that it can be financed at market OECD Arrangement rates." This "commercially viable" project rule did not apply to the poorest countries, which the OECD concluded often had trouble securing any financing. The Helsinki Package also strengthened OECD notification and consultation procedures for tied aid.[86]

Leading up to the Helsinki Package the Bank used its War Chest in an "offensive operation" to force an agreement.[87] Bank officials employed the War Chest funds twelve times for authorizations of $53.4 million in 1990 and $145.4 million in 1991 (Appendix B). In the latter year, the Bank was especially aggressive in using the $150 million War Chest appropriated by Congress, virtually exhausting it before the agreement on the Helsinki Package.[88] Ex-Im supported exports of telecommunications, power, transportation, and construction equipment in Indonesia, Mauritius, Pakistan, Papua New Guinea, and Thailand.[89]

85 John E. Ray, *Managing Official Export Credits: The Quest for a Global Regime* (Washington, DC: Institute for International Economics, 1995), pp. 85–96.

86 Ray, pp. 96–9; *Export Finance*, pp. 50–2.

87 "Transition Briefing Book," 1992, Section E-2, pp. 4–5, POF.

88 Ibid., pp. 4–6. Besides the aggressive use of the War Chest in May 1990, AID and the Bank established a $500 million joint program combining AID grant funds and Bank export credits, essentially a U.S. tied aid program directed at four so-called spoiled markets where tied aid credits were used by foreign ECAs. These countries were Indonesia, Pakistan, Thailand, and the Philippines; "Transition Briefing Book, 1992," Section F-2, POF.

89 *Export Finance*, p. 6.

After agreement on the Helsinki Package, Congress appropriated $115 million for the War Chest in fiscal year 1992, but the Bank only used $5.1 million in one case. The figures for fiscal year 1993 were a $200 million War Chest of which the Bank used $26.7 million. There were concerns within the Bank about the future of the War Chest after credit reform. Because of the Helsinki Package, the tied aid War Chest would be employed in riskier markets. This would increase the cost of the program per transaction under credit reform budget rules.[90]

Interested members of Congress, however, complained that War Chest authority was not used extensively enough in the wake of the Helsinki Package. They cited the limited expenditures in fiscal years 1992 and 1993. Consequently, the incoming Clinton administration and the new Bank chairman Brody took a much more aggressive posture. They saw the War Chest as an instrument to enforce the OECD Arrangements and to maintain the competiveness of U.S. exporters, not just the tied aid provisions of the Helsinki Package. The administration's stance was also a reflection of Commerce Secretary Ron Brown's emphasis on the U.S. energetically promoting big export sectors.[91]

In September 1993, President Clinton announced an aggressive export strategy, including new funding "to counter the tied aid policies of our competitors." In April 1994, the Bank began to administer the Tied-Aid Capital Projects Fund (TACPF) and implemented a new strategy designed to counter the tied aid efforts of other ECAs. Ex-Im would match competing offers, whether or not they were violations of the Arrangement and would even initiate soft loans in targeted countries when it was permissible under the Arrangement. According to John Ray, a leading student of export credit, "the United States softened this move toward 'preemptive matching' by an ingenious innovation; it would only extend soft loans after it had first attempted and failed to reach agreement with other [OECD] participants on a common line [even before formal OECD notification] that would forbid aid credits for the transaction in question.... In other words, when the United States could be sure in advance that its exporters would not find themselves facing competition from aid credits, it would not extend an aid credit itself."[92]

90 "Transition Briefing Book," 1992, Section E-2, p. 6, POF.

91 Cruse Interview, August 15, 2000, pp. 21–3.

92 Ray, pp. 106–7.

In the year and a half following the initiation of the TACPF (April 12, 1994), Ex-Im used the fund to counter over $2 billion in actual and potential tied aid credits. In terms of actual expenditures, there was only one disbursement of $22 million.[93] The new strategy, which was a significant departure from past practice, seemed to work. The 1994 annual report quoted an exporter (President Peter A. Bowe of Ellicott Machine International of Baltimore) as saying that in the past before agreeing to make a counteroffer the Ex-Im would wait until there was firm evidence of a foreign ECA offer involving concessional finance. As a result, U.S. exporters often lost the sale. But the new policy gave exporters a better chance.[94]

The Helsinki Package and the United States' vigorous enforcement of it resulted in a dramatic decline in the type of tied aid curtailed by the changes in the Arrangement. Before 1992, there was $8 to $10 billion annually in Helsinki-type aid credits. That declined and averaged between $4.1 billion and $5.3 billion between 1993 and 1995 and was even less in the manufacturing, power, and communication sectors that were of primary interest to the United States. It continued to use War Chest funds between 1996 and 1999 – in 1996 there were nine authorizations (for $136 million); in 1997 there were two ($75.2 million); in 1998 there was one ($16.6 million); and in 1999 there were three ($54.5 million) to support total exports of much higher dollar value.[95]

The Helsinki Package expanded the exclusive coverage of CIRR (Commercial Interest Reference Rate) to Category II developing countries. Thus it limited export subsidies Matrix or SDR-based rates to Category III (relatively poor) countries. It also raised the minimum interest rate for these countries by 30 basis points. At the time of the agreement, countries in Category II received the bulk of the officially supported export credit (54 percent of all medium- and long-term export credits reported to the OECD).[96] Subsequently, in 1994 (effective 1995) the OECD's "Schaerer Package" made the application of the CIRR universal, and eliminated the use of matrix rates.[97] Thus, in effect, it

93 Kamarck Statement, p. 5.
94 Annual Report for 1994, p. 14.
95 Harmon Senate Testimony, pp. 13–14.
96 Ray, pp. 96–7.
97 Ibid., p. 111.

squeezed much of the last subsidy out of the funding element of commercial export credit activities (but not in conjunction with aid).

Soon after the Helsinki Package was in place the OECD turned to the last area of unrestrained ECA competition. In 1994, the OECD established a working group on risk premiums or exposure fees. In many respects, attention to the issue was a consequence of the increased demands of business in riskier sectors and countries, although other factors had driven it to the head of the OECD agenda. Important in the United States was the discipline of credit reform and the realization that for budget purposes risk needed to be realistically priced. Additionally, the new markets in Russia and the Newly Independent States of the former Soviet Union, as well as the realities of the post-debt-crisis world, made demand for credit risk premiums and exposure fees much more important. Credit reform subsidies in newly emerging markets averaged 12 percent, according to one former Bank director.[98]

Furthermore, all the ECAs, including Ex-Im, had incurred substantial losses during the debt crisis in the 1980s. Their treasuries were "bleeding" as a result of bad loans. Finance ministry officials pressured their ECAs to reduce losses, raise fees, and reach some type of accommodation at the OECD. Much of the "blood" could be attributed to risk fee policies that did not reflect the cost of risk undertaken. Germany, for example, charged a flat 2 percent fee. According to Rita Rodriguez, who was the Ex-Im director negotiating at OECD, the Germans were "literally giving it away."[99] For its part, Ex-Im had used flat fees until the mid 1980s, and the Bank's premiums had been underpriced in certain markets prior to credit reform. For political risk (for credits, guarantees, and insurance) in low-risk developing countries, the Bank's coverage was priced at more than what it was worth before 1987 and at approximately what it was worth from 1987 through 1992. But for higher-risk developing countries, the Bank had significantly underpriced during these periods, as no doubt had other ECA competitors.[100]

Britain was the driving force in the negotiations. The government of Prime Minister John Major had told its ECA (Exports Credit Guarantee Department or ECGD) that it had to break even. For its part, the United

98 Rodriguez Interview, August 15, 2000, pp. 9–12.

99 Ibid., pp. 11–13.

100 Ray, pp. 145–51.

States maintained pressure on the negotiations because charges were extremely low.[101] Two and one-half years of negotiations resulted in a June 1997 OECD agreement on minimum risk premium benchmarks that would be applied two years later to all OECD participants and to all transactions other than aircraft, military equipment, ships, and agricultural products.[102]

Chairman Harmon explained the new arrangement to a Senate committee in July 1997: "The new rules establish a transparent, uniform system that will provide exporters with a clear and fair trade-off between quality and extent of coverage, on the one hand, and price on the other. Hence, Ex-Im can create a menu of programs from which exporters can choose, for each individual transaction, the best program and associated exposure fees to meet case-specific needs." Harmon concluded that the system would prevent a future "fare war" of fee cuts. It would provide budget savings in the immediate term because, on average across all risk categories and terms, the Bank would increase fees about 15 percent or one percentage point. This resulted in savings, after phase in, of approximately $50 million to $75 million a year.[103]

Despite these efforts to level the playing field in the work of ECAs, a new source of competition arose outside the disciplines of the OECD Arrangements. In the 1990s, the so-called market window – as opposed to "government window" – financing of exports became a source of new competition for the Bank, and other ECAs. The Germans and Canadians aggressively expanded the use of market windows. Ostensibly, the German Kreditanstalt für Wiederaufbau (KfW) and the Canadian Export Development Corporation (EDC) provide financing at commercial or market terms, after their governments determine that there is a national interest in a particular transaction. Because KfW and EDC can borrow with the full faith and credit of their governments, and do not pay taxes or interest to them, there appears to be a subsidy element in their transactions. They challenged the premise behind OECD Arrangements that export decisions should not be distorted by nonmarket

101 Rodriguez Interview, August 15, 2000, pp. 11–15.

102 Competitiveness Report 1998, p. 72.

103 Harmon Senate Testimony, pp. 15–17; Pierre Knaepen, "The 'Knaepen Package': Towards Convergence in Pricing Risk," in OECD, *The Export Credit Arrangement: Achievements and Challenges 1978–1998* (Paris: OECD, 1998), pp. 75–80.

considerations. How the Bank would respond to the challenge of market windows remained an open question at the end of 2000. Commercial banks in Canada and Germany have complained about EDC and KfW competition, respectively. Ex-Im's long history, and statutory mandates, seemed to rule out an approach to financing that would compete with the private sector. In responding to the challenge posed by the Germans and Canadians, however, other ECAs might create a situation that undermined the OECD understandings so painstakingly negotiated over a quarter century.[104]

"REINVENTING" THE BANK

For much of the late 1980s and 1990s, the Bank had to adjust to major changes resulting from the debt crisis of the 1980s, the collapse of the Soviet Union, and alterations in the conduct of finance driven by the deregulation of financial markets and the revolution in information technology. But the Bank in these years also found itself influenced generally by American management's passion to restructure, reinvent, and reengineer corporate organization, as well as more specifically by a major initiative of the Clinton administration to "reinvent" government. Much of the interest in reinvention was driven by the need to mesh organizational operations with the possibilities of the new information technology. But it also reflected the need to rework how organizations conducted business in new environments, especially in organizations like the Bank involved in fast-changing financial markets.

Of course, the Bank had needed to change in response to new circumstances over the course of its history, and its leaders adjusted the organization accordingly. But the new information technologies of the 1990s, to say nothing of the mergers and restructurings in corporate America, lent a sense of urgency to the need to adapt. Then, too, there was a growing industry of consultants and advisers committed to convincing managers of the need for change.

When John Macomber arrived as chairman and president in 1989, he introduced the ideas of Total Quality Management, a popular set of

[104] Allan I. Mendelowitz, "The New World of Government-Supported International Finance," in Gary Clyde Hufbauer and Rita M. Rodriguez, eds., *The Ex-Im Bauk in the 21st Century: A New Approach?* Special Report 14 (Washington, DC: Institute for International Economics, 2001), pp. 159–89.

concepts focusing on improving every aspect of an enterprise's contacts with it customers. Earlier in his career, Macomber had directed the European operations of the well-known management consulting firm of McKinsey and Company, a leader in many of the newest ideas about organizational effectiveness. Macomber was well-liked by Bank staff. Many thought that his working relationship with his vice chairman was as frictionless as such an arrangement could be. Macomber was a consolidator and conciliator. He made the Bank work well. Perhaps, this came at the expense of dealing with some of the deeper, underlying issues of the time, in particular the need to cope with the "exploding demand" for the Bank's services and the special requirements of the new kind of project lending.[105]

Macomber was followed by Kenneth D. Brody, a leader with a very different style. In fact, the Brody years, and that of his successor, Martin A. Kamarck, were tumultuous. The last of Clinton's appointments, James A. Harmon, remained for the duration of the president's term and had a calming influence on the institution. Adjusting the Ex-Im culture to fast-paced changes in its outside environment was not a simple task. Understanding what needed to be done, and then doing it, are among the toughest tasks for any organization. Because the Bank had three chairmen who had different views on how to manage change, the process of adjustment perhaps became even more difficult.

Brody became Bank chairman and president in May 1993. When he left at the end of 1995, after little more than two and a half years, many in the Bank remembered his blunt – some thought undiplomatic – speech, probing questions regarding the fundamental ways the institution operated, and high level of nervous energy. Brody came from a twenty-year career at the investment banking firm of Goldman Sachs, where he has served as a member of the management committee from 1990.

Many of his colleagues at Ex-Im strongly believed that Brody wanted to turn Ex-Im into a first-class investment banking agency. But from the first he was critical of the institution and the skill levels of the professionals at the Bank. He complained, for instance, that when he arrived the Bank's computing system still relied on a mainframe computer. Brody's point of reference for this judgment was Goldman Sachs, an institution at the pinnacle of American investment banks, where its amply rewarded

[105] Rodriguez Interview, August 15, 2000, pp. 20–2.

professional investors and traders were among the best in the country. Few in the industry were on a par with them for drive, energy, and intelligence. In any event, Brody focused on procedures and wanted to shake up the existing credit culture at the Bank. Following the debt crisis of the 1980s, the collapse of business, and the controversies during the Reagan years, Ex-Im had become risk averse.

Even so, Ex-Im had fine-tuned its operations under Macomber as demand picked up late in the 1980s and the early 1990s and as the Bank was called on to move into riskier markets. But processing times remained comparatively slow, and customer service was a concern. Brody thought the process of change too slow. His vice chairman Martin A. Kamarck believed that the Bank was stymied in its own procedures and that in some respects it had taken on a British "National Health Service model" in terms of its service to the public.[106] Brody's provocative style seemed to him to be the only way to achieve a quick change in thinking in the Bank.[107]

In any event, Brody assigned Kamarck, as vice chairman and chief operating officer, the task of spearheading procedural changes that were to be generated by "Reinventing Export-Import Bank." Kamarck, an attorney, had come to the Bank from Financial Guarantee Insurance Corporation. He took to heart Vice President Albert Gore's interest in "reinventing" government to make it smaller, but "smarter" and more efficient. Both Brody and Kamarck knew reinvention would be unsettling. Such processes had proved difficult in the corporate sector but were likely to be even more so in the civil service. The latter was a stable culture unaccustomed to the tumult that accompanied restructuring in private business enterprise in the 1980s and 1990s.[108]

The concept of reinvention, according to Kamarck, was to get the Bank's people to reflect on how to improve service to customers. Ex-Im called in professional management consultants to assist in the reinvention effort and used the Federal Quality Institute (FQI) to facilitate the process.[109]

[106] Kamarck Interview, September 14, 2000, pp. 5–6; Brody Interview, October 3, 2000, pp. 5–6.

[107] Cruse Interview, August 15, 2000, pp. 28–34.

[108] Kamarck Interview, September 14, 2000, pp. 9–11; Brody Interview, October 3, 2000, pp. 5–6.

[109] Kamarck Interview, September 14, 2000, pp. 9–11.

There were nevertheless significant changes in the way the Bank did business. Processing times became an issue in the 1990s. These circumstances only exacerbated a problem that first surfaced in the late 1980s during the debt crisis. The 1986 reauthorization mandated that the Bank make its guarantees completely transferable, and that in general the Bank tailor its programs to reengage the private sector in export credit markets. The effort to construct a "clean" guarantee to enhance private marketability increased staff processing time. But slack demand in the mid/late 1980s offset the increased workload. These requirements in regard to guarantees became more onerous as lending operations accelerated and diversified in the early 1990s.[110]

Dealing with the mushrooming medium- and long-term guarantee issues also prompted Macomber to create a policy review committee (PRC) in July 1990. It was an effort to coordinate and guide the growing technical aspects of operating Bank programs and policies. Ultimate authority to set Bank policies remained with the board of directors, but the PRC served as a "consultative tool to interpret, implement and fine tune policies and programs sanctioned by the Board of Directors." It was composed of one or two members of the board (and headed by Macomber's vice chairman) and several other senior-level managers meeting on an as-needed basis.[111]

One of the earliest, and probably most important, was the introduction of the "letter of interest" procedure in 1993. Consideration of this procedure had begun under Macomber, so it was not technically a result

110 Cruse Interview, August 15, 2000, pp. 3–6. Note that Macomber made still more changes to the Ex-Im guarantee to make it more attractive to private banks. The Bank increased the interest cover on bank guaranteed loans to 100 percent on October 1, 1991, and eliminated a 2 percent "counter guarantee" on nonsovereign guaranteed midterm financing that had been required from the exporter or guaranteed lender. Ex-Im accelerated the shift of the administrative burden from commercial lenders to itself as part of the continuing effort to reengage the private sector. Fees, including lending and investment banking fees, could be included in the Bank financing package. It gave commercial lenders a choice of payment options at the time of claim. In addition, at any time during the term of the loan guarantee the lender of record had a one-time option of switching the interest rate basis on the total amount of outstanding principal from a floating rate to a fixed rate. See Congress, Senate, Committee on Banking, Housing, and Urban Affairs, Subcommittee on International Finance and Monetary Policy, *Reauthorization of the Export-Import Bank – 1992*, 102nd Congress, 2nd Session, 1992, pp. 49–50.

111 "Transition Briefing Book" 1992, Section B-5, POF.

of the reinvention process. In designing the procedure, the Bank hoped to increase efficiency and improve service to customers. Prior to this time, Bank loan officers spent a significant percentage of their time – perhaps as much as 80 percent – in lengthy, detailed credit analyses required for a preliminary commitment that did not necessarily result in a loan authorization.[112] The time required for issuance of a PC averaged three months, and a smaller percentage of them ultimately resulted in credit/guarantee authorizations. In contrast, a letter of interest essentially indicated that Ex-Im was open for and interested in the type of transaction that the American exporter was investigating. It did not bind the Bank to any further action and had a six month expiration date. The letter of interest could be issued in an average of under seven days. It proved helpful for exporters seeking orders, while it did not require any major expenditure of staff time.[113] It was simply an indication of future Bank support if the exporter was successful in winning a contract from a foreign buyer.[114]

Other changes were made in addition to those resulting from reinvention. Until this time, the line staff (loan officers) had been entirely responsible for gathering information for, consultation about, and the processing of deals. These functions were split. The Business Development Division separated the line function of processing the applications and took responsibility for assembling information and counseling. The establishment of the distinct Project Finance Division in 1994 reflected changes in the Ex-Im's customer base. Brody retained two managers with private sector experience to run it. They promised to stay two years to train Bank personnel to take charge of the operation after they left. He also hired five leading project finance firms to assist the Bank in project evaluation.[115] Additionally, Brody created the separate Aircraft Finance Division. Thus, some of the Bank's fastest-growing, interesting work (in terms of risk analysis) was taken out of geographic divisions and put in separate divisions. During the 1990s, airlines increased the pace by which they were replacing aging aircraft, a process that heightened competition with Airbus. Also under Brody, Ex-Im increased its fees for aircraft, raising them to the level of their European ECA competition,

[112] Harmon Senate Testimony, pp. 29–30; Cruse Interview, August 15, 2000, pp. 25–8.
[113] Harmon Senate Testimony, pp. 29–30.
[114] "Transition Briefing Book," 1992, Section D-1, p. 1, POF.
[115] Annual Report for 1995, p. 4; Kamarck Interview, September 14, 2000, pp. 13–16.

allowing greater credit at the same cost.[116] In 1996 and 1997, the Bank supported $3.3 billion in aircraft finance, over three quarters of which was in Asia. Between 1993 and 1997, total aircraft financing came to $10.7 billion.[117]

The decision in the fall of 1995 to evaluate most individual transaction risk separately reflected the changing nature of the Bank's business. It demonstrated the importance of fees in the post-credit-reform period. The Bank referred to this as "transaction pricing," part and parcel of the trends that led Ex-Im to deemphasize organizational geographic divisions, which were finally disposed of under Harmon in 1999.[118] In the changing mix of Bank customers in the 1990s, geographic market knowledge was not nearly as important as the ability to analyze special and complex deals.

Of course, for some in the Bank, the Brody years were an uncertain and hence stressful time. Clearly the reinvention exercise proved controversial. There were those who thought that the process did not accomplish much, especially after the devotion of a significant amount of time and the expenditure of high levels of emotional energy. For others, though, Brody spearheaded a refreshing reexamination of first principles about how and why the Bank conducted its business as it did. Brody, in addition to championing new initiatives in project finance, also in many ways changed the public appearance of the Bank. He brought in new faces (female in many instances) into key positions. Bank senior executives had been staffed almost exclusively by white males up to that time.[119] In fact, lack of gender and racial diversity characterized the professional staff and had been a source of increasing concern in the Bank in previous administrations.

Ex-Im had to face other troublesome personnel issues in the 1990s. Overall, the Bank had an increasingly difficult time in attracting and keeping quality professional employees as the gap between private sector and federal pay widened after the 1970s. Other federal institutions, such as the Federal Reserve, Federal Home Loan Bank Board (now,

[116] Statement, Kenneth Brody, Subcommittee on Foreign Operations, Committee on Appropriations, Senate, 103rd Congress, 2nd Session, May 24, 1994; Brody Interview, October 3, 2000, pp. 10–12.

[117] Harmon Senate Testimony, pp. 26–7; Competitiveness Report 1998, pp. 45–50.

[118] Harmon Senate Testimony, pp. 17–18.

[119] Brody Interview, October 3, 2000, pp. 3–5.

Federal Housing Finance Board), Controller of the Currency, and the Federal Deposit Insurance Corporation, had statutory exceptions to the standard federal pay scale and were allowed to compensate employees at rates well above that scale. Ex-Im did not have such authority, although it had gained a limited exception in its 1992 reauthorization.[120] Congress allowed the Bank to exempt thirty-five positions from federal compensation rules in a pilot program. Ultimately, Brody and Kamarck determined that this program was essentially unworkable and looked for other solutions.[121]

With available opportunities in the private banking sector expanding in the 1990s, the Brody administration believed that large numbers of Bank employees might leave the agency.[122] Ex-Im's response was to use "retention allowance" authority created by the Federal Employees Pay Comparability Act of 1990. This legislation, and the Office of Personnel Management (OPM) regulations implementing it, allowed federal agencies to make supplemental payments (up to 25 percent above base pay) to employees. Such payments were to be based on a determination that the employee possessed unique skills needed by the agency. To justify the payment of such allowances, OPM regulations specified narrow criteria and detailed documentation, including that the potential recipient was likely to leave government service.[123]

The Bank made extensive use of retention allowances during the Brody administration. A December 1995 General Accounting Office report of the government-wide use of retention allowances observed that "as of September 30, 1994, 354 of the 1.9 million civilian executive branch employees were receiving retention allowances." One hundred Ex-Im employees received the allowances, out of a staff of 462. The average retention allowance paid to Bank employees was under $5,000, and the highest amount was under $13,000. Ex-Im did not pay the allowances to political appointees or those managers in the equivalent grade of Senior Executive Service (SES).[124]

[120] Mendelowitz Interview, February 13, 2001, pp. 58–9.
[121] Kamarck Interview, September 14, 2000, pp. 39–41.
[122] Ibid., pp. 40–2.
[123] Letter, Report, General Accounting Office, to Senator David Pryor, Report to Ranking Minority Member, Subcommittee on Post Office and Civil Service, Committee on Government Affairs, US Senate, 106th Congress, 1st Session, December 1995, p. 1.
[124] Ibid., pp. 1–5.

GAO noted that "Ex-Im Bank did not appear to comply with the statutory requirement that it must determine that prospective recipients would be likely to leave the agency if they did not receive an allowance. We informed OPM of our preliminary compliance concerns. Subsequently, in furtherance of its oversight responsibility, OPM initiated an in-depth review of Ex-Im Bank's use of retention allowances and recruitment bonuses."[125] OPM's subsequent report criticized Ex-Im's wholesale use of retention allowances and its inadequate justification and documentation. The report provided time for the Bank to justify payments if it submitted the appropriate documentation required by the statute and OPM's regulations. In response, the Bank immediately ended the payment of retention allowances, reevaluated its criteria in light of OPM criticism, and dramatically reduced the number of its employees that received the allowances.[126]

The controversy over retention allowances began immediately before Brody's departure at the end of December 1995, and the installation of his vice chair, Martin Kamarck, as acting chair. A convergence of many factors would make Kamarck's short tenure (through April 1997) a troubled one. In his role as vice chair, Kamarck had assumed the traditional role as manager of internal operations at the Bank. This included responsibility for the retention allowances policy. He and others around Brody knew that this authority had been used very judiciously government wide and that they were "making a stretch" and "might get our hands slapped," as Kamarck himself observed.[127] And, as the person in charge of the Bank's effort at "reinvention," Kamarck was associated with the discord resulting from that effort.

Other factors clouded Kamarck's tenure. In 1995, the Republicans gained control of both houses of Congress. Scrutiny of Democratic-run agencies increased, and the appointment process for government officials was accompanied by increased tension. Kamarck's immediate predecessors had excellent relations with Congress. Macomber benefitted from a long "honeymoon" that followed settlement of the contentious

[125] Ibid., p. 2. Ironically, Pryor – the sponsor of the 1990 legislation to allow the payment of retention allowances – had asked GAO for a report because he was concerned that the authority was being underutilized.

[126] Mendelowitz Interview, February 13, 2001, pp. 60–4.

[127] Kamarck Interview, September 14, 2000, pp. 41–2; Mendelowitz Interview, February 13, 2001, pp. 46–7; Brody Interview, October 3, 2000, p. 33.

loss reserve question and an increased focus on small business concerns.[128] Brody also enjoyed good relations with Congress, having cultivated key staff members at the committees overseeing the Bank. Thus when problems developed over the retention allowances, he had a reservoir of goodwill on Capitol Hill to draw on.[129]

But Brody's departure coincided with the GAO/OPM reports on retention allowances. Even though the total amounts of money involved were small – under $2 million – and Kamarck responded quickly to the OPM criticisms, the practice became grist for attacks on the Bank in Congress. In the context of increasing executive–congressional tensions, matters were exacerbated when President Clinton used a recess appointment to make Kamarck the Bank's chairman in April 1996. This circumstance would have placed obstacles in the way of even the most politically experienced and savvy of appointees, something that Kamarck was not. The new chairman did not help matters by getting into a dispute – at times highly personal – with Senator Mitch McConnell of Kentucky, chairman of the Senate Banking Committee. These circumstances soured Kamarck's relations more generally with Capitol Hill, which contributed to Congress reducing the Bank's administrative budget for fiscal year 1997.[130]

Kamarck's original term expired in January 1997. By that time, he had decided not to seek reappointment as chairman. He promised the White House that he would stay until a successor was installed. But things proceeded slowly, and he left the Bank in April 1997.[131]

Kamarck's difficult tenure also saw a major case involving the Bank's new environmental guidelines. In the 1992 reauthorization, Congress required the Bank to consider potential environmental effects of goods and services for which long-term financial support of $10 million or more was requested from the Bank. The legislation explicitly allowed the board to withhold financing for environmental reasons, according to guidelines it devised. Ex-Im issued environmental guidelines in 1995, following extensive discussions with exporter groups and environmental activists. Development of these guidelines had begun during 1993 under Brody through the supervision of Carol Lee, Ex-Im's

[128] Lawson Interview, September 21, 2000, pp. 6, 8–11.
[129] Mendelowitz Interview, February 13, 2001, pp. 42–3.
[130] Kamarck Interview, September 14, 2000, pp. 47, 48–9, 50–2, 56.
[131] Ibid., pp. 51–2.

general counsel; John Wisniewski, the vice president of the Engineering Division; and subsequently Bank Director Julie Belaga, who had been a regional administrator at the Environmental Protection Agency. Under the guidelines, the Bank's engineering staff, which was renamed the Engineering and Environmental Division after the hiring of an environmental specialist in 1994, conducted the environmental reviews of foreign projects. From the time the guidelines were approved through 2000, Ex-Im reevaluated the environmental effects of 193 transactions involving projects. Of these, twenty were upgraded during the review process to meet Ex-Im's guidelines, and all but one of the 193 were approved.

That was the Three Gorges Project on the Yangtze River in China, which was not actually turned down. Rather, the Bank simply declined to issue a letter of interest with the facts available at the time. The case involved a large dam in China (a 18,000-megawatt hydroelectric dam that would supply 10 percent of China's electricity) that would have required Ex-Im support for $414 million in exports. Three exporters, Caterpillar Company, Vioth Hydro, and Rotec Industries, had requested Bank financing.[132]

The Yangtze Three Gorges Corporation did not have a plan to address major environmental issues concerning water quality in the proposed reservoir. Essentially, unofficial sources of information suggested that the project would dam sewage and industrial waste from Chungking – a city of 10 million people – which was already being dumped into the Yangtze. Nor did the corporation address the relocation of 1.3 million people in the building of the dam and the project's impact on endangered species. The Bank wanted Chinese officials to address these issues through the provision of authoritative official information. Kamarck visited Beijing, where he and Bank staff from the Asia and Engineering and Environmental divisions met with senior government representatives. When ultimately the official data was not forthcoming, Ex-Im refused to issue a letter of interest; it announced the decision on May 30, 1996.[133] Even without Bank assistance, the Chinese awarded contracts

[132] "Ex-Im Bank Makes Ruling of Three Gorges Dam Project," "Three Gorges" folder, Temelin files, Archives, Ex-Im.

[133] "Statement of Export-Import Bank of the United States by Martin Kamarck for Three Gorges Press Briefing," May 30, 1996, "Three Gorges" folder, Temelin files, Archives, Ex-Im.

to the American exporters. In this way Kamarck believed that his visit, and his reassurances that the Bank valued China's business, was able to defuse a difficult situation, while allowing the Bank to remain true to its environmental standards.[134]

Harmon's arrival in July 1997 had a calming effect on the Bank. An experienced financier and manager, Harmon was not the target of the intense political battling that plagued Kamarck. Even so, his term was filled with dramatic challenges, in particular the Asian financial crisis (1997–8). He and his senior colleagues used the occasion of a new millennium to examine where the Bank stood and where it might go in a new century.

[134] Ibid.; Kamarck Interview, September 14, 2000, pp. 31–7.

EPILOGUE

To mark sixty-five years of work, the Washington-based Institute for International Economics (IIE), with the full support of the Bank, sponsored a conference in May 2000 to assess Ex-Im's effectiveness and to explore its role in the twenty-first century.[1] While the theme of the conference was looking toward a new century, conference participants nevertheless also focused heavily on the Bank's situation at the end of the 1990s. In fact, the tenor of the conference – and the book made up of selected papers published in 2001 – was in large measure one of taking stock. To plan for the future, one needed to put the recent past into perspective. Thus, the conference presentations generally addressed the challenges the Bank faced at the end of the century. Together these challenges represented, as was so often the case in the past, the need for the Bank to determine how to adjust its internal operations and policies to yet another set of shifts in the public and private, domestic and international, environments in which it operated. In many respects, of course, the process of adjustment was already underway at the time of the meetings in Washington.[2]

But, as the century ended, it was not entirely clear how the Bank would ultimately respond to some of the other challenges that it faced.

[1] "Ex-Im Bank in the 21st Century: A New Approach," a conference sponsored by the Institute for International Economics, on the 65th anniversary of the Export-Import Bank, May 15–16, 2000, Washington, DC (hereafter IIE Conference). Papers presented at the conference have been published in Gary Clyde Hufbauer and Rita M. Rodriguez, eds., *The Ex-Im Bank in the 21st Century: A New Approach?* (Special Report 14; Washington, DC: Institute for International Economics, 2001) (hereafter *The Ex-Im Bank in the 21st Century*).

[2] James A. Harmon, "A Chairman's Perspective on the Future of Ex-Im Bank," *The Ex-Im Bank in the 21st Century*, pp. 39–45.

This, of course, was one of the reasons for the conference. Some of the difficult issues needed careful analysis before the Bank, its constituencies, Congress, and White House officials would be able to determine what course to take in the future.

Ex-Im confronted the continuing consequences of several ongoing trends in the international economy: growing risk aversion among commercial banks despite increasing private capital flows to emerging markets; new competitive challenges from other ECAs; the on-going movement toward privatization of formerly state-owned enterprises in many regions of the world; a "market revolution" in the former communist countries of the USSR and in still-communist China; a high-tech revolution in computer, information, and communication technologies; and the on-going vulnerabilities of the international economic system as demonstrated in the financial crises in Mexico (1994–5), Southeast Asia (1997–8), and Russia (1998).

Together these developments had the Bank's leadership thinking anew about Ex-Im's role and direction and how, in a new century, it would meet its fundamental mandates to counteract market imperfections in financing exports and to level the international playing field upon which export credit agencies operated. They also prompted renewed attention to the Bank itself and to the restraints public policy put on its operations and procedures.

THE HARMON YEARS

Many of the issues the Bank began to confront in the late 1980s and 1990s did not abate during the term of the Bank's last chairman in the twentieth century, James A. Harmon. He and his senior colleagues used the occasion of the new millennium, and the Bank's sixty-fifth anniversary, to put into perspective the consequential developments in his term and those of his immediate predecessors. Harmon and his senior colleagues believed that the Bank faced major turning points in the last years of the century.

President Clinton in 1997 turned to Harmon, a seasoned Wall Street professional, after the stormy tenure of his predecessor Martin A. Kamarck. Harmon, with almost thirty-five years of experience as an investment banker, also had substantial managerial and international experience as the chairman and CEO of Wertheim Schroder and Company, an enterprise formed in 1986 through a trans-Atlantic merger of a leading bank in London and in New York. Clinton nominated Harmon on May 6, 1997, along with Jackie M. Clegg, as vice chairman. She had joined the Bank in 1993, after having served in several senior staff positions on Capitol Hill. At the Bank she held the position of chief of staff and later as acting vice president for Congressional and External Affairs.[3]

Harmon, looking back on his tenure in April 2001, saw his chairmanship as encompassing three chapters. The first focused on the Bank's response to the Asian and Russian financial crises, 1997–8; the second, opening up new markets for U.S. exports in emerging markets; and the third, strengthening the Bank as an institution.[4]

Soon after taking office in June 1997, Harmon devoted his attention to preparations for the Bank's reauthorization. While he was focused on the rechartering, there were in mid July the beginnings of a major currency and financial crisis in Asia. Events over the next year threatened a meltdown of the entire international financial system. Few experts in government or the private sector, as Harmon pointed out, saw the crisis coming. For the Bank, its immediate effect was to threaten the economies of countries – in particular Indonesia – where Ex-Im had substantial loan and guarantee commitments. Outside of China, Indonesia represented one of the highest percentages of Bank authorizations in fiscal year 1997. Bank loans and guarantees to China in fiscal 1997 were $1.3 billion and to Indonesia, $610 million. Indonesia, with $3.8 billion in total Bank exposure at the end of fiscal year 1997, ranked only behind Mexico, China, and Brazil.[5]

The Asian crisis began in July 1997, when the Thai government allowed its currency to float free of the dollar to which it had been pegged. This implicit devaluation also forced other countries to abandon their dollar pegs, beginning a process of competitive devaluations. The currency crisis became a financial debacle because large numbers of

[3] Press Release, "New Leadership Team at Export-Import Bank," July 9, 1997, Library, Export-Import Bank of the United States, Washington, DC (hereafter Library, Ex-Im).

[4] Remarks of James A. Harmon, Export-Import Bank Annual Conference, April 5, 2001, Files, Office of the Chairman, Ex-Im Bank of the United States, Washington, DC (hereafter Harmon Remarks).

[5] Export-Import Bank of the United States Annual Report for 1997 (Washington, DC: Export-Import Bank of the United States, 1997), pp. 46–52; Transcript, James A. Harmon, Remarks to Professional Bankers Association (PBA), March 4, 1999, Chairman's Files, Library, Ex-Im [p. 3] (hereafter Remarks, PBA, Chairman's Files).

short-term loans, denominated in hard currency (usually dollars or yen), suddenly became more expensive to service for banks and enterprises conducting business in depreciating local currencies. Consequently, as numerous banks and businesses in Southeast Asia failed, Japanese and Western commercial bank capital fled the region. Thailand, South Korea, and Indonesia were most seriously hurt by the crisis, while its effects were also felt in Malaysia, Singapore, Hong Kong, and to some extent the Phillippines. At the behest of the governments in Thailand, South Korea, and Indonesia, the International Monetary Fund stepped in with multibillion dollar assistance packages. Later the World Bank also devised programs to mitigate the crisis' social fallout on the countries in the region.

But neither the IMF nor the World Bank provided a quick fix to the problems in Asia. In fulfilling one of its primary roles – addressing periodic market imperfections – the Bank stepped in to provide trade finance when private capital had an exaggerated perception of risk. The Ex-Im initiated a program, announced by Harmon on a trip to the region in January 1998, with the fifteen most creditworthy Korean banks to confirm their letters of credit.[6] This program changed the character of Ex-Im's lending to Korea. The latter, after graduating from its status as one of the Bank's major customers in the 1960s and 1970s, had utilized Ex-Im in the decade and a half before the crisis to finance aircraft purchases. At the time of the crisis, the Bank's exposure in Korea was $1.6 billion. Between April and July 1998, Ex-Im introduced a short-term $1 billion program to allow for the purchase of raw materials and spare parts.[7] And in July 1998, Ex-Im also offered up to $2 billion in a medium-term facility, supported by a sovereign guarantee, for the purchase of U.S. capital goods and services.[8]

At the same time, Indonesia's precarious position was a cause for alarm. During the 1990s, the Bank had supported substantial private sector projects involving power generation, telecommunications facilities, mining equipment, and refining operations. In order to continue

[6] Interview with James A. Harmon, September 22, 2000, pp. 15–16, Library, Ex-Im (hereafter Harmon Interview, September 22, 2000); Annual Report for 1998, pp. 9–10.

[7] Annual Report for 1998, pp. 9–10; Text, Testimony of James A. Harmon, House Appropriations Committee, Subcommittee on Foreign Relations, February 11, 1999, 111th Congress, 2nd Session, 1999, Chairman's Files, Library, Ex-Im, p. 5.

[8] Remarks, PBA (pp. 4–5).

support for U.S. exports to Indonesia, the Bank structured $1 billion in short-term trade finance that underwrote letters of credit, much like the program in Korea. Subsequently, Ex-Im worked out a similar $1 billion short-term credit for Thailand.[9]

Coping with the Asian crisis consumed a considerable amount of the Bank's energy in 1998. In the summer, there were fears of a "contagion" from Asia's problems that would cripple key countries in Latin America – Brazil in particular was having problems – and Russia. Harmon and other Bank officials made trips to Brazil and Mexico to demonstrate Ex-Im's commitment to these countries, as well as to the other two major borrowers in the hemisphere, Argentina and Venezuela.[10]

Ultimately, the fears of contagion were not borne out in Latin America. Russia, in contrast, confronted a major crisis in August 1998 that resulted in the government defaulting on its internal debt, which further damaged an already crippled economy. Nevertheless, by early 1999, there was reason for some hope of recovery in Asia, especially in Korea. That country's economy turned around relatively quickly. There were also positive signs in other parts of the region, such as Thailand. Indonesia, however, remained troubled economically, a situation exacerbated by political turmoil that led to the resignation of long-time President Suharto in May 1998. The change in political leadership did little to improve the economic situation in the country.

As contagion was avoided in Latin America, and the situation seemed brighter in several parts of Asia, the Bank turned to longer-term issues. In what Harmon described as the second chapter of his term, Bank officials focused on cultivating new markets in developing countries, areas where in the twenty-first century they anticipated there would be substantial growth.[11] Sub-Saharan Africa proved ripe for a test of their commitment to areas that might be the world's future emerging markets. Congress had in the fall 1997 mandated a greater Bank effort in Africa. Soon after, the Clinton administration embraced the goal of enlarging United States business with Africa.

9 Annual Report for 1998, p. 10. Neither of the credits to Indonesia and Thailand was used.

10 Annual Report for 1998, p. 10; Harmon Interview, pp. 33–5.

11 Presentation, James A. Harmon, World Power Conference, New York, May 4, 1999, p. 7, Chairman's Files, Archives, Ex-Im.

For its part, the Bank's chairman and board of directors signed onto a Clinton administration initiative begun in 1998 to increase exports to Africa. The program – the Partnership for Economic Growth and Opportunity for Africa – was part of a larger administration initiative to encourage American exports, an effort that received substantial bipartisan congressional support.[12] Because Harmon held that the U.S. government and private business had been too cautious and conservative in dealing with Sub-Saharan Africa (SSA), he welcomed Clinton's initiative.[13]

Even so, whatever the Bank's efforts in SSA would have to be built on a modest base of previous support. In fiscal year 1998, Ex-Im only authorized $56 million in loans to SSA. Nevertheless, the Bank had shown an increasing interest in the region in the mid 1990s; starting in 1995, the Bank's directors began to make trips to SSA. By 1997, the Bank was open for traditional export financing in eighteen of the forty-eight SSA countries. That number rose to thirty-two in 1999.[14] In 1998, the Bank appointed a coordinator-counselor for Africa to head a task force on increasing export financing in SSA and, as a result of the congressional mandate, established a Sub-Saharan Africa Advisory Committee to guide the Bank in these efforts.[15] By 1999, support for exports to SSA grew to $587 million, and in 2000 they were over $900 million. To demonstrate the Bank's increased interest in the region, Harmon made three trips to Africa to meet with both public and private sector officials. From the Ex-Im's perspective, SSA presented an opportunity to assist U.S. exporters in creating new markets. He was the first sitting president of the Bank to visit SSA in fifteen years, and the first ever to go to southern Africa while in office.[16]

Underlying the new-found interest in SSA and other potential markets in risky environments was Harmon's belief that the Bank could accept more risk. Following the avalanche of claims from the debt crisis in the 1980s, the Bank had tightened underwriting standards and practices. The Ex-Im's losses as a percentage of disbursements had been modest as a result, at a rate of less than 3 percent of disbursements.[17] But

[12] Annual Report for 1997, p. 8.
[13] Harmon Interview, September 22, 2000, pp. 33–40.
[14] Annual Report for 1998, p. 12; Annual Report for 1997, p. 8; Annual Report for 1999, p. 2.
[15] Annual Report for 1998, p. 12.
[16] Harmon Interview, September 22, 2000, pp. 45–50; Annual Report for 2000, p. 10.
[17] Annual Report for 2000, p. 10; Harmon Interview, September 22, 2000, pp. 37–8, 45–50.

the Asian financial crisis had induced additional caution, an outlook strengthened following Russia's debt crisis in August 1998. Harmon and other senior Bank officials saw future possibilities in Russia and the NIS, as well as in central and southeastern Europe. The countries of these regions all appeared to be promising, if difficult and somewhat risky, places for the Bank to offer its financing.[18] Since mid 1993, Ex-Im had begun to assist American exporters' interested in Russia. By 1997, the Bank had an exposure there of about $2 billion, only about half of which enjoyed a sovereign guarantee. The rest, about $900 million, was for equipment to upgrade diamond mining operations and oil and gas production. This was part of a new pattern. Overall, the Bank's limited recourse, nonsovereign-based lending had increased from 22 percent of the total dollar value of authorizations in 1990 to 55 percent in 1999.[19]

The initial euphoria following the collapse of communism in the USSR had long since dissipated by the fall of 1998, when Harmon made his first trip to Russia as chairman. The Russian road to market reform had been very difficult, and the immediate possibilities for Bank business in the region in 1997 were clouded.[20] Ex-Im's role, in Harmon's opinion, was to reassure private capital markets that future opportunities existed in Russia, although personally he remained uncertain about the immediate future in 1997 and 1998.[21]

The Bank did not add new exposure in Russia until December 1999. At that time, it concluded a deal for $500 million of guarantees with the Tyumen Oil Company. In fiscal year 2000, there were also other substantial guarantees to Aeroflot Russian International Airlines for aircraft engines and related equipment, as well as for the purchase of medical equipment.[22]

Guarantees to the Tyumen Oil Company provoked a sharp political and diplomatic battle. These developments illustrated the political

18 Memorandum, James Cruse, "(Part of) An Introduction to Eximbank – Transition Issues," February 21, 1997, Policy Office Files, Archives, Export-Import Bank of the United States, Washington, DC; Harmon Interview, September 22, 2000, pp. 42–51; Interview with Stephen Glazer, August 7, 2000, pp. 48–9, Library, Ex-Im.

19 Annual Report for 1999, pp. 5, 21–3, 25–6.

20 "Report on Visit to Russia, November 1–9, 1997, to President Clinton," Chairman's Files, Library, Ex-Im.

21 Harmon Interview, September 22, 2000, pp. 56–7.

22 Harmon Interview, September 22, 2000, pp. 23–4; Annual Report for 2000, pp. 11, 29.

and foreign policy dimension of the difficulties the Bank could face in supporting exporters in emerging markets. Representatives of the European Bank for Reconstruction and Development (EBRD) and BP Amoco charged Tyumen's management with corruption. These critics convinced the Department of State to postpone the transaction for 90 days by invoking the 1978 Chafee Amendment (Public Law 95-630). After an investigation, the secretary of state determined that the arrangement was not detrimental to American foreign policy interests, and the final documents were signed in September 2000.[23]

Chapter three of Harmon's tenure focused on strengthening the Bank as an institution. This effort proceeded on several fronts. Picking up on initiatives begun in earlier administrations, the Bank increased its efforts to assist small business exporters. The efforts undertaken at the end of the 1990s included not only familiarizing smaller companies with the Bank's services but also focusing on increasing their speed and efficiency.[24] The numbers of small businesses receiving assistance from the Bank grew in the 1990s. Indeed by 2000, in terms of numbers (not volume), more than 80 percent of the Bank's customers were small businesses.[25]

In the late 1990s, Bank officials promoted several efforts to streamline procedures. Ex-Im delegated greater authority to insurance or trade finance division vice presidents to approve qualifying medium-term transactions. The goal was to make the Bank "user-friendly" and speedier in approving financing. In addition, the Bank simplified the documentation for its Working Capital Guarantee Program, which proved an important source of export financing for small- and medium-sized businesses. Ex-Im also expanded the numbers of lenders in its Delegated Authority Lenders Program to over 100 members.[26]

Some of the growth in the Bank's small business portfolio came from companies making goods or providing services that benefitted the environment. Generally, Bank officials viewed environmental products and services as a growth area for U.S. exporters. In promoting such exports,

[23] Harmon Interview, September 22, 2000, pp. 25–33; Neela Baneerjee, "Tuymen Oil of Russia Seeks Links to Old Foes After Winning Fight," New York *Times*, December 2, 1999.

[24] Harmon Interview, September 22, 2000, p. 15.

[25] Harmon Remarks, p. 4.

[26] Harmon Interview, September 22, 2000, pp. 13–14, 16.

the Bank was also responding to congressional mandates to increase its support for this new sector of American business. Since the introduction of its Environmental Exports Program in fiscal year 1994, the number of transactions related to the sector went from thirteen to sixty-two in fiscal year 2000; by then, the portfolio of loans and guarantees was over $2 billion. As part of this effort, the Bank had to follow guidelines earlier developed at the behest of Congress. Essentially, they required Ex-Im to ensure that negative environmental impacts were limited in projects sponsoring fossil fuel power plants, petroleum refineries, and mining operations. The Bank was also to promote U.S. renewable energy exports that did not increase greenhouse gases. Accordingly, Ex-Im identified markets for wind, solar, and geothermal energy. There was also a growing interest in facilitating the exports of the information technology industries, companies that produced the computers, software, and communications equipment that fired the information technology and Internet revolutions of the 1990s.[27]

In talking about the third chapter of his term, Harmon observed that streamlining the Bank would require continuing attention. Congressionally imposed restraints on the Bank's activities simply limited its ability to speed operations to the same degree as private sector institutions. These constraints involved assurances by way of documentation that export sales met certain standards in regard to the environment, domestic content, and U.S. merchant vessels. Worthy as these requirements might be, they nevertheless impeded – and probably always would – bringing the Bank to a par with private sector institutions in making decisions about loans and guarantees. Even so, the Bank continued to address how to streamline its operations and meet its congressional mandate to be fully competitive with other ECAs. In 2000, for example, it made its first changes in domestic content procedures in more than fifteen years, introducing a greater degree of flexibility.[28]

Improving operations was not the only issue that Harmon saw needing more work at the end of his term. In speaking to the May 2000 IIE conference, he referred to large issues that had developed during the 1990s and that would need full attention in the years ahead. Harmon was not alone in remarking about the growing aversion to risk among

[27] Ibid., p. 17.
[28] Harmon Remarks, p. 2.

private sector providers of finance to exporters.[29] Nor was he the only senior official to express concern about threats to the OECD Arrangements that had ultimately set the framework for the competition among ECAs in official export financing.[30]

TAKING STOCK AND LOOKING FORWARD

In looking toward a new century, it was clear from the Bank's experiences in the 1990s that there were fundamental questions about the direction Ex-Im might have to take in the future. The resolution of these turn-of-the-century issues would determine how Ex-Im would continue to meet two of its essential mandates: compensating for market imperfections and keeping American exporters' financing packages competitive with those offered by other ECAs to their exporters. As a government institution, the Bank could accept a higher level of risk to achieve a public policy purpose as opposed to a private sector financial organization responsible to making a profit for its stockholders.

First, the experience of the 1990s illustrated the continuing relevance of the Bank's mandate to compensate for market imperfections, especially in emerging markets, among the most promising areas for new U.S. export business.[31] In the face of the Mexican crisis in 1994–5, and the Asian and Russian financial crises of 1997–8, private commercial capital fled. In the Mexican emergency, the Bank continued to provide credit to private sector firms when it could find reasonable reassurance of payment, while paying claims of other private sector enterprises having financial difficulties.[32] Ex-Im played a similar role as a lender of last resort by providing export credit in the Asian crisis in 1997–8.

29 John P. Lipsky, "Can Trade Finance Attract Commercial Banks," in *The Ex-Im Bank in the 21st Century*, pp. 205–8.

30 Rita M. Rodriguez, "Ex-Im Bank: Overview, Challenges, and Policy Options," in *The Ex-Im Bank in the 21st Century*, pp. 7–9.

31 In the 1990s, the major emerging markets were, on the basis of net capital flows from commercial banks and nonbank creditors, China, India, Indonesia, Malaysia, Philippines, South Korea, Thailand, Argentina, Brazil, Chile, Colombia, Equador, Mexico, Peru, Uruguay, Venezuela, Bulgaria, Czech Republic, Hungary, Poland, Romania, Russia, Slovakia, Turkey, Algeria, Egypt, Morocco, South Africa, and Tunisia. See William R. Cline, "Ex-Im, Exports, and Private Capital: Will Financial Markets Squeeze the Bank?" in *The Ex-Im Bank in the 21st Century*, pp. 107–10.

32 Ibid., pp. 101–3.

But there was a new dimension to market imperfections by the end of the 1990s. It appeared to be as much a systemic as simply a cyclical problem in emerging markets. Traditional commercial bank lending shrank during the decade, even though the total of private capital flows to emerging markets increased. By 1999, 97 percent of the capital going to those regions originated from the private sector. These flows remained relatively high even in the crisis years of 1997 and 1998 when public aid increased; net private capital represented 81 percent of net flows in those troubled years. But the composition of the private capital directed toward emerging markets changed. During the decade, the percentage of direct investment in these net private flows increased to 90 percent in 1999, from 32 percent in 1991. The tendency for reduced commercial lending to be replaced in part by strategic investment in emerging markets began following the Latin American debt crisis of the 1980s. It intensified following the difficulties in the 1990s in Mexico, Asia, Russia, and Brazil.[33]

Despite these trends of growing risk aversion following crises, there were other factors at work that kept private sector lending low, even after conditions improved. In the 1980s and 1990s, large international banks came under shareholder pressure to produce better returns. As a result, by the late 1990s, to better manage risk these institutions acted more like investment than commercial banks. That is, instead of making loans, they preferred to collect fees as a cross-border intermediary for equities and bonds, as well as an arranger of syndicated bank loans in emerging markets. These trends in risk management make it likely that large international banks' new practices will outlast changes in the business cycle.[34]

[33] Ibid., pp. 103–10.

[34] Ibid., pp. 108–10; see also Lipsky, pp. 205–8. Lipsky is chief economist and director of research for Chase Manhattan Bank, New York. He observed in his piece that Chase Manhattan was the single largest provider of Bank guaranteed credits of $6 billion between 1997 and 1999, but that on balance trade finance was not attractive to commercial banks. Harmon and his senior colleagues explored ways to keep the private sector engaged with export finance in emerging markets. In 1999, the Bank developed a program for private sector risk-sharing arrangements in the Bank's export guarantee portfolio. In June 2000, the Board approved a proposal from Citibank to set up a facility by which the private sector bank would share risk under the Bank's medium- and long-term guarantee and medium-term insurance programs. In return for taking on some of the Bank's risk of loss, Citibank would receive a part of the Ex-Im's exposure fees. Both the treasury and the OMB raised questions about the appropriateness of the U.S. government transferring some of its risk to the private sector.

To enlarge financing opportunities for exporters, the Bank explored cofinancing with other ECAs. In such a joint arrangement, the ECA financing the largest part of the transaction would take the lead and accept the risk. Other ECAs joining in would provide a guarantee or reinsurance for their share. By the time the Clinton administration left office, cofinancing arrangements had been completed with the British and Canadian ECAs. Cofinancing enjoyed the support of organized exporter groups and the Bank's advisory board, made up of representatives of business and labor. Many corporations had manufacturing and warehousing facilities overseas, so cofinancing appeared to be a businesslike way to source orders from those facilities. To facilitate cofinancing among ECAs, the Bank indicated a willingness in principle to change some of its procedures to avoid the need for exporters to produce two different sets of documentation.[35]

However the Bank meets the increased demand for assistance to exporters in emerging markets, it's clear that its mandate to provide finance for exports unsupported by the private sector remains as relevant as ever. Indeed, the logic of this mandate appears as strong at the beginning of the new century as at the time the Bank was founded. Exports were an increasing part of United States GDP, moving from 7 percent in 1985 to 12 percent in 2000. These exports support about 12 million domestic jobs. To be sure, the Bank's total export supported authorizations of $15.5 billion (in 2000) represented only a modest (less than 2) percent of the United States' aggregate exports for that year. Nonetheless, this represented 10 percent of capital goods exported to the developing world. In some higher-risk markets, the Bank supported over 40 percent of capital goods exported to these areas. Thus, the Bank continued to support the goods and services of the United States' capital goods sector, where exports often represent a significant share of an industry's total sales and are concentrated in emerging markets.[36]

Equally relevant in the new century was the Bank's mandate to promote the competitiveness of U.S. exporters. In coping with new competition in the 1990s, the Bank has been presented with a series of difficult

[35] Allan I. Mendelowitz, "The New World of Government-Supported International Financing," in *The Ex-Im Bank in the 21st Century*, p. 167.

[36] Cline, pp. 100, 106; Robert E. Rubin, "Ex-Im Bank and International Economic Policy Leadership," in *The Ex-Im Bank in the 21st Century*, pp. 35–8; see Appendix B for authorizations.

challenges that raise fundamental policy issues about the direction it should take in responding to initiatives from other ECAs. In 1997, with the agreements on risk premia, the OECD's financial arrangements governing the activities of ECAs came full circle. With this arrangement, the United States could say that it had become fully competitive with the terms offered by other providers of official export credit, at least in regard to interest rates, tenor, and risk premia.[37]

But by the time the risk premia arrangement went into effect in 1999, it was clear that the United States was already facing serious new challenges from overseas. In particular, public agencies in Germany (KfW) and in Canada (EDC) sharpened the competition for American exporters in emerging markets through "market windows," an approach first introduced in the 1980s by Sweden. Under market windows, KfW and EDC could offer better terms than either the private sector was prepared to extend in emerging markets or ECAs were permitted to advance under OECD Arrangements. By the 1990s, several governments had market windows, although only in the fast-growing German and Canadian agencies did market window credits outweigh the provision of official credits through "government windows."[38]

These developments jeopardized over twenty years of effort at the OECD to standardize practices in the government provision of export credits. As such, they challenge the basic approach the Bank has taken to meet its mandate to promote the competitiveness of U.S. exporters. American critics of the KfW and EDC do not accept that these agencies were acting strictly according to market principles. Indeed, they maintained that the use of market windows continued to provide – in a perhaps subtle and indirect but nevertheless distinct way – subsidized credits to exporters. The KfW and EDC paid no taxes nor dividends to their governments on the profits they earned. Moreover, they could borrow their funds at the best available rates using the full faith and credit of their governments.[39]

Market window practices have alarmed U.S. exporters, bankers, and government officials. Yet, by the year 2000, no consensus had developed in the Bank on how to cope with the challenge. Perhaps the most common view about strategy among U.S. officials was to pursue negotiations

[37] Rodriguez, p. 10.
[38] Ibid., pp. 10–11; Mendelowitz, pp. 169–80.
[39] Mendelowitz, pp. 173–5, 179–80.

to create another OECD, or perhaps World Trade Organization, regime. The goal would be to articulate and manage a new set of "rules of the game." This was the position of Secretary of the Treasury Lawrence H. Summers, who spoke at the May 2000 IIE conference. To force other governments to cooperate with such a rule-making exercise, other U.S. officials supported using the Bank's tied aid war chest to match or if necessary to overmatch market windows offers made by other ECAs. This strategy had worked at crucial points in the history of OECD rule-making negotiations. The Germans, Canadians, and Japanese countered such suggestions with the argument that, in fact, the OECD Arrangements needed to be amended to better conform to market discipline. Indeed, the Japanese argued that market windows were a response to the rigid and punitive OECD rules.[40]

Challenges to U.S. export competitiveness did not just arise from overseas. As the international competitive environment sharpened, exporters increasingly criticized congressional requirements that hampered the Bank's operations. These included rules, regulations, and international agreements having to do with terrorism, nuclear proliferation, and human rights violations. To protect U.S. jobs, the Bank also maintained fairly strict domestic content rules, which limited its financing to goods substantially of U.S. origin. Even though the Bank revised these rules in 2001, they remained more stringent than those of other major ECAs. Similarly, there were shipping regulations that many exporters complained about. On long-term transactions (over $10 million and with a term beyond five years), preference had to be given to U.S. flag vessels in shipping. Exceptions could be granted, but they required a waiver from the U.S. Maritime Administration, another step in what exporters complained was an already drawn-out process in dealing with the Bank.[41]

Prompting particularly sharp criticism was the U.S. government's propensity to act unilaterally in imposing economic sanctions. These often included specific prohibitions against Ex-Im offering credits to sanctioned countries. While some countries sanctioned by the United

[40] Rodriguez, pp. 15–16; the views of the German, Canadian, and Japanese ECAs can be found in essays in *The Ex-Im Bank in the 21st Century*: Hans W. Reich, "A German Perspective, pp. 221–5; A. Ian Gillespie, "A Canadian Perspective," pp. 227–34; Fumio Hoshi, "A Japanese Perspective,"pp. 235–44.

[41] Rodriguez, pp. 20–3.

States, such as Syria, were not creditworthy anyway, others, such as India and Colombia, were. It was, of course, not so much that exporters and their allies in Congress approved of the behavior that led to the sanctions. Rather it was that other governments did not believe that sanctions were an effective tool of diplomacy in any case and so refused as a rule to impose them. Certainly, Bank officials believed that sanctions did not achieve their objectives when other countries refused to join the United States in imposing them. In the view of Bank officials, sanctions hindered the work of the Bank and disadvantaged American exporters.[42]

On the environmental front, there were similar complaints about the United States standing alone. Congress in the 1992 reauthorization mandated that the Bank take into account the negative and positive environmental impacts of the transactions it was prepared to support. Ex-Im alone among the major ECAs was required to meet such strict standards by its government. Again, Bank officials were not, in principle, opposed to the environmental goals at issue. They were, however, concerned that other ECAs did not have to adhere to similar principles, putting U.S. exporters at a disadvantage. To mitigate the resulting negative consequences for U.S. exporters, the United States has pressed at meetings of the Group of 7 (G7) to support common environmental guidelines, something that has received generalized support in the communiques issued at the end of recent annual summits. Additionally, the Bank has advocated OECD negotiations to develop uniform environmental standards. Ex-Im proposed that ECAs accept common environmental guidelines on the impact of potential projects based on World Bank procedures. Although these efforts met with resistance among other ECAs, nongovernmental organizations (NGOs) committed to protecting the environment pressed the governments of other ECAs to accept common, substantive standards on the impact of projects on the environment.[43]

Clearly, in the future, the Bank would continue to support changes in policies that from its point of view negatively affected the competitiveness of U.S. exporters. Bank officials would have to work through Congress, the Department of the Treasury, the Office of Management

[42] Ibid., pp. 23–6.
[43] Ibid., pp. 26–7.

and Budget, and the OECD, as in the past. Indeed, international discussions, hearings, and negotiations were underway at the turn of the century on many of these issues that affected competitiveness.

Nevertheless, other governments have adopted a more state-oriented approach to export competitiveness, the emphasis on the "market" in market windows notwithstanding. The entire market windows effort bespeaks a statist approach to export credits out of step with the efforts of the Ex-Im to engage and cooperate with the private sector in its work. In contrast, the Ex-Im has, because of its mandate, avoided competing with its private sector. In fact, one strain of its history has been to encourage the private sector to provide more export financing through joint arrangements and the provision of guarantees.

What the United States faces in the twenty-first century, then, is the prospect of a very different competitive world in export finance. Ex-Im might become an entity isolated among other ECAs in its philosophy and approach to export finance. To meet that circumstance, the challenge will be for the United States to devise a strategy compatible with its own history and principles.

THE BANK, THE STATE, AND THE MARKET IN PERSPECTIVE

The May 2000 IIE conference brought into sharp focus the overarching themes of the Bank's history. Over the decades, the Bank – like many other long-lived public or private institutions – had to adjust itself periodically to changing environments, domestic and foreign, public and private. Essentially, the Bank had to respond to its changing environment within the confines of congressionally determined mandates that imposed restraints – and also at times offered opportunities – on how it behaved. In providing financial services, as set forth in one of its earliest mandates, the Bank had to have a reasonable assurance of repayment. That essential stricture demanded that the Bank discipline itself according to market principles, which resulted in this public institution structuring its procedures, and ultimately its culture, along the lines of the private financial sector.

Another of its essential mandates was to compensate for market imperfections without competing with private sector commercial banks. This dictate reinforced Ex-Im's orientation toward the private sector.

Over the years, the Bank came to use private commercial banks as agents for its services. Invariably, Bank officials had to ask themselves whether a proposed activity might reduce the involvement of private commercial banks in export finance. Consequently, the Bank remained attuned to their interests. Thus, when the private sector failed the needs of export finance, Ex-Im stepped in to meet the market failure. On occasion, Ex-Im also sought ways to reengage commercial banks in export finance.

Inherently, the Bank's private financial sector orientation created tensions with the Congress and the White House. Congressional and administration officials at various times in the Bank's history insisted that the Bank focus on meeting public policy goals. For many years in the Bank's first decades, U.S. government officials expected Ex-Im to serve the interests of American foreign policy. Achieving those goals was not always consistent with what Bank leaders saw as their market-oriented requirements to offer assistance to creditworthy borrowers likely to repay their loans.

During the course of the Bank's history, there were also occasions when it was in conflict with the Department of the Treasury and White House budget officials. These tensions arose when Ex-Im policies diverged from the varying interests of those agencies. Thus, Bank leaders had the task of managing relations with key government bureaucracies, as well as Congress.

Even though in recent decades the Bank has been less overtly utilized as a tool of foreign policy, Congress has restricted its activities on the basis of civil society concerns for the environment, terrorism, narcotics trafficking, and human rights violations. These strictures have created a new set of conflicting institutional tensions because, since 1971, Congress mandated that Ex-Im help ensure the competitiveness of American exporters. Since most other governments did not require their ECAs to restrict lending on the basis of borrowers' adherence to standards extraneous to market-based decisions, U.S. exporters needing Ex-Im services were put at a disadvantage.

Nevertheless, ensuring U.S. competitiveness became a major focus of the Bank's history in the last quarter of the twentieth century. To be sure, government-supported export finance had been a characteristic of the international economy beginning in the 1920s. In fact, Congress originally established the Bank in part to satisfy U.S. exporters who believed that they were handicapped by European competitors assisted by government export credit agencies. But such public-supported finance became a more prominent aspect of international markets following the oil crises of the 1970s. Increasing costs of oil imports in particular, and commodity imports in general, focused many governments on the need to increase exports. The increasing subsidies offered by foreign ECAs to their countries' exporters threatened to injure U.S. export interests.

The policies of foreign ECAs also posed a challenge to the United States' commitment to promoting free trade. As a result of the 1971 mandate that the Bank attend to the competitive position of U.S. exporters, Bank representatives joined Treasury Department officials at the OECD in negotiating the rules of the game governing public-supported export finance. The arrangements arduously worked out over the next 25 years significantly reduced the subsidies that distorted export markets and ultimately created a more level playing field in government-supported export finance.

While these long-term efforts were underway at the OECD, the international economy underwent enormous changes that affected almost every financial institution engaged in overseas business. The 1980s debt crisis in Latin America led to a serious rethinking of state-directed, import-substitution development policy there. Following the death of Mao Tse-tung in 1976, China's new leadership began in 1979 a market revolution, still on-going, to transform its command economy. In 1989, the Soviet Union began to lose control of its satellite countries in Eastern Europe and then itself collapsed in 1991. The move to democratic governments in many of these countries was accompanied by a commitment to creating market economies. Parallel to these political and economic developments were vast technological changes in computer and communications technology. As a result, by the 1990s, markets worldwide were almost in instant contact because of an information technology revolution that harnessed the data-manipulating capabilities of computers to vast improvements in communications technology.

One of the major consequences of these paradigm-shifting economic developments was a rush to privatization, that is, a shift away from government-owned enterprises. Privatization opened up vast possibilities for capital goods industries worldwide, as the enterprises comprising the infrastructure of many countries in the developing world were turned over to private management. As a result, the Bank had to reorient how it structured its provision of loans and guarantees. Ex-Im increasingly had to deal with private borrowers rather than governments that provided sovereign guarantees of repayment. The resulting growth of limited-recourse project borrowing increased demands on the Bank to hone its credit analysis skills. The latter was an essential capability as Ex-Im did more and more business in the many emerging markets that appeared after the revolutionary international changes of the 1980s and 1990s.

The Bank's essential market orientation in its operations made these adjustments possible, if not without friction, at least without major contention. What these recent market-oriented demands pointed up, however, was a need for new kinds of professional financial expertise. This proved a difficult issue for the Bank, in large part because the private sector financial markets could easily attract the required talent with salaries and benefits well beyond what a government agency could hope to offer.

In adjusting to the new international environment of the last two decades, the Bank took on enhanced international responsibilities, as well as acceding to new demands from Congress and the White House. On the international scene, during the financial crises in Latin America in the 1980s, Mexico in 1994–5, and Asia in 1997–8, the Bank moved aggressively when private capital dried up. Additionally, the U.S. government generally had encouraged and supported the market revolutions that began in the 1980s. These developments were very much in step with the long-held free market views of policy makers in Washington. Because the government wanted to support the market revolutions in Latin America, Russia, the Newly Independent States, Eastern Europe, and Asia, the Bank found itself at times pressed to move perhaps faster than it would have liked in some markets. But, in contrast, there were also times when foreign policy considerations restrained the Bank. This happened when Congress and the Clinton administration showed its displeasure with some of Russia's political and economic policies by restricting access to finance. On the policy front in another part of the world, both Congress and the White House in the 1990s wanted to engage the United States more with Africa, which led to the Bank's increased interest and activity there.

Thus, overall, the Bank's history has demonstrated a flexibility in adjusting to the changing environments in which it found itself. As a government institution, with a market-oriented culture, this has not produced a record without tension and contention. Its experience, though, is instructive in an era that, beginning in the 1980s with the Reagan administration, has come to emphasize the need for government to adopt market-oriented solutions to public policy problems. The Bank's history demonstrates the difficulties and limits, as well as the successes, of such an effort.

The Bank's history also illustrates its role in the larger effort of the United States to create a freer international trade. Recent developments suggest, though, that the Bank may be an exception to trends being set by the ECAs of other major countries. Ex-Im played an important part in the development of an articulated set of rules and regulations through the OECD to govern public-supported export finance. At the turn of a new century, Canada, Germany, and Japan are challenging that regime through the reintroduction of what appears to be a new form of subsidized trade finance in the guise of market windows. Apparently these and other countries have adopted a more statist, rather than market-oriented, approach to export finance. The issue for the Bank at the beginning of the twenty-first century is how to deal with that challenge in the face of resistance to the creation of a new regulatory regime through the OECD or perhaps the WTO.

In the last decade or so, the Ex-Im has been swept along with the rest of the world by the information technology revolution, the globalization of markets, the collapse of communism, and market revolutions in formerly command economies. It was thus in the wake of these consequential developments that the Bank entered the new century to face yet again the need to confront rapid change and adjust to new circumstances.

Ex-Im has responded to these changes by moving on several fronts. One is to leverage the advantage the United States has in its highly developed capital markets by creating private-public partnerships in which private investors share in Ex-Im's portfolio risk. Another tactic is to develop markets where private capital remains risk averse. The Bank's historic success in minimizing its losses has provided it with the expertise to structure deals in some places commercial banks find too risky. In addition, the Bank continues to encourage smaller American business to get involved in export markets. Finally, the financial crises in Mexico in 1994–5 and in Asia in 1997–8, demonstrated that the Bank has a continued role to play as a lender of last resort in supporting exports in an economic emergency. Private commercial capital fled affected countries during these crises and would probably do the same in similar circumstances in the future.

Thus, an institution established in the state-building era of the New Deal continued to adjust itself to increasingly market-driven circumstances in the domestic and international economies of the 1990s. Because it has usually adhered to market principles, Ex-Im has not found the adjustment difficult. But in the beginning of a new century, the challenges are as large as the Bank has ever faced in terms of intensifying ECA competition, leveraging the strengths of American capital markets in private-public partnerships, maximizing the benefits of the IT revolution, and attracting to public service younger professionals beckoned by well-paying private sector opportunities. The Bank is also faced with a change in the international competitive environment that challenges the very principles upon which it has operated in coping with its competitiveness mandate.

APPENDIX A

BOARD OF DIRECTORS

Export-Import Bank of the United States Board of Directors, Inception through July 31, 2001[a]

Name	Position	Date Sworn in	Depature Date
R. Walton Moore	Chairman	Feb. 13, 1934	Feb. 8, 1941
Jesse H. Jones	Chairman	July 30, 1941	Aug. 18, 1943
Leo T. Crowley	Chairman	Aug. 18, 1943	Oct. 8, 1945
William McC. Martin, Jr.	Chairman	Feb. 13, 1946	Feb. 7, 1949
Herbert E. Gaston	Chairman	Feb. 10, 1949	Jan. 19, 1953
Glen E. Edgerton	Chairman	April 7, 1953	Aug. 4, 1953
Glen E. Edgerton	Managing director	Aug. 5, 1953	Oct. 8, 1954
Glen E. Edgerton	Chairman	Oct. 11, 1954	Sept. 30, 1955
Samuel C. Waugh	Chairman	Oct. 4, 1955	Jan. 20, 1961
Harold F. Linder	Chairman	March 3, 1961	July 31, 1968
Henry Kearns	Chairman	March 20, 1969	Oct. 31, 1973
William J. Casey	Chairman	March 14, 1974	Jan. 2, 1976
Stephen M. DuBrul, Jr.	Chairman	Jan. 5, 1976	May 2, 1977
John L. Moore, Jr.	Chairman	May 3, 1977	March 31, 1981
William H. Draper III	Chairman	July 14, 1981	Feb. 28, 1986
John A. Bohn, Jr.	Chairman	April 11, 1986	Feb. 28, 1989
John D. Macomber	Chairman	July 25, 1989	Nov. 30, 1992
Rita M. Rodriguez	Acting chairman	Jan. 9, 1993	May 9, 1993
Kenneth D. Brody	Chairman	May 10, 1993	Dec. 31, 1995
Martin A. Kamarck	Chairman	April 12, 1996	March 31, 1997
Rita M. Rodriguez	Acting chairman	April 1, 1997	June 16, 1997
James A. Harmon	Chairman	June 17, 1997	May 29, 2001
John Robson	Chairman	May 30, 2001	March 20, 2002
George N. Peek	President	Feb. 13, 1934	Nov. 30, 1935
Warren Lee Pierson	President	Feb. 21, 1936	April 12, 1945
Lynn U. Stambaugh	Vice chairman	Oct. 11, 1954	July 31, 1960
Tom Killefer	Vice chairman	Aug. 1, 1960	Sept. 23, 1962
Walter C. Sauer	Vice chairman	Sept. 28, 1962	Aug. 15, 1976
Delio E. Gianturco	Vice chairman	Aug. 16, 1976	Nov. 4, 1977
H. K. Allen	Vice chairman	March 31, 1978	April 3, 1981
Charles E. Lord	Vice chairman	May 2, 1982	Sept. 30, 1983
John A. Bohn	Vice chairman	March 18, 1984	April 10, 1986
William F. Ryan	Vice chairman	Aug. 12, 1986	July 20, 1989
Eugene K. Lawson	Vice chairman	Oct. 4, 1989	Jan. 8, 1993
Martin A. Kamarck	Vice chairman	Nov. 23, 1993	April 11, 1996
Jackie M. Clegg	Vice chairman	June 17, 1997	July 20, 2001

Appendix A (cont.)

Name	Position	Date Sworn in	Depature Date
William McC. Martin, Jr.	Director	Dec. 3, 1945	Feb. 12, 1946
Clarence E. Gauss	Director	Jan. 2, 1946	June 30, 1952
Wilson L. Townsend	Director	July 24, 1952	April 6, 1953
Hawthorne Arey	Director	April 11, 1949	Aug. 4, 1953
Hawthorne Arey	Director	Oct. 11, 1954	Jan. 29, 1961
George A. Blowers	Director	Dec. 31, 1954	March 13, 1961
Vance Brand	Director	Nov. 5, 1954	Sept. 1, 1959
James S. Bush	Director	Sept. 2, 1959	Aug. 31, 1963
George Docking	Director	Jan. 29, 1961	Jan. 20, 1964
Charles M. Meriwether	Director	March 14, 1961	Sept. 30, 1965
Elizabeth S. May	Director	June 17, 1964	April 18, 1969
Hobart Taylor	Director	Sept. 21, 1965	Jan. 31, 1968
Tom Lilley	Director	Oct. 25, 1965	Dec. 31, 1972
John C. Clark	Director	June 3, 1969	Aug. 31, 1976
R. Alex McCullough	Director	May 21, 1969	Dec. 20, 1977
Mitchell P. Kobelinski	Director	July 17, 1973	Feb. 12, 1976
Margaret W. Kahliff	Director	Oct. 8, 1976	Aug. 10, 1982
Donald E. Stingel	Director	Nov. 14, 1977	Aug. 4, 1981
Thibaut de Saint Phalle	Director	Dec. 21, 1977	June 15, 1981
Richard W. Heldridge	Director	Aug. 11, 1982	June 3, 1988
Rita M. Rodriguez	Director	Oct. 12, 1982	March 15, 1999
James E. Yonge	Director	Oct. 12, 1982	July 1, 1984
Richard H. Hughes	Director	June 1, 1985	Sept. 30, 1985
Simon C. Fireman	Director	Nov. 10, 1986	Aug. 11, 1989
Richard Houseworth	Director	Sept. 8, 1988	Jan. 20, 1991
Constance B. Harriman	Director	July 25, 1991	March 25, 1994
Cecil B. Thompson	Director	March 27, 1991	Sept. 13, 1994
Maria Luisa Haley	Director	April 7, 1994	July 20, 1999
Julie Belaga	Director	May 3, 1994	Jan. 20, 1999
Dan Renberg	Director	Nov. 19, 1999	
Dorian Venessa Weaver	Director	Nov. 19, 1999	

[a] Date derived from information collected by Dr. Rita Rodriquez. All other dates are from official personnel records.

APPENDIX B

SUMMARY OF AUTHORIZATIONS

Export-Import Bank of the United States Summary of Authorizations, 1934–1946 (millions of dollars)

	FY 1934	FY 1935	FY 1936	FY 1937	FY 1938	FY 1939	FY 1940	FY 1941	FY 1942	FY 1943	FY 1944	FY 1945	FY 1946
Loan Authorization Summary													
Regular Direct Loans	3.8	42.3	52.2	15.1	28.6	91.0	217.6	308.6	357.9	22.2	36.8	70.4	294.1
Development Project Credits	0.0	0.0	0.0	0.0	0.0	0.0	0.0	0.0	0.0	0.0	0.0	0.0	0.0
MT/Small Business Credits	0.0	0.0	0.0	0.0	0.0	0.0	0.0	0.0	0.0	0.0	0.0	0.0	0.0
Lend-Lease Credits	0.0	0.0	0.0	0.0	0.0	0.0	0.0	0.0	0.0	0.0	0.0	0.0	655.0
Emergency Reconstruction Credits	0.0	0.0	0.0	0.0	0.0	0.0	0.0	0.0	0.0	0.0	0.0	0.0	1115.0
Intermediary Loans	0.0	0.0	0.0	0.0	0.0	0.0	0.0	0.0	0.0	0.0	0.0	0.0	0.0
CFF/Relending Loans	0.0	0.0	0.0	0.0	0.0	0.0	0.0	0.0	0.0	0.0	0.0	0.0	0.0
Commodity Credits	0.0	3.6	4.2	7.8	2.7	6.6	2.4	0.0	0.0	0.0	0.0	0.0	133.0
Balance of Payments Loans	0.0	0.0	0.0	0.0	0.0	19.2	0.0	0.0	0.0	0.0	0.0	0.0	0.0
Exporter Credits	0.0	0.0	0.0	0.0	0.0	0.0	0.0	0.0	0.0	0.0	0.0	0.0	0.0
Military Credits	0.0	0.0	0.0	0.0	0.0	0.0	0.0	0.0	0.0	0.0	0.0	0.0	0.0
Special Foreign Trade Credits	0.0	0.0	0.0	0.0	0.0	0.0	0.0	0.0	0.0	0.0	0.0	0.0	0.0
War Chest	0.0	0.0	0.0	0.0	0.0	0.0	0.0	0.0	0.0	0.0	0.0	0.0	0.0
Discount Loans	0.0	0.0	0.0	0.0	0.0	0.0	0.0	0.0	0.0	0.0	0.0	0.0	0.0
Interest Equalization Program	0.0	0.0	0.0	0.0	0.0	0.0	0.0	0.0	0.0	0.0	0.0	0.0	0.0
Total Loan Program	3.8	45.9	56.4	22.9	31.3	116.8	220.0	308.6	357.9	22.2	36.8	70.4	2,197.1
Pre Credit Reform Grants													
Guarantee and Insurance Authorization Summary													
ST Insurance	0.0	0.0	0.0	0.0	0.0	0.0	0.0	0.0	0.0	0.0	0.0	0.0	0.0
ST War Risk and Expropriation Insurance	0.0	0.0	0.0	0.0	0.0	0.0	0.0	0.0	0.0	0.0	0.0	0.0	0.0

Export-Import Bank of the United States Summary of Authorizations, 1934–1946 (millions of dollars)

	FY 1934	FY 1935	FY 1936	FY 1937	FY 1938	FY 1939	FY 1940	FY 1941	FY 1942	FY 1943	FY 1944	FY 1945	FY 1946
MT Insurance	0.0	0.0	0.0	0.0	0.0	0.0	0.0	0.0	0.0	0.0	0.0	0.0	0.0
LT Guarantees	0.0	0.0	0.0	0.0	0.0	0.0	0.0	0.0	0.0	0.0	0.0	0.0	0.0
MT Guarantees	0.0	0.0	0.0	0.0	0.0	0.0	0.0	0.0	0.0	0.0	0.0	0.0	0.0
CFF Guarantees	0.0	0.0	0.0	0.0	0.0	0.0	0.0	0.0	0.0	0.0	0.0	0.0	0.0
Exporter Guarantees	0.0	0.0	0.0	0.0	0.0	0.0	0.0	0.0	0.0	0.0	0.0	0.0	0.0
ST Guarantees	0.0	0.0	0.0	0.0	0.0	0.0	0.0	0.0	0.0	0.0	0.0	0.0	0.0
Working Capital	0.0	0.0	0.0	0.0	0.0	0.0	0.0	0.0	0.0	0.0	0.0	0.0	0.0
Total Guarantees and Insurance	0.0	0.0	0.0	0.0	0.0	0.0	0.0	0.0	0.0	0.0	0.0	0.0	0.0
Total Authorizations													
Loans	3.8	45.9	56.4	22.9	31.3	116.8	220.0	308.6	357.9	22.2	36.8	70.4	2,197.1
Guarantees	0.0	0.0	0.0	0.0	0.0	0.0	0.0	0.0	0.0	0.0	0.0	0.0	0.0
Insurance	0.0	0.0	0.0	0.0	0.0	0.0	0.0	0.0	0.0	0.0	0.0	0.0	0.0
TOTAL	3.8	45.9	56.4	22.9	31.3	116.8	220.0	308.6	357.9	22.2	36.8	70.4	2,197.1
Aircraft, Nuclear Power, All Other Aircraft – Commercial Jet	0.0	0.0	0.0	0.0	0.0	0.0	0.0	0.0	0.0	0.0	0.0	0.0	0.0
Nuclear Power	0.0	0.0	0.0	0.0	0.0	0.0	0.0	0.0	0.0	0.0	0.0	0.0	0.0
Other LT Loans and Guarantees	3.8	45.9	56.4	22.9	31.3	116.8	220.0	308.6	357.9	22.2	36.8	70.4	2,197.1
MT Loans, Guarantees, and Insurance	0.0	0.0	0.0	0.0	0.0	0.0	0.0	0.0	0.0	0.0	0.0	0.0	0.0
ST Guarantees	0.0	0.0	0.0	0.0	0.0	0.0	0.0	0.0	0.0	0.0	0.0	0.0	0.0
ST Insurance	0.0	0.0	0.0	0.0	0.0	0.0	0.0	0.0	0.0	0.0	0.0	0.0	0.0
Working Capital Guarantees	0.0	0.0	0.0	0.0	0.0	0.0	0.0	0.0	0.0	0.0	0.0	0.0	0.0
GRAND TOTAL	3.8	45.9	56.4	22.9	31.3	116.8	220.0	308.6	357.9	22.2	36.8	70.4	2,197.1

Export-Import Bank of the United States Summary of Authorizations, 1947–1959 (millions of dollars)

	FY 1947	FY 1948	FY 1949	FY 1950	FY 1951	FY 1952	FY 1953	FY 1954	FY 1955	FY 1956	FY 1957	FY 1958	FY 1959
Loan Authorization Summary													
Regular Direct Loans	269.2	436.7	167.8	268.6	395.3	167.9	230.3	173.0	497.2	375.9	498.0	672.7	512.4
Development Project Credits	0.0	0.0	0.0	0.0	0.0	0.0	0.0	0.0	0.0	0.0	0.0	0.0	0.0
MT/Small Business Credits	0.0	0.0	0.0	0.0	0.0	0.0	0.0	0.0	0.0	0.0	0.0	0.0	0.0
Lend-Lease Credits	0.0	0.0	0.0	0.0	0.0	0.0	0.0	0.0	0.0	0.0	0.0	0.0	0.0
Emergency Reconstruction Credits	3.0	0.0	0.0	100.0	0.0	0.0	0.0	0.0	0.0	0.0	0.0	0.0	0.0
Intermediary Loans	0.0	0.0	0.0	0.0	0.0	0.0	0.0	0.0	0.0	0.0	0.0	0.0	0.0
CFF/Relending Loans	0.0	0.0	0.0	0.0	0.0	0.0	0.0	0.0	0.0	0.0	0.0	0.0	0.0
Commodity Credits	7.0	29.0	6.1	36.8	0.0	183.0	40.0	75.0	0.0	0.0	68.0	0.0	66.0
Balance of Payments Loans	0.0	0.0	0.0	0.0	0.0	0.0	300.0	0.0	0.0	0.0	0.0	0.0	0.0
Exporter Credits	0.0	0.0	0.0	0.0	0.0	0.0	0.0	0.0	131.3	32.8	0.0	17.4	17.0
Military Credits	0.0	0.0	0.0	0.0	0.0	200.0	0.0	0.0	0.0	0.0	0.0	0.0	0.0
Special Foreign Trade Credits	0.0	0.0	0.0	0.0	0.0	0.0	0.0	0.0	0.0	0.0	500.0	165.5	289.8
War Chest	0.0	0.0	0.0	0.0	0.0	0.0	0.0	0.0	0.0	0.0	0.0	0.0	0.0
Discount Loans	0.0	0.0	0.0	0.0	0.0	0.0	0.0	0.0	0.0	0.0	0.0	0.0	0.0
Interest Equalization Program	0.0	0.0	0.0	0.0	0.0	0.0	0.0	0.0	0.0	0.0	0.0	0.0	0.0
Total Loan Program	279.2	465.7	173.9	405.4	395.3	550.9	570.3	248.0	628.5	408.7	1,066.0	855.6	885.2
Pre Credit Reform Grants													
Guarantee and Insurance Authorization Summary													
ST Insurance	0.0	0.0	0.0	0.0	0.0	0.0	0.0	0.0	0.0	0.0	0.0	0.0	0.0
ST War Risk and Expropriation Insurance	0.0	0.0	0.0	0.0	0.0	0.0	0.0	0.0	4.5	0.0	0.0	0.0	0.0

Export-Import Bank of the United States Summary of Authorizations, 1947–1959 (millions of dollars)

	FY 1947	FY 1948	FY 1949	FY 1950	FY 1951	FY 1952	FY 1953	FY 1954	FY 1955	FY 1956	FY 1957	FY 1958	FY 1959
MT Insurance	0.0	0.0	0.0	0.0	0.0	0.0	0.0	0.0	0.0	0.0	0.0	0.0	0.0
LT Guarantees	0.0	0.0	0.0	0.0	0.0	0.0	0.0	0.0	0.0	0.0	0.0	0.0	0.0
MT Guarantees	0.0	0.0	0.0	0.0	0.0	0.0	0.0	0.0	0.0	0.0	0.0	0.0	0.0
CFF Guarantees	0.0	0.0	0.0	0.0	0.0	0.0	0.0	0.0	0.0	0.0	0.0	0.0	0.0
Exporter Guarantees	0.0	0.0	0.0	0.0	0.0	0.0	0.0	0.0	0.0	0.0	0.0	0.0	0.0
ST Guarantees	0.0	0.0	0.0	0.0	0.0	0.0	0.0	0.0	0.0	0.0	0.0	0.0	0.0
Working Capital	0.0	0.0	0.0	0.0	0.0	0.0	0.0	0.0	0.0	0.0	0.0	0.0	0.0
Total Guarantees and Insurance	0.0	0.0	0.0	0.0	0.0	0.0	0.0	0.0	4.5	0.0	0.0	0.0	0.0
Total Authorizations													
Loans	279.2	465.7	173.9	405.4	395.3	550.9	570.3	248.0	628.5	408.7	1,066.0	855.6	885.2
Guarantees	0.0	0.0	0.0	0.0	0.0	0.0	0.0	0.0	0.0	0.0	0.0	0.0	0.0
Insurance	0.0	0.0	0.0	0.0	0.0	0.0	0.0	0.0	4.5	0.0	0.0	0.0	0.0
TOTAL	279.2	465.7	173.9	405.4	395.3	550.9	570.3	248.0	633.0	408.7	1,066.0	855.6	885.2
Aircraft, Nuclear Power, All Other													
Aircraft – Commercial Jet	3.1	24.6	0.0	0.0	0.0	0.0	1.5	1.6	0.0	0.0	17.2	46.0	13.7
Nuclear Power	0.0	0.0	0.0	0.0	0.0	0.0	0.0	0.0	0.0	0.0	0.0	0.0	135.4
Other LT Loans and Guarantees	276.1	441.1	173.9	405.4	395.3	550.9	568.8	246.4	628.5	408.7	1,048.8	809.6	736.1
MT Loans, Guarantees, and Insurance	0.0	0.0	0.0	0.0	0.0	0.0	0.0	0.0	0.0	0.0	0.0	0.0	0.0
ST Guarantees	0.0	0.0	0.0	0.0	0.0	0.0	0.0	0.0	0.0	0.0	0.0	0.0	0.0
ST Insurance	0.0	0.0	0.0	0.0	0.0	0.0	0.0	0.0	0.0	0.0	0.0	0.0	0.0
Working Capital Guarantees	0.0	0.0	0.0	0.0	0.0	0.0	0.0	0.0	4.5	0.0	0.0	0.0	0.0
GRAND TOTAL	279.2	465.7	173.9	405.4	395.3	550.9	570.3	248.0	633.0	408.7	1,066.0	855.6	885.2

Export-Import Bank of the United States Summary of Authorizations, 1960–1972 (millions of dollars)

	FY 1960	FY 1961	FY 1962	FY 1963	FY 1964	FY 1965	FY 1966	FY 1967	FY 1968	FY 1969	FY 1970	FY 1971	FY 1972
Loan Authorization Summary													
Regular Direct Loans	69.5	0.0	555.0	0.0	570.2	435.2	738.7	1,396.7	891.4	730.6	1,187.1	1,451.7	1,951.7
Development Project Credits	296.0	707.0	0.0	525.0	0.0	0.0	0.0	0.0	0.0	0.0	0.0	0.0	0.0
MT/Small Business Credits	0.0	0.0	0.0	0.0	0.0	0.0	0.0	0.0	0.0	0.0	0.0	0.0	0.0
Lend-Lease Credits	0.0	0.0	0.0	0.0	0.0	0.0	0.0	0.0	0.0	0.0	0.0	0.0	0.0
Emergency Reconstruction Credits	0.0	0.0	0.0	0.0	0.0	0.0	0.0	0.0	0.0	0.0	0.0	0.0	0.0
Intermediary Loans	0.0	0.0	0.0	0.0	0.0	0.0	0.0	0.0	0.0	0.0	0.0	0.0	0.0
CFF/Relending Loans	0.0	0.0	0.0	0.0	0.0	0.0	0.0	0.0	0.0	29.5	76.1	22.4	69.5
Commodity Credits	70.0	63.5	3.5	79.8	178.0	76.3	76.0	76.0	75.0	75.0	75.0	112.6	84.8
Balance of Payments Loans	0.0	0.0	0.0	0.0	0.0	0.0	0.0	0.0	0.0	0.0	0.0	0.0	0.0
Exporter Credits	29.1	145.0	32.2	39.9	30.9	0.0	6.6	31.6	4.2	0.0	0.0	0.0	0.0
Military Credits	0.0	0.0	0.0	0.0	0.0	0.0	237.7	972.8	827.6	225.0	286.4	253.0	190.0
Special Foreign Trade Credits	35.0	327.2	500.0	35.0	0.0	340.0	90.0	175.0	525.0	50.0	0.0	0.0	0.0
War Chest	0.0	0.0	0.0	0.0	0.0	0.0	0.0	0.0	0.0	0.0	0.0	0.0	0.0
Discount Loans	0.0	0.0	0.0	0.0	0.0	0.0	0.0	71.5	203.1	185.1	584.2	522.4	988.6
Interest Equalization Program	0.0	0.0	0.0	0.0	0.0	0.0	0.0	0.0	0.0	0.0	0.0	0.0	0.0
Total Loan Program	499.6	1,242.7	1,090.7	679.7	779.1	851.5	1,149.0	2,723.6	2,526.3	1,295.2	2,208.8	2,362.1	3,284.6
Pre Credit Reform Grants													
Guarantee and Insurance Authorization Summary													
ST Insurance	0.0	0.0	0.0	860.2[a]	686.3	669.3	589.6	599.7	620.9	666.3	801.4	1,202.0	1,628.6
ST War Risk and Expropriation Insurance	0.0	0.0	0.0	0.0	0.0	0.0	0.0	0.0	0.0	0.3	1.1	1.1	1.9

Export-Import Bank of the United States Summary of Authorizations, 1960–1972 (millions of dollars)

	FY 1960	FY 1961	FY 1962	FY 1963	FY 1964	FY 1965	FY 1966	FY 1967	FY 1968	FY 1969	FY 1970	FY 1971	FY 1972
MT Insurance	0.0	0.0	Incl in 1963	30.0[a]	61.1	55.3	103.2	91.0	96.8	158.0	345.4	412.8	571.8
LT Guarantees	0.0	Incl in 1963	Incl in 1963	280.9[a]	96.5	128.2	94.2	23.4	59.2	112.3	335.5	1,076.7	1,190.5
MT Guarantees	0.0	Incl in 1963	Incl in 1963	153.2[a]	118.8	150.4	203.7	168.1	230.0	277.5	265.1	302.9	493.4
CFF Guarantees	0.0	0.0	0.0	0.0	0.0	0.0	0.0	0.0	0.0	0.0	0.0	incl in L/T	29.3
Exporter Guarantees	0.0	Incl in 1963	Incl in 1963	30.9[a]	1.5	4.3	2.2	1.5	0.9	7.1	11.9	40.0	30.2
ST Guarantees	17.2	144.0	0.0	0.0	0.0	0.0	0.0	0.0	0.0	0.0	0.0	0.0	0.0
Working Capital	0.0	0.0	0.0	0.0	0.0	0.0	0.0	0.0	0.0	0.0	0.0	0.0	0.0
Total Guarantees and Insurance	17.2	144.0	0.0	1,355.2	964.2	1,007.5	992.9	883.7	1,007.8	1,221.5	1,760.4	3,035.5	3,945.7
Total Authorizations													
Loans	499.6	1,242.7	1,090.7	679.7	779.1	851.5	1,149.0	2,723.6	2,526.3	1,295.2	2,208.8	2,362.1	3,284.6
Guarantees	17.2	144.0	0.0	465.0	216.8	282.9	300.1	193.0	290.1	396.9	612.5	1,419.6	1,743.4
Insurance	0.0	0.0	0.0	890.2	747.4	724.6	692.8	690.7	717.7	824.6	1,147.9	1,615.9	2,202.3
TOTAL	516.8	1,386.7	1,090.7	2,034.9	1,743.3	1,859.0	2,141.9	3,607.3	3,534.1	2,516.7	3,969.2	5,397.6	7,230.3
Aircraft, Nuclear Power, All Other													
Aircraft – Commercial Jet	87.2	107.2	32.6	35.5	62.6	83.0	100.3	748.0	344.3	328.3	673.3	846.7	689.5
Nuclear Power	34.0	0.0	0.0	0.0	2.0	24.5	40.0	145.3	9.5	115.3	208.4	530.3	1,024.3
Other LT Loans and Guarantees	378.4	1,135.5	1,058.1	925.1	811.0	872.2	1,102.9	1,782.2	2,028.6	749.3	1,002.3	1,517.0	1,703.2
MT Loans, Guarantees, and Insurance	0.0	0.0	0.0	214.1	181.4	210.0	309.1	332.1	530.8	657.2	1,282.7	1,300.5	2,182.8
ST Guarantees	17.2	144.0	0.0	0.0	0.0	0.0	0.0	0.0	0.0	0.0	0.0	0.0	0.0
ST Insurance	0.0	0.0	0.0	860.2	686.3	669.3	589.6	599.7	620.9	666.6	802.5	1,203.1	1,630.5
Working Capital Guarantees	0.0	0.0	0.0	0.0	0.0	0.0	0.0	0.0	0.0	0.0	0.0	0.0	0.0
GRAND TOTAL	516.8	1,386.7	1,090.7	2,034.9	1,743.3	1,859.0	2,141.9	3,607.3	3,534.1	2,516.7	3,969.2	5,397.6	7,230.3

[a] Represents total authorizations for fiscal year 1961 through 1963. Breakdown by fiscal year not available.

Export-Import Bank of the United States Summary of Authorizations, 1973–1982 (millions of dollars)

	FY 1973	FY 1974	FY 1975	FY 1976	*TQ*	FY 1977	FY 1978	FY 1979	FY 1980	FY 1981	FY 1982
Loan Authorization Summary											
Regular Direct Loans	2,046.5	3,486.8	2,449.9	2,141.4	267.3	700.0	2,872.4	3,724.7	4,045.3	5,045.5	3,104.2
Development Project Credits	0.0	0.0	0.0	0.0	0.0	0.0	0.0	0.0	0.0	0.0	0.0
MT/Small Business Credits	0.0	0.0	0.0	0.0	0.0	0.0	0.0	0.0	0.0	0.0	0.0
Lend-Lease Credits	0.0	0.0	0.0	0.0	0.0	0.0	0.0	0.0	0.0	0.0	0.0
Emergency Reconstruction Credits	0.0	0.0	0.0	0.0	0.0	0.0	0.0	0.0	0.0	0.0	0.0
Intermediary Loans	0.0	0.0	0.0	0.0	0.0	0.0	0.0	0.0	0.0	0.0	0.0
CFF/Relending Loans	92.4	212.6	166.8	143.7	14.9	47.1	54.9	100.2	41.7	33.8	0.0
Commodity Credits	75.0	81.7	84.0	0.0	0.0	0.0	0.0	0.0	0.0	0.0	0.0
Balance of Payments Loans	0.0	0.0	0.0	0.0	0.0	0.0	0.0	0.0	0.0	0.0	0.0
Exporter Credits	0.0	0.0	0.0	0.0	0.0	0.0	0.0	0.0	0.0	0.0	0.0
Military Credits	200.0	200.0	0.0	0.0	0.0	0.0	0.0	0.0	0.0	0.0	0.0
Special Foreign Trade Credits	0.0	0.0	0.0	0.0	0.0	0.0	0.0	0.0	0.0	0.0	0.0
War Chest	0.0	0.0	0.0	0.0	0.0	0.0	0.0	0.0	0.0	0.0	0.0
Discount Loans	1,639.6	923.5	1,111.9	1,203.7	166.0	473.5	497.3	650.0	490.8	351.6	412.1
Interest Equalization Program	0.0	0.0	0.0	0.0	0.0	0.0	0.0	0.0	0.0	0.0	0.0
Total Loan Program	4,053.5	4,904.6	3,812.6	3,488.8	448.2	1,220.6	3,424.6	4,474.9	4,577.8	5,430.9	3,516.3
Pre Credit Reform Grants				78.1	7.6						
Guarantee and Insurance Authorization Summary											
ST Insurance	1,928.1	2,141.1	2,456.2	2,762.5	590.8	2,949.5	2,835.0	3,559.5	4,795.7	5,396.0	4,666.5
ST War Risk and Expropriation Insurance	0.0	0.0	0.0	0.0	0.0	0.0	0.0	0.0	0.0	0.0	0.0

Export-Import Bank of the United States Summary of Authorizations, 1973–1982 (millions of dollars)

	FY 1973	FY 1974	FY 1975	FY 1976	TQ	FY 1977	FY 1978	FY 1979	FY 1980	FY 1981	FY 1982
MT Insurance	544.7	460.2	472.6	707.4	139.7	408.8	527.4	548.9	726.0	514.0	438.2
LT Guarantees	1,490.1	1,151.0	1,105.9	1,035.5	149.9	483.7	230.5	479.5	1,892.2	890.4	239.5
MT Guarantees	360.1	323.9	422.7	564.0	115.4	531.7	346.8	399.2	473.1	557.4	468.6
CFF Guarantees	39.5	40.0	38.2	47.0	7.0	5.3	12.1	26.1	12.7	13.8	0.0
Exporter Guarantees	98.3	78.7	6.7	14.7	0.0	0.0	0.0	3.1	131.7	51.6	18.9
ST Guarantees	0.0	0.0	0.0	0.0	0.0	0.0	0.0	0.0	0.0	0.0	0.0
Working Capital	0.0	0.0	0.0	0.0	0.0	0.0	0.0	0.0	0.0	0.0	0.0
Total Guarantees and Insurance	4,460.8	4,194.9	4,502.3	5,131.1	1,002.8	4,379.0	3,951.8	5,016.3	8,031.4	7,423.2	5,831.7
Total Authorizations											
Loans	4,053.5	4,904.6	3,812.6	3,488.8	448.2	1,220.6	3,424.6	4,474.9	4,577.8	5,430.9	3,516.3
Guarantees	1,988.0	1,593.6	1,573.5	1,661.2	272.3	1,020.7	589.4	907.9	2,509.7	1,513.2	727.0
Insurance	2,472.8	2,601.3	2,928.8	3,469.9	730.5	3,358.3	3,362.4	4,108.4	5,521.7	5,910.0	5,104.7
TOTAL	8,514.3	9,099.5	8,314.9	8,619.9	1,451.0	5,599.6	7,376.4	9,491.2	12,609.2	12,854.1	9,348.0
Aircraft, Nuclear Power, All Other											
Aircraft – Commercial Jet	969.9	1,129.1	840.3	663.7	93.8	354.4	304.5	1,704.0	2,482.9	3,051.2	262.2
Nuclear Power	322.9	598.8	350.9	647.7	81.5	275.8	994.3	671.3	589.4	235.0	24.9
Other LT Loans and Guarantees	2,518.8	3,191.6	2,448.6	1,865.5	241.9	553.5	1,804.1	1,828.9	2,865.2	2,649.7	3,056.6
MT Loans, Guarantees, and Insurance	2,774.6	2,038.9	2,218.9	2,680.5	443.0	1,466.4	1,438.5	1,727.5	1,876.0	1,522.2	1,337.8
ST Guarantees	0.0	0.0	0.0	0.0	0.0	0.0	0.0	0.0	0.0	0.0	0.0
ST Insurance	1,928.1	2,141.1	2,456.2	2,762.5	590.8	2,949.5	2,835.0	3,559.5	4,795.7	5,396.0	4,666.5
Working Capital Guarantees	0.0	0.0	0.0	0.0	0.0	0.0	0.0	0.0	0.0	0.0	0.0
GRAND TOTAL	8,514.3	9,099.5	8,314.9	8,619.9	1,451.0	5,599.6	7,376.4	9,491.2	12,609.2	12,854.1	9,348.0

Export-Import Bank of the United States Summary of Authorizations, 1983–2000 (millions of dollars)

	FY 1983	FY 1984	FY 1985	FY 1986	FY 1987	FY 1988	FY 1989	FY 1990	FY 1991	FY 1992
Loan Authorization Summary										
Regular Direct Loans	684.7	1,122.1	320.2	370.5	331.6	464.9	517.1	318.0	424.6	660.9
Development Project Credits	0.0	0.0	0.0	0.0	0.0	0.0	0.0	0.0	0.0	0.0
MT/Small Business Credits	160.2	0.0	339.2	206.9	227.8	0.2	0.0	0.0	0.0	0.0
Lend-Lease Credits	0.0	0.0	0.0	0.0	0.0	0.0	0.0	0.0	0.0	0.0
Emergency Reconstruction Credits	0.0	0.0	0.0	0.0	0.0	0.0	0.0	0.0	0.0	0.0
Intermediary Loans	0.0	0.0	0.0	0.0	39.5	220.2	201.7	240.6	206.2	150.5
CFF/Relending Loans	0.0	0.0	0.0	0.0	0.0	0.0	0.0	0.0	0.0	0.0
Commodity Credits	0.0	0.0	0.0	0.0	0.0	0.0	0.0	0.0	0.0	0.0
Balance of Payments Loans	0.0	0.0	0.0	0.0	0.0	0.0	0.0	0.0	0.0	0.0
Exporter Credits	0.0	0.0	0.0	0.0	0.0	0.0	0.0	0.0	0.0	0.0
Military Credits	0.0	0.0	0.0	0.0	0.0	0.0	0.0	0.0	0.0	0.0
Special Foreign Trade Credits	0.0	0.0	0.0	0.0	0.0	0.0	0.0	0.0	0.0	0.0
War Chest	0.0	0.0	0.0	0.0	0.0	0.0	0.0	53.4	145.4	5.1
Discount Loans	0.0	0.0	0.0	0.0	0.0	0.0	0.0	0.0	0.0	0.0
Interest Equalization Program	0.0	0.0	0.0	0.0	0.0	0.0	0.0	2.1	0.0	0.0
Total Loan Program	844.9	1,465.0	659.4	577.4	598.9	685.3	718.8	614.1	776.2	816.5
Pre Credit Reform Grants										
Guarantee and Insurance Authorization Summary										
ST Insurance	6,492.6	5,513.2	6,323.6	4,227.0	6,177.6	4,963.3	3,954.4	4,214.7	4,045.4	3,398.1
ST War Risk and Expropriation Insurance	0.0	0.0	0.0	0.0	0.0	0.0	0.0	0.0	0.0	0.0

Export-Import Bank of the United States Summary of Authorizations, 1983–2000 (millions of dollars)

	FY 1983	FY 1984	FY 1985	FY 1986	FY 1987	FY 1988	FY 1989	FY 1990	FY 1991	FY 1992
MT Insurance	291.1	304.4	205.9	152.9	266.4	170.3	390.4	626.4	508.1	822.1
LT Guarantees	1,202.7	899.2	779.3	716.0	1,019.6	324.8	870.5	2,713.1	3,845.8	4,218.6
MT Guarantees	527.6	415.6	514.1	386.3	467.3	200.7	366.9	531.0	2,121.7	2,939.0
CFF Guarantees	0.0	0.0	0.0	0.0	0.0	0.0	0.0	0.0	0.0	0.0
Exporter Guarantees	0.7	0.0	0.0	0.0	0.0	0.0	0.0	0.0	0.0	0.0
ST Guarantees	0.0	0.0	0.0	0.0	0.0	0.0	0.0	0.0	0.0	0.0
Working Capital	9.6	18.4	26.7	25.6	18.6	75.5	54.8	88.6	66.7	143.4
Total Guarantees and Insurance	8,524.3	7,150.8	7,849.6	5,507.8	7,949.5	5,734.6	5,637.0	8,173.8	10,587.7	11,521.2
Total Authorizations										
Loans	844.9	1,465.0	659.4	577.4	598.9	685.3	718.8	614.1	776.2	816.5
Guarantees	1,740.6	1,333.2	1,320.1	1,127.9	1,505.5	601.0	1,292.2	3,332.7	6,034.2	7,301.0
Insurance	6,783.7	5,817.6	6,529.5	4,379.9	6,444.0	5,133.6	4,344.8	4,841.1	4,553.5	4,220.2
TOTAL	9,369.2	8,615.8	8,509.0	6,085.2	8,548.4	6,419.9	6,355.8	8,787.9	11,363.9	12,337.7
Aircraft, Nuclear Power, All Other										
Aircraft – Commercial Jet	208.6	0.0	301.5	323.7	821.5	73.4	643.1	230.2	621.4	1,542.5
Nuclear Power	692.1	1,195.9	64.5	0.0	8.9	0.0	0.0	0.0	0.0	0.0
Other LT Loans and Guarantees	979.6	1,062.9	733.5	762.8	520.8	716.3	744.5	2,856.4	3,794.4	3,342.1
MT Loans, Guarantees, and Insurance	0.0	0.0	1,059.2	746.1	1,001.0	591.4	959.0	1,398.0	2,836.0	3,911.6
ST Guarantees	0.0	0.0	0.0	0.0	0.0	0.0	0.0	0.0	0.0	0.0
ST Insurance	9,369.2	8,615.8	8,509.0	6,085.2	8,548.4	6,419.9	6,355.8	8,787.9	11,363.9	12,337.7
Working Capital Guarantees	9.6	18.4	26.7	25.6	18.6	75.5	54.8	88.6	66.7	143.4
GRAND TOTAL	9,369.2	8,615.8	8,509.0	6,085.2	8,548.4	6,419.9	6,355.8	8,787.9	11,363.9	12,337.7

Export-Import Bank of the United States Summary of Authorizations, 1983–2000 (millions of dollars)

	FY 1993	FY 1994	FY 1995	FY 1996	FY 1997	FY 1998	FY 1999	FY 2000
Loan Authorization Summary								
Regular Direct Loans	1,634.7	2,979.8	1,562.4	1,100.3	1,473.4	86.0	848.1	932.6
Development Project Credits	0.0	0.0	0.0	0.0	0.0	0.0	0.0	0.0
MT/Small Business Credits	0.0	0.0	0.0	0.0	0.0	0.0	0.0	0.0
Emergency Reconstruction Credits	0.0	0.0	0.0	0.0	0.0	0.0	0.0	0.0
Intermediary Loans	86.6	36.6	13.9	0.0	0.0	0.0	0.0	0.0
CFF/Relending Loans	0.0	0.0	0.0	0.0	0.0	0.0	0.0	0.0
Commodity Credits	0.0	0.0	0.0	0.0	0.0	0.0	0.0	0.0
Balance of Payments Loans	0.0	0.0	0.0	0.0	0.0	0.0	0.0	0.0
Exporter Credits	0.0	0.0	0.0	0.0	0.0	0.0	0.0	0.0
Military Credits	0.0	0.0	0.0	0.0	0.0	0.0	0.0	0.0
Special Foreign Trade Credits	0.0	0.0	0.0	0.0	0.0	0.0	0.0	0.0
War Chest	26.7	0.0	22.0	136.0	75.5	16.6	54.6	0.0
Discount Loans	0.0	0.0	0.0	0.0	0.0	0.0	0.0	0.0
Interest Equalization Program	0.0	0.0	0.0	0.0	0.0	0.0	0.0	0.0
Total Loan Program	1,748.0	3,016.4	1,598.3	1,236.3	1,548.9	102.6	902.7	932.6
Pre Credit Reform Grants								
Guarantee and Insurance Authorization Summary								
ST Insurance	3,754.6	3,634.8	3,801.9	3,134.7	2,317.3	3,582.8	3,276.4	2,410.7
ST War Risk and Expropriation Insurance	0.0	0.0	0.0	0.0	0.0	0.0	0.0	0.0

Export-Import Bank of the United States Summary of Authorizations, 1983–2000 (millions of dollars)

	FY 1993	FY 1994	FY 1995	FY 1996	FY 1997	FY 1998	FY 1999	FY 2000
MT Insurance	474.4	626.6	753.1	733.4	531.5	713.5	589.5	880.4
LT Guarantees	6,252.2	5,843.0	4,677.8	5,314.6	6,745.1	5,123.7	7,238.4	6,911.0
MT Guarantees	2,682.6	1,585.0	728.0	720.9	572.7	639.3	644.7	914.1
CFF Guarantees	0.0	0.0	0.0	0.0	0.0	0.0	0.0	0.0
Exporter Guarantees	0.0	0.0	0.0	0.0	0.0	0.0	0.0	0.0
ST Guarantees	0.0	0.0	0.0	0.0	0.0	0.0	0.0	0.0
Working Capital	159.7	180.6	305.8	377.8	443.3	387.7	415.9	588.3
Total Guarantees and Insurance	13,323.5	11,870.0	10,266.6	10,281.4	10,609.9	10,447.0	12,164.9	11,704.5
Total Authorizations								
Loans	1,748.0	3,016.4	1,598.3	1,236.3	1,548.9	102.6	902.7	932.6
Guarantees	9,094.5	7,608.6	5,711.6	6,413.3	7,761.1	6,150.7	8,299.0	8,413.4
Insurance	4,229.0	4,261.4	4,555.0	3,868.1	2,848.8	4,296.3	3,865.9	3,291.1
TOTAL	15,071.5	14,886.4	11,864.9	11,517.7	12,158.8	10,549.6	13,067.6	12,637.1
Aircraft, Nuclear Power, All Other								
Aircraft – Commercial Jet	3,448.6	2,958.6	977.0	1,154.8	2,132.9	2,553.1	6,311.1	3,142.1
Nuclear Power	0.0	0.0	0.0	0.0	0.0	0.0	0.0	0.0
Other LT Loans and Guarantees	4,425.0	5,864.2	5,285.2	5,396.1	6,161.1	2,673.2	1,830.0	4,701.5
MT Loans, Guarantees, and Insurance	3,243.6	2,248.2	1,495.0	1,454.3	1,104.2	1,352.8	1,234.2	1,794.5
ST Guarantees	0.0	0.0	0.0	0.0	0.0	0.0	0.0	0.0
ST Insurance	15,071.5	4,261.4	4,555.0	3,838.1	2,848.8	4,296.3	3,865.9	3,291.1
Working Capital Guarantees	159.7	180.6	305.8	377.8	443.3	387.7	415.9	588.3
GRAND TOTAL	15,071.5	14,886.4	11,864.9	11,517.7	12,158.8	10,549.6	13,067.6	12,637.1

APPENDIX C

NUMBER OF AUTHORIZATIONS

Export-Import Bank of the United States Number of Authorizations Approved, 1934–1946

	FY 1934	FY 1935	FY 1936	FY 1937	FY 1938	FY 1939	FY 1940	FY 1941	FY 1942	FY 1943	FY 1944	FY 1945	FY 1946
Regular Direct Loans	1	22	16	19	43	61	33	34	43	3	7	16	33
Development Project Credits	0	0	0	0	0	0	0	0	0	0	0	0	0
MT/Small Business Credits	0	0	0	0	0	0	0	0	0	0	0	0	0
Lend-Lease Credits	0	0	0	0	0	0	0	0	0	0	0	0	3
Emergency Reconstruction Credits	0	0	0	0	0	0	0	0	0	0	0	0	15
Intermediary Loans	0	0	0	0	0	0	0	0	0	0	0	0	0
CFF/Relending Loans	0	0	0	0	0	0	0	0	0	0	0	0	0
Commodity Credits	0	3	6	4	0	0	0	0	0	0	0	0	2
Balance of Payments Loans	0	0	0	0	0	0	0	0	0	0	0	0	0
Exporter Credits	0	0	0	0	0	0	0	0	0	0	0	0	0
Military Credits	0	0	0	0	0	0	0	0	0	0	0	0	0
Special Foreign Trade Credits	0	0	0	0	0	0	0	0	0	0	0	0	0
War Chest	0	0	0	0	0	0	0	0	0	0	0	0	0
Discount Loans	0	0	0	0	0	0	0	0	0	0	0	0	0
Interest Equalization Program	0	0	0	0	0	0	0	0	0	0	0	0	0
Total Loans	1	25	22	23	43	61	33	34	43	3	7	16	53
ST Insurance	0	0	0	0	0	0	0	0	0	0	0	0	0
ST War Risk and Expropriation Insurance	0	0	0	0	0	0	0	0	0	0	0	0	0
MT Insurance	0	0	0	0	0	0	0	0	0	0	0	0	0
LT Guarantees	0	0	0	0	0	0	0	0	0	0	0	0	0
MT Guarantees	0	0	0	0	0	0	0	0	0	0	0	0	0
CFF Guarantees	0	0	0	0	0	0	0	0	0	0	0	0	0
Exporter Guarantees	0	0	0	0	0	0	0	0	0	0	0	0	0
ST Guarantees	0	0	0	0	0	0	0	0	0	0	0	0	0
Working Capital	0	0	0	0	0	0	0	0	0	0	0	0	0
Total Guarantees & Insurance	0	0	0	0	0	0	0	0	0	0	0	0	0
TOTAL ALL PROGRAMS	1	25	22	23	43	61	33	34	43	3	7	16	53

Export-Import Bank of the United States Number of Authorizations Approved, 1947–1958

	FY 1947	FY 1948	FY 1949	FY 1950	FY 1951	FY 1952	FY 1953	FY 1954	FY 1955	FY 1956	FY 1957	FY 1958
Regular Direct Loans	27	17	21	22	22	24	21	23	54	156	181	46
Development Project Credits	0	0	0	0	0	0	0	0	0	0	0	0
MT/Small Business Credits	0	0	0	0	0	0	0	0	0	0	0	0
Lend-Lease Credits	0	0	0	0	0	0	0	0	0	0	0	0
Emergency Reconstruction Credits	1	0	0	1	0	0	0	0	0	0	0	0
Intermediary Loans	0	0	0	0	0	0	0	0	0	0	0	0
CFF/Relending Loans	0	0	0	0	0	0	0	0	0	0	0	0
Commodity Credits	2	1	0	0	0	7	1	2	0	0	0	0
Balance of Payments Loans	0	0	0	0	0	0	1	0	0	0	0	0
Exporter Credits	0	0	0	0	0	0	0	0	90	51	0	141
Military Credits	0	0	0	0	0	1	0	0	0	0	0	0
Special Foreign Trade Credits	0	0	0	0	0	0	0	0	0	0	1	4
War Chest	0	0	0	0	0	0	0	0	0	0	0	0
Discount Loans	0	0	0	0	0	0	0	0	0	0	0	0
Interest Equalization Program	0	0	0	0	0	0	0	0	0	0	0	0
Total Loans	30	18	21	23	22	32	23	25	144	207	182	191
ST Insurance	0	0	0	0	0	0	0	0	0	0	0	0
ST War Risk and Expropriation Insurance	0	0	0	0	0	0	0	55	118	0	0	0
MT Insurance	0	0	0	0	0	0	0	0	0	0	0	0
LT Guarantees	0	0	0	0	0	0	0	0	0	0	0	0
MT Guarantees	0	0	0	0	0	0	0	0	0	0	0	0
CFF Guarantees	0	0	0	0	0	0	0	0	0	0	0	0
Exporter Guarantees	0	0	0	0	0	0	0	0	0	0	0	0
ST Guarantees	0	0	0	0	0	0	0	0	0	0	0	0
Working Capital	0	0	0	0	0	0	0	0	0	0	0	0
Total Guarantees & Insurance	0	0	0	0	0	0	0	55	118	0	0	0
TOTAL ALL PROGRAMS	30	18	21	23	22	32	23	80	262	207	182	191

Export-Import Bank of the United States Number of Authorizations Approved, 1959–1968

	FY 1959	FY 1960	FY 1961	FY 1962	FY 1963	FY 1964	FY 1965	FY 1966	FY 1967	FY 1968
Regular Direct Loans	38	107	60	49	0	64	56	58	120	78
Development Project Credits	0	Incl above	Incl above	0	44	0	0	0	0	0
MT/Small Business Credits	0	0	0	0	0	0	0	0	0	0
Lend-Lease Credits	0	0	0	0	0	0	0	0	0	0
Emergency Reconstruction Credits	0	0	0	0	0	0	0	0	0	0
Intermediary Loans	0	0	0	0	0	0	0	0	0	0
CFF/Relending Loans	0	0	0	0	0	0	0	0	0	0
Commodity Credits	3	2	2	0	5	3	3	2	2	1
Balance of Payments Loans	0	0	0	0	0	0	0	0	0	0
Exporter Credits	72	67	228	339	38	3	0	Incl in LT above	Incl in LT above	Incl in LT above
Military Credits	0	0	0	0	0	0	0	13	7	19
Special Foreign Trade Credits	5	2	1	4	2	0	2	1	1	2
War Chest	0	0	0	0	0	0	0	0	0	0
Discount Loans	0	0	0	0	0	0	0	0	19	16
Interest Equalization Program	0	0	0	0	0	0	0	0	0	0
Total Loans	118	178	291	392	89	70	61	74	149	116
ST Insurance	0	0	0	0	0	0	5,266[a]	1,352	1,320	1,256
ST War Risk and Expropriation Insurance	0	0	0	0	0	0	0	5	19	121
MT Insurance	0	0	0	0	0	0	2,079[a]	1,059	987	849
LT Guarantees	0	0	0	0	0	0	108[a]	12	3	5
MT Guarantees	0	0	541	324	0	0	2,234[a]	645	700	798
CFF Guarantees	0	0	0	0	0	0	0	0	0	0
Exporter Guarantees	0	0	0	41	0	0	130[a]	28	10	7
ST Guarantees	0	28	Incl above	0	0	0	0	0	0	0
Working Capital	0	0	0	0	0	0	0	0	0	0
Total Guarantees & Insurance	0	28	541	365	0	0	9,817	3,101	3,039	3,036
TOTAL ALL PROGRAMS	118	206	832	757	89	70	9,878	3,175	3,188	3,152

[a] Represents total from fiscal years 1961–5. Breakdown by fiscal year not available.

Export-Import Bank of the United States Number of Authorizations Approved, 1969–1977

	FY 1969	FY 1970	FY 1971	FY 1972	FY 1973	FY 1974	FY 1975	FY 1976	TQ	FY 1977
Regular Direct Loans	77	126	198	614	274	353	239	150	17	52
Development Project Credits	0	0	0	0	0	0	0	0	0	0
MT/Small Business Credits	0	0	0	0	0	0	0	0	0	0
Lend-Lease Credits	0	0	0	0	0	0	0	0	0	0
Emergency Reconstruction Credits	0	0	0	0	0	0	0	0	0	0
Intermediary Loans	0	0	0	0	0	0	0	0	0	0
CFF/Relending Loans	7	24	38	0	975	1,495	978	696	127	305
Commodity Credits	1	1	4	0	1	0	3	0	0	0
Balance of Payments Loans	0	0	0	0	0	0	0	0	0	0
Exporter Credits	0	0	0	0	0	0	0	0	0	0
Military Credits	3		4		2				0	0
Special Foreign Trade Credits	1	0	0	0	0	0	0	0	0	0
War Chest	0	0	0	0	0	0	0	0	0	0
Discount Loans	45	765	543	885	2,008	1,846	1,672	1,226	242	609
Interest Equalization Program	0	0	0	0	0	0	0	0	0	0
Total Loans	134	916	787	1,499	3,260	3,694	2,892	2,072	386	966
ST Insurance	1,145	1,147	1,142	1,206	1,250	1,156	1,045	1,077	279	1,008
ST War Risk and Expropriation Insurance	24	38	41	46	0	0	0	0	0	0
MT Insurance	1,115	1,536	1,645	1,470	1,756	1,520	1,093	1,080	252	684
LT Guarantees	6	52	159	202	213	193	88	62	9	28
MT Guarantees	903	834	716	802	971	1,111	765	737	185	662
CFF Guarantees	0	0	Incl in LT above	227	566	350	247	348	77	63
Exporter Guarantees	11	16	27	25	25	20	3	7	0	0
ST Guarantees	0	0	0	0	0	0	0	0	0	0
Working Capital	0	0	0	0	0	0	0	0	0	0
Total Guarantees & Insurance	3,204	3,623	3,730	3,978	4,781	4,350	3,241	3,311	802	2,445
TOTAL ALL PROGRAMS	3,338	4,539	4,517	5,477	8,041	8,044	6,133	5,383	1,188	3,411

Export-Import Bank of the United States Number of Authorizations Approved, 1978–1989

	FY 1978	FY 1979	FY 1980	FY 1981	FY 1982	FY 1983	FY 1984	FY 1985	FY 1986	FY 1987	FY 1988	FY 1989
Regular Direct Loans	66	99	137	131	68	21	29	13	15	19	25	14
Development Project Credits	0	0	0	0	0	0	0	0	0	0	0	0
MT/Small Business Credits	0	0	0	0	0	154	263	239	225	221	0	0
Lend-Lease Credits	0	0	0	0	0	0	0	0	0	0	0	0
Emergency Reconstruction Credits	0	0	0	0	0	0	0	0	0	0	0	0
Intermediary Loans	0	0	0	0	0	0	0	0	0	72	158	120
CFF/Relending Loans	296	468	178	226	0	0	0	0	0	0	0	0
Commodity Credits	0	0	0	0	0	0	0	0	0	0	0	0
Balance of Payments Loans	0	0	0	0	0	0	0	0	0	0	0	0
Exporter Credits	0	0	0	0	0	0	0	0	0	0	0	0
Military Credits	0	0	0	0	0	0	0	0	0	0	0	0
Special Foreign Trade Credits	0	0	0	0	0	0	0	0	0	0	0	0
War Chest	0	0	0	0	0	0	0	0	0	0	0	0
Discount Loans	527	753	875	527	752	0	0	0	0	0	0	0
Interest Equalization Program	0	0	0	0	0	0	0	0	0	0	0	0
Total Loans	889	1,320	1,190	884	820	175	292	252	240	312	183	134
ST Insurance	960	1,362	1,769	1,803	1,454	1,256	1,025	919	648	1,047	995	1,001
ST War Risk and Expropriation Insurance	0	0	0	0	0	0	0	0	0	0	0	0
MT Insurance	831	953	978	656	332	96	85	74	103	47	32	66
LT Guarantees	10	14	28	47	17	32	29	24	27	19	13	19
MT Guarantees	477	573	576	635	444	217	195	140	138	116	87	134
CFF Guarantees	123	233	82	83	0	0	0	0	0	0	0	0
Exporter Guarantees	0	3	11	7	0	0	0	0	0	0	0	0
ST Guarantees	0	0	0	0	0	0	0	0	0	0	0	0
Working Capital	0	0	0	0	0	7	10	32	27	23	85	72
Total Guarantees & Insurance	2,401	3,138	3,444	3,231	2,247	1,608	1,344	1,189	943	1,252	1,212	1,292
TOTAL ALL PROGRAMS	3,290	4,458	4,634	4,115	3,067	1,783	1,636	1,441	1,183	1,564	1,395	1,426

Export-Import Bank of the United States Number of Authorizations Approved, 1990–2000

	FY 1990	FY 1991	FY 1992	FY 1993	FY 1994	FY 1995	FY 1996	FY 1997	FY 1998	FY 1999	FY 2000
Regular Direct Loans	16	17	49	32	31	29	29	15	4	13	8
Development Project Credits	0	0	0	0	0	0	0	0	0	0	0
MT/Small Business Credits	0	0	0	0	0	0	0	0	0	0	0
Lend-Lease Credits	0	0	0	0	0	0	0	0	0	0	0
Emergency Reconstruction Credits	0	0	0	0	0	0	0	0	0	0	0
Intermediary Loans	184	106	70	37	16	4	0	0	0	0	0
CFF/Relending Loans	0	0	0	0	0	0	0	0	0	0	0
Commodity Credits	0	0	0	0	0	0	0	0	0	0	0
Balance of Payments Loans	0	0	0	0	0	0	0	0	0	0	0
Exporter Credits	0	0	0	0	0	0	0	0	0	0	0
Military Credits	0	0	0	0	0	0	0	0	0	0	0
Special Foreign Trade Credits	0	0	0	0	0	0	0	0	0	0	0
War Chest	4	8	1	1	0	1	9	2	1	3	0
Discount Loans	0	0	0	0	0	0	0	0	0	0	0
Interest Equalization Program	2	0	0	0	0	0	0	0	0	0	0
Total Loans	206	131	120	70	47	34	38	17	5	16	8
ST Insurance	1,043	1,072	1,107	1,207	1,803	1,691	1,590	1,384	1,431	1,436	1,528
ST War Risk and Expropriation Insurance	0	0	0	0	0	0	0	0	0	0	0
MT Insurance	66	73	77	67	234	279	324	347	261	246	373
LT Guarantees	30	46	58	81	70	62	73	88	73	71	65
MT Guarantees	182	189	208	245	136	141	111	180	147	124	194
CFF Guarantees	0	0	0	0	0	0	0	0	0	0	0
Exporter Guarantees	0	0	0	0	0	0	0	0	0	0	0
ST Guarantees	0	0	0	0	0	0	0	0	0	0	0
Working Capital	86	54	130	130	155	208	286	332	275	330	361
Total Guarantees & Insurance	1,407	1,434	1,580	1,730	2,398	2,381	2,384	2,331	2,187	2,207	2,521
TOTAL ALL PROGRAMS	1,613	1,565	1,700	1,800	2,445	2,415	2,422	2,348	2,192	2,223	2,529

APPENDIX D

CHARGES AGAINST STATUTORY LIMITATIONS ON TOTAL ACTIVITY

Export-Import Bank of the United States Charges Against Statutory Limitations on Total Activity, 1934–1946 (millions of dollars)

	FY 1934[a]	FY 1935[a]	FY 1936	FY 1937[a]	FY 1938	FY 1939	FY 1940	FY 1941	FY 1942	FY 1943	FY 1944	FY 1945	FY 1946
Lending Authority	0.0	0.0	0.0	0.0	0.0	100.0[g]	200.0[g]	700.0[g]	700.0	700.0	700.0	700.0	3,500.0[g]
Balances Charged @ 100%													
Outstanding Loans	0.0	0.2	0.1	0.0	14.6	63.9	130.4	186.7	178.3	200.5	217.0	214.1	727.2
Undisbursed Loans	0.0	0.0	0.2	0.0	0.0	0.0	0.0	335.3	436.4	434.6	348.2	336.3	1,953.2
Portfolio Certificates sold with Recourse	0.0	0.0	0.0	0.0	0.0	0.0	0.0	0.0	0.0	0.0	0.0	0.0	0.0
Loans Sold with Recourse	0.0	0.0	0.0	0.0	0.0	0.0	0.0	0.0	0.0	0.0	0.0	0.0	0.0
Outstanding Balance of Paid Claims[b]	N/A	N/A	N/A	N/A	N/A	N/A	N/A	N/A	N/A	N/A	N/A	N/A	N/A
Guarantees	0.0	0.0	0.0	0.0	0.0	0.0	0.0	0.0	0.0	0.0	0.0	0.0	0.0
Insurance	0.0	0.0	0.0	0.0	0.0	0.0	0.0	0.0	0.0	0.0	0.0	0.0	0.0
Guar & Ins in Excess of Fractional Reserve	0.0	0.0	0.0	0.0	0.0	0.0	0.0	0.0	0.0	0.0	0.0	0.0	0.0
Total Charges at 100%	0.0	0.2	0.3	0.0	14.6	63.9	130.4	522.0	614.7	635.1	565.2	550.4	2,680.4
Guarantee & Insurance charges at 25% (see below)	N/A	N/A	N/A	N/A	N/A	N/A	N/A	N/A	N/A	N/A	N/A	N/A	N/A
Total Charges against Overall Authority	N/A	N/A	N/A	N/A	N/A	63.9	130.4	522.0	614.7	635.1	565.2	550.4	2,680.4
Uncommited Authority	N/A	N/A	N/A	N/A	N/A	36.1	69.6	178.0	85.3	64.9	134.8	149.6	819.6
Limitation on Outstanding Guarantees & Insurance which can be charged at 25% against authority	N/A	N/A	N/A	N/A	N/A	N/A	N/A	N/A	N/A	N/A	N/A	N/A	N/A
100% of Balances Charged at 25%													
Loans sold with recourse	N/A	N/A	N/A	N/A	N/A	N/A	N/A	N/A	N/A	N/A	N/A	N/A	N/A
Guarantees	N/A	N/A	N/A	N/A	N/A	N/A	N/A	N/A	N/A	N/A	N/A	N/A	N/A
Insurance	N/A	N/A	N/A	N/A	N/A	N/A	N/A	N/A	N/A	N/A	N/A	N/A	N/A
Total Charged at 25%	N/A	N/A	N/A	N/A	N/A	N/A	N/A	N/A	N/A	N/A	N/A	N/A	N/A
Less 75%	N/A	N/A	N/A	N/A	N/A	N/A	N/A	N/A	N/A	N/A	N/A	N/A	N/A
Net 25% Charge to Lending Authority	N/A	N/A	N/A	N/A	N/A	N/A	N/A	N/A	N/A	N/A	N/A	N/A	N/A
Guarantee and Insurance charged at 100%	N/A	N/A	N/A	N/A	N/A	N/A	N/A	N/A	N/A	N/A	N/A	N/A	N/A
Total Charges to Fractional Reserve Limitation	N/A	N/A	N/A	N/A	N/A	N/A	N/A	N/A	N/A	N/A	N/A	N/A	N/A
Uncommited Fractional Reserve Limitation	N/A	N/A	N/A	N/A	N/A	N/A	N/A	N/A	N/A	N/A	N/A	N/A	N/A

Export-Import Bank of the United States Charges Against Statutory Limitations on Total Activity, 1947–1958 (millions of dollars)

	FY 1947	FY 1948	FY 1949	FY 1950	FY 1951	FY 1952	FY 1953	FY 1954	FY 1955	FY 1956	FY 1957	FY 1958
Lending Authority	3,500.0	3,500.0	3,500.0	3,500.0	3,500.0	4,500.0[g]	4,500.0	4,500.0	5,000.0[g]	5,000.0	5,000.0[g]	7,000.0[g]
Balances Charged @ 100%												
Outstanding Loans	1,750.0	2,229.4	2,164.7	2,226.3	2,321.6	2,395.9	2,552.9	2,761.8	2,740.1	2,649.1	2,603.1	3,040.3
Undisbursed Loans	938.6	642.7	381.6	560.1	685.9	911.9	791.3	444.4	746.2	739.2	1,535.6	1,424.3
Portfolio Certificates sold with Recourse	0.0	0.0	0.0	0.0	0.0	0.0	0.0	0.0	0.0	0.0	0.0	0.0
Loans Sold with Recourse	0.0	0.0	0.0	0.0	0.0	0.0	0.0	0.0	0.0	0.0	0.0	0.0
Outstanding Balance of Paid Claims[b]	N/A	N/A	N/A	N/A	N/A	N/A	N/A	N/A	N/A	N/A	N/A	N/A
Guarantees	0.0	0.0	0.0	0.0	0.0	0.0	0.0	0.6	0.0	0.0	3.5	3.3
Insurance	0.0	0.0	0.0	0.0	0.0	0.0	0.0	0.0	0.0	0.0	0.0	0.0
Guar & Ins in Excess of Fractional Reserve	0.0	0.0	0.0	0.0	0.0	0.0	0.0	0.0	0.0	0.0	0.0	0.0
Total Charges at 100%	2,689.5	2,872.1	2,546.3	2,786.4	3,007.5	3,307.8	3,344.2	3,206.8	3,486.3	3,388.3	4,142.2	4,467.9
Guarantee & Insurance charges at 25% (see below)	N/A	N/A	N/A	N/A	N/A	N/A	N/A	N/A	N/A	N/A	N/A	N/A
Total Charges against Overall Authority	2,689.5	2,872.1	2,546.3	2,786.4	3,007.5	3,307.8	3,344.2	3,206.8	3,486.3	3,388.3	4,142.4	4,467.9
Uncommited Authority	810.5	627.9	953.7	713.6	492.5	1,192.2	1,155.8	1,293.2	1,513.7	1,611.7	857.8	2,532.1
Limitation on Outstanding Guarantees & Insurance which can be charged at 25% against authority	N/A	N/A	N/A	N/A	N/A	N/A	N/A	N/A	N/A	N/A	N/A	
100% of Balances Charged at 25%												
Loans sold with recourse	N/A	N/A	N/A	N/A	N/A	N/A	N/A	N/A	N/A	N/A	N/A	N/A
Guarantees	N/A	N/A	N/A	N/A	N/A	N/A	N/A	N/A	N/A	N/A	N/A	N/A
Insurance	N/A	N/A	N/A	N/A	N/A	N/A	N/A	N/A	N/A	N/A	N/A	N/A
Total Charged at 25%	N/A	N/A	N/A	N/A	N/A	N/A	N/A	N/A	N/A	N/A	N/A	N/A
Less 75%	N/A	N/A	N/A	N/A	N/A	N/A	N/A	N/A	N/A	N/A	N/A	N/A
Net 25% Charge to Lending Authority	N/A	N/A	N/A	N/A	N/A	N/A	N/A	N/A	N/A	N/A	N/A	N/A
Guarantee and Insurance charged at 100%	N/A	N/A	N/A	N/A	N/A	N/A	N/A	N/A	N/A	N/A	N/A	N/A
Total Charges to Fractional Reserve Limitation	N/A	N/A	N/A	N/A	N/A	N/A	N/A	N/A	N/A	N/A	N/A	N/A
Uncommited Fractional Reserve Limitation	N/A	N/A	N/A	N/A	N/A	N/A	N/A	N/A	N/A	N/A	N/A	N/A

Export-Import Bank of the United States Charges Against Statutory Limitations on Total Activity, 1959–1970 (millions of dollars)

	FY 1959	FY 1960	FY 1961	FY 1962	FY 1963	FY 1964	FY 1965	FY 1966	FY 1967	FY 1968	FY 1969	FY 1970
Lending Authority	7,000.0	7,000.0	7,000.0	7,000.0	7,000.0	9,000.0[g]	9,000.0	9,000.0	9,000.0	13,500.0[g]	13,500.0	13,500.0
Balances Charged @ 100%												
Outstanding Loans	3,462.5	3,231.8	3,367.7	3,610.5	3,295.6	2,706.3	2,489.6	2,226.8	4,151.4	5,058.6	5,421.5	5,713.8
Undisbursed Loans	1,310.2	1,570.0	2,107.0	2,048.8	1,590.7[c]	1,725.3	1,820.4	1,876.6	2,832.0	3,460.3	2,462.3	2,976.6
Portfolio Certificates sold with Recourse	0.0	0.0	0.0	300.0	520.0	826.8	1,022.3	1,385.0	0.0	0.0	0.0	0.0
Loans Sold with Recourse	0.0	0.0	0.0	0.0	5.0	5.0	38.4	50.4	0.0	0.0	475.2	393.0
Outstanding Balance of Paid Claims[b]	N/A	N/A	N/A	N/A	N/A	N/A	N/A	N/A	N/A	N/A	N/A	N/A
Guarantees	0.5	17.9	164.7	13.5	3.7	2.9	0.0	12.2	34.7	19.4	2.2	0.2
Insurance	0.0	0.0	0.0	0.0	0.0	0.0	0.0	0.0	0.0	0.0	0.0	0.0
Guar & Ins in Excess of Fractional Reserve	0.0	0.0	0.0	0.0	0.0	0.0	0.0	0.0	0.0	0.0	0.0	0.0
Total Charges at 100%	4,764.2	4,819.7	5,639.4	5,972.8	5,415.0	5,266.3	5,370.7	5,551.0	7,018.1	8,538.3	8,361.2	9,083.6
Guarantee & Insurance charges at 25% (see below)	N/A	N/A	N/A	181.6	221.0	274.4	330.8	365.1	369.9	382.0	369.5	625.1
Total Charges against Overall Authority	4,764.2	4,819.7	5,639.4	6,154.4	5,636.0	5,540.7	5,701.5	5,916.1	7,388.0	8,920.3	8,730.7	9,708.7
Uncommited Authority	2,235.8	2,180.3	1,360.8	845.6	1,364.0	3,459.3	3,298.5	3,083.9	1,612.0	4,579.8	4,769.4	3,791.3
Limitation on Outstanding Guarantees & Insurance which can be charged at 25% against authority	N/A	N/A	N/A	1,000.0[g]	1,000.0	2,000.0[g]	2,000.0	2,000.0	2,000.0	3,500.0[g]	3,500.0	3,500.0
100% of Balances Charged at 25%												
Loans sold with recourse	N/A	N/A	N/A	0.0	0.0	0.0	0.0	0.0	151.7	162.3	16.3	22.0
Guarantees	N/A	N/A	N/A	226.3	260.6	350.6	511.1	594.2	459.0	488.1	533.4	912.1
Insurance	N/A	N/A	N/A	500.0	623.5	747.0	812.0	866.1	869.0	877.4	928.1	1,566.4
Total Charged at 25%	N/A	N/A	N/A	726.3	884.1	1,097.6	1,323.1	1,460.3	1,479.7	1,527.8	1,477.8	2,500.5
Less 75%	N/A	N/A	N/A	544.7	663.1	823.2	992.3	1,095.2	1,109.8	1,145.9	1,108.4	1,875.4
Net 25% Charge to Lending Authority	N/A	N/A	N/A	181.6	221.0	274.4	330.8	365.1	369.9	382.0	369.5	625.1
Guarantee and Insurance charged at 100%	N/A	N/A	N/A	0	0.0	0.0	0.0	12.2[b]	0.0	0.0	0.0	0.0
Total Charges to Fractional Reserve Limitation	N/A	N/A	N/A	726.3	884.1	1,097.6	1,323.1	1,472.5	1,479.7	1,365.5	1,477.8	2,500.5
Uncommited Fractional Reserve Limitation	N/A	N/A	N/A	273.7	115.9	902.4	676.9	527.5	520.3	2,134.5	2,022.2	999.5

Export-Import Bank of the United States Charges Against Statutory Limitations on Total Activity, 1971–1981 (millions of dollars)

	FY 1971	FY 1972	FY 1973	FY 1974	FY 1975	FY 1976	Transition Quarter[c]	FY 1977	FY 1978	FY 1979	FY 1980	FY 1981
Lending Authority	13,500.0	20,000.0[g]	20,000.0	20,000.0	25,000.0[g]	25,000.0	25,000.0	25,000.0	25,000.0	40,000.0[g]	40,000.0	40,000.0
Balances Charged @ 100%												
Outstanding Loans	5,664.7	5,956.2	6,585.8	7,910.5	9,408.9	10,830.4	11,092.5	11,538.5	11,550.1	11,859.1	13,765.2	15,802.4
Undisbursed Loans	3,512.7	4,567.7	5,778.9	7,331.8	7,043.6	7,231.1	6,563.6	4,015.1	5,435.2	7,292.2	7,647.5	9,147.0
Portfolio Certificates sold with Recourse	0.0	0.0	0.0	0.0	0.0	0.0	0.0	0.0	0.0	0.0	0.0	0.0
Loans Sold with Recourse	527.7	398.7	514.7	492.4	425.0	0.0	0.0	0.0	0.0	0.0	0.0	0.0
Outstanding Balance of Paid Claims[b]	N/A	N/A	N/A	N/A	N/A	N/A	N/A	N/A	N/A	N/A	N/A	N/A
Guarantees	0.0	0.0	0.0	0.0	0.0	0.0	0.0	0.0	0.0	0.0	0.0	0.0
Insurance	0.0	0.0	0.0	0.0	0.0	0.0	0.0	0.0	0.0	0.0	0.0	0.0
Guar & Ins in Excess of Fractional Reserve	0.0	0.0	0.0	0.0	0.0	0.0	0.0	0.c	0.0	0.0	0.0	0.0
Total Charges at 100%	9,892.1	10,922.6	12,879.4	15,734.7	16,877.5	18,061.5	17,656.1	15,553.6	16,985.3	19,151.3	21,412.7	24,949.4
Guarantee & Insurance charges at 25% (see below)	875.0	1,437.3	1,763.6	2,028.8	2,249.6	2,581.5	2,602.6	2,511.0	2,351.6	2,387.0	2,937.3	3,364.2
Total Charges against Overall Authority	10,767.1	12,359.9	14,643.0	17,763.5	19,127.1	20,643.0	20,258.7	18,064.6	19,336.9	21,538.3	24,350.0	28,313.6
Uncommited Authority	2,732.9[d]	7,460.1	5,357.0[d]	2,236.6[f]	5,872.9	4,357.0	4,741.4	6,935.4	5,663.1	18,461.7	15,650.1	11,686.4
Limitation on Outstanding Guarantees & Insurance which can be charged at 25% against authority	3,500.0	10,000.0	10,000.0	10,000.0	20,000.0	20,000.0	20,000.0	20,000.0	20,000.0	25,000.0[g]	25,000.0	25,000.0
100% of Balances Charged at 25%												
Loans sold with recourse	26.9	27.8	28.2	51.2	62.4	0.0	0.0	0.0	0.0	0.0	0.0	0.0
Guarantees	1,706.3	3,054.0	4,040.0	4,515.2	5,260.7	5,986.3	5,980.0	5,803.1	5,357.2	4,961.3	6,178.2	6,702.7
Insurance	1,766.8	2,667.5	2,986.3	3,548.8	3,675.3	4,339.8	4,430.2	4,240.6	4,049.1	4,586.7	5,570.8	6,754.1
Total Charged at 25%	3,500.0	5,749.3	7,054.5	8,115.2	8,998.3	10,326.1	10,410.2	10,043.7	9,406.3	9,548.0	11,749.0	13,456.8
Less 75%	2,625.0	4,312.0	5,290.9	6,086.4	6,748.8	7,744.6	7,807.7	7,532.8	7,054.7	7,161.0	8,811.8	10,092.6
Net 25% Charge to Lending Authority	875.0	1,437.3	1,763.6	2,028.8	2,249.6	2,581.5	2,602.6	2,511.0	2,351.6	2,387.0	2,937.3	3,364.2
Guarantee and Insurance charged at 100%	0.0	0.0	0.0	0.0	0.0	0.0	0.0	0.0	0.0	0.0	0.0	0.0
Total Charges to Fractional Reserve Limitation	3,500.0	5,749.3	7,054.5	8,115.2	8,998.4	10,326.1	10,410.2	10,043.7	9,406.3	9,548.0	11,749.0	13,456.8
Uncommited Fractional Reserve Limitation	0.0	4,250.7	2,945.5	1,884.8	11,001.6	9,673.9	9,589.8	9,956.3	10,593.7	15,452.0	13,251.0	11,543.2

Export-Import Bank of the United States Charges Against Statutory Limitations on Total Activity, 1982–1993 (millions of dollars)

	FY 1982	FY 1983	FY 1984	FY 1985	FY 1986	FY 1987	FY 1988	FY 1989	FY 1990	FY 1991	FY 1992	FY 1993
Lending Authority	40,000.0	40,000.0	40,000.0	40,000.0	40,000.0	40,000.0	40,000.0	40,000.0	40,000.0	40,000.0	40,000.0	75,000.0[g]
Balances Charged @ 100%												
Outstanding Loans	16,565.2	16,882.6	17,503.8	15,875.6	14,341.2	11,213.3	9,905.3	9,381.9	9,366.9	8,947.4	8,717.1	8,209.1
Undisbursed Loans	9,445.8	6,829.2	5,479.6	3,435.8	2,380.2	2,378.5	1,944.9	1,925.0	1,726.8	1,730.1	1,813.2	2,688.7
Portfolio Certificates sold with Recourse	0.0	0.0	0.0	0.0	0.0	0.0	0.0	0.0	0.0	0.0	0.0	0.0
Loans Sold with Recourse	0.0	0.0	0.0	0.0	0.0	0.0	0.0	0.0	0.0	0.0	0.0	0.0
Outstanding Balance of Paid Claims[b]	N/A	N/A	N/A	N/A	N/A	N/A	1,796.2	1,942.7	2,166.1	2,358.8	2,463.6	2,760.7
Guarantees	0.0	0.0	0.0	0.0	0.0	0.0	0.0	0.0	0.0	0.0	0.0	24,094.2
Insurance	0.0	0.0	0.0	40.0	0.0	0.0	0.0	0.0	0.0	0.0	0.0	9,152.2
Guar & Ins in Excess of Fractional Reserve	0.0	0.0	0.0	0.0	0.0	0.0	0.0	0.0	0.0	0.0	3,817.2	0.0
Total Charges at 100%	26,011.1	23,711.8	22,983.4	20,487.9	17,998.4	15,182.8	13,646.4	13,249.6	13,259.8	13,036.3	12,993.9	46,904.9
Guarantee & Insurance charges at 25% (see below)	3,038.3	3,630.9	3,815.6	3,628.5	3,553.8	3,822.0	3,565.8	3,393.0	4,174.6	5,611.8	6,250.0	
Total Charges against Overall Authority	29,049.3	27,342.7	26,799.0	24,116.4	21,552.2	19,004.8	17,212.2	16,642.6	17,434.4	18,648.1	19,243.9	#VALUE!
Uncommited Authority	10,950.7	12,627.3	13,201.0	15,883.6	18,447.8	20,995.2	22,787.8	23,357.4	22,565.6	21,351.9	20,756.1	#VALUE!
Limitation on Outstanding Guarantees & Insurance which can be charged at 25% against authority	25,000.0	25,000.0	25,000.0	25,000.0	25,000.0	25,000.0	25,000.0	25,000.0	25,000.0	25,000.0	25,000.0	N/A 7/
100% of Balances Charged at 25%												
Loans sold with recourse	0.0	0.0	0.0	0.0	0.0	0.0	0.0	0.0	0.0	0.0	0.0	N/A
Guarantees	6,210.4	6,675.2	6,599.9	6,394.9	6,278.1	6,948.6	5,730.3	5,381.1	7,733.8	12,306.9	17,990.1	N/A
Insurance	5,942.7	7,848.4	8,662.6	8,119.1	7,937.2	8,339.4	8,533.0	8,190.8	8,964.7	10,140.3	7,009.9	N/A
Total Charged at 25%	12,153.1	14,523.6	15,262.5	14,514.0	14,215.3	15,288.0	14,263.3	13,571.9	16,698.5	22,447.2	25,000.0	N/A
Less 75%	9,114.8	10,892.7	11,446.9	10,885.5	10,661.5	11,466.0	10,697.5	10,178.9	12,523.9	16,835.4	18,750.0	N/A
Net 25% Charge to Lending Authority	3,038.3	3,630.9	3,815.6	3,628.5	3,553.8	3,822.0	3,565.8	3,393.0	4,174.6	5,611.8	6,250.0	N/A
Guarantee and Insurance charged at 100%	0.0	0.0	0.0	0.0	0.0	0.0	0.0	0.0	0.0	0.0	0.0	Incl above
Total Charges to Fractional Reserve Limitation	12,153.1	14,523.6	15,262.5	14,514.0	14,215.3	15,288.0	14,263.3	13,571.9	16,698.5	22,447.2	25,000.0	N/A
Uncommited Fractional Reserve Limitation	12,846.9	10,476.4	9,737.5	10,486.0	10,784.7	9,712.0	10,736.7	11,428.1	8,301.5	2,552.8	0.0	N/A

Export-Import Bank of the United States Charges Against Statutory Limitations on Total Activity, 1988–2000 (millions of dollars)

	FY 1994	FY 1995	FY 1996	FY 1997	FY 1998	FY 1999	2000
Lending Authority	75, 000.0[g]						
Balances Charged @ 100%							
Outstanding Loans	7, 484.6	7, 627.6	7, 887.6	7, 978.0	8, 566.1	10, 125.7	9, 948.5
Undisbursed Loans	4, 754.4	5, 041.0	4, 809.4	4, 778.6	3, 611.8	2, 901.9	2, 612.2
Portfolio Certificates sold with Recourse	0.0	0.0	0.0	0.0	0.0	0.0	0.0
Loans Sold with Recourse	0.0	0.0	0.0	0.0	0.0	0.0	0.0
Outstanding Balance of Paid Claims[b]	2, 831.9	3, 714.5	3, 690.1	3, 363.2	3, 342.5	4, 511.0	4, 233.3
Guarantees	29, 167.5	29, 805.4	31, 709.1	32, 112.7	33, 352.9	34, 063.1	36, 944.2
Insurance	7, 914.1	7, 347.3	7, 713.2	6, 433.1	5, 712.1	6, 816.0	7, 857.5
Guar & Ins in Excess of Fractional Reserve	0.0	0.0	0.0	0.0	c.0	0.0	0.0
Total Charges at 100%	52, 152.5	53, 535.8	55, 809.4	54, 665.6	54, 585.4	58, 417.7	61, 595.7
Guarantee & Insurance charges at 25% (see below)	N/A	N/A	N/A	N/A	N/A	N/A	N/A
Total Charges against Overall Authority	52, 152.5	53, 535.8	55, 809.4	54, 665.6	54, 585.4	58, 417.7	61, 595.7
Uncommited Authority	22, 847.5	21, 464.2	19, 190.6	20, 334.4	20, 414.6	16, 582.3	13, 404.3
Limitation on Outstanding Guarantees & Insurance which can be charged at 25% against authority	N/A	N/A	N/A	N/A	N/A	N/A	N/A
100% of Balances Charged at 25%							
Loans sold with recourse	N/A	N/A	N/A	N/A	N/A	N/A	N/A
Guarantees	N/A	N/A	N/A	N/A	N/A	N/A	N/A
Insurance	N/A	N/A	N/A	N/A	N/A	N/A	N/A
Total Charged at 25%	N/A	N/A	N/A	N/A	N/A	N/A	N/A
Less 75%	N/A	N/A	N/A	N/A	N/A	N/A	N/A
Net 25% Charge to Lending Authority	N/A	N/A	N/A	N/A	N/A	N/A	N/A
Guarantee and Insurance charged at 100%	Incl above	Incl above	Incl above	Incl above	Incl above	Incl above	Incl above

N/A – Not Applicible.

[a] Fiscal 1934 data are as of 2/12/35; fiscal 1935 data are as of 10/28/35; and fiscal 1937 data were unavailable because GAO report could not be found.

Table notes (*cont.*)

[b] Outstanding balance of paid claims not charged against lending authority until fiscal year 1985.

[c] Includes $29.2 million representing $25 million charge to entertain loan applications, $.1 million advance commitment to commercial Banks for Political Risk Guarantees and $4.1 million shown in Published Budget as Guaranteed Loans.

[d] Uncommitted lending authority in annual report off by $140.2 million represents $140.2 million adjustment to fractional reserve (75% of $187 million over fractional reserve limit).

[e] Uncommited Balance in Annual Report higher by $7 million representing 25% of $28.2 million for Loans Sold with Recourse not included in overall charges.

[f] Uncommited Balance in Annual Report higher by $12.8 million representing 25% of $51.2 million for Loans Sold with Recourse not included in overall charges.

[g] Covered under the following legislation:

Export-Import Bank established under District of Columbia Banking Laws February 12, 1934.

April 4, 1939, Bank's lending authority limited to $100 million.

March 2, 1940, lending authority increased to $200 million.

September 26, 1940, lending authority increased to $700 million.

July 31, 1945, Export-Import Bank Act of 1945 established (12 U.S.C. 635), also increased lending authority to $3.5 billion.

October 3, 1951, Export-Impot Bank Act amended to increase lending authority to $4.5 billion.

August 9, 1954, Export-Import Bank Act amended to increase lending authority to $5 billion.

May 22, 1958, Export-Import Bank Act amended to increase lending authority to $7 billion.

October 4, 1961, Export-Import Bank Act amended to set up 25% fractional reserve charge to overall lending authority and limited to $1 billion amount to be charged at 25%.

Public Law 88-101 effective August 20, 1963, increased overall lending authority to $9 billion and increased fractional reserve to $2 billion.

Public Law 90-267 effective March 13, 1968, increased overall lending authority to $13.5 billion and increased fractional reserve to $3.5 billion.

Public Law 92-116 effective August 17, 1971, increased overall lending authority to $20 billion and fractional reserve to $10 billion.

Public Law 93-646 effective January 4, 1975, increased overall lending authority to $25 billion and fractional reserve charge to $20 billion.

Public Law 95-630 effective November 10, 1978, increased overall lending authority to $40 billion and fractional reserve charge to $25 billion.

Public Law 102-429 effective October 21, 1992, eliminated the fractional reserve charge for guarantees and insurance and increased overall lending authority to $75 billion.

[h] $12.2 million shown in printed budget as guarantees issued at 100% and included in charge to fractional reserve limitation. $34.7 million guarantees outstanding at 100% as of June 30, 1967 not included in fractional reserve limitation calculation in printed budget.

[i] Represents transition period between end of fiscal year 1976, which ended June 30, 1976, and beginning of fiscal year 1977, which started on October 1, 1976. Beginning in fiscal year 1977, the fiscal year was moved to an October 1 to September 30 cycle.

INDEX